Lonely Planet

D0028407

CALIFORNIA'S
BEST TRIPS
35 AMAZING ROAD TRIPS

This edition written and researched by

Sara Benson
Nate Cavalieri
Beth Kohn

SYMBOLS IN THIS BOOK

✓ Top Tips	📖 History & Culture	📷 Essential Photo
🔗 Link Your Trips	👪 Family	🏃 Walking Tour
💬 Tips from Locals	🍷 Food & Drink	✕ Eating
➡ Trip Detour	🌳 Outdoors	🛏 Sleeping

📞 Telephone Number	@ Internet Access	📖 English-Language Menu
🕐 Opening Hours	📶 Wi-Fi Access	👪 Family-Friendly
P Parking	🥗 Vegetarian Selection	🐾 Pet-Friendly
🚭 Nonsmoking	🏊 Swimming Pool	
❄ Air-Conditioning		

MAP LEGEND

Routes
Trip Route
Trip Detour
Linked Trip
Walk Route
Tollway
Freeway
Primary
Secondary
Tertiary
Lane
Unsealed Road
Plaza/Mall
Steps
Tunnel
Pedestrian Overpass
Walk Track/Path

Boundaries
--- International
---- State/Province
—— Cliff

Population
✪ Capital (National)
◉ Capital (State/Province)
● City/Large Town
○ Town/Village

Transport
✈ Airport
Cable Car/Funicular
P Parking
Train/Railway
Tram
Ⓤ Underground Train Station

Trips
1 Trip Numbers
9 Trip Stop
🏃 Walking tour
➡ Trip Detour

Highway Route Markers
97 US National Hwy
5 US Interstate Hwy
44 California State Hwy

Hydrography
River/Creek
Intermittent River
Swamp/Mangrove
Canal
Water
Dry/Salt/Intermittent Lake
Glacier

Areas
Beach
Cemetery (Christian)
Cemetery (Other)
Park
Forest
Reservation
Urban Area
Sportsground

PLAN YOUR TRIP

Welcome to California 7

California Classic Trips 8

California Highlights 12

If You Like... 22

Need to Know 24

City Guide 26

ON THE ROAD

NORTHERN CALIFORNIA TRIPS 31

1 Pacific Coast Highways .... 7–10 Days 35

2 San Francisco, Marin & Napa Loop .... 4–5 Days 49

3 Earthquake Trail .... 3 Days 61

4 Alice Waters' Culinary Tour .... 3 Days 69

5 Napa Valley .... 2–3 Days 79

6 Sonoma Valley .... 2 Days 91

7 Russian River & the Bohemian Highway .. 2 Days 99

8 Mendocino & Anderson Valley ... 3–4 Days 107

9 Lost Coast & Southern Redwoods .... 4 Days 115

CONTENTS

10 **Northern Redwood Coast** .... 5 Days 125

11 **Trinity Scenic Byway** .... 3 Days 133

12 **Volcanic Legacy Scenic Byway** .... 3 Days 141

CENTRAL CALIFORNIA TRIPS 149

13 **Big Sur** .... 2 Days 153

14 **Along Highway 1 to Santa Cruz** .... 2–3 Days 161

15 **Around Monterey & Carmel** .... 2–3 Days 169

16 **Around San Luis Obispo** .... 2–3 Days 179

17 **Santa Barbara Wine Country** .... 2–3 Days 187

18 **Lake Tahoe Loop** .... 2–3 Days 197

19 **Yosemite, Sequoia & Kings Canyon National Parks** .... 5–7 Days 205

20 **Eastern Sierra Scenic Byway** ...... 3–5 Days 217

21 **Highway 49 Through Gold Country** .... 3–4 Days 227

Northern
California
p31

Central
California
p149

Southern
California
p269

Contents cont.

22 Ebbetts Pass
Scenic Byway .... **2 days** 237

23 Feather River
Scenic Byway ...... **3–4 Days** 245

24 Lazy Delta
Dawdle .... **2 Days** 253

25 Highway 99 Through
Central Valley .... **3 Days** 261

SOUTHERN CALIFORNIA
TRIPS 269

26 Disneyland & Orange
County Beaches ... **2–4 Days** 273

27 Fun on the San
Diego Coast .... **2–4 Days** 283

28 Mission
Trail .... **5 Days** 295

29 SoCal Pop
Culture .... **3 Days** 303

30 Route
66 .... **3–4 Days** 313

31 Big Bear & Rim of the World
Scenic Byway ...... **2–3 Days** 323

32 Life in
Death Valley .... **3 Days** 331

33 Palm Springs &
Joshua Tree
Oases .... **2–3 Days** 341

34 Palms to Pines
Scenic Byway .... **2 Days** 349

35 Temecula, Julian &
Anza-Borrego .... **3 Days** 357

CALIFORNIA
DRIVING
GUIDE 364

Classic Trips

Look out for the Classic Trips stamp on our favorite routes in this book.

1 Pacific Coast Highways .... 7–10 Days 35

5 Napa Valley .... 2–3 Days 79

19 Yosemite, Sequoia & Kings Canyon National Parks .... 5–7 Days 205

21 Highway 49 Through Gold Country .... 3–4 Days 227

26 Disneyland & Orange County Beaches ... 2–4 Days 273

30 Route 66 .... 3–4 Days 313

32 Life in Death Valley .... 3 Days 331

Yosemite National Park Waterfall (Trip 19)

WELCOME TO
CALIFORNIA

Starry-eyed newbies head to the Golden State to find fame and fortune, but you can do better. Come for the landscapes, stay for the farm-fresh and global fusion food, and glimpse the future in the making on America's creative coast. Live in California? Rest assured there's a gold mine of mom-and-pop restaurants, scenic routes and swimming holes yet to be discovered.

The 35 trips in this book will take you from the breezy, wildlife-rich Pacific coast, to the towering redwoods of Big Sur and Northern California, to off-the-beaten-track SoCal desert and Gold Rush towns, to landmark national parks such as Yosemite and Death Valley, and through the vine-strewn valleys of celebrated wine countries, starting with Sonoma and Napa.

From backcountry lanes to beachside highways, we've got something for you. If it's your first time here, pick one of our seven Classic Trips, which highlight California's most unforgettable, must-do experiences. Turn the page for more.

→

CALIFORNIA
Classic Trips

5

PIETRO CANALI / SOPA / CORBIS ©

32

WHAT IS A CLASSIC TRIP?

All the trips in this book show you the best of California, but we've chosen seven as our all-time favorites. These are our Classic Trips – the ones that lead you to the best of the iconic sights, the top activities and the unique California experiences. Turn the page to see the map, and look out for the Classic Trip stamp throughout the book

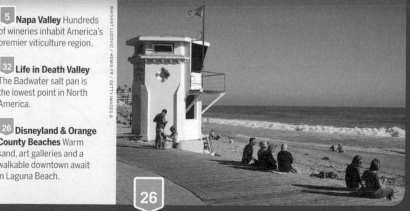

5 Napa Valley Hundreds of wineries inhabit America's premier viticulture region.

32 Life in Death Valley The Badwater salt pan is the lowest point in North America.

26 Disneyland & Orange County Beaches Warm sand, art galleries and a walkable downtown await in Laguna Beach.

MAISANT LUDOVIC / HEMIS.FR / GETTY IMAGES ©

26

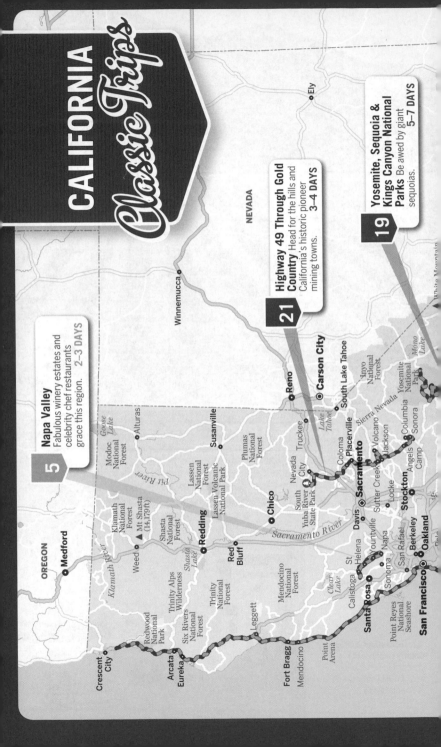

CALIFORNIA Classic Trips

5 Napa Valley Fabulous winery estates and celebrity chef restaurants grace this region. 2–3 DAYS

21 Highway 49 Through Gold Country Head for the hills and California's historic pioneer mining towns. 3–4 DAYS

19 Yosemite, Sequoia & Kings Canyon National Parks Be awed by giant sequoias. 5–7 DAYS

OREGON

NEVADA

Medford

Crescent City

Arcata
Eureka

Redwood National Park

Six Rivers National Forest

Klamath River

Trinity Alps Wilderness

Weed

Mt Shasta (14,179ft)

Klamath National Forest

Shasta National Forest

Shasta Lake

Trinity National Forest

Redding

Red Bluff

Mendocino National Forest

Leggett

Fort Bragg

Mendocino

Point Arena

Clear Lake

Calistoga

St Helena

Yountville

Sonoma

Santa Rosa

Napa

San Rafael

Point Reyes National Seashore

Berkeley
Oakland

San Francisco

Modoc National Forest

Alturas

Goose Lake

Pit River

Lassen National Forest

Lassen Volcanic National Park

Chico

Sacramento River

Susanville

Plumas National Forest

Truckee

Nevada City

South Yuba River State Park

Coloma

Placerville

Davis

Sacramento

Sutter Creek

Locke

Stockton

Volcano

Jackson

Angels Camp

Columbia

Sonora

Winnemucca

Ely

Reno

Carson City

South Lake Tahoe

Lake Tahoe

Sierra Nevada

Inyo National Forest

Mono Lake

Yosemite National Park

White Mountain

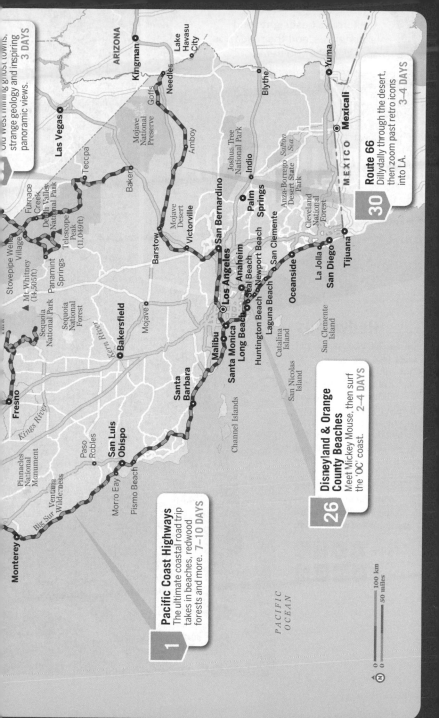

Pacific Coast Highways
The ultimate coastal road trip takes in beaches, redwood forests and more. **7–10 DAYS**

1

Disneyland & Orange County Beaches
Meet Mickey Mouse, then surf the 'OC' coast. **2–4 DAYS**

26

Route 66
Dillydally through the desert, then zoom past retro icons into LA. **3–4 DAYS**

30

... old west mining ghost towns, strange geology and inspiring panoramic views. **3 DAYS**

California's best sights and experiences, and the road trips that will take you there.

CALIFORNIA
HIGHLIGHTS

Redwoods

Ditch the cell phone and hug a tree, dude. California's towering giants grow along much of the coast, from Big Sur north to the Oregon border. It's possible to cruise past the trees – or even drive right through them at old-fashioned tourist traps – but nothing compares to the awe you'll feel while walking underneath these ancient ones. Explore Redwood National Park on **Trip 10: Northern Redwood Coast**.

TRIPS

MARK NEWMAN / GETTY IMAGES ©

Redwoods A tree in Jedediah Smith Redwoods State Park (Trip 10)

13

Golden Gate Bridge

Golden Gate Bridge

Sashay out onto San Francisco's iconic bridge. Spy on cargo ships threading through the pylons and memorize 360-degree views of the rugged Marin Headlands, far-off downtown skyscrapers and the speck that is Alcatraz Island. Get another perspective on this 20th-century engineering feat by driving across it on **Trip 1: Pacific Coast Highways**.

TRIPS 1 2 28

Palm Springs

A chic desert oasis ever since the early days of Hollywood and Frank Sinatra's Rat Pack. Do like A-list stars do here: lounge by your hotel's swimming pool, then drink cocktails from sunset till dawn. Break a sweat in hot-springs spas or on hiking trails that wind through desert canyons or mountain forests atop the head-spinning aerial tramway on **Trip 34: Palms to Pines Scenic Byway**.

TRIPS 33 34

Disneyland

Where orange groves once grew, there Walt Disney built his fantasy Magic Kingdom in 1955. Beloved cartoon characters still waltz arm-in-arm down Main Street, USA, and fireworks explode over Sleeping Beauty's Castle. If you're a kid, or just hopelessly young-at-heart, who are we to say this can't really be 'the Happiest Place on Earth'? Make a date with Mickey on **Trip 26: Disneyland & Orange County Beaches**.

TRIP 26

Yosemite National Park View from Glacier Point

BEST SCENIC ROUTES

Pacific Coast Highway (PCH) Put the convertible top down while cruising Hwy 1 in Orange County. **Trips** 1 26

Avenue of the Giants Wind past the world's biggest old-growth redwood groves. **Trips** 1 9

Kings Canyon Scenic Byway Descend into the Sierra Nevada's deepest river canyon. **Trip** 19

Rim of the World Scenic Byway Curve past lakes on this hair-raising highway. **Trip** 31

Ebbetts Pass Scenic Byway Climb over high-elevation peaks from Gold Country to Lake Tahoe. **Trip** 22

Yosemite National Park

In what conservationist John Muir called his 'great temple,' everything looks bigger, whether you're getting splashed by thunderous waterfalls, staring up at granite domes or walking in ancient groves of sequoia. For sublime views, perch at Glacier Point under a full moon or motor along high-elevation Tioga Rd on **Trip 19: Yosemite, Sequoia & Kings Canyon National Parks**.

TRIP 19

15

Big Sur Pacific Coast Hwy

Big Sur

Hidden by redwood forests, the bohemian Big Sur coast keeps its secrets for those who will savor them: hidden hot springs, waterfalls and beaches where the sand is tinged purple or where gigantic chunks of jade have been found. Don't forget to look skyward to catch sight of endangered California condors soaring above craggy sea cliffs on **Trip 13: Big Sur**.

TRIPS

BEST SMALL TOWNS

- -

Bolinas This end-of-the-road coastal hamlet in Marin County isn't really a secret. **Trip 2**

- -

Calistoga For Napa Valley's blue-jeans-and-boots crowd and hot-springs lovers. **Trip 5**

Avila Beach Sunny beach boardwalk, quaint shops and a creaky fishing pier. **Trips 1 16**

- -

Bodie California's official Old West mining ghost town. **Trip 20**

- -

Arcata NorCal bohemian counter-culture in the heart of the Redwood Empire. **Trips 1 11**

Lake Tahoe Kayaking on the lake

Santa Monica Pacific Park's Ferris wheel on Santa Monica Pier

Lake Tahoe

In summer, startlingly clear blue waters invite splashing around, kayaking and boating, while mountain bikers careen and hikers stride along trails threading through pine forests. In winter, after a thrilling day of skiing Olympic-worthy runs or snowshoe trekking, retreat to your cozy lakefront cottage to toast s'mores by the fire pit. **Trip 18: Lake Tahoe Loop** is ready to roll year-round.

TRIP 18

Monterey

Forget Hollywood visions of sun soaked SoCal beaches. Instead imagine John Steinbeck and his novels of American realism set on this rugged peninsula. To meet local wildlife, hop aboard a whale-watching cruise in the marine sanctuary or step inside Cannery Row's renowned aquarium. Then soak up the atmosphere at the West Coast's oldest lighthouse on **Trip 15: Around Monterey & Carmel**.

TRIPS 1 15

Santa Monica

Who needs LA traffic? Hit the beach instead. Santa Monica can grant instant happiness. Learn to surf, ride a solar-powered Ferris wheel, dance under the stars on an old-fashioned pier, amaze the kids at the aquarium's tidal touch pools or just dip your toes in the water and let your troubles float away. Did we mention jaw-dropping sunsets? Experience it all on **Trip 30: Route 66**.

TRIPS 1 30

19

Joshua Tree National Park

Whimsical-looking Joshua trees define this park, where the Colorado and Mojave Deserts converge. This is one of California's top places to climb, but even kids can scramble around the boulders. Hikers seek out fan-palm oases fed by springs and streams. Come in spring to see wildflowers bloom on **Trip 33: Palm Springs & Joshua Tree Oases**.

TRIP 33

Sonoma Valley

Sun-dappled vineyards surrounded by pastoral ranchlands, where the uniqueness of *terroir* is valued more than a winery's fine-art collection. In this down-to-earth wine country, you may taste new vintages straight from the barrel inside a shed. Who cares if it's not noon yet? Relax; conventions need not apply on **Trip 6: Sonoma Valley**.

TRIP 6

(left) **Joshua Tree National Park** Joshua trees;

(below) **San Diego's Beaches** Roller coaster at Mission Beach

OCEAN / CORBIS ©

San Diego's Beaches

Cruise past impossibly white sands on Coronado's Silver Strand, then stop for cotton candy and a roller-coaster ride at Mission Beach. Farther north, La Jolla sits pretty atop rocky bluffs, a whisper's breath from the sea, while beyond stretches an eclectic line-up of North County beach towns. Whatever you've been dreaming of for your ultimate SoCal beach vacation, find it on **Trip 27: Fun on the San Diego Coast**.

TRIPS

BEST ROADSIDE ODDITIES

Trees of Mystery Animatronic Paul Bunyan in the redwoods. **Trip** 10

Solvang Where windmills collide with Danish village kitsch. **Trips** 17 28

Elmer's Place Folk-art 'bottle trees' on Route 66. **Trip** 30

Cabazon Dinosaurs Concrete behemoths outside Palm Springs. **Trip** 34

Sonoma Valley Wine tasting (Trip 6)

Beaches

California spoils you with over 1100 miles of Pacific coastline. Northern beaches are all about crashing waves, rocky tidepools and solitary strolls along the continent's edge. If you're dreaming of golden strands lapped by frothy surf and bronzed bods hanging out in lifeguard huts, head to SoCal.

26 Disneyland & Orange County Beaches Over 40 miles of surf, sand and sun in the OC.

27 Fun on the San Diego Coast Take your pick of ritzy or bohemian beach towns.

16 Around San Luis Obispo Steal away to the Central Coast's laidback beaches.

10 Northern Redwood Coast Walk the rocky headlands past tidepools and barking sea lions.

History

Gold mining is the usual reason given for the madcap course of California's history. Yet Native Americans, Spanish missions, Mexican *pueblos* (towns) and later waves of global immigration have all left traces to dig deeper for, too.

21 Highway 49 Through Gold Country Follow the footsteps of 19th-century gold seekers, bordello keepers and outlaws.

28 Mission Trail Trace the path of Spanish colonialists and Catholic priests through 'Alta California.'

32 Life in Death Valley Where the dreams of miners and pioneers are just ghosts today.

3 Earthquake Trail San Francisco's 1906 quake is not the only time California's fault lines have really shaken things up.

Fabulous Food & Wine

Rock-star chefs' menus feature produce from local farmers, fishers, ranchers and artisan food makers. And wine? Although Napa and Sonoma Valley are the most famous, California's other wine countries more than hold their own.

4 Alice Waters' Culinary Tour Loop the Bay Area, sampling farmers markets and California cuisine.

6 Sonoma Valley Napa's rustic-chic country cousin is a patchwork of farms and vineyards.

7 Russian River & the Bohemian Hwy Pop champagne corks and tipple biodynamic pinot noir and old-vine zinfandel.

17 Santa Barbara Wine Country Where the hit movie *Sideways* romped, find a gateway to seriously sophisticated vintages.

Alabama Hills Road through the hills with view of Sierra Nevada (Trip 20)

Bringing Kids

The Golden State welcomes pint-sized travelers with open arms. Just keep them covered in sunblock and make sure they see something beyond just SoCal's thrilling theme parks.

26 Disneyland & Orange County Beaches
Multigenerational families all find fun at Disneyland and California Adventure, then cruise sunny coastal Hwy 1

19 Yosemite, Sequoia & Kings Canyon National Parks Amaze your kids with sequoia trees, huge waterfalls and wildlife spotting.

18 Lake Tahoe Loop No worries, no hurry: take a slow-moving drive around the 'Big Blue' for swimming in summer or winter skiing.

27 Fun on the San Diego Coast Tour the zoo's wild safari park, then treat tots to Legoland and teens to endless surf beaches.

National & State Parks

Wilderness parklands protect an astonishing diversity of life zones, from misty redwood forests and snowy mountain peaks to marine sanctuaries where migratory whales breach.

19 Yosemite, Sequoia & Kings Canyon National Parks Don't miss the Sierra Nevada's prime-time parks, with wildflower meadows, forests and mountain vistas.

10 Northern Redwood Coast See sandy beaches, calm lagoons where migratory birds flock, and the tallest trees on earth.

12 Volcanic Legacy Scenic Byway Alpine lakes, volcanic peaks, hot-springs 'hells'and waterfalls await.

33 Palm Springs & Joshua Tree Oases
Clamber through J-Tree's wonderland of rocks and flowering desert gardens.

Backwoods Byways

Far from coastal California's bumper-to-bumper freeways, these scenic backroads let you finally lose the crowds – and maybe yourself – in cinematic landscapes of jagged peaks, rushing rivers and placid lakes.

11 Trinity Scenic Byway Watch for bald eagles (or Bigfoot!) as you dangle your fishing pole in lakes.

20 Eastern Sierra Scenic Byway Explore real Wild West landscapes, from Mt Whitney to the ghost town of Bodie and beyond.

22 Ebbetts Pass Scenic Byway Take the rugged back-door route over the Sierra Nevada toward Lake Tahoe.

31 Big Bear & Rim of the World Scenic Byway
Navigate hairpin turns and dizzying canyon drop-offs en route to Big Bear Lake.

NEED ^{TO} KNOW

CELL PHONES

The only foreign phones that will work in the USA are GSM multiband models. Network coverage is often spotty in remote areas (eg mountains, deserts).

INTERNET ACCESS

Wi-fi is available at most coffee shops and lodgings. Some accommodations have free guest computers. Cybercafes ($6 to $12 per hour) are common in cities.

FUEL

Gas stations are everywhere, except in national parks and remote areas. Expect to pay $4 to $5 per US gallon.

RENTAL CARS

Alamo (www.alamo.com)

Car Rental Express (www.carrentalexpress.com)

Simply Hybrid (www.simplyhybrid.com)

Zipcar (www.zipcar.com)

IMPORTANT NUMBERS

American Automobile Association (AAA; ☎877-428-2277)

Emergencies (☎911)

Highway conditions (☎800-427-7623)

Traffic updates (☎511)

Climate

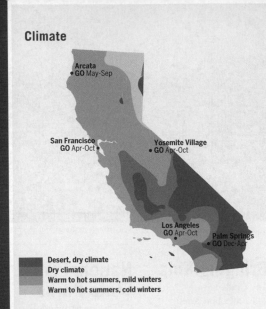

Arcata
● GO May-Sep

San Francisco
GO Apr-Oct ●

Yosemite Village
● GO Apr-Oct

Los Angeles
GO Apr-Oct ●

Palm Springs
● GO Dec-Apr

- Desert, dry climate
- Dry climate
- Warm to hot summers, mild winters
- Warm to hot summers, cold winters

When to Go

High Season (Jun–Aug)

» Accommodations prices up 50% to 100%.

» Major holidays are even busier and more expensive.

» Summer is low season in the desert: temperatures exceed 100°F (38°C).

Shoulder Season (Apr–May & Sep–Oct)

» Crowds and prices drop, especially along the coast and in the mountains.

» Typically wetter in spring, drier in autumn.

» Milder temperatures and sunny, cloudless days.

Low Season (Nov–Mar)

» Accommodations rates drop in cities and by the coast.

» Many attractions open fewer days and shorter hours.

» Chilly temperatures and rainstorms; mudslides occasionally wash out coastal highways.

» In the mountains, carry tire chains; heavy snowfall closes higher-elevation roads.

» Winter is peak season in SoCal's desert regions.

Daily Costs

Budget: less than $75

» Camping: $20–40

» Meals in roadside diners and cafes: $10–20

» Graze farmers markets for cheaper eats

» Hit the beach and find 'free days' at museums

Midrange: $75–200

» Two-star motel or hotel double room: $75–150

» Meals in casual and midrange restaurants: $20–40

» Theme-park admission: $40–100

Top end: over $200

» Three-star lodging: from $150 per night in high season, more for ocean views

» Three-course meal in top restaurant: $75 plus wine

Eating

Roadside diners & cafes Cheap and simple; abundant only outside cities.

Beach shacks Casual burgers, shakes and seafood meals with ocean views.

National, state & theme parks Mostly so-so, overpriced cafeteria-style or deli picnic fare.

Vegetarians Food restrictions and allergies can usually be catered for at restaurants.

Eating price indicators represent the average cost of a main dish:

$	less than $10
$$	$10–$20
$$$	more than $20

Sleeping

Motels & hotels Ubiquitous along well-trafficked highways and in major tourist areas.

Camping & cabins Ranging from rustic campsites to luxury 'glamping' resorts.

B&Bs Quaint, romantic and pricey inns, found in most coastal and mountain towns

Hostels Cheap and basic, but almost exclusively in cities.

Sleeping price indicators represent the average cost of a double room with private bathroom:

$	less than $100
$$	$100–$200
$$$	more than $200

Arriving in California

Los Angeles International Airport

Rental cars Major companies offer shuttles to off-airport lots.

Door-to-door shared-ride shuttles $16 to $25 one-way (reservations recommended).

Taxis $30 to $50 plus tip to Santa Monica, Hollywood or Downtown LA; 30 minutes to one hour.

Buses Take Shuttle C (free) to LAX City Bus Center or Metro FlyAway bus ($7) to Downtown LA.

San Francisco International Airport

Rental cars Take free AirTrain blue line to SFO Rental Car Center.

Door-to-door shared-ride shuttles $15 to $18 one-way (reservations recommended).

Taxis $35 to $50 plus tip to most San Francisco neighborhoods; 30 to 50 minutes.

Train BART ($8.10, 30 minutes to downtown SF) leaves every 20 minutes (take free AirTrain from any terminal to BART station).

Money

ATMs are widely available. Credit cards are accepted almost universally.

Tipping

Tipping is expected, not optional. Standard tips: 18% to 20% in restaurants; 15% for taxis; $1 per drink in bars; $2 per bag for porters.

Opening Hours

Banks 8:30am–4:30pm Mon–Fri, some to 5:30pm Fri, 9am–12:30pm Sat

Business hours (general) 9am–5pm Mon–Fri

Post offices 9am–5pm Mon–Fri, some 9am–noon Sat

Restaurants 7am–10:30am, 11:30am–2:30pm & 5–9:30pm daily, some later Fri & Sat

Shops 10am–6pm Mon-Sat, noon–5pm Sun (malls open later)

Useful Websites

Lonely Planet (www.lonelyplanet.com/usa/california) Destination info, hotel bookings, travelers' forums and more.

California Travel and Tourism Commission (www.visitcalifornia.com) Multilingual trip-planning guides and an events calendar.

For more, see Driving in California (p364).

SAN FRANCISCO

Ride the clanging cable cars up unbelievably steep hills, snake down Lombard St's famous hairpin turns, cruise through Golden Gate Park and drive across the arching Golden Gate Bridge. Then go get lost in the creatively offbeat neighborhoods of California's capital of weird.

Getting Around

Avoid driving downtown. Cable cars are slow and scenic (single rides $6). MUNI streetcar and bus are faster but infrequent after 9pm (fares $2). BART (tickets from $1.75) run high-speed Bay Area trains. Taxis cost $2.75 per mile; meters start at $3.50.

Parking

Street parking is scarce and meter readers ruthless. Meters take coins, sometimes credit cards; central pay stations accept coins or cards. Overnight hotel parking averages $35 to $50; downtown parking garages start at $2.50 per hour or $25 per day.

THOMAS WINZ / GETTY IMAGES ©

San Francisco Colorful buildings

Where to Eat

The Ferry Building, Mission District and South of Market (SoMa) are foodie faves. Don't miss the city's outdoor farmers markets either. Head to North Beach for Italian, Chinatown for dim sum, the Mission District for Mexican, and the Sunset or Richmond for pan-Asian.

Where to Stay

The Marina is near the family-friendly waterfront and Fisherman's Wharf. Downtown and Union Square are more expensive, but conveniently located for walking. Avoid the rough-edged Civic Center and Tenderloin neighborhoods.

Useful Websites

San Francisco Travel (www.sanfrancisco. travel) Destination info, events calendar and accommodations bookings.

SF Station (www.sfstation.com) Nightlife, restaurants, shopping and the arts.

Lonely Planet (www. lonelyplanet.com/usa/ san-francisco) Travel tips and travelers' forums.

Trips Through San Francisco:

1 2 3 4 28

For more, check out our city and country guides.
www.lonelyplanet.com

Los Angeles Elvis impersonator on Hollywood Blvd

LOS ANGELES

Loony LA, land of starstruck dreams and Hollywood Tinseltown magic. You may think you know what to expect: celebrity worship, Botoxed beach blondes, endless traffic and earthquakes. But it's also California's most ethnically diverse city, with new immigrants arriving daily, evolving the boundary-breaking global arts, music and food scenes.

Getting Around

Angelenos drive everywhere. Freeway traffic jams are endless, but worst during extended morning and afternoon rush hours. LA's Metro operates slower buses and speedier subway and light-rail trains (fares $1.50), with limited night and weekend services. DASH minibuses (single-ride 50¢) zip around downtown; Santa Monica's Big Blue Bus (fares $1) connects West LA. Taxis cost $2.80 per mile; meters start at $2.85.

Parking

Street parking is tough. Meters take coins, sometimes credit cards; central pay stations accept coins or cards. Valet parking is ubiquitous, typically $5 to $10 plus tip. Overnight hotel parking averages $25 to $40.

Where to Eat

Food trucks and pop-up kitchens are a local obsession. Downtown cooks up a worldly mix, with Little Tokyo, Chinatown, Thai Town, Koreatown and Latin-flavored East LA nearby. Trend-setting eateries inhabit Hollywood, Mid-City, Santa Monica and Venice.

Where to Stay

For beach life, escape to Santa Monica or Venice. Long Beach is convenient to Disneyland and Orange County. Party people adore Hollywood and West Hollywood (WeHo); culture vultures, Downtown LA.

Useful Websites

LA Inc (http://discoverlosangeles.com) City's official tourism website for trip planning and events.

LA Weekly (www.laweekly.com) Arts, entertainment, dining and events calendar.

Lonely Planet (www.lonelyplanet.com/usa/los-angeles) Travel tips, hotel reservations and travelers' forums.

Trips Through Los Angeles: 1 28 30

San Diego View of the city from Coronado

SAN DIEGO

San Diegans shamelessly promote their hometown as 'America's Finest City.' Smug? Maybe, but it's easy to see why. The weather is idyllic, with coastal high temperatures hovering around 72°F year-round. Wander the museums and gardens of Balboa Park, laze on the beaches, then party in the Gaslamp Quarter after dark.

Getting Around

Driving is how most people get around. MTS operates a metro-area network of buses, trolleys and trains (one-way fare $2.25 or $2.50, day pass $5) with limited night and weekend services. Taxi meters start at $2.20, plus $2.30 per mile.

Parking

Street parking is crowded. Meters take mostly coins; central pay stations accept coins or cards. Valet parking, public lots and garages downtown cost from $10. Overnight hotel parking runs $20 to $40.

Where to Eat

Hit the Gaslamp Quarter for creative cuisine, Hillcrest for casual ethnic and fusion eats, and beach towns for seafood and microbrews. Mexican food and the city's famous fish tacos are everywhere.

Where to Stay

Boutique and luxury hotels are downtown and in the Gaslamp Quarter. Old Town has chain hotels and motels, as does Mission Valley inland. Beach towns nearby kid-friendly attractions have the biggest range of lodgings, from Coronado north to Carlsbad.

Useful Websites

San Diego.org (www.sandiego.org) City's official tourism site for trip planning and events.

San Diego Reader (www.sandiegoreader.com) Nightlife, arts, entertainment and events calendar.

Lonely Planet (www.lonelyplanet.com/usa/san-diego) Travel tips, hotel reservations and travelers' forums.

Trips Through San Diego: `1` `27` `28`

Northern California Trips

SAN FRANCISCO IS THE ANCHOR OF CALIFORNIA'S MOST DIVERSE REGION, even if earthquakes have shown it isn't rock solid. From exploring the rugged beaches of the Lost Coast to floating down the isolated bends of the Russian River, from poking around (and through) the redwoods to surmounting volcano summits, there's no shortage of natural places to explore and scenic roads to drive.

Then there is the wine and food... Many visitors seek out the iconic Napa Valley for cabernets and sparkling wines, but you can sip equally impressive vintages in Sonoma, Dry Creek and Anderson Valleys. Then soak in some hot springs, where conversations start with, 'Hey, dude!' and end hours later.

Point Reyes National Seashore (Trip 1 Detour)
NIK WHEELER / CORBIS ©

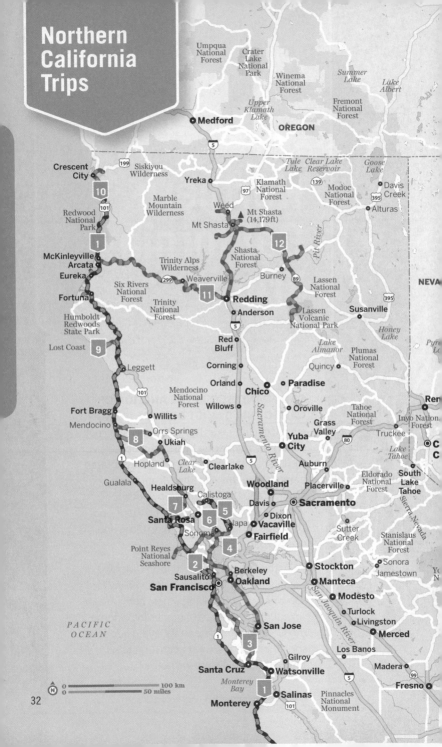

Northern California Trips

Classic Trip

1 Pacific Coast Highways 7–10 Days
The ultimate coastal road trip takes in beaches, redwood forests and more. (p35)

2 San Francisco, Marin & Napa Loop 4–5 Days
A taste of city, an eyeful of wildlife, plus the heady nectar of Wine Country. (p49)

3 Earthquake Trail 3 Days
Explore some cracks, shaken buildings and fissures found around the Bay Area. (p61)

4 Alice Waters' Culinary Tour 3 Days
The mother of America's Slow Food movement introduces the source of life-affirming food. (p69)

Classic Trip

5 Napa Valley 2–3 Days
Fabulous winery estates and celebrity chef restaurants grace this grand wine-producing region. (p79)

6 Sonoma Valley 2 Days
Tour this down-to-earth part of Wine Country and time travel through historic Sonoma. (p91)

7 Russian River & the Bohemian Highway 2 Days
Meander ocean-bound back roads, float in the river and sample regional wines. (p99)

8 Mendocino & Anderson Valley 3–4 Days
Navigate byways lined with vines, redwoods and spectacular Pacific bluffs near dreamy Mendocino. (p107)

9 Lost Coast & Southern Redwoods 4 Days
Get lost on this wild coastal frontier, home to Roosevelt elk, redwood and offbeat towns. (p115)

10 Northern Redwood Coast 5 Days
Stand agape at colossal primeval forests and drop in on kitschy mid-20th-century roadside attractions. (p125)

11 Trinity Scenic Byway 3 Days
From Shasta to the sea, this route traces a path through the heart of Bigfoot country. (p133)

12 Volcanic Legacy Scenic Byway 3 Days
Dormant volcanoes, thermal springs and quiet wilderness lakes dominate the agenda of this naturalist excursion. (p141)

 DON'T MISS

Point Arena
Ascend 145 corkscrew steps inside the tallest lighthouse in California that you can still climb to the top of on Trip **1**

Conzelman Rd
Gawk at million-dollar views of San Francisco and the Pacific while exploring abandoned military bunkers tucked into hillsides on Trip **2**

Gundlach-Bundschu Winery
At one of Sonoma's oldest wineries, sample sustainably grown wines, tour a mammoth barrel cave and enjoy a picnic alongside a lake on Trip **6**

Red Door Cottage
Stay overnight at this Philo Apple Farm cottage, where you can take a private, open-air shower amid the apple blossoms on Trip **8**

Heart Lake
After a simple hike, take a dip in Heart Lake, sun-warm in July and offering an amazing view of Mt Shasta on Trip **12**

Big Sur coast Precipitous cliffs dominate the seascape

Pacific Coast Highways

1

Our top pick for classic California dreamin' snakes along the Pacific coast for 1000 miles. Uncover beaches, seafood shacks and piers for catching sunsets over boundless ocean horizons.

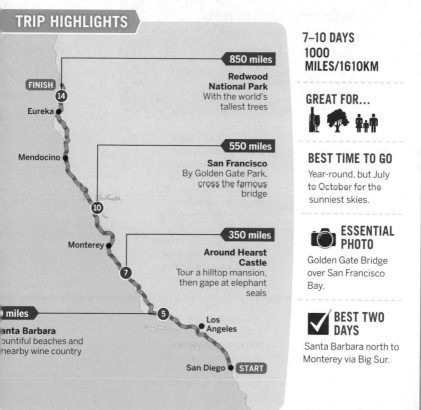

850 miles
Redwood National Park
With the world's tallest trees

550 miles
San Francisco
By Golden Gate Park, cross the famous bridge

350 miles
Around Hearst Castle
Tour a hilltop mansion, then gape at elephant seals

miles
anta Barbara
ountiful beaches and nearby wine country

FINISH
14
Eureka

Mendocino

10

Monterey
7

5
Los Angeles

San Diego • START

7–10 DAYS
1000 MILES/1610KM

GREAT FOR...

BEST TIME TO GO
Year-round, but July to October for the sunniest skies.

ESSENTIAL PHOTO
Golden Gate Bridge over San Francisco Bay.

BEST TWO DAYS
Santa Barbara north to Monterey via Big Sur.

Classic Trip

1 Pacific Coast Highways

Make your escape from California's tangled, traffic-jammed freeways and cruise in the slow lane. Once you get rolling, it'll be almost painful to leave the ocean behind for too long. Officially, only the short, sun-loving stretch of Hwy 1 through Orange and Los Angeles Counties can legally call itself Pacific Coast Highway (PCH). But never mind those technicalities, because equally bewitching ribbons of Hwy 1 and Hwy 101 await all along this route.

1 San Diego

Begin at the bottom of the state map, where the pretty peninsular beach town of **Coronado** is connected to the San Diego mainland by the white-sand beaches of the **Silver Strand**. If you've seen Marilyn Monroe cavort in *Some Like It Hot,* you'll recognize the **Hotel Del Coronado**, which has hosted US presidents, celebrities and royalty, including the Prince of Wales who gave up his throne to marry a Coronado divorcée. Wander the turreted palace's labyrinthine corridors, then quaff tropical cocktails at ocean-view Babcock & Story Bar.

Be thrilled by driving over the 2.1-mile-long **Coronado Bay Bridge**. Detour inland to Balboa Park (for our self-guided walking tour, see p292). Head west, then south to Point Loma's **Cabrillo National Monument** (www.nps.gov/cabr; per car $5; ⊘9am-5pm, last entry 4:30pm; ⚐) for captivating

bay panoramas from the 19th-century lighthouse and monument to the West Coast's first Spanish explorers. Rolling north of **Mission Beach**, where an old-fashioned amusement park is dwarfed by SeaWorld, suddenly you're in hoity-toity **La Jolla**, beyond which lie North County's beach towns.

✕ 🛏 p46

The Drive » It's a 50-mile trip from La Jolla north along coastal roads then the I-5 into Orange County (aka the 'OC'), passing Camp Pendleton Marine Corps Base and buxom-shaped San Onofre Nuclear Generating Station. Exit at San Clemente and follow Avenida del Mar downhill to the beach.

LINK YOUR TRIP

13 Big Sur

Get lost on the rugged Big Sur coast, stretched between Hearst Castle and the painterly scenery of Carmel-by-the-Sea on the Monterey Peninsula.

27 Fun on the San Diego Coast

Start your California coastal road trip slowly with an extra couple of days in sunny San Diego.

Classic Trip

② San Clemente

Life behind the conservative 'Orange Curtain' is far different than in most other laid-back, liberal California beach towns. Apart from glamorous beaches where famous TV shows and movies have been filmed, you can still uncover the California beach culture of yesteryear here in off-the-beaten-path spots like San Clemente. Home to living surfing legends, top-notch surfboard companies and *Surfer* magazine, this may be the last place in the OC where you can authentically live the surf lifestyle. Ride your own board or swim at the city's main beach beside San Clemente Pier. A fast detour inland, the community's **Surfing Heritage Foundation** (www.surfingheritage.com; 101 Calle Iglesia; admission by donation; ⊙11am-5pm) exhibits surfboards ridden by the greats, from Duke Kahanamoku to Kelly Slater.

The Drive ≫ Slingshot north on I-5, exiting onto Hwy 1 near Dana Point. Speed by the wealthy artists colony of Laguna Beach, wild Crystal Cove State Park, Newport Beach's yacht harbor and 'Surf City USA' Huntington Beach (see p273 and p303). Turn west off Hwy 1 near Naples toward Long Beach, about 45 miles from San Clemente.

③ Long Beach

In Long Beach, the biggest stars are the **Queen Mary** (www.queenmary.com; 1126 Queens Hwy; adult/child from $25/14; ⊙10am-6pm Mon-Thu, to 7pm Fri-Sun), a grand (and allegedly haunted) British ocean liner permanently moored here, and the giant **Aquarium of the Pacific** (www.aquariumofpacific.org; 100 Aquarium Way; adult/child $25/14; ⊙9am-6pm; 👣), a high-tech romp through an underwater world in which sharks dart and jellyfish float. Often overlooked, the **Long Beach Museum of Art** (www.lbma.org; 2300 E Ocean Blvd; adult/child $7/free; ⊙11am-5pm Fri-Sun, to 8pm Thu) focuses on California modernism and contemporary mixed-media inside a 20th-century mansion by the ocean, while the urban **Museum of Latin American Art** (www.molaa.org; 628 Alamitos Ave; adult/child $9/free; ⊙11am-5pm Wed & Fri-Sun, to 9pm Thu) shows off contemporary south-of-the-border art.

🛏 p46

The Drive ≫ Wind slowly around the ruggedly scenic Palos Verdes Peninsula. Follow Hwy 1 north past the South Bay's primetime beaches.

Curving around LAX airport and Marina del Rey, Hwy 1 continues north to Venice (see p303), Santa Monica (see p313) and all the way to Malibu, over 50 miles from Long Beach.

④ Malibu

Leaving traffic-jammed LA behind, Hwy 1 breezes northwest of Santa Monica to Malibu. You'll feel like a movie star walking around on the public beaches, backing against gated compounds owned by Hollywood celebs. One mansion you can actually get a look inside is the **Getty Villa** (www.getty.edu; 17985 Pacific Coast Hwy; per car $15, parking reservation required; ⊙10am-5pm Wed-Mon), a hilltop showcase of Greek, Roman and Etruscan antiquities and manicured gardens. Next to Malibu Lagoon State Beach, west of the surfers by Malibu Pier, **Adamson House** (www.adamsonhouse.org; 23200 Pacific Coast Hwy; adult/child $7/2; ⊙11am-3pm Wed-Sat, last tour 2pm) is a Spanish-Moorish villa lavishly decorated with locally made hand-painted tiles. Motoring further west along the coast, where the Santa Monica Mountains plunge into the sea, take time out for a frolic on Malibu's mega-popular beaches like sandy Point Dume, Zuma or Leo Carrillo.

🍴 p46

The Drive » Hwy 1 crosses into Ventura County, winding alongside the ocean and windy Point Mugu. In Oxnard, join Hwy 101 northbound beyond Ventura, a jumping-off point for boat trips to Channel Islands, to Santa Barbara, just over 70 miles from Malibu Pier.

TRIP HIGHLIGHT

⑤ Santa Barbara

Seaside Santa Barbara has almost perfect weather and a string of idyllic beaches, where surfers, kite flyers, dog walkers and surfers mingle (for our walk, see p194). Get a close-up of the city's iconic Mediterranean-style architecture along **State St** downtown or from the **county courthouse** (www. santabarbaracourthouse.org; 1100 Anacapa St; admission free; 8:30am-4:30pm Mon-Fri, 10am-4:30pm Sat & Sun), its tower rising above the red-tiled rooftops. Gaze south toward the busy harborfront and **Stearns Wharf** (www.stearnswharf. org; 🚻) or north to the historic Spanish mission church (see p295). Santa Barbara's balmy climate is also perfect for growing grapes. A 45-minute drive northwest along Hwy 154, visit the Santa Ynez Valley wine country (see p187), made famous by the 2004 movie *Sideways*. Hit wine-tasting rooms in **Los Olivos**, then take Foxen Canyon Rd north past

more wineries to rejoin Hwy 101.

🍴 🏠 p16

The Drive » Keep following fast Hwy 101 northbound or detour west onto slow Hwy 1, which squiggles along the Pacific coastline past Guadalupe, gateway to North America's largest sand dunes. Both highways meet up again in Pismo Beach, 100 miles northwest of Santa Barbara.

----

⑥ Pismo Beach

A classic California beach town, Pismo Beach has a long, lazy stretch of sand for swimming, surfing and strolling out onto the pier at sunset. After digging into bowls of clam chowder and baskets of fried seafood at surf-casual cafes, check out the retro family fun at the bowling alley, billiards halls and bars uphill from the beach, or dash 10 miles up Hwy 101 to the vintage **Sunset Drive-In** (www.fairoakstheatre.net; 255 Elks Lane, San Luis Obispo; 🚻), where you can put your feet up on the dash and munch on bottomless bags of popcorn while watching

Hollywood blockbuster double-features.

🍴 p10

The Drive » Follow Hwy 101 north past San Luis Obispo, exiting onto Hwy 1 west to landmark Morro Rock in Morro Bay (see p179). North of Cayucos, Hwy 1 rolls through bucolic pasture lands, only swinging back to the coast at Cambria. Ten miles further north stands Hearst Castle, about 60 miles from Pismo Beach.

TRIP HIGHLIGHT

⑦ Around Hearst Castle

Hilltop **Hearst Castle** (info 805-927-2020, reservations 800-444-4445; www.hearstcastle. org; tours adult/child from $25/12; daily, call for hr) is California's most famous monument to wealth and ambition. William Randolph Hearst, the early-20th-century newspaper magnate, entertained Hollywood stars and royalty at this fantasy estate furnished with European antiques, accented by shimmering pools and surrounded by flowering gardens. Try to

TROUBLE-FREE ROAD TRIPPING

In coastal areas, thick fog may impede driving – slow down and if it's too soupy, get off the road. Along coastal cliffs, watch out for falling rocks and mudslides that could damage or disable your car if struck. For current highway conditions, including road closures (which aren't uncommon during the rainy winter season) and construction updates, call 800-427-7623 or visit www.dot.ca.gov.

LOCAL KNOWLEDGE
AMY STARBIN, LA
SCREENWRITER &
MOM

For a fun way to cool off when driving through LA along the coast, bring the family out to **Santa Monica Pier** (www.santamonicapier.org). Not only do you get a great view of the ocean, you can also get up close and personal with sea life at the **aquarium** (www.healthebay.org). Then head up top for a spin on the carousel used in *The Sting* or the solar-powered Ferris wheel.

Top: Pool, Hearst Castle,
Left: Lighthouse, Trinidad
Right: Redwoods

DAVID MUENCH/CORBIS ©

make tour reservations in advance, especially for living-history evening programs during the Christmas holiday season.

About 4.5 miles further north along Hwy 1, park at the signposted vista point and amble the boardwalk to view the enormous **elephant seal colony** that breeds, molts, sleeps, plays and fights on the beach. Seals haul out year-round, but the winter birthing and mating season peaks on Valentine's Day. Nearby, **Piedras Blancas Light Station** (www. piedrasblancas.org; tour adult/ child $10/5; ☺ call for hr) is an outstandingly scenic spot.

✕ ⊨ p47

The Drive ⟩⟩ Fill your car's gas tank before plunging north into the redwood forests of the remote Big Sur coast (see p153), where precipitous cliffs dominate the seascape, and tourist services are few and far between. Hwy 1 keeps curving north to the Monterey Peninsula (see p169), approximately a three-hour, 100-mile trip from Hearst Castle.

⑧ Monterey

As Big Sur loosens its condor's talons on the coastal highway, Hwy 1 rolls gently downhill towards Monterey Bay. The fishing community of Monterey is the heart of Steinbeck country, and although Cannery Row today is touristy

Classic Trip

claptrap, it's worth strolling down to step inside the mesmerizing **Monterey Bay Aquarium** (☎tickets 866-963-9645; www.montereybayaquarium. org; 886 Cannery Row; adult/ child $33/20; ⏰10am-5pm or 6pm daily, extended summer hr; 🛜📶), inhabiting a converted sardine cannery on the shores of a national marine sanctuary. All kinds of aquatic denizens swim in giant tanks here, from sea stars to pot-bellied seahorses and comical sea otters. Afterwards, explore historic Old Monterey on our self-guided walking tour (see p176).

🍴 p47

DETOUR: POINT REYES

Start: ⑩ San Francisco

A rough-hewn beauty, **Point Reyes National Seashore** (www.nps.gov/pore; admission free; ⏰sunrise-midnight; 📶) lures marine mammals and birds, as well as scores of shipwrecks. It was here that Sir Francis Drake repaired his ship the *Golden Hind* in 1579 and, while he was at it, claimed the indigenous land for England. Follow Sir Francis Drake Blvd west out to the point's edge-of-the-world lighthouse, whipped by ferocious winds, where you can observe migrating whales in winter. The lighthouse is about 10 miles west of Point Reyes Station off Hwy 1 along the Marin County coast.

The Drive » It's a relatively quick 45-mile trip north to Santa Cruz. Hwy 1 traces the crescent shoreline of Monterey Bay, passing Elkhorn Slough wildlife refuge near Moss Landing boat harbor, Watsonville's strawberry and artichoke farms, and a string of tiny beach towns in Santa Cruz County.

---

⑨ Santa Cruz

Here, the flower power of the 1960s lives on, and bumper stickers on surfboard-laden woodies shout, 'Keep Santa Cruz weird.' Next to the ocean, **Santa Cruz Beach Boardwalk** (☎831-423-5590; www.beachboardwalk. com; 400 Beach St; admission free, rides $3-5; ⏰seasonal schedules vary, call for hr; 📶) has a glorious old-school Americana vibe and a 1911 Looff carousel. Its fun-for-all atmosphere is punctuated by squeals from nervous nellies on the stomach-turning Giant Dipper, a 1920s wooden roller coaster that's a national historic landmark, as seen in the vampire cult-classic movie *The Lost Boys*.

A kitschy, old-fashioned tourist trap, the **Mystery Spot** (☎831-423-8897; www. mysteryspot.com; 465 Mystery Spot Rd; admission $5, parking $5; ⏰daily, hr vary; 📶) makes compasses point crazily, while mysterious forces push you around and buildings lean at odd angles; call for directions, opening hours and tour reservations.

🛏 p47

The Drive » It's a blissful 75-mile coastal run from Santa Cruz up to San Francisco past Pescadero, Half Moon Bay and Pacifica, where Hwy 1 encounters washout-prone Devil's Slide (see p161). Merge with heavy freeway traffic in Daly City, staying on Hwy 1 north through the city into Golden Gate Park.

TRIP HIGHLIGHT

⑩ San Francisco

Gridlock may shock your system after hundreds of lazy miles of wide-open, rolling coast. But don't despair. Hwy 1 runs straight through the city's biggest, most breathable greenspace: **Golden Gate Park** (www. golden-gate-park.com; admission free; 📶🎭). You could easily spend all day in the conservatory of flowers, arboretum and botanical gardens, perusing the **California Academy of Sciences** (www.calacademy.org; 55 Music Concourse Dr; adult/child $30/20; ☻9:30am-5pm Mon-Sat, 11am-5pm Sun; 🚻) and the **de Young Museum** (www.famsf.org/deyoung; 50 Hagiwara Tea Garden Dr; adult/child $10/free; ☻9:30am-5:15pm Tue-Sun) of fine arts. (For our self-guided walking tour of Chinatown and North Beach, see p58). Then follow Hwy 1 north over the **Golden Gate Bridge**. Guarding the entry to San Francisco Bay, this iconic bridge is named after the straits it spans, not for its 'International Orange' paint job. Park in the lot on the bridge's south or north side, then traipse out onto the pedestrian walkway for a photo.

🍴 🛏 p47

The Drive » Past Sausalito, leave Hwy 101 in Marin City for slow-moving, wonderfully twisted Hwy 1 along the Marin County coast (see p49). Over the next 210 miles to Mendocino via Bodega Bay, revel in a remarkably uninterrupted stretch of coastal highway. Just over halfway along, watch for the lighthouse road turnoff north of Point Arena town.

⑪ Around Point Arena

The fishing fleets of Bodega Bay and Jenner's harbor-seal colony are the last things you'll see before PCH dives into California's great rural northlands. Hwy 1 twists and turns past the Sonoma Coast's state parks packed with hiking trails, sand dunes and beaches, as well as underwater marine reserves, rhododendron groves and a 19th-century, Russian fur-trading fort. At Sea Ranch, don't let exclusive-looking vacation homes prevent you from following public-access trailhead signs and staircases down to empty beaches and across ocean bluffs. Further north, guarding an unbelievably windy point since 1908, **Point Arena Lighthouse** (www.pointarenalighthouse.com; 45500 Lighthouse Rd; adult/child $7.50/1; ☻10am-3:30pm, to 4:30pm late May-early Sep; 🚻) is the only lighthouse in California where you can actually climb to the top. Check in at the museum, then ascend the 115ft tower to inspect the Fresnel lens and panoramas of the sea and the jagged San Andreas Fault below.

🛏 p47

The Drive » It's an hour-long, 35-mile drive north along Hwy 1 from the Point Arena Lighthouse turnoff to Mendocino, crossing the Navarro, Little and Big Rivers. Feel free to stop and stretch at wind-tossed state beaches, parklands criss-crossed by hiking trails and tiny coastal towns along the way.

⑫ Mendocino & Fort Bragg

Looking more like Cape Cod than California, the quaint maritime town of **Mendocino** has white picket fences surrounding New England–style cottages with blooming gardens and redwood-built water towers. Its dramatic headlands jutting into the Pacific, this

---

LOCAL KNOWLEDGE: GRIZZLY CREEK REDWOODS STATE PARK

To find the best hidden redwood groves, **Grizzly Creek Redwoods State Park** (www.parks.ca.gov; per car $8; ☻sunrise-sunset; 🚻) is the place to go. It's smaller than other parks, but so out of the way that it's pristine. Head to Cheatham Grove for lush sorrel carpets under the trees, then take a dip in summer swimming holes along the Van Duzen River. Bonus factoid: *Return of the Jedi* scenes were shot here. North of the Avenue of the Giants, exit Hwy 101 onto Hwy 36, then drive east for 17 miles.

Richard Stenger, retired park ranger

yesteryear timber town and shipping port was 'discovered' by artists and bohemians in the 1950s and has served as a scenic backdrop in over 50 movies. Once you've browsed the souvenir shops and art galleries selling everything from driftwood carvings to homemade fruit jams, escape north to workaday **Fort Bragg**, with its simple fishing harbor and brewpub, stopping first for a short hike on the ecological staircase and pygmy forest trail at oceanfront **Jug Handle State Natural Reserve** (www.parks.ca.gov; Hwy 1; admission free; ☉ sunrise-sunset; 👫).

✕ 🛏 p47

The Drive ≫ About 25 miles north of Mendocino, Westport is the last hamlet along this rugged stretch of Hwy 1. Rejoin Hwy 101 northbound at Leggett for another 90 miles to Eureka, detouring along the Avenue of the Giants and, if you have more time to spare, to the Lost Coast (for both, see p115).

⑬ Eureka

Hwy 101 trundles alongside **Humboldt Bay National Wildlife Refuge** (www.fws.gov/humboldtbay), a major stopover for migratory birds on the Pacific Flyway. Next comes the sleepy railroad town of Eureka. As you wander downtown, check the ornate **Carson Mansion** (143 M St), built in the 1880s by a timber baron and adorned with dizzying Victorian turrets, towers, gables and gingerbread details. Also a historical park, **Blue Ox Millworks** (www.blueoxmill.com; 1 X St; self-guided tour adult/child $7.50/3.50; ☉9am-5pm Mon-Fri, to 5pm Sat) still creates Victorian detailing by hand using traditional carpentry and 19th-century equipment. Back by Eureka's harborfront, climb aboard the blue-and-white 1910 **Madaket** (📞707-445-1910; www.humboldtbaymaritimemuseum.com; foot of C St; adult/child $18/10; ☉mid-May–early Oct, call for hr). Sunset cocktail cruises serve from California's smallest licensed bar.

🛏 p47

The Drive ≫ Follow Hwy 101 north past the Rastafarian-hippie college town of Arcata (for our self-guided walking tour, see p122) and turnoffs for Trinidad State Beach and Patrick's Point State Park (for both, see p125). Hwy 101 drops out of the trees beside marshy Humboldt Lagoons State Park (see p128), rolling north towards Orick, just over 40 miles from Eureka.

TRIP HIGHLIGHT

⑭ Redwood National Park

At last, you'll reach **Redwood National Park** (www.nps.gov/redw, www.parks.ca.gov; state park day-use per car $8; 👫). Get oriented to the tallest trees on earth at the coastal **Kuchel Visitor Center** (☉10am-4pm, to 5pm Nov-Mar; 👫), just south of Orick. Then commune with the coastal giants on their own mossy turf inside **Lady Bird Johnson Grove** or the majestic **Tall Trees Grove** (free drive-and-hike permit required). For more untouched redwood forests, wind along the 8-mile **Newton B Drury Scenic Parkway**, passing grassy meadows where Roosevelt elk roam, then follow Trip 10 all the way north to Crescent City, the last pit-stop before the Oregon border.

Eureka Carson Mansion

Eating & Sleeping

San Diego ❶
See also Trip 27, p290.

✕ C Level — Seafood $$
(☎619-298-6802; www.islandprime.com; 880 Harbor Island Dr; mains $15-30; ⊙11am-late) Be mesmerized by bay views as you bite into carefully crafted salads, grilled seafood or the ultra-rich lobster sandwich on jalapeño-cheddar sourdough bread.

⊨ Pearl Hotel — Boutique Hotel $$
(☎619-226-6100, 877-732-7573; www.thepearlsd.com; 1410 Rosecrans Ave, Point Loma; r $129-205; ✳🐾🛁) At this Mid-Century Modern motor lodge, rooms have soothing aquamarine hues, trippy surf motifs and fish bowls. With a lively pool scene, it's not for light sleepers.

Long Beach ❸

⊨ Hotel Varden — Boutique Hotel $$
(☎562-432-8950, 877-382-7336; www.thevardenhotel.com; 335 Pacific Ave; r $119-149; ✳@🛁) Diminutive rooms at this historic art-deco hotel downtown have tiny sinks, cushy beds, white, white and more white. It's two blocks from Pine Ave's restaurant row.

Malibu ❹

✕ Neptune's Net — Seafood $$
(www.neptunesnet.com; 42505 Pacific Coast Hwy; mains $6-20; ⊙10:30am-8pm Mon-Thu, to 9pm Fri, to 8:30pm Sat & Sun; 🐾🛁) Order fish and chips at this 1950s roadhouse, where Harley riders and sand-covered kids chow down together at picnic tables.

Santa Barbara ❺
See also Trip 17, p193.

✕ Santa Barbara Shellfish Company — Seafood $$
(www.sbfishhouse.com; 230 Stearns Wharf; dishes $5-19; ⊙11am-9pm) 'From sea to skillet to plate' best describes this end-of-the-wharf counter joint. Great lobster bisque, ocean views and the same location for 25 years.

⊨ El Capitán Canyon — Cabin, Campground $$
(☎805-685-3887, 866-352-2729; www.elcapitancanyon.com; 11560 Calle Real, Goleta; safari tents $155, yurts $205, cabins $225-355; 🛁🐾🍴) Go 'glamping' in this car-free zone near El Capitán State Beach, a 25-minute drive from downtown on Hwy 101. Creekside cabins come with heavenly mattresses, kitchenettes and outdoor fire pits.

⊨ Hotel Indigo — Boutique Hotel $$
(☎805-966-6586, 877-270-1392; www.indigosantabarbara.com; 121 State St; r $155-250; ✳@🛁🐾) Poised between downtown and the beach, this petite Euro-chic boutique hotel has all the right touches: curated contemporary-art displays, rooftop patios and ecofriendly green-design elements like the living-plant wall.

Pismo Beach ❻
See also Trip 16, p185.

✕ Splash Cafe — Seafood $
(www.splashcafe.com; 197 Pomeroy Ave; dishes $4-12; ⊙8am-8:30pm Sun-Thu, to 9pm Fri & Sat, shorter winter hr; 🐾) Uphill from the pier, lines go out the door and wrap around this scruffy hole-in-the-wall, famous for its clam chowder in fresh-baked sourdough-bread bowls.

Around Hearst Castle ⑦

🍴 Sebastian's
General Store Deli, Market $

(442 San Simeon Rd, off Hwy 1; mains $6-12; ⊙11am-5pm Wed-Sun, kitchen till 4pm) **Across** Hwy 1 from Hearst Castle, this tiny historic market sells cold drinks, Hearst Ranch beef burgers and wines, giant deli sandwiches and salads for beach picnics at San Simeon Cove.

🛏 Blue Dolphin Inn Hotel $$

(☎805-927-3300; www.cambriainns.com; 6470 Moonstone Beach Dr; d incl breakfast $159-329; 🛜📶🎦) Sand-colored, slate-sided, two-story building across from the ocean boardwalk has cozy rooms with romantic fireplaces.

Monterey ⑧
See also Trip 15, p175.

🍴 Monterey's Fish House Seafood $$$

(☎831-373-4647; 2114 Del Monte Ave, mains $12-35; ⊙11:30am-2:30pm Mon-Fri, 5-9:30pm daily; 📶) Watched over by photos of Sicilian fishermen, dig into dock-fresh seafood with some fusion twists. Try the barbecued oysters or the Mexican squid steak. The vibe is casual, but reservations are essential (it's *so* crowded).

Santa Cruz ⑨

🛏 Pelican Point Inn Inn $$

(☎831-475-3381; www.pelicanpointinn -santacruz.com; 21345 E Cliff Dr; ste $109-199; 📶) Simple but roomy retro apartments near kid-friendly Twin Lakes State Beach come with everything you'll need for a coastal getaway, including kitchenettes and high-speed internet.

San Francisco ⑩
See also Trip 2, p56.

🍴 Greens Vegetarian $$

(☎415-771-6222; www.greensrestaurant. com; Fort Mason Center, Bldg A; mains $7-20; ⊙11:45am-2:30pm Tue-Fri, 11am-2:30pm Sat & 10:30am-2pm Sun, plus 5:30-9pm Mon-Sat; 🥗) In a converted army barracks, savor the Golden

Gate Bridge views and meat-free, organic California cuisine, mostly sourced from a Zen Buddhist farm in Marin County.

🛏 Argonaut Hotel Boutique Hotel $$$

(☎415-563-0800; www.argonauthotel.com; 495 Jefferson St; r from $300; 🅿️@🛜📶🎦) Inhabiting a converted cannery near Fisherman's Wharf, this nautical-themed hotel has century-old wooden beams, porthole-shaped mirrors and 'Tall Rooms' with extra-long beds.

Around Point Arena ⑪

🛏 Mar Vista Cottages Cottage $$

(☎707-884-3522, 877-855-3522; www. marvistamendocino.com; 35101 S Hwy 1, Gualala; cottage $175-295; 🛜📶🎦) Stylishly renovated 1930s fishing cabins, south of Point Arena at Anchor Bay, make a perfectly relaxing coastal escape in a harmonious environment.

Mendocino & Fort Bragg ⑫
See also Trip 8, p113.

🍴 North Coast Brewing Co Brewpub $$

(www.northcoastbrewing.com; 444 N Main St; mains $10-30; ⊙11:30am-9:30pm Sun-Thu, to 10pm Fri & Sat) Classic burgers and garlic waffle fries soak up locally handcrafted brews. Arrive early to get a table, or join the party in the bar. Thursday is souvenir pint night.

🛏 Shoreline Cottages Motel, Cottage $$

(☎707-964-2977; www.shoreline-cottage.com; 18725 Shoreline Hwy, Fort Bragg; d $115-165; 🛜📶🎦) Low-key rooms and cottages with kitchens surround a grassy lawn where dogs play. All are stocked with DVD players and complimentary snacks.

Eureka ⑬

🛏 Carter House Inns Hotel, B&B $$

(☎707-444-8062; www.carterhouse.com; 301 L St; r/ste incl breakfast from $180/295; 🛜) Hotel Carter's rooms are outfitted with top-quality linens and mod cons. Alternatively, reserve a romantic roost in a nearby historic home. Restaurant 301 is Eureka's top table for seasonal North Coast dinners with wine pairings.

San Francisco Saunter through the busy streets of Chinatown

San Francisco, Marin & Napa Loop

2

Loop your way around the Bay Area, drinking in the sights of hilly San Francisco, the stunning wild vistas of Marin and the world-renowned wineries of Napa Valley and Sonoma County.

TRIP HIGHLIGHTS

65 miles

Point Reyes
Home to grazing deer, circling hawks and breaching whales

153 miles

Napa Valley
The premiere wine-producing region in the country

Glen Ellen

Sonoma

9

Petaluma

Point Reyes Station

Olema

6

20 miles

Muir Woods
A canopy of massive ancient redwoods obscures the sun

4

2

START/ FINISH
San Francisco

Marin Headlands
Panoramic hilltop views from bay to breakers

8 miles

4–5 DAYS
253 MILES/407KM

GREAT FOR...

BEST TIME TO GO
April to October for dry and warmer days.

ESSENTIAL PHOTO

Views of Alcatraz, the Pacific Ocean, the Golden Gate Bridge and shimmering San Francisco unfold from Conzelman Rd.

BEST BIG TREES

Feel small under the rocketing redwoods of Muir Woods.

49

2 San Francisco, Marin & Napa Loop

Begin by exploring the heady sights of cosmopolitan San Francisco before crossing north on the windswept passageway of the Golden Gate Bridge. From here, the scenery turns untamed, and Marin County's undulating hills, redwood forest and crashing coastline prove a welcome respite from urban living. Continue north to Napa and Sonoma Wine Country, basking in the warmer temperatures and tasting some of the best wines in the state.

❶ San Francisco

In two action-packed days, explore Golden Gate Park, spy on lolling sea lions at Fisherman's Wharf and saunter through the busy streets of Chinatown to the Italian sidewalk cafes in North Beach. Feast on an overstuffed burrito in the Mission District and then wander its mural-splashed alleys.

Queue up at Powell and Market Sts for a ride on a bell-clanging **cable car** (www.sfmta.com; ride $6), and then cruise to the

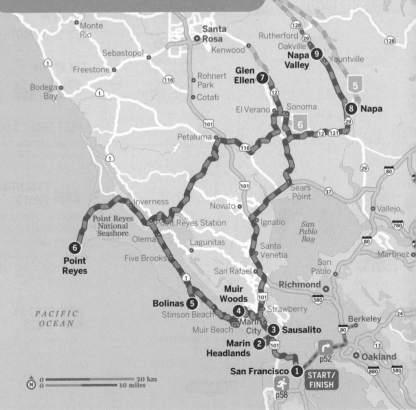

infamous prison island of **Alcatraz** (☑415-981-7625; www.alcatrazcruises.com, www.nps.gov/alcatraz; adult/child day $28/17, night $35/20.50; ☻call center 8am-7pm, ferries depart Pier 33 every 30min 9am-3:55pm, plus 6:10pm & 6:45pm). In summer, book Alcatraz tickets online at least two weeks ahead.

At the foot of Market St, indulge your inner epicure at the **Ferry Building** (www.ferrybuildingmarketplace.com; Embarcadero; ☻approximately 10am-6pm) food stalls, and stop by its farmers market on Tuesday, Thursday and Saturday mornings year-round to wallow in the bounty of

California-grown organic produce and gourmet prepared foods.

At the historic **Castro Theatre** (☑415-621-6120; www.castrotheatre.com; 429 Castro St; adult/child $10/7.50), the crowd goes wild when the giant organ rises from the floor and pumps out show tunes until the movie starts, and the sumptuous chandeliered decor complements a repertory of silver-screen classics.

If you have extra time to cavort about town, see p58 for more ideas.

 p56

The Drive » Aim north over the turret-topped Golden Gate Bridge, pausing to stroll around the Marin-side Vista Point area. Exit at Alexander Ave and bear left before swinging back under the highway to ascend the bayview ridgeline of Conzelman Rd. It's 2 miles to Hawk Hill, located just before the road becomes one-way.

TRIP HIGHLIGHT

❷ Marin Headlands

Near echoey WWII battery tunnels, bird-watchers should make a mandatory stop to hike up **Hawk Hill**. Thousands of migrating birds of prey soar here from late summer to early fall, straddling a windy ridge with views of Rodeo Lagoon all the way to Alcatraz.

Stay west on Conzelman Rd until it ends in about 2 miles and

then bear left towards the bay. The third lighthouse built on the West Coast, the **Point Bonita Lighthouse** (www.nps.gov/goga/pobo.htm; ☻12:30-3:30pm Sat-Mon) was completed in 1855, but after complaints about its performance in fog, it was scooted down to the promontory about 20 years later. Three afternoons a week you can cross through a dark rock tunnel – carved out with hand tools only – and traverse a steep half-mile trail to inspect the lighthouse beacon. A bouncy suspension bridge delivers you to the Fresnel lens tower, and harbor seals sun themselves on the rocks below.

The Drive » Continue north along the oceanview bluffs of Field Rd, joining westbound Bunker Rd (signed San Francisco) after passing the Marin Headlands Visitor Center. Pass through the timed one-way tunnel and turn left onto Alexander Ave towards Sausalito.

❸ Sausalito

Perfectly arranged on a secure little harbor on the bay, Sausalito's pretty houses tumble neatly down a green hillside into a well-heeled downtown, and much of the town affords uninterrupted views of San Francisco and Angel Island.

LINK YOUR TRIP

5 **Napa Valley**
From Napa, continue further north through Napa Valley along Hwy 29 for destination restaurants, a fabulous spa town and even more tempting wineries.

6 **Sonoma Valley**
Venture north or south from Glen Ellen along Hwy 12 for low-key wine tasting and the historic sights clustered in downtown Sonoma.

Just under the north tower of the Golden Gate Bridge, at East Fort Baker, families should stop by the **Bay Area Discovery Museum** (www.baykidsmuseum.org; adult/child $10/8; ⏰9am-4pm Tue-Fri, 10am-5pm Sat & Sun; 👶), an excellent hands-on activity museum specifically designed for children. Exhibits include a wave workshop, a small underwater tunnel and a large outdoor play area.

✗ p56

The Drive » Follow Hwy 101 north to Hwy 1, passing a stretch of Richardson Bay packed with funky houseboats. Ascend a mostly residential section of two-lane Hwy 1, and after 3 miles follow signs to Muir Woods via Panoramic Hwy.

GEOFF KUCHERA / ISTOCKPHOTO ©

TRIP HIGHLIGHT

❹ Muir Woods

Walking through an awesome stand of the world's tallest trees is an experience to be had only in Northern California and a small part of southern Oregon. The old-growth redwoods at **Muir Woods** (www.nps.gov/muwo; adult/child $7/free; ⏰8am-sunset) are the closest redwood stand to San Francisco. Logging plans were halted when congressman and naturalist William Kent bought a section of Redwood Creek, and in 1907 he donated 295 acres to the federal government. President Theodore Roosevelt made the site a national monument in 1908, the name honoring John Muir, naturalist and founder of the environmental organization the Sierra Club.

Muir Woods can become quite crowded, especially on weekends. But even at busy times, a short hike will get you out of the densest crowds and onto trails with huge trees and stunning vistas. A lovely cafe serves local and organic goodies and hot drinks that hit the spot on foggy days.

The Drive » Head southwest on Muir Woods Dr (signed

DETOUR: CHEZ PANISSE

Start: ❶ San Francisco

The soul and anchor of Berkeley's 'Gourmet Ghetto,' Alice Waters' famed **Chez Panisse** (🍴restaurant 510-548-5525, cafe 510-548-5049; www.chezpanisse.com; 1517 Shattuck Ave, Berkeley; restaurant meals $65-100, cafe mains $18-29; ⏰restaurant dinner Mon-Sat, cafe lunch & dinner Mon-Sat) gave birth to modern California cuisine and is a bucket-list destination for gourmands who prize fresh, local and organic ingredients. Upscale but unpretentious, its two dining rooms inhabit a welcoming Arts and Crafts house. The downstairs restaurant serves more formal prix-fixe meals, while the cafe upstairs is slightly less expensive. Reserve weeks ahead.

Cross the Bay Bridge to I-80, exiting at University Ave. At 2 miles, turn north onto Shattuck Ave.

Sausalito

Muir Beach/Stinson Beach) and rejoin Hwy 1/Shoreline Hwy, winding north along this spectacularly scenic and curvy Pacific Ocean byway. Trace Bolinas Lagoon, where waterfowl prowl during low tide and harbor seals often frolic, and take the very first left after the lagoon. Go left onto Olema–Bolinas Rd into central Bolinas.

- - - - - - - - - - - - -

⑤ Bolinas

Don't look for any signs directing you here. Residents from this famously private town tore the road sign down so many times that state highway officials finally gave in and stopped replacing it years ago.

Known as 'Jugville' during the Gold Rush days, the sleepy beachside community is home to writers, musicians and fisherfolk. Stroll along the sand from access points at Wharf Rd or Brighton Ave.

Hikers should veer off Olema–Bolinas Rd to Mesa Rd and follow it 5 miles to road's end at Palomarin Trailhead, the tromping-off point for coastal day hikes into the Point Reyes National Seashore. On a toasty day, pack some water and a towel and hightail it out from here to **Bass Lake**, a popular freshwater swimming

spot reached by way of a 3-mile hike skirting the coast. Another 1.5 miles of walking brings you to the a fantastic flume of **Alamere Falls**, which tumbles 50ft off a cliff to the beach below.

✗ p56

The Drive ›› Return to Hwy 1 and continue 12 miles north through Olema Valley. Just past Olema, drive 23 miles west on Sir Francis Drake Blvd (towards Inverness), following the 'lighthouse' signs. Raptors perch on fence posts of historic cattle ranches, and the road bumps over rolling hills as it twists towards the sea.

❻ Point Reyes

At the very end of Sir Francis Drake Blvd, and jutting 10 miles out into the Pacific, this wild tip of land endures ferocious winds that can make it feel like the edge of the world. The **Point Reyes Lighthouse** (☎415-669-1534; www.nps.gov/pore; ⊙lens room 2:30-4pm Thu-Mon, visitor center & other chambers 10am-4:30pm Thu-Mon) sits below the headlands at the base of over 300 stairs. Not merely a beautiful beacon site, it's also one of the best whale-watching spots along the coast, as gray whales pass the shore during their annual migration from Alaska to Baja. Gray-whale sightings tend to peak in mid-January and mid-March, with the season lasting from about January through to April.

However, the occasional spout or spy-hop of humpbacks and minkes can occur year-round.

Note that on weekends and holidays from late December through to mid-April, the road to the lighthouse is closed to private vehicles, and visitors must take a shuttle from Drakes Beach.

✖ 🛏 p57

The Drive ≫ Retrace Sir Francis Drake Blvd to Hwy 1 north and through the tiny village of Point Reyes Station. Soon after, go right onto Point Reyes–Petaluma Rd for 19 miles to Petaluma, stopping en route to sample brie at Marin French Cheese. At the railroad crossing, go right on Lakeville St, which becomes Hwy 116. Drive to Arnold Dr, turn right onto Petaluma Ave and pick up Hwy 12 north.

- - - - - - - - - - - -

❼ Glen Ellen

In Sonoma Valley, picnic like a rock star at the perpetually busy **BR Cohn** (www.brcohn.com; 15000 Sonoma Hwy; tasting $10 & applicable to purchase, bottles $16-55; ⊙10am-5pm), whose founder managed '70s superband the Doobie Brothers before moving on to make outstanding organic olive oils and fine wines – including excellent cabernet sauvignon. In autumn, he throws benefit concerts, amid the olives, by the likes of Skynyrd and the Doobies.

The name **Little Vineyards** (www.littlevineyards.com; 15188 Sonoma Hwy; tastings $5, bottles $17-35; ⊙11am-4:30pm Thu-Mon; 🐾) fits at this family-owned small-scale winery. It's long on atmosphere, with a lazy dog to greet you and a weathered, cigarette-burned tasting bar, which Jack London drank at (before it was moved here). The tasting room is good for folks who dislike crowds, and there's good picnicking on the terrace with a vineyard view. The big reds include syrah, petite sirah, zinfandel, cab and several blends.

✖ p57

The Drive ≫ Double back south on Hwy 12 and then east on Hwy 12/121. Make your way north on Hwy 29, exiting at Downtown Napa/First St. Follow the signs to the Oxbow Public Market.

WILDLIFE WATCHING

Want to see marine wildlife in Marin? Here are a few choice spots suggested by Anne Bauer, Director of Education at the **Marine Mammal Center** (www.tmmc.org).

≫ Point Reyes National Seashore (Chimney Rock & Point Reyes Lighthouse) for gray whales

≫ Bolinas (Duxbury Reef, Bolinas Lagoon), Marin Headlands (around Point Bonita) and Point Reyes National Seashore (Limantour Estero) for harbor seals

≫ Point Reyes National Seashore (Sea Lion Overlook) for sea lions

8 Napa

Near the river in downtown Napa, the stands inside the **Oxbow Public Market** (www. oxbowpublicmarket.com; 610 & 644 First St; ⊙9am-7pm Mon-Sat, 10am-5pm Sun; 🚻🐾) offer everything from fresh-roasted organic coffee to cranberry baguette sandwiches with pea shoots and fontina. Sample a beef frank at the counter of **Five Dot Ranch** (www.fivedotranch. com), an all-natural beef purveyor with a holistic, sustainable, open-pasture program combined with low-stress handling. The family has been raising California livestock for seven generations. Top it off a couple of stands over with the funky, creative and organic flavors of **Three Twins Ice Cream** (www. threetwinsicecream.com) – try the Strawberry Je Ne Sais Quoi, where the creaminess is cut with an unexpected dash of balsamic vinegar.

The Drive » Leaving Napa, take picturesque Hwy 29 (St Helena Hwy) 12 miles north to Oakville, driving past the Napa Valley foodie destination of Yountville.

WINE TASTING 101

Even if you know nothing about wine, you can enjoy it with gusto. Inhale the wine's aroma by burying your nose deep in the glass. Swirl it and look at its color before letting it hit every part of your tongue. It's OK not to drain every glass (in fact, it'll dull your taste buds if you do). Use the containers on the counter to empty your glass and prepare for your next taste. You won't be offending anyone!

TRIP HIGHLIGHT

9 Napa Valley

The huge, corporate-owned winery of **Robert Mondavi** (www. robertmondavi.com; 7801 Hwy 29, Oakville; tours $15-25, bottles $19-150; ⊙10am-5pm) draws oppressive crowds, but if you know nothing about wine, the worthwhile tours provide excellent insight into wine making. Otherwise, skip it – unless you're here for one of the wonderful summer concerts, ranging from classical and jazz to R&B and Latin.

A half-mile south, just after the Oakville Grocery, take a left onto Oakville Cross Rd and drive 2.5 miles, passing through vineyards to Silverado Trail. For hilltop views and food-friendly wines, head south another 2.5 miles to visit chef-owned **Robert Sinskey** (🕿707-944-9090; www. robertsinskey.com; 6320 Silverado Trail, Napa; tastings $25, bottles $22-95; ⊙10am-4:30pm), whose discreetly dramatic tasting room of stone, redwood and teak resembles a small cathedral. The winery specializes in organically grown pinot, merlot and cabernet, great Alsatian varietals, vin gris, cabernet franc and dry rosé, and small bites accompany the *vino*.

✖ 🛏 p57

The Drive » Continue south on Silverado Trail to Napa, picking up southbound Hwy 121 (Sonoma)/Hwy 29 (Vallejo) and turning right as it merges into westbound Hwy 12 (Sonoma). Stay on Hwy 121 until Hwy 37, and take it west. From Hwy 101, it's 20 miles back to San Francisco via the Golden Gate Bridge.

Eating & Sleeping

San Francisco ❶

✖ Bi-Rite Creamery — Ice Cream $

(www.biritecreamery.com; 3692 18th St; ice cream $3.25-7; ⊙11am-10pm Sun-Thu, to 11pm Fri & Sat) Velvet ropes at clubs seem pretentious in laid-back San Francisco, but at organic Bi-Rite Creamery they make perfect sense: lines wrap around the corner for legendary salted-caramel ice cream with housemade hot fudge.

✖ Cotogna — Italian $$

(📞415-775-8508; www.cotognasf.com; 490 Pacific Av; mains $14-24; ⊙noon-3pm & 7-10pm Mon-Sat; 🍴) No wonder chef-owner Michael Tusk won the 2011 James Beard Award: his rustic Italian pastas and toothsome pizzas magically balance a few pristine, local flavors. Book ahead; the $24 prix-fixe is among SF's best dining deals.

✖ Slanted Door — Vietnamese, Californian $$

(📞415-861-8032; www.slanteddoor.com; 1 Ferry Bldg; lunch mains $13-24, dinner mains $18-36; ⊙lunch & dinner) California ingredients, Continental influences and Vietnamese flair with a sparkling bay outlook, from award-winning chef-owner Charles Phan. Reserve ahead or picnic on takeout from the Open Door stall.

⌂ Galleria Park — Boutique Hotel $$

(📞415-781-3060; www.jdvhotels.com; 191 Sutter St; r $189-229; ❄ @ 🛜) Exuberant staff greet you at this downtown boutique charmer, a 1911 hotel styled with contemporary art and handsome furnishings in soothing jewel tones. Some rooms (and bed sizes) run small, but include Frette linens, down pillows, high-end bath amenities, free evening wine hour and – most importantly – good service. Rooms on Sutter St are noisier, but get more light; interior rooms are quietest.

⌂ Good Hotel — Hotel $$

(📞415-621-7001; www.thegoodhotel.com; 112 7th St; r $109-169; @ 🛜 ⛱) A revamped motor lodge attached to a restyled apartment hotel, Good Hotel places a premium on green, with reclaimed wood headboards, light fixtures of repurposed bottles, and fleece bedspreads made of recycled soda bottles and cast-off fabrics. The aesthetic is like a smartly decorated college dorm room: youthful and fun. The big drawbacks are a sometimes-sketchy neighborhood and street noise; book a room in the back. Also has bikes for rent. The pool is across the street at the Americana.

Sausalito ❸

✖ Avatar's — Indian $$

(www.enjoyavatars.com; 2656 Bridgeway Blvd; mains $10-17; ⊙11am-3pm & 5-9:30pm Mon-Sat; 🍴 ♿) Boasting a cuisine of 'ethnic confusion,' the Indian fusion dishes here incorporate Mexican, Italian and Caribbean ingredients and will bowl you over with their flavor and creativity. Think Punjabi enchilada with curried sweet potato or spinach and mushroom ravioli with mango and rose petal alfredo sauce. All diets (vegan, gluten-free etc) are graciously accommodated.

✖ Fish — Seafood $$

(www.331fish.com; 350 Harbor Dr; mains $13-25; ⊙11:30am-8:30pm; ♿) Chow down on seafood sandwiches, oysters and Dungeness crab rolls with organic local butter at redwood picnic tables facing Richardson Bay. A local leader in promoting fresh and sustainably caught fish, this place has wonderful wild salmon in season, and refuses to serve the farmed stuff. Cash only.

Bolinas ❺

✖ Bolinas People's Store — Market $

(14 Wharf Rd; ⊙8:30am-6:30pm; 🍴) An awesome little co-op grocery store hidden behind the community center, the People's Store serves Fair Trade coffee and sells organic produce, fresh soup and excellent tamales. Eat at the tables in the shady courtyard, and have a rummage through the Free Box, a shed full of clothes and other waiting-to-be-reused items.

✕ Coast Café American $$

(www.bolinascafe.com; 46 Wharf Rd; mains $10-22; ⏰11:30am-3pm & 5-8pm Tue & Wed, to 9pm Thu & Fri, 8am-3pm & 5-9pm Sat, to 8pm Sun; 🍴🚹👪) The only 'real' restaurant in town, so everyone jockeys for outdoor seats among the flower boxes for fish and chips, barbecued oysters, or buttermilk pancakes with damn good coffee.

Point Reyes ❻

✕ Tomales Bay Foods & Cowgirl Creamery Market $$

(www.cowgirlcreamery.com; 80 4th St, Point Reyes Station; ⏰10am-6pm Wed-Sun; 🍴) A local market in an old barn selling picnic items, including gourmet cheeses and organic produce. All of the milk is local and organic, with vegetarian rennet in all its soft cheeses, and you can often watch cheese being made from a large view window near the entryway.

🛏 Point Reyes Hostel Hostel $

(☎415-663-8811; www.norcalhostels.org/reyes; dm/r $24/68; @) Just off Limantour Rd, this rustic HI property has bunkhouses with warm and cozy front rooms, big-view windows and outdoor areas with hill vistas, and a brand new LEED-certified building with four private rooms. It's in a beautiful secluded valley 2 miles from the ocean and surrounded by lovely hiking trails, and the only lodging in the park.

Glen Ellen ❼

✕ Vineyards Inn Bar & Grill Spanish, Tapas $$

(www.vineyardsinn.com; 8445 Sonoma Hwy 12, Kenwood; mains $8-20; ⏰11:30am-9:30pm; 🍴) Though nothing fancy, this roadside tavern's food is terrific – succulent organic burgers, line-caught seafood, paella, ceviche and biodynamic produce from the chef's ranch. Full bar.

Napa Valley ❾

✕ Ad Hoc Modern American $$$

(☎707-944-2487; www.adhocrestaurant. com, 6476 Washington St, Yountville; set menu $48; ⏰dinner Wed-Mon, 10:30am-2pm Sun) A winning formula by Yountville's culinary oligarch, Thomas Keller, Ad Hoc serves the master's favorite American home-cooking in four-course family-style menus, with no variations except for dietary restrictions. There's also weekend lunchtime takeout behind the restaurant at Keller's latest venture, **Addendum** (⏰11am-2pm Thu-Sat), which also serves barbecue; get the daily menu on Twitter at @AddendumatAdHoc.

🛏 Hotel St Helena Historic Hotel $$

(☎707-963-4388; www.hotelsthelena.net; 1309 Main St, St Helena; r with bath $125-235, without bath $105-165; �──🖵) Decorated with period furnishings, this frayed-at-the-edges 1881 hotel sits right in St Helena's downtown. Rooms are tiny, but good value, especially those with shared bathroom. No elevator.

🛏 Maison Fleurie B&B $$$

(☎707-944-2056; www.maisonfleurienapa. com; 6529 Yount St, Yountville; r incl breakfast $145-295; �──🖵🏊) Rooms at this ivy-covered country inn are in a century-old home and carriage house, decorated in French-provincial style. There's a big breakfast, and afternoon wine and hors d'oeuvres. Hot tub.

STRETCH YOUR LEGS
SAN FRANCISCO

Start/Finish Chinatown Gate

Distance 2.7 miles

Duration 4–5 hours

Limber up and look sharp: on this walk, you'll pass hidden architectural gems, navigate the winding alleys of Chinatown and catch shimmering views of the bay. Along the way, enjoy controversial art, savory street snacks and a flock of parrots.

Take this walk on Trips

Chinatown Gate

The first steps of this tour are through the elaborate threshold of the **Dragon Gate** (at Bush St & Grant Ave), which was donated by Taiwan in 1970 and announces the entrance to Chinatown. The street, beyond the gate, was once a notorious red-light district, but forward-thinking Chinatown businessmen reinvented the area in the 1920s, hiring architects to create a signature 'Chinatown Deco' look. The jumble of glittering shops is the perfect place to pick up a cheap souvenir.

The Walk >> Huff it uphill from Chinatown Gate, past Grant Ave gilded dragon lamps to Old St Mary's Square. A few blocks beyond the noble Old St Mary's Church take a left on Clay St.

Chinese Historical Society of America Museum

At this intimate museum, visitors picture what it was like to be Chinese during the Gold Rush, the transcontinental railroad construction and the Beat heyday. The **Chinese Historical Society of America Museum** (415-391-1188; www.chsa.org; 965 Clay St; adult/child $5/2, first Tue of month free; noon-5pm Tue-Fri, 11am-4pm Sat) hosts rotating exhibits across the courtyard in a graceful building, built as Chinatown's YWCA in 1932.

The Walk >> Backtrack past Stockton St and turn left down Spofford Alley where mah-jongg tiles click and Sun Yat-sen plotted the 1911 overthrow of China's last dynasty. At Washington, take a right. Then go left on Ross Alley.

Golden Gate Fortune Cookie Factory

Ross Alley (sometimes marked as Old Chinatown Alley) might seem familiar to movie buffs; it's been the backdrop for flicks like *Karate Kid, Part II* and *Indiana Jones and the Temple of Doom*. The humble little warehouse at No 56 is where to get your fortune while it's hot, folded into warm cookies at the **Golden Gate Fortune Cookie Factory** (56 Ross Alley; admission free; 8am-7pm). For a small fee you can even print custom fortunes.

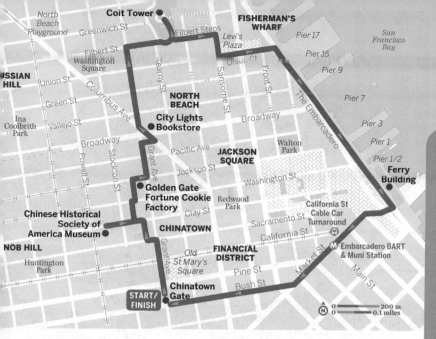

The Walk >> Go right on Jackson and left on Grant. You'll pass a number of Chinese bakeries with piping hot *char siu bao* (BBQ pork buns). Take a shortcut through Jack Kerouac Alley, where the poetic vagabond once strolled.

City Lights Bookstore

Ever since manager Shigeyoshi Murao and Beat poet Lawrence Ferlinghetti successfully defended their right to 'willfully and lewdly print' Allen Ginsberg's magnificent *Howl and Other Poems* in 1957, **City Lights Bookstore** (www.citylights.com; 261 Columbus Ave; ⊙10am–midnight) has been a landmark. Snuggle into the Poet's Chair upstairs overlooking Jack Kerouac Alley or entertain radical ideas downstairs in the Muckracking and Stolen Continents sections. If reading makes you thirsty, grab a pint at Vesuvio next door.

The Walk >> Leave City Lights front door and go right on Columbus. Make a slight right on Grant and walk for 5 blocks, then take a right and hoof it up the Greenwich St steps.

Coit Tower

Adding an exclamation mark to San Francisco's landscape, a visit to **Coit Tower** (☎415-362-0808; Telegraph Hill; admission free, elevator rides $5; ⊙10am–6pm) ends the walk atop Telegraph Hill. This peculiar 210ft-projectile is a monument to San Francisco firefighters. When it was completed in 1934, the Diego Rivera–style murals lining the lobby were denounced as Communist. To see more murals hidden inside Coit Tower's stairwell, take a free guided tour at 11am on Saturdays.

The Walk >> Take the Filbert Steps downhill past wild parrots and hidden cottages to Levi's Plaza. Head right on Embarcadero to the Ferry Building.

Ferry Building

The historic **Ferry Building** was once a thriving hub of commuters; these days it has transformed itself into a destination for foodies. Artisan food producers, organic produce and boutique suppliers make it a mouth-watering stop.

The Walk >> Walk down Market St. Turn right on Bush St back to Chinatown Gate.

Great 1906 Earthquake and Fire

105th Anniversary

San Francisco Lotta's Fountain, a meeting spot for survivors of the 1906 quake

Earthquake Trail

3

Fascinated by the famed rock and roll California lifestyle? Loop around the Bay Area, tracing the San Andreas and Hayward Faults, and tip toe along their scenic natural creations.

TRIP HIGHLIGHTS

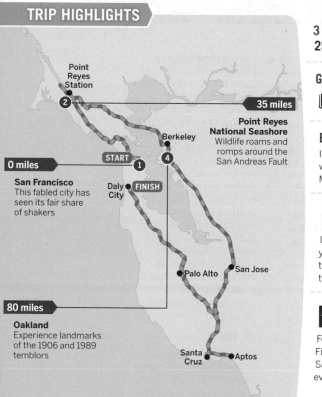

Point Reyes Station

2

35 miles

Berkeley

START **1**

4

0 miles

San Francisco
This fabled city has seen its fair share of shakers

Daly City **FINISH**

Point Reyes National Seashore
Wildlife roams and romps around the San Andreas Fault

San Jose

Palo Alto

80 miles

Oakland
Experience landmarks of the 1906 and 1989 temblors

Santa Cruz • Aptos

**3 DAYS
250 MILES/402KM**

- - -

GREAT FOR...

- - -

BEST TIME TO GO
Infrequent rain and warmer days between March and October.

- - -

 ESSENTIAL PHOTO

In Point Reyes, spread your arms between the two fence sections on the Earthquake Trail.

- - -

 BEST BAR

Feel tipsy at Heinold's First & Last Chance Saloon before you've even raised a glass.

61

3 Earthquake Trail

Although earthquakes occur across California, the 1906 San Francisco quake remains a defining moment in the state's history. Unseen faults, such as the one responsible for the 1989 quake, crisscross the Bay Area. The evidence is there if you know where to look. So don your Sherlock hat and sleuth out some cracks in the earth.

TRIP HIGHLIGHT

❶ San Francisco

For earthquake tourists, the entire city is a location, as most of it either tumbled down or went up in smoke during the raging fires that followed the quake of 1906.

Walk down Market St towards the iconic Ferry Building and pause where Kearny and 3rd Sts converge. **Lotta's Fountain** dates from 1875, and in 1906 was a meeting spot for survivors. Today people gather here on each anniversary of the quake at the fateful time of 5:12am. Continue to the end of Market St and the **Ferry Building**, which figured in the 1989 Loma Prieta earthquake. The 7.1 temblor caused widespread damage in the Bay Area and fatally damaged a multilevel highway that ran like a scar down the middle of the Embarcadero. The eyesore freeway was eventually torn down, the lavish landscaping you now see was installed and the Ferry Building was turned into one of the nation's premier marketplaces for organic and artisan foods.

For our walking tour, see p58.

✕ 🎽 p67

The Drive » Drive north across the Golden Gate Bridge and exit on Hwy 1. After Stinson

PACIFIC OCEAN

Beach the road follows the San Andreas Fault, which runs through the rift valley like an arrow. Just past the stop sign in Olema, follow the brown Point Reyes National Seashore sign to the visitor center on Bear Valley Rd.

TRIP HIGHLIGHT

2 Point Reyes National Seashore

A national park that covers much of the peninsula, wind-blown Point Reyes National Seashore shelters free-ranging elk, scores of marine mammals and all manner of raptors and wild cats. Near Olema, the Earthquake Trail begins by the park's **Bear Valley Visitor Center** (www.nps.gov/pore; Bear Valley Rd, Point Reyes Station; admission free; 🕘9am-5pm Mon-Fri, 8am-5pm Sat & Sun; 🚻), with reconstructed evidence

---

🔗 LINK YOUR TRIP

2 San Francisco, Marin & Napa Loop

Add wine tasting to your to-do list by continuing north on Hwy 101 from Point Reyes or San Francisco.

14 Along Highway 1 to Santa Cruz

Join Hwy 1 for the beacons of historic lighthouses, organic farms and your pick of sandy cove beaches.

of the 1906 quake. The short paved trail reaches a 16ft gap between the two halves of a once-connected fence line, a lasting testimonial to the power of earthquakes.

A few miles north, the 12-mile long Tomales Bay estuary straddles the San Andreas Fault. The thin channel teems with curious harbor seals, and **Blue Waters Kayaking** (☎415-669-2600; www. bwkayak.com; kayak rental 2/4hr $50/60), in Inverness and across the bay in Marshall, offers various bay tours. Or you can rent a kayak and paddle around the secluded beaches and rocky crevices on your own.

✗ 🛏 p67

The Drive >> Backtrack to the stop sign in Olema and take Sir Francis Drake Blvd 15 miles southeast to San Rafael, where you can join I-580 and head to the East Bay over the Richmond–San Rafael Bridge. Continue south on Hwy 580/80, and take the University Ave exit to the campus of UC Berkeley.

❸ Berkeley

A national hot spot of (mostly left-of-center) intellectual discourse, and with one of the most vocal activist populations in the country, this infamous college town has an interesting mix of graying progressives and idealistic undergrads. The campus is good for a stroll, and nearby Telegraph Ave is chock-a-block with shops and cheap eateries.

Talk about *baaad* planning. **Memorial Stadium**, which dates from 1923, is UC Berkeley's 71,000-seat sporting venue, and the Hayward Fault lurks just beneath it. Modeled on the Roman Coliseum, it boasts a spectacular setting in Strawberry Canyon with a backdrop of the forested Berkeley Hills. A recent $321-million retrofit and renovation project tackled the stadium's ability to withstand a major temblor. On alternate years, the iconic facility hosts the famous football frenzy between the UC Berkeley and Stanford teams.

✗ p67

The Drive >> Head south on College Ave and then Claremont Ave to get onto Hwy 24/980. Take the freeway about 3.5 miles south and exit on Jackson St to reach the waterfront at Oakland's Jack London Sq.

TRIP HIGHLIGHT

❹ Oakland

In Jack London Sq, try to get your bearings at **Heinold's First & Last Chance Saloon** (www. firstandlastchance.com; 48 Webster St). You really have to hold on to your beer at this 1883 bar constructed from wood scavenged from an old whaling ship. Keeled to a severe slant during the 1906 earthquake, the building's 20% grade might make you feel self-conscious about stumbling before you even order. Its other big claim to fame is that author Jack London was a regular patron.

A mile and a half northwest, 42 people died when the Cypress Fwy collapsed in West Oakland, one of the most horrifying and enduring images of the 1989 Loma Prieta quake. The **Cypress Freeway Memorial Park** at 14th St and Mandela Pkwy commemorates those who perished as well as those who helped rescue survivors. A large

FAULTY TOWERS

One of the region's biggest earthquake sites sits in the middle of the San Francisco Bay. The **Bay Bridge** (www.baybridgeinfo.org) was rendered useless during the 1989 quake, when a small segment of the east portion collapsed. More than two decades later, much of the structural steel on the suspension side has been restored, while the entire eastern portion is simply being replaced. The cost has shot past $6 billion.

Oakland Heinhold's First & Last Chance Saloon

twisted metal sculpture on the corner recalls the destruction of the double-decker concrete freeway, and a lavishly landscaped – and nonelevated – parkway opened here in 2005. Look for the wall bearing the inscription '15 seconds.'

The Drive » Continue south on I-880 to San Jose and join up with Hwy 17, which narrows down to a curvy four-lane nail biter. In Santa Cruz, pick up Hwy 1 South for 6 miles, exiting at State Park Dr. Cut north over the highway and go right on Soquel Dr. After half a mile, turn left on Aptos Creek Rd and drive 4 miles to the park.

5 Aptos

Adjacent to the posh little village of Aptos, the **Forest of Nisene Marks State Park** (www.parks. ca.gov; Aptos Creek Rd; parking $8; 🚹 👫) boasts trails that stretch through old logging camps and redwood groves all the way to the summit of the coastal mountains and the peak that gave the 1989 earthquake its name: Loma Prieta. On the Aptos Creek Trail, a sign marks the actual epicenter of the Loma Prieta quake, and on the Big Slide Trail a number of fissures can

be spotted. Pause in the quiet, surrounded by the impossibly green trees, and ponder when the San Andreas will next let rip.

The Drive » Backtrack to Hwy 1 North and follow it west to Santa Cruz.

6 Santa Cruz

The old brick buildings of the downtown area, which were built on dubious river sand, were no match for the 1989 quake, and much of the Pacific Garden Mall was destroyed or had to be demolished later. Yet Santa Cruz hung on, and thriving

65

LOCAL KNOWLEDGE: DEROSE WINERY

The **DeRose Winery** (www.derosewine.com) in Hollister is my favorite stop on a fault-finding tour of northern California. The winery is in a beautiful valley that has been carved by the creeping San Andreas Fault. The main building sits squarely on the fault – keeping the structure supported has been a challenge. But gosh, the wine is good. To me, it serves as metaphor: Californians not just surviving, but thriving in earthquake country.

Susan Elizabeth Hough, author of Finding Fault in California, An Earthquake Tourist's Guide

veteran businesses like **Bookshop Santa Cruz** (www.bookshopsantacruz.com; 1520 Pacific Ave; ⏰9am-10pm Sun-Thu, 9am-11pm Fri & Sat; 🍴), which operated out of a tent in a parking lot for months after the earthquake, are proof of the town's rebirth.

A block away at the intersection of Water St, Pacific Ave and Knight St, a small plaza showcases the city's historic **Town Clock**. While not destroyed in 1989, its hands stopped at exactly 5:04am, a haunting reminder of that day's devastation until the timepiece was repaired weeks later. A plaque on the red-brick base memorializes those who died that day.

🍴 🛏 p67

The Drive » Return north on Hwy 17, and exit at Summit Rd, approximately 13 miles north of Hwy 1. Cross west over the highway and take Skyline Blvd/ Hwy 35 north for 20 miles to Page Mill Rd, a breathtaking journey along the scenic ridge road of the Santa Cruz Mountains. Take Page Mill Rd east about 1.5 miles to the Los Trancos parking lot.

❼ Palo Alto

One of a number of attractive and bucolic parks cluster around dreamy Skyline Blvd, and the **Los Trancos Open Space Preserve** (www.openspace.org; Page Mill Rd; 🍴🐕) spans the San Andreas Fault as it bisects the tree-dotted rolling hills. Lined with stations explaining the movements of the fault, the easy 1.5-mile San Andreas Fault Trail uses the landscape to illustrate the effects of seismic activity.

🍴 p67

The Drive » Follow winding and pastoral Page Mill Rd north to Hwy 280 North, another scenic route of crystal-blue reservoirs framed by fog-combed ridges. After 20 miles, exit back onto Skyline Blvd/ Pacifica, where a glorious coastal panorama peeks through the trees. Turn west on Manor Dr and then north on Palmetto Ave. Bear left onto Westline Dr for Mussel Rock Park.

❽ Daly City

The epicenter for the 1906 San Francisco earthquake is marked by mangy **Mussel Rock**, which sits amid the thrashing surf just offshore from Daly City. It was here on April 18 that the San Andreas Fault let loose a couple of centuries of built-up pressure. The resulting quake – estimated at 8.3 on the Richter scale – is among the most powerful of all time.

The site is overlooked by **Mussel Rock Park** (120 Westline Dr; 🍴🐕), a grassy coastal expanse that easily stirs up images of geologic chaos. The sandy ground is unstable and surrounding streets are riddled with offshoot faults from the San Andreas. Many homes on Westline Dr have been undermined by the unstable earth. End your adventure by scouting out the secret cave by the water's edge.

Eating & Sleeping

San Francisco ❶

✖ Ferry
Building   Market, International $$

(www.ferrybuildingmarketplace.com; 1 Ferry Building; 🚇) This sustainable-food temple houses several foodie shrines under one roof. It features chef-operated lunch counters, high end takeout and a farmers market on Tuesday and Thursday from 10am to 2pm, and Saturdays from 8am to 2pm.

🛏 Orchard
Garden Hotel   Boutique Hotel $$

(☎415-399-9807; www.theorchardgardenhotel. com; 466 Bush St; r $179-249; ❋ @ 🛜) San Francisco's first all-green-practices hotel uses sustainably grown wood, chemical-free cleaning products and recycled fabrics in its soothingly quiet rooms. Don't think you'll be trading comfort for conscience: rooms have unexpectedly luxe touches like high-end down pillows and Egyptian-cotton sheets. Don't miss the sunny rooftop terrace.

Point Reyes National Seashore ❷

✖ Bovine Bakery   Bakery $

(11315 Hwy 1; 🕑6:30am-5pm Mon-Thu, 7am-5pm Sat & Sun) Don't leave town without sampling something from possibly the best bakery in Marin. A bear claw (large, sweet pastry) and an organic coffee are a good way to kick off your morning.

✖ Osteria Stellina   Italian $$

(☎415-663-9988; www.osteriastellina.com; 11285 Hwy 1; mains $15-25; 🕑11:30am-2:30pm & 5-9pm; 🍴) This place specializes in rustic Italian cuisine, with pizza and pasta dishes and Niman Ranch meats. Head over on Tuesday nights for lasagna and live music, and definitely make reservations for the weekend.

🛏 Holly Tree Inn   Inn, Cottage $$

(☎415-663-1554; www.hollytreeinn.com; Silver Hills Rd, Point Reyes Station; r incl breakfast $130-180, cottages $190-265) The Holly Tree Inn, off Bear Valley Rd, has four rooms and three private cottages in a beautiful country setting. The Sea Star Cottage is a romantic refuge at the end of a small pier on Tomales Bay.

Berkeley ❸

✖ Gather   American $$

(☎510-809-0400; www.gatherrestaurant.com; 2200 Oxford St; lunch mains $10-17, dinner mains $14-19; 🕑11:30am-2pm Mon-Fri, 10am-2:30pm Sat & Sun, plus 5-10pm daily; 🍴) When vegan foodies and passionate farm-to-table types dine out together, they often end up here. Inside a salvaged wood interior punctuated by green vines streaking down over an open kitchen, patrons swoon over dishes created from locally sourced ingredients and sustainably raised meats. Reserve for dinner.

Santa Cruz ❻

✖ El Palomar   Mexican $$

(1336 Pacific Ave; mains $7-27; 🕑11am-11pm; 🚇) Always packed and consistently good (if not great), El Palomar serves tasty Mexican staples – try the seafood ceviche – and fruity margaritas. Tortillas are made fresh by charming women in the covered courtyard.

🛏 Sunny Cove Motel   Motel $$

(☎831-475-1741; www.sunnycovemotel.com; 21610 E Cliff Dr; r $90-200; ❋ 🐾) It's nothing fancy, but this tidy little hideaway east of downtown is a staunch budget fave. The long-time Santa Cruzian owner rents retro beach-house rooms and kitchenette suites.

Palo Alto ❼

✖ Palo Alto Creamery   Diner $$

(www.paloaltocreamery.com; 566 Emerson St; mains $7-20; 🕑7am-10pm, longer hr Sat & Sun) An upmarket downtown institution, this sparkling chrome and red booth beauty from 1923 is famous for its frothy milkshakes, hefty hamburgers and scratch-made pies.

Ferry Building Marketplace *Hosts a broad selection of gourmet organics*

Alice Waters' Culinary Tour

4

Filled with the explosive tastes of California, chef and food revolutionary Alice Waters' tour is a deeply satisfying taste of her home turf, ending with dinner at her own Chez Panisse.

TRIP HIGHLIGHTS

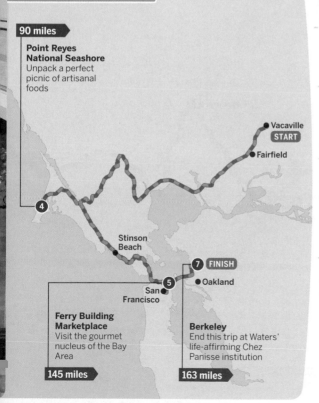

90 miles

Point Reyes National Seashore
Unpack a perfect picnic of artisanal foods

4

Stinson Beach

Vacaville
START

Fairfield

7 **FINISH**

San Francisco

Oakland

Ferry Building Marketplace
Visit the gourmet nucleus of the Bay Area

145 miles

Berkeley
End this trip at Waters' life-affirming Chez Panisse institution

163 miles

3 DAYS
157 MILES/253KM

GREAT FOR...

BEST TIME TO GO
Late summer, when farms deliver their tastiest bounty.

ESSENTIAL PHOTO
The lighthouse, bluffs and endless horizon at Point Reyes National Seashore.

BEST PICNIC
Briny oysters, Acme bread and Cowgirl Creamery cheese at the Hog Island Oyster Company.

69

4 Alice Waters' Culinary Tour

Making a delicious loop around the Bay Area, this trip wanders through the aisles of celebrated farmers markets and drops in on artisanal food producers – all hand-picked by the reigning queen of California cuisine, Alice Waters. Thankfully, a stroll through Point Reyes National Seashore will work up a healthy appetite. You'll need it on this deeply satisfying trip to foodie heaven.

❶ Vacaville

The journey begins down on the farm – the inspiration for Chez Panisse's pioneering menu, and most California culinary triumphs since. Run by Alexis Koefoed, **Soul Food Farm** (www. soulfoodfarm.com; 6046 Pleasant Valley Rd; 🚶) supplies chickens and eggs to select restaurateurs throughout the Bay Area, including Waters herself. Waters reminisces about Soul Food's humanely raised

'Freedom Rangers' breed, which peck around the 15 acres. If made it at home, this simple chicken, and you know what, I'm pretty used to good chicken. It tasted like no other chicken I've had in the United States. The dark meat was richer, more flavorful, and it was a revelation. It reminded me of the chicken I had 35 years ago in France.' Pick up some eggs from the cooler at the end of the drive and leave your money in the jar. 'Her eggs are fantastic,'

Waters says. 'I just feel like I'm making a donation to the cause.'

The Drive >> From Vacaville, go south on I-80 for 20 minutes and follow the exit for Hwy 37, which skirts the marshes of the San Pablo Bay and leads into Novato. Head north on Hwy 101 for 20 miles to Petaluma.

- - - - - - - - - - - -

❷ Petaluma

Near the elegantly slouching Victorians of Petaluma is another Alice Waters standby, **Green String Farm** (www.greenstringfarm.com; 3571 Old Adobe Rd; ⊙10am-5pm winter, to 6pm summer). Bob Cannard has pioneered sustainable farming in the North Bay for 30 years, and you can taste the chemical-free fruits of his labors at the on-site farm store, which serves seasonal produce, local cheese and nuts. Instead of battling weeds with herbicides, Green String's lets them coexist with cover vegetation

and planted crops, creating a symbiotic ecosystem that yields a smaller crop but richer soil. The only weed eaters on hand are the fluffy sheep you can pet near the store. You may also meet strutting chickens, members of the Green String Farm Band (theme song: 'Favorite Chicken'), and Bob himself. 'Bob is doing amazing things with that land,' Waters says with admiration.

The Drive >> Take the Point Reyes–Petaluma Rd 19 miles west of town to Point Reyes Station.

- - - - - - - - - - - -

❸ Point Reyes Station

Surrounded by dairies and ranches, Point Reyes Station became a hub for artists in the 1960s and offers a pleasant collection of art galleries, tourist shops and excellent food. The tour of Point Reyes'

❶ **Vacaville**
START

○ Fairfield

○ Port Chicago

○ Pittsburg

Concord

alnut eek

⑤ LINK YOUR TRIP

5 Napa Valley

Cruise the winding back roads of America's most celebrated wine region, home to several of California's best restaurants. Connect to this trip by crossing into the North Bay on I-80 and going west on the Lincoln Hwy.

7 Russian River & the Bohemian Highway

Sink into the slow pace of the North Bay's rural charms, by traveling north over the Golden Gate Bridge and touring the Bohemian Hwy's orchards, vineyards and country hotels.

DETOUR: HOG ISLAND OYSTER COMPANY

Start: ❸ **Point Reyes Station**

Only 10 minutes north of Point Reyes Station, you'll find the salty turnout for the **Hog Island Oyster Company** (☎415-663-9218; www.hogislandoysters.com; 20215 Hwy 1, Marshall; 12 oysters $13-$16, picnic area fee $8; ⏱9am-5pm Mon-Sun). There's hardly much to see – just a few picnic tables, some barbeque grills and a small window selling their famously silky oysters and a few other provisions. And while they sell oysters to go (by the pound), for Waters, 'There's nothing better than eating them right there on the beach.' For a fee you can arrange for a table and borrow shucking tools and take a lesson on how to crack open and grill the oysters. A picnic at the farm is an unforgettable lunch – and popular, so make reservations. Take the Hwy 1 north from Point Reyes Station and look for the sign for Hog Island Oyster Company, on the bay.

edibles begins by fighting your way through the spandex-clad crowd of weekend cyclist to grab a crusty loaf of fire-baked Brickmaiden Bread at the **Bovine Bakery** (11315 Hwy 1; ⏱6:30am-5pm Mon-Thu, 7am-5pm Sat & Sun). Next, step down the block to the restored barn that houses **Tomales Bay Foods & Cowgirl Creamery** (www.cowgirlcreamery.com; 80 4th St; ⏱10am-6pm Wed-Sun; 🍴🐾), one of the nation's most sought-after cheese makers. In spring the must-buy is their St Pat's, a smooth, mellow round wrapped in nettle leaves; the Mt Tam (available year-round) is pretty damn good too. There is also a gourmet deli and tour on Friday mornings.

✕ 🛏 p76

The Drive ⟩⟩ Follow signs for the Point Reyes National Seashore, which is south on Hwy 1, just on the other side of Tomales Bay.

TRIP HIGHLIGHT

❹ Point Reyes National Seashore

For the perfect picnic spot, Waters says to look just down the coast, to the **Point Reyes National Seashore** (www.nps.gov/pore; Bear Valley Rd; ⏱9am-5pm Mon-Fri, from 8am Sat & Sun). 'Go up there in the headlands and find a little spot on the way out by Bolinas and Inverness and along the Point Reyes National Seashore,' she says. 'I think that is one of the greatest park areas I've ever been in.' The windswept

peninsula is rough-hewn beauty that lures marine mammals and migratory birds. The 110 sq miles of pristine ocean beaches also offer excellent hiking and camping opportunities. For an awe-inspiring view, follow the Earthquake Trail from the park headquarters at Bear Valley.

🛏 p76

The Drive ⟩⟩ Leaving the park, you'll follow the eucalyptus-lined curves of Hwy 1 south toward Stinson Beach and past one stunning Pacific view after the next. If you don't pause for some beach combing, you'll be back across the Golden Gate Bridge in about an hour and a half. From the bridge, follow Hwy 101 through the city to Broadway, then go right to the waterfront.

TRIP HIGHLIGHT

❺ Ferry Building Marketplace

From the center of the Golden Gate Bridge, it's possible to view the clock tower of the city's Ferry Building Marketplace which hosts a broad selection of gourmet organics and is a one-stop destination for many of Waters' recommendations. 'The day to go, of course, is Saturday,' she says. That's when the landmark is encircled by some 80 family farmers and 40 food artisans. From dry-farmed tomatoes

Hog Island Oyster Company Oysters

to organic kimchi, this bounty may seem like an embarrassment of riches – but not to Waters. 'We have to start looking at food as a right and not a privilege,' she says flatly. 'That is important.' Smaller market days are on Tuesdays and Thursdays, but if your trip doesn't coincide with a market day, never fear: 35 local food purveyors are indoors. 'Inside there are really quite exceptional vendors,' she says. 'It's one of the only places where you can get real food all in one place – real meat, real chicken, raised at Soul Food Farm and Prather Meat. There's obviously Cowgirl Creamery and Acme Bread and McEvoy Olive Oil.' When it comes to McEvoy, she offers high praise. 'I just think they've put a lot of energy into figuring out what varietals of tree can grow up there, south of Petaluma. There are loads of little boutique producers of olive oil that are happening now, but they've set the standard.' For a self-guided walking tour of more of San Francisco, see p58.

✕ 🛏 p76

The Drive » From the bustle of the Ferry Building, head south on Market St and right on Valencia, the colorful heart of the Mission District.

- - - - - - - - - - - - -

❻ Mission District

This hip neighborhood is home to many of the restaurants by Waters' protégés and has emerged as one of the most exciting restaurant hubs in the city. No place exemplifies all these qualities as well as **Zuni Café**, (📞415-552-2522; www.zunicafe.com; 1658 Market St, San Francisco; mains $15-30; ⏱11:30am-midnight Tue-Sat, 11am-11pm Sun), an excellent spot for mesquite-grilled meats, brick-oven pizzas and people watching. This is a place Waters merrily refers to as her 'home away from home.' She'll quickly admit that it's a distinctively different atmosphere from the one at Chez Panisse, but adds, 'Zuni is run in the right spirit. It's real food.' By the way she offers these straightforward compliments – her voice going from a kind of

DETOUR: MUIR WOODS

Start: ❹ Point Reyes National Seashore

The old-growth redwoods at **Muir Woods** (www.nps.gov/muwo; adult/child under 16 $7/free; ⏱8am-sunset), just 12 miles north of the Golden Gate Bridge, is the closest redwood stand to San Francisco. The easiest stroll is the gentle 1-mile **Main Trail Loop**, which passes 1000-year-old trees at **Cathedral Grove** and returns via **Bohemian Grove**, where the tallest tree in the park stands 254ft high. For something more challenging, try the 7-mile **Dipsea Trail**, which climbs over the coastal range and down to Stinson Beach, cutting through a corner of Muir Woods.

A lovely cafe serves local and organic goodies and hot drinks, but the real reward here is hiking up to the gorgeous beer garden overlooking Muir Woods and Mt Tamalpais at the **German Tourist Club** (www.touristclubsf.org; ⏱1-5pm 1st, 3rd & 4th weekends of the month), or Nature Friends (*Die Naturefreunde*).

By car, follow Hwy 1 to Muir Beach, then turn onto Ridge Ave from Panoramic Hwy, park in the gravel driveway at the end of the road and start the 0.3-mile walk downhill. You can also hike in on the Sun Trail from Panoramic – a half-hour of mostly flat trail with views of the ocean and Muir Woods.

For a bit more background on Muir Woods, see p52.

PANISSE PROTÉGÉS

'When you operate a restaurant for 37 years, a whole lot of people come through the kitchen,' Waters says. Of her alumni in San Francisco, try Michael Tusk, who offers shrewd Italian-French fusions at Quince, or Gayle Pirie, who operates Foreign Cinema, a gourmet movie house in the Mission District. More casual eateries are across the bay, where Charlie Hallowell offers immaculate wood-fired pizzas at a pair of Oakland restaurants: Pizzaiolo and Boot & Shoe Service. You can tuck into earthy California cuisine at Camino or visit Alison Barakat, who serves what may be the best chicken sandwich on earth at Bakesale Betty.

gregarious, playful lilt to dead-serious in a second – it's clear that a declaration of 'real food' is her highest praise. It's reserved for a select handful of students who have passed through the kitchen of her restaurant and other like-minded chefs in what she calls 'the cause.' Asked about menus she admires, her response is uncomplicated: 'It's about seasonality, no question,' she says. 'And obviously locality. I'm looking for people who are using organic produce and meat. So I want grass-fed beef. I want organic vegetables. I want organic breads. I want people who care about farmers and ranchers. I'm looking,' and she pauses just a beat, 'for the *purists.*'

✖️ 🛏️ p77

The Drive ❯❯ From the Mission District it is a straight shot over the Bay Bridge and into Berkeley via I-80.

TRIP HIGHLIGHT

❼ Berkeley

San Francisco might host a handful of banner dining rooms, but the heart of Waters' food revolution is across the Bay, in Berkeley. Start at the **Berkeley farmers market** (Center St; 🕙10am-3pm Sat), run by the Ecology Center since 1987. Alice Waters herself may be here, in her element and in raptures. 'You have to try Prima Vera's organic tortillas,' she urges, 'and Annabelle's stand [La Tercera] has wonderful Italian greens. Oh, that *puntarella...*' On the western end of the so-called 'Gourmet Ghetto' – a neighborhood that married the revolutionary '60s ideals of Berkeley with a haute dining sensibility – follow the scent of cinnamon bread to the **Acme Bread Company** (📞510-524-1327; 1601 San Pablo; 🕙8am-6pm Mon-Sat, 8:30am-3pm Sun), where Chez Panisse alum Steve Sullivan sparked

what local foodies call the 'San Francisco bread revolution.' The crown jewel of the Gourmet Ghetto, and appropriate final stop, is **Chez Panisse** (📞restaurant 510-548-5525, cafe 510-548-5049; www.chezpanisse.com; 1517 Shattuck Ave; restaurant meals $65-100, cafe mains $18-29; 🕙restaurant dinner Mon-Sat, cafe lunch & dinner Mon-Sat). It's casual and unpretentious, and every mind-altering, soul-sanctifying bite of the food served in the dining room downstairs and the slightly less formal cafe upstairs is emblematic of Waters' principles. The kitchen is even open so diners can peek behind the scenes (ask nicely at the end of the night and you might even get a tour). Reserve weeks ahead.

✖️ 🛏️ p77

Eating & Sleeping

Point Reyes Station ❸

✘ Bovine Bakery   Bakery $

(11315 Hwy 1; ⏱6:30am-5pm Mon-Thu,
7am-5pm Sat & Sun) Don't leave town without
sampling something buttery from possibly the
best bakery in Marin. A bear claw (large, sweet
pastry) and an organic coffee are a good way to
kick off your morning.

✘ Tomales Bay
Foods & Cowgirl Creamery   Market $$

(☎415-663-9335; www.cowgirlcreamery.
com; 80 4th St; ⏱10am-6pm Wed-Sun; ♨)
A local market in an old barn sells picnic
items, gourmet cheeses and organic produce.
Reserve in advance for the small-scale artisanal
cheesemaker's demonstration and tasting ($5).
The milk is local and organic, with vegetarian
rennet in all its soft cheeses.

⌂ Point Reyes Hostel   Hostel $

(☎415-663-8811; www.norcalhostels.org/reyes;
dm/r $24/68; 🛜@♨) Just off Limantour Rd,
this rustic HI property has bunkhouses with
warm and cozy front rooms, big-view windows
and outdoor areas with hill vistas. It's in a
beautiful secluded valley 2 miles from the ocean
and surrounded by lovely hiking.

Point Reyes
National Seashore ❹

⌂ Point Reyes National
Seashore Campgrounds   Campground $

(☎415-663-8054; www.nps.gov/pore/
planyourvisit/campgrounds.htm; tent sites $15)
Wake up to deer nibbling under a blanket of
fog at one of Point Reyes' four popular hike-in
areas, each with pit toilets, water and tables.
Reservations accepted up to three months in
advance. Reaching the campgrounds requires a
2- to 6-mile hike.

Ferry Building Marketplace ❺

✘ Ferry Building
Farmers Market   Market $

(☎415-693-0996; www.ferrybuildingmarket
place.com; One Ferry Building; ⏱10am-2pm Tue
& Thu, 8am-2pm Sat; ♨) Fanning out around
the south end of the building like a fabulous
garnish, this year-round market brings in the
best produce of the region.

✘ Ferry Building
Marketplace   Market $$

(☎415-693-0996; www.ferrybuildingmarket
place.com; One Ferry Building; ⏱Mon-Fri 10am-
6pm, Sat 9am-6pm, Sun 11am-5pm; ♨) Once a
transportation hub, this remodeled landmark
now houses a gourmet emporium – all a tribute
to San Francisco's monumental good taste.

✘ McEvoy Ranch   Market $

(☎415-291-7224; www.mcevoyranch.com; One
Ferry Building; ⏱9am-6pm Mon-Sat, 10am-5pm
Sun) In addition to their famous olive oils, this
marketplace inside the Ferry Building sells
organic produce and potted olive trees.

✘ Prather Ranch
Meat Company   Market $

(☎415-391-0420; www.prmeatco.com; One Ferry
Building; ⏱10am-7pm Sun-Fri, 8am-6pm Sat) For
carnivores this is the highest quality outlet in the
Bay Area. Look no further for humanely raised,
all-natural, dry-aged organic beef.

⌂ Orchard
Garden Hotel   Boutique Hotel $$

(☎415-399-9807; www.theorchardgardenhotel.
com; 466 Bush St; r $179-249; ✳@🛜) San
Francisco's first all-green-practices hotel has
soothingly quiet rooms with luxe touches, like
Egyptian-cotton sheets, plus an organic rooftop
garden.

Mission District ⑥

✕ Foreign Cinema California $$$

(☎415-648-7600; www.foreigncinema.com;
2524 Mission St; mains from $25) Reliably
tasty dishes like truffled swordfish are the
main attraction, but Luis Buñuel and François
Truffaut provide an entertaining backdrop, with
movies screened in the courtyard.

✕ Quince Italian $$$

(☎415 278 3700; www.quincerestaurant.com;
470 Pacific Ave; 4-course/chef's tasting menu
$95/140; ☺5:30-10pm Mon-Fri) The tasting
menu is an event for deep-pocketed foodies, but
those who can't swallow the price can still enjoy
an exceptional à la carte menu in the lounge.
The four-course stunner might include Liberty
Duck with radish and local honey.

✕ Zuni Café American $$$

(☎415-552-2522; www.zunicafe.com; 1658
Market St; mains $15-30; ☺11:30am-midnight
Tue-Sat, 11am-11pm Sun) A lively vibe is
accompanied by excellent comfort-food
wonders. Their brunch is also among San
Francisco's best.

⊨ Hotel Vitale Luxury Hotel $$$

(☎415-278-3700; www.hotelvitale.com; 8
Mission St; r from $319; ☎) The ugly exterior
disguises a fashion-forward hotel with echoes of
Mid-Century Modern design, up-to-the-minute
luxuries and a soothing spa.

Berkeley ⑦

✕ Bakesale Betty Bakery $

(www.bakesalebetty.com; 2228 Broadway;
pastries from $2, sandwiches $6.50-9; ☺11am-
2pm Tue-Fri; ✍) An Aussie expat and Chez
Panisse alum, Betty Barakat (in signature blue
wig) has patrons lining up out the door for
heavenly scones, strawberry shortcake and
fried-chicken sandwiches.

✕ Boot & Shoe Service Pizzeria $$

(☎510-763-2668; www.bootandshoeservice.
com; 3308 Grand Ave; pizza from $10; ☺5:30-
10pm Tue-Thu, 5-10:30pm Fri & Sat, to 10pm Sun)
Patrons pack this place for wood-fired pizzas,
original cocktails and creative antipasti made
from sustainably sourced, fresh ingredients.

✕ Camino American $$$

(☎510-547-5035; www.caminorestaurant.
com; 3917 Grand Ave, Oakland; mains $13-26;
☺10am-2pm Sat & Sun, 5:30-10pm Mon &
Wed-Sat, 5-10pm Sun) Gather around the roaring
fire at reclaimed-wood communal tables for
sophisticated rustic fare and seasonal cocktails.

⊨ Hotel
Shattuck Plaza Boutique Hotel $$$

(☎510-845-7300; www.hotelshattuckplaza.com;
2086 Allston Way; r $219-259; ✳ @ ☎) Newly
remodeled, this 100-year-old downtown jewel
has a foyer of red Italian glass lighting, flocked
Victorian-style wallpaper – and yes, a peace
sign tiled into the floor.

Napa Valley Swaths of vineyards
carpet hillsi...

Napa Valley

5

The birthplace of modern-day Wine Country is famous for regal cabernet sauvignons, château-like wineries and fabulous food. Expect to be wined, dined and tucked between crisp linens.

TRIP HIGHLIGHTS

46 miles

Silverado Trail
Explore dozens of wineries along this tranquil transvalley road

6

St Helena

8 FINISH

Yountville

1 START

Calistoga
Spa town famous for mud baths and hot spring soaks

25 miles

Napa
The region's main city boasts a tempting food market

0 miles

**2–3 DAYS
76 MILES/122KM**

GREAT FOR...

BEST TIME TO GO
May for a presummer lull, and September and October to experience 'the crush.'

ESSENTIAL PHOTO
Three...two...one! Get ready for an eruption at Old Faithful Geyser.

BEST SPLURGE
If you can get a table, tantalize your taste buds at Thomas Keller's French Laundry.

Classic Trip

5   Napa Valley

America's premier viticulture region has earned its reputation among the world's best. Rolling hills, dotted with century-old oaks, turn the color of lion's fur under the summer sun and swaths of vineyards carpet hillsides as far as the eye can see. Hundreds of wineries inhabit Napa Valley, but it's quality, not quantity, that sets the region apart — it competes with France and doubles as an outpost of San Francisco's top-end culinary scene.

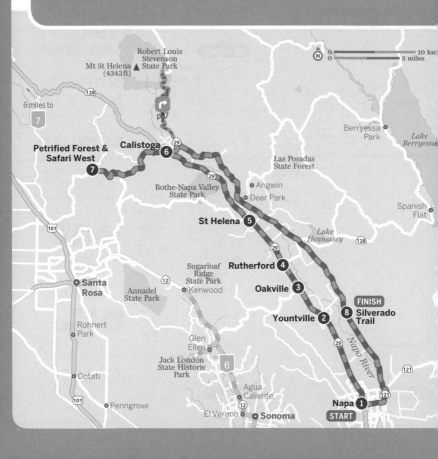

❶ Napa

The valley's workaday hub was once a nothing-special city of storefronts, Victorian cottages and riverfront warehouses, but booming real-estate values caused an influx of new money that has transformed Napa into a growing city of arts and food. Its number-one attraction, the **Oxbow Public Market** (www. oxbowpublicmarket.com; 610 1st St; ⏰9am-7pm Mon & Wed-Sat, to 8pm Tue, 10am-6pm Sun; 🚻🎏) showcases all things culinary – from produce stalls to kitchen stores to fantastic edibles. It's foodie central, with an emphasis on seasonal and regional ingredients, grown sustainably. Graze your way through this gourmet market and plug into the Northern California food scene. Standouts include fresh oysters, Venezuelan cornbread sandwiches, excellent Cal-Mexican and certified organic ice cream. Tuesday is locals night, with many discounts. On Tuesday and Saturday mornings, there's a farmers market. Friday nights bring live music.

West of downtown, scrap-metal sheep graze Carneros vineyards at 217-acre **Di Rosa** (📞707-226-5991; www.dirosaart. org; 5200 Carneros Hwy 121; ⏰gallery 9:30am-3pm Wed-Fri, by appointment Sat), a stunning collection of Northern California art displayed indoors in galleries and outdoors in sculpture gardens. Reservations are recommended for tours.

🍴 🛏 p88

The Drive » From Napa, Yountville is 9 miles north on Hwy 29, a divided four-lane road surrounded by vineyards and framed by low hills.

❷ Yountville

This one-time stagecoach stop is now a major foodie destination, with more Michelin stars per capita than any other American town. There are some good inns here, but it's deathly boring at night. You stay in Yountville to drink with dinner without having to drive afterward – but make reservations or you might not eat!

Ma(i)sonry (📞707-944-0889; www.maisonry.com; 6711 Washington St; ⏰9am-10pm) occupies a 1904 stone house, now transformed into a rustic-modern showplace for furniture, art and wine. The garden is a swank postdinner fireside gathering spot for *vino*.

Yountville's modernist 40,000-sq-ft **Napa Valley Museum** (📞707-944-0500; www.napavalleymuseum.org; 55 Presidents Circle; adult/child $5/2.50; ⏰10am-5pm Wed-Mon), off California Dr, chronicles cultural history and showcases local paintings, and has good picnicking outside.

🍴 🛏 p88

The Drive » Go north to Oakville via another 4 miles of vineyard vistas on Hwy 29, which slims to two lanes just outside of Yountville. Tracks for the Napa Valley Wine Train line the west side of the road.

❸ Oakville

But for its famous grocery, you'd drive through the tiny settlement of Oakville (population 71) and never know you'd missed it. This is the middle of the grapes – vineyards sprawl in every direction.

The behemoth **Robert Mondavi Winery**

LINK YOUR TRIP

6 Sonoma Valley
For lower-key wineries and Sonoma's early California historical sites, Hwy 12/121 is the main connector between the Napa and Sonoma Valleys.

7 Russian River & the Bohemian Highway
From Calistoga, continue west on Hwy 128 for river dips, rural wineries and wildlife watching along rugged undeveloped coastline.

(📞888-766-6328; www.
robertmondavi.com; 7801
Hwy 29; tours $15-25, bottles
$19-150; ⊙10am-5pm) is
somewhat of a corporate-
winery experience
and you can expect a
lot of company. That
said, the grounds are
gorgeous and it offers a
good menu of tours and
tastings for those who
are new to wine. The
winery also uses careful
environmental practices
in its farming, managing
1000 acres of naturally
farmed vineyards.

✕ p88

The Drive ≫ Rows of
grapevines recede into the
distance as you continue 2 miles
north on Hwy 29.

- - - - - - - - - - -

❹ Rutherford

Another blip of a town,
Rutherford (population
164) is more conspicuous,

with its wineries putting
it on the map. The valley
views are spectacular at
Mumm Napa (📞800-686-
6272; www.mummnapa.com;
8445 Silverado Trail; tasting
$7-25; ⊙10am-4:45pm; 🐾),
which makes respectable
sparkling wines that you
can sample while seated
on a vineyard-view
terrace. No appointment
necessary, and you can
dodge crowds by paying
$7 extra for the reserve-
tasting terrace. Check
the website for discount
tasting coupons.

Meandering paths
wind through the
magical gardens and
fruit-bearing orchards
of **Frog's Leap** (📞707-
963-4704; www.frogsleap.
com; 8815 Conn Creek Rd;
tours & tastings $20, bottles
$18-42, ⊙by appointment;
👶🐾) – pick peaches in
July – surrounding an
1884 barn and farmstead
with cats and chickens.
But more than anything,
it's the vibe that's
wonderful: casual and
down-to-earth, with
a major emphasis on

fun. Sauvignon blanc
is its best-known wine,
but the merlot merits
attention, and all are
organic. There's also a
dry, restrained cabernet,
atypical in Napa.

Round Pond (📞888-
302-2575; www.roundpond.
com; 875 Rutherford Rd;
tastings $25, bottles $24-
95; ⊙by appointment)
tantalizes with fantastic
food pairings on a
vineyard-view stone
patio. We especially love
the olive-oil and wine-
vinegar tastings, which
are included with guided
tours of the olive mill
($30).

The Drive ≫ St Helena is
another 4 miles north on Hwy
29, though you may be slowing
to a crawl before hitting the first
stoplight in the center of town.

- - - - - - - - - - -

❺ St Helena

You'll know you're
arriving here when
traffic halts. St Helena
(ha-*lee*-na) is the
Rodeo Dr of Napa, with
fancy boutiques lining
Main St (Hwy 29). The
historic downtown is
good for a stroll, with
great window-shopping,
but parking is next to
impossible on summer
weekends.

Owned by Bill
Clinton's former
ambassador to Austria,
Hall (📞707-967-2626; www.
hallwines.com; 401 St Helena
Hwy; tastings $15-25, bottles
$22-80; ⊙10am-5:30pm; 🐾)
specializes in cabernet

NAPA VALLEY WINERIES

Cab is king in Napa. No varietal captures imaginations
like the fruit of the cabernet sauvignon vine –
Bordeaux is the French equivalent – and no wine
fetches a higher price. Napa farmers can't afford *not*
to grow cabernet. Other heat-loving varietals, such as
sangiovese and merlot, also thrive here.

Napa's wines merit their reputation among the
world's finest – complex, with luxurious finishes.
Napa wineries sell many 'buy-and-hold' wines,
versus Sonoma's 'drink-now' wines.

DRIVING IN NAPA VALLEY

» Napa Valley is 30-miles long and 5-miles wide at its widest point (the city of Napa), 1 mile at its narrowest (Calistoga). Two roads run north–south: Hwy 29 (St Helena Hwy) and the more scenic Silverado Trail, a mile east. Drive up one, and down the other.

» The American Automobile Association determined Napa Valley to be America's eighth-most congested rural vacation destination. Summer and fall weekend traffic is unbearable, especially on Hwy 29 between Napa and St Helena. Plan accordingly.

» Cross-valley roads that link Silverado Trail with Hwy 29 – including Yountville, Oakville and Rutherford crossroads – are bucolic and get less traffic. For scenery, the Oakville Grade and rural Trinity Rd (which leads southwest to Hwy 12 in Sonoma Valley) are narrow, curvy and beautiful – but treacherous in rainstorms. Mt Veeder Rd leads through pristine countryside west of Yountville.

» Police watch like hawks for traffic violators. Don't drink and drive.

franc, sauvignon blanc, merlot and cabernet sauvignon. There's a cool abstract-sculpture garden and a lovely picnic area shaded by mulberry trees (with wines by the glass) at this LEED–gold-certified winery – California's first (tours $45, including barrel tastings).

The **Silverado Museum** (✆707-963-3757; www. silveradomuseum.org; 1490 Library Lane; admission free; ⊙noon-4pm Tue-Sat) contains a fascinating collection of Robert Louis Stevenson memorabilia. In 1880, the author – then sick, penniless and unknown – stayed in an abandoned bunkhouse at the old Silverado Mine on Mt St Helena with his wife, Fanny Osbourne; his novel *The Silverado Squatters* is based on his time there. To reach Library Lane, turn east off Hwy 29 at the Adams St traffic light and cross the railroad tracks.

Hushed and regal, the 1889 stone château of the **Culinary Institute of America at Greystone** (✆707-967-2320; www. ciachef.edu/california; 2555 Main St; mains $25-29, cooking demonstration $20; ⊙restaurant 11:30am-9pm, cooking demonstrations 1:30pm Sat & Sun) houses a gadget- and cookbook-filled culinary shop; an upscale restaurant and a new cafe; weekend cooking demonstrations; and wine-tasting classes by luminaries in the field,

including Karen MacNeil, author of *The Wine Bible*.

 p89

The Drive ›› Trees begin to reappear on the landscape, breaking up the vineyard views as you head 8 miles north on Hwy 29.

- - - - - - - - - -

TRIP HIGHLIGHT

❻ Calistoga

The least gentrified town in Napa Valley feels refreshingly simple, with an old-fashioned main street lined with shops, not boutiques, and diverse characters wandering the sidewalks.

BOOKING WINERY APPOINTMENTS

Because of strict county zoning laws, many Napa wineries cannot legally receive drop-in visitors; unless you've come strictly to buy, you'll have to call ahead. This is *not* the case with all wineries. We recommend booking one appointment and planning your day around it.

LOCAL KNOWLEDGE
DALIA CEJA, CEJA VINEYARDS

Indian Springs
(☎707-942-4913; www.
indianspringscalistoga.com; 1712 Lincoln Ave,
Calistoga; ☉8am-9pm) **is the perfect
place to relax either as a couple
or with a group of friends. You
can take a bath with mud infused
with lavender and chamomile,
and afterwards take a dip in the
Olympic-size natural mineral pool.
On a chilly fall day, swimming in
the pool – the temperature reaches
about 100°F at one end – is my
number-one favorite thing to do.**

Top: Castello di Amorosa
Left: Mud bath, Indian Springs
Right: Wine tasting, Robert Mondavi Winery

EMILY RIDDELL / GETTY IMAGES ©

CATHERINE KARNOW / CORBIS ©

Calistoga is synonymous with the mineral water bearing its name, bottled here since 1924, and its springs and geysers have earned it the nickname the 'hot springs of the West.' Plan to visit one of the town's spas, where you can indulge in the local specialty: a hot-mud bath, made of the volcanic ash from nearby Mt St Helena.

It took 14 years to build the perfectly replicated 12th-century Italian castle at **Castello di Amorosa** (☎707-967-6272; www.castellodiamorosa. com; 4045 Hwy 29; tasting $18-28, bottles $20-125, tour adult/child $33/23; ⊙by appointment; 🚼🐾), complete with moat, hand-cut stone walls, ceiling frescoes by Italian artisans, Roman-style cross-vault brick catacombs, and a torture chamber with period equipment. You can taste without an appointment, but this is one tour worth taking. Wines include some respectable Italian varietals, including a velvety Tuscan blend.

Calistoga's mini-version of Yellowstone, the **Old Faithful Geyser** (☎707-942-6463; www. oldfaithfulgeyser.com; 1299 Tubbs Lane; adult/child $10/ free; ⊙9am-6pm summer, to 5pm winter; 🚼) shoots boiling water 60ft to 100ft into the air, every 30 minutes. The vibe is pure roadside Americana, with

folksy hand-painted interpretive exhibits, picnicking and a little petting zoo, where you can come nose-to-nose with llamas. It's north of Calistoga, via Hwy 128 west to Tubbs Lane, and discount coupons are available around town.

✕ ⊨ p89

The Drive » Backtrack east on Hwy 128 and go 4 miles west on forested and curvy Petrified Forest Rd.

----

❼ Petrified Forest & Safari West

Three million years ago, a volcanic eruption at nearby Mt St Helena blew down a stand of redwoods between Calistoga and Santa Rosa. The trees fell in the same direction, away from the blast, and were covered in ash and mud. Over the millennia, the mighty giants' trunks turned to stone. Gradually the overlay eroded, exposing them, and the first stumps of **Petrified Forest** (📞707-942-6667; www.petrifiedforest. org; 4100 Petrified Forest Rd; adult/child $10/5; ⊕9am-7pm summer, to 5pm winter) were discovered in 1870. A monument marks Robert Louis Stevenson's 1880 visit. He describes it in *The Silverado Squatters*. Check online for 10%-off coupons.

CALISTOGA SPAS

Calistoga is famous for hot-spring spas and mud-bath emporiums, where you're buried in hot mud and emerge feeling supple, detoxified and enlivened. (The mud is made with volcanic ash and peat; the higher the ash content, the better the bath.)

Packages take 60 to 90 minutes and cost $70 to $90. You start semisubmerged in hot mud, then soak in hot mineral water. A steam bath and blanket-wrap follow. The treatment can be extended with a massage, increasing the cost to $130 and up.

Baths can be taken solo or, at some spas, as couples. Variations include thin, painted-on clay-mud wraps (called 'fango' baths, good for those uncomfortable sitting in mud), herbal wraps, seaweed baths and various massage treatments. Discount coupons are sometimes available from the visitors center. Reservations essential at all spas, especially on summer weekends.

Indian Springs (📞707-942-4913; www.indianspringscalistoga.com; 1712 Lincoln Ave; ⊕8am-9pm) The longest continually operating spa and original Calistoga resort has concrete mud tubs and mines its own ash. Treatments include use of the huge, hot-spring-fed pool.

Spa Solage (📞707-226-0825; www.solagecalistoga.com; 755 Silverado Trail; ⊕8am-8pm) Chichi, austere, top-end spa, with couples' rooms and a fango-mud bar for DIY paint-on treatments. Also has zero-gravity chairs for blanket wraps, and a clothing-optional pool.

Dr Wilkinson's Hot Springs (📞707-942-4102; www.drwilkinson.com; 1507 Lincoln Ave; ⊕8:30am-5:30pm) Operational for 50 years, 'the doc' uses more peat in its mud.

Mount View Spa (📞707-942-6877; www.mountviewhotel.com; 1457 Lincoln Ave; ⊕9am-9pm) Traditional full-service, 12-room spa, good for clean-hands gals who prefer painted-on mud to submersion.

Calistoga Spa Hot Springs (📞707-942-6269; www.calistogaspa.com; 1006 Washington St; ⊕appointments 8:30am-4:30pm Tue-Thu, to 9pm Fri-Mon; 🚻) Traditional mud baths and massage at a motel complex with two huge **swimming pools** (⊕10am-9pm) where kids can play while you soak (pool passes $25).

DETOUR:
ROBERT LOUIS STEVENSON STATE PARK

Start: ❻ **Calistoga**

Eight miles north of Calistoga via curvaceous Hwy 29, the long-extinct volcanic cone of Mt St Helena marks the Napa Valley's end. Encircled within undeveloped **Robert Louis Stevenson State Park** (☎707-942-4575; www.parks.ca.gov), the crest often gets snow in winter. It's a strenuous 5-mile climb to the peak's 4343ft summit, but what a view – 200 miles on a clear winter's day. Check conditions before setting out. Also consider 2.2-mile one-way Table Rock Trail (go south from the summit parking area) for drop-dead valley views. Temperatures are best in wildflower season, February to May; fall is prettiest, when the vineyards change colors.

The park includes the site of the Silverado Mine where Stevenson and his wife honeymooned in 1880.

Giraffes in Wine Country? Whadya know! Just 4 miles west (Petrified Forest Rd becomes Porter Creek Rd), **Safari West** (☎707-579-2551; www.safariwest.com; 3115 Porter Creek Rd; adult $68-78, child 3-12 $32, child under 2 $15; ⊕) covers 400 acres and protects zebras, cheetahs and other exotic animals, who mostly roam free. See them on a guided three-hour safari in open-sided jeeps; reservations required. You'll also walk through an aviary and lemur condo. The reservations-only cafe serves lunch and dinner. If you're feeling adventurous, stay overnight in nifty canvas-sided **tent cabins** (cabins incl breakfast $200-295), right in the preserve.

The Drive » Return east back to Calistoga and drive 1 mile south on Hwy 29/128 and 1 mile north on Lincoln Ave to the Silverado Trail. Lined with row after row of grapevines, journey 21 miles southeast along lovely Silverado Trail.

TRIP HIGHLIGHT

❽ Silverado Trail

The Napa Valley winery jackpot, Silverado Trail runs from Calistoga to Napa and counts approximately three-dozen wineries along its bucolic path. At the northernmost reaches of the Silverado Trail, and breaking ranks with Napa snobbery, the party kids at **Lava Vine** (☎707-942-9500; www.lavavine.com; 965 Silverado Trail; tasting $10, refundable with purchase; ⊕10am-5pm, appointment suggested; ⊕⊕) take a lighthearted approach to their seriously good wines, all paired with small bites, including some hot off the barbecue. Children and dogs play outside, while you let your guard down in the tiny tasting room. Bring a picnic.

One of Napa's oldest wineries, unfussy **Regusci** (☎707-254-0403; www.regusciwinery.com; 5584

Silverado Trail; tasting $15-25, bottles $36-125; ⊕10am-5pm; ⊕) dates to the late 1800s, with 173 acres of vineyards unfurling around a century-old stone winery that makes Bordeaux-style blends. Located along the valley's quieter eastern side, it's a good bet when traffic up-valley is bad. No appointments are necessary, and the oak-shaded picnic area is lovely.

Like a modern-day Persian palace, **Darioush** (☎707-257-2345; www.darioush.com; 4240 Silverado Trail; tastings $18-35, bottles $40-80; ⊕10:30am-5pm) ranks high on the fabulosity scale, with towering columns, Le Corbusier furniture, Persian rugs and travertine walls. Though known for cabernet, Darioush also bottles chardonnay, merlot and shiraz, all made with 100% of their respective varietals. Reserve in advance for its wine-and-cheese pairings.

Eating & Sleeping

Napa ❶

✖ Alexis Baking Co　Cafe $

(☎707-258-1827; www.alexisbakingcompany.
com; 1517 3rd St; dishes $6-10; ⏰7:30am-3pm
Mon-Fri, 7am-3pm Sat, 8am-2pm Sun; 🚼🍷)
Our fave spot for scrambles, granola, focaccia
sandwiches, big cups of joe and boxed lunches
to go.

✖ Ubuntu　Vegetarian $$

(☎707-251-5656; www.ubuntunapa.com; 1140
Main St; dishes $14-18; ⏰dinner nightly, lunch
Sat & Sun; 🍷) The Michelin-starred, seasonal,
vegetarian menu features artfully presented
natural wonders from the biodynamic kitchen
garden, satisfying hearty eaters with four-
to-five inspired small plates, and eco-savvy
drinkers with 100-plus sustainably produced
wines.

🛏 Avia Hotel　Hotel $$

(☎707-224-3900; www.aviahotels.com; 1450
1st St; r $149-249; 🌡@🛜) Downtown Napa's
newest hotel opened in 2009 and feels like a
big-city hotel, with business-class-fancy rooms,
styled in sexy retro-'70s chic. Walkable to
restaurants and bars.

Yountville ❷

✖ Bouchon Bakery　Bakery $

(☎707-944-2253; www.bouchonbakery.com;
6528 Washington St; dishes $3-9; ⏰7am-7pm)
Bouchon makes perfect French pastries and
strong coffee. Order at the counter and sit
outside, or pack a bag to go.

✖ Étoile　Californian $$$

(☎707-944-8844; www.chandon.com; 1
California Dr; lunch mains $26-31, dinner mains
$32-36; ⏰11:30am-2:30pm & 6-9pm Thu-Mon)
Within the Chandon winery, Michelin-starred

Étoile's is perfect for a lingering white-
tablecloth lunch in the vines; ideal when you
want to visit a winery and eat a good meal with
minimal driving.

✖ French Laundry　Californian $$$

(☎707-944-2380; www.frenchlaundry.com;
6640 Washington St; prix-fixe incl service charge
$270; ⏰dinner daily, lunch Sat & Sun) The
pinnacle of California dining, Thomas Keller's
French Laundry is epic, a high-wattage culinary
experience on par with the world's best. Book
two months ahead at 10am sharp, or log onto
OpenTable.com precisely at midnight. Avoid
tables before 7pm; first-service seating moves
faster than the second – sometimes too fast.

🛏 Napa Valley Railway Inn　Theme Inn $$

(☎707-944-2000; www.napavalleyrailwayinn.
com; 6523 Washington St; r $125-260;
🌡@🛜🏊) Sleep in a converted railroad car,
part of two short trains parked at a central
platform. They have little privacy, but are
moderately priced. Bring earplugs.

🛏 Poetry Inn　Inn $$$

(☎707-944-0646; www.poetryinn.com; 6380
Silverado Trail; r incl breakfast $650-1400;
🌡🛜🏊) There's no better view of Napa Valley
than from this understatedly chic, three-room
inn, high on the hills east of Yountville. Rooms
are decorated in Arts and Crafts–inspired style,
and have private balconies, wood-burning
fireplaces, 1000-thread-count linens and
enormous baths with indoor-outdoor showers.
Bring a ring.

Oakville ❸

✖ Oakville Grocery & Cafe　Deli $$

(www.oakvillegrocery.com; 7856 Hwy 29;
⏰8am-5:30pm) The once-definitive Wine
Country deli has gotten ridiculously overpriced,
with less variety than in previous years, but still

carries excellent cheeses, charcuterie, bread, olives and wine. There are tables outside, but ask where to picnic nearby.

St Helena ❺

✗ Farmstead   Modern American $$$
(☎707-963-9181; www.farmsteadnapa.com; 738 Main St; mains $16-26; ⏰11:30am-9pm) A cavernous open-truss barn with big leather booths and rocking-chair porch, Farmstead grows many of its own ingredients – including grass-fed beef – for its earthy menu that highlights wood-fired cooking.

✗ Gott's Roadside
(Taylor's Auto Refresher)   Burgers $$
(☎707-963-3486; www.gottsroadside.com; 933 Main St; dishes $8-15; ⏰10:30am-9pm; 🚻) Wiggle your toes in the grass and feast on all-natural burgers, Cobb salads and fried calamari at this classic roadside drive-in, whose original name, 'Taylor's Auto Refresher,' is still listed on the roadside sign. Avoid big weekend waits by calling in your order.

🛏 El Bonita Motel   Motel $$
(☎707-963-3216; www.elbonita.com; 195 Main St; $119-179; ❄ @ 🛜 🏊 🐾) Book in advance to secure a room at this sought-after motel, with up-to-date rooms (quietest are in back), attractive grounds, hot tub and sauna.

🛏 Meadowood   Resort $$$
(☎707-963-3646; www.meadowood.com; 900 Meadowood Lane; r from $600; ❄ @ 🛜 🏊 🚻) Hidden in a wooded dell with towering pines and miles of hiking, Napa's grandest resort has cottages and rooms in satellite buildings surrounding a croquet lawn. We most like the hillside fireplace cottages; lawn-view rooms lack privacy but are good for families, with space to play outside. The vibe is country club, with white-clapboard buildings reminiscent of New England.

Calistoga ❻

✗ Calistoga Inn & Brewery   American $$
(☎707-942-4101; www.calistogainn.com; 1250 Lincoln Ave; lunch mains $9-13, dinner mains $14-26; ⏰11:30am-3pm & 5:30-9pm) Locals crowd the outdoor beer garden on Sundays. Midweek we prefer the country dining room and its big oakwood tables, a homey spot for pot roast and other simple American dishes. There's live music on summer weekends.

✗ Jolé   Californian $$
(☎707-942-5938; www.jolerestaurant.com; 1457 Lincoln Ave; mains $15-20; ⏰5-9pm Sun-Thu, to 10pm Fri & Sat) The earthy and inventive farm-to-table small plates at chef-owned Jolé evolve seasonally, and may include such dishes as local sole with tangy miniature Napa grapes, caramelized Brussels sprouts with capers, and organic Baldwin apple strudel with burnt-caramel ice cream. Four courses cost $50. Reservations essential.

🛏 Dr Wilkinson's Motel
& Hideaway Cottages   Motel, Cottage $$
(☎707-942-4102; www.drwilkinson.com; 1507 Lincoln Ave; r $149-255, cottages $165-270; ❄ 🛜 🏊) This good-value vintage-1950s motel has well-kept rooms facing a swimming-pool courtyard. No hot tub, but three pools (one indoors) and mud baths. Dr Wilkinson's also rents simple stand-alone cottages, with kitchens, at the affiliated Hideaway Cottages.

🛏 Indian Springs Resort   Resort $$$
(☎707-942-4913; www.indianspringscalistoga. com; 1712 Lincoln Ave; motel r $229-299, bungalow $259-349, 2-bedroom bungalow $359-419; ❄ 🛜 🏊 🚻) The definitive old-school Calistoga resort, Indian Springs has bungalows facing a central lawn with palm trees, shuffleboard, bocce, hammocks and Weber grills – not unlike a vintage Florida resort. Some bungalows sleep six. There are also top-end motel-style rooms and a huge hot-springs-fed swimming pool.

Sonoma Valley Explore vineyards a
farms in this folksy, bucolic reg.

Sonoma Valley 6

Flanked by sun-drenched hills and vast vineyard landscapes, the bountiful roadside farms and unassuming top-notch wineries along this trip make for a relaxing excursion.

TRIP HIGHLIGHTS

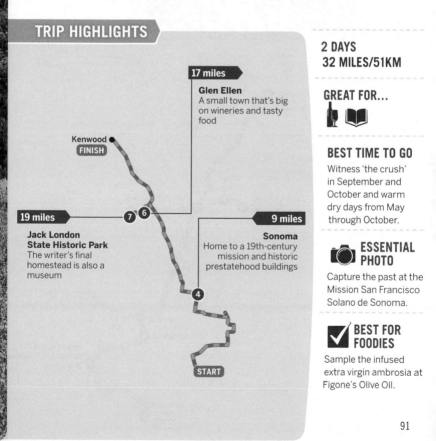

17 miles

Glen Ellen
A small town that's big on wineries and tasty food

Kenwood
FINISH

19 miles

Jack London State Historic Park
The writer's final homestead is also a museum

7 **6**

9 miles

Sonoma
Home to a 19th-century mission and historic prestatehood buildings

4

START

2 DAYS
32 MILES/51KM

GREAT FOR...

BEST TIME TO GO

Witness 'the crush' in September and October and warm dry days from May through October.

ESSENTIAL PHOTO

Capture the past at the Mission San Francisco Solano de Sonoma.

BEST FOR FOODIES

Sample the infused extra virgin ambrosia at Figone's Olive Oil.

6 Sonoma Valley

Locals call it 'Slow-noma.' Unlike fancy Napa, nobody in folksy Sonoma cares if you drive a clunker and vote Green. Anchoring the bucolic, 17-mile-long Sonoma Valley, the town of Sonoma makes a great jumping-off point for exploring Wine Country – it's only an hour from San Francisco – and has a marvelous sense of place, with storied 19th-century historical sights surrounding the state's largest town square.

❶ Cornerstone Gardens

There's nothing traditional about **Cornerstone Gardens** (☎707-933-3010; www.cornerstonegardens. com; 23570 Arnold Dr; admission free; ⊙10am-4pm; 👪), which showcases the work of renowned avant-garde landscape designers. Set aside an hour to stroll through the thought-provoking and conceptual plots. Look for the enormous blue chair at road's edge.

✗ p97

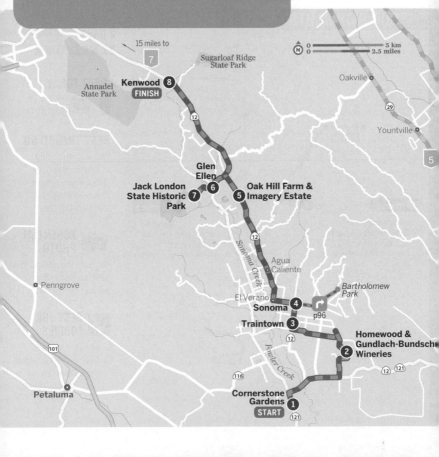

The Drive » Go north on Hwy 121 and follow it for 3 miles as it bears east. Turn south on Burndale Rd. Homewood winery is on your left, at the flagpole.

❷ Homewood & Gundlach-Bundschu Wineries

A stripy rooster named Steve chases dogs in the parking lot of **Homewood** (☏707-996-6353; www.homewoodwinery.com; 23120 Burndale Rd at Hwy 121/12; tastings free, bottles $18-32; ⊙10am-4pm; 🐾), a down-home winery whose motto sums it up: 'Da redder, da better.' The tasting room is a garage, and the winemaker crafts standout ports and

LINK YOUR TRIP

5 Napa Valley
For upscale wineries, spa resorts and top notch restaurants, Hwy 12/121 is the main connector between the Napa and Sonoma Valleys.

7 Russian River & the Bohemian Highway
From Kenwood, go west on Hwy 12 for summertime river dips, delightful wineries and rambles in redwood forest or pristine Pacific beach.

Rhône-style grenache, mourvèdre and syrah. Ask about 'vertical tastings,' and sample wines from the same vineyards but different years. From Homewood, go north on Burndale Rd, jog left briefly onto Napa Rd and then right onto Denmark St.

One of Sonoma Valley's oldest and prettiest wineries, **Gundlach-Bundschu** (☏707-938-5277; www.gunbun.com; 2000 Denmark St; tastings $10, bottles $22-40; ⊙11am-4:30pm) looks like a storybook castle. Founded in 1858 by Bavarian immigrant Jacob Gundlach, it's now at the cutting edge of sustainability. Signature wines are rieslings and gewürztraminers, but 'Gun-Bun' was the first American winery to produce 100% merlot. Tours of the 2000-barrel cave ($20) are available by reservation. Down a winding lane and with a small lake, it's also pleasant for picnicking and hiking.

The Drive » Follow Denmark St back to Napa Rd, and go west to Hwy 12. Drive Hwy 12/Broadway north a quarter mile to Traintown.

❸ Traintown

If you're traveling with young children, make a beeline to **Traintown** (☏707-938-3912; www.traintown.com; 20264

Broadway; ⊙10am-5pm daily summer, Fri-Sun only mid-Sep–late May). A miniature steam engine makes 20-minute loops ($5.25), and there are vintage amusement-park rides ($2.75 per ride), including a carousel and a Ferris wheel.

The Drive » Drive north on Hwy 12/Broadway about one mile.

TRIP HIGHLIGHT

❹ Sonoma

Kick back for a few hours in Sonoma's town square, with tree-lined paths and a playground, surrounded by shops, restaurants and tasting rooms. Comprising multiple sites, the **Sonoma State Historic Park** (☏707-938-1519; www.parks.ca.gov; adult/child $3/2; ⊙10am-5pm Tue-Sun) is a must-see for California history buffs. The **Mission San Francisco Solano de Sonoma** (E Spain St), at the plaza's northeast corner, was built in 1823, in part to forestall the Russian coastal colony at Fort Ross from moving inland. The mission was the 21st and final California mission, and the only one built during the Mexican period (the rest were founded by the Spanish). The not-to-be-missed chapel dates from 1841.

The adobe **Sonoma Barracks** (E Spain St; ⊙daily) was built by Vallejo between 1836 and 1840 to house Mexican troops, but it became the capital of a rogue nation on June 14, 1846, when American settlers, of varying sobriety, surprised the guards and declared an independent 'California Republc' [sic] with a homemade flag featuring a blotchy bear. The US took over the republic a month later, but abandoned the barracks during the Gold Rush, leaving Vallejo to turn them into (what else?) a winery in 1860.

Walk just round the corner to stock up for an afternoon picnic. Known for its dry-jack cheeses (made here since the 1930s), **Vella Cheese Co** (☏707-928-3232; www. vellacheese.com; 315 2nd St E) also makes delectable Mezzo Secco with cocoa powder-dusted rind.

✕ 🏠 p97

The Drive ›› Head north on Hwy 12 for about five miles to Oak Hill Farm along tree-lined vineyards.

WALTER BIBIKOW/JAI / CORBIS ©

⑤ Oak Hill Farm & Imagery Estate

At the southern end of Glen Ellen, **Oak Hill Farm** (☏707-996-6643; www. oakhillfarm.net; 15101 Sonoma Hwy; ⊙11am-6pm Wed-Sun Apr-Dec; 🚻) contains acres upon acres of organic flowers and produce, hemmed in by lovely steep oak and manzanita woodland. The farm's Red Barn Store is a historic dairy barn filled with handmade wreaths, herbs and organic goods reaped from the surrounding fields. Try the heirloom tomatoes, pumpkins and blue plums.

Just farther north on Sonoma Hwy, **Imagery Estate** (☏707-935-4515, 877-550-4278; www. imagerywinery.com; 14335 Sonoma Hwy; tastings $10-15; ⊙10am-4:30pm) boasts bottle labels designed by local artists; the art changes with each vintage and varietal. A gallery houses the entire collection of artwork – over 200 pieces with interpretations of the winery's signature Parthenon symbol. The heavy-sweet viognier and moscato are popular, and

THE BEAR FLAG REPUBLIC

Sonoma has a rich history. In 1846 it was the site of a second American revolution, this time against Mexico, when General Mariano Guadalupe Vallejo deported all foreigners from California, prompting outraged American frontiersmen to occupy the Sonoma Presidio and declare independence. They dubbed California the Bear Flag Republic after the battle flag they'd fashioned.

The republic was short-lived. The Mexican–American War broke out a month later, and California was annexed by the US. The revolt gave California its flag, which remains emblazoned with the words 'California Republic' beneath a muscular brown bear. Vallejo was initially imprisoned, but ultimately returned to Sonoma and played a major role in the region's development.

Jack London State Historic Park Ruins of Wolf House

all wines are certified biodynamic.

The Drive » Continue half a mile north before dipping 1.5 miles west and then south on Arnold Dr to the Jack London Village complex.

- - - - - - - - - - -

TRIP HIGHLIGHT

6 Glen Ellen

Try not to drool as you compare chocolates with varying percentages of cacao at **Wine Country Chocolates Tasting Bar** (☏707-996-1010; www. winecountrychocolates.com; 14301 Arnold Dr; 🚻). Pick up some champagne- or cabernet-infused truffles for the drive, or do your best to save them for gifts.

If you're new to wine, take a crash course in winemaking and biodynamic vineyard practices at **Benziger Winery** (☏888-490-2739; www.benziger.com; 1883 London Ranch Rd, Glen Ellen; tasting $10-20, tram tour adult incl tasting/child $15/5, bottles $15-80; ⊙10am-5pm; 🚻). The worthwhile, nonreservable tour includes an open-air tram ride through biodynamic vineyards, and a four-wine tasting. Afterward, you can check out the caves – and the cabernets.

You'll also learn about the difference between organic and biodynamic farming – biodynamic systems work to achieve a balance with the entire ecosystem, going beyond organic practices. Kids love the peacocks. The large-production wine's OK (head for the reserves), but the tour's the draw.

✕ 🛏 p97

The Drive » From Benziger, go half a mile farther west on London Ranch Rd to reach Jack London State Historic Park.

DETOUR: BARTHOLOMEW PARK

Start: ❹ **Sonoma Plaza**

The top close-to-town outdoors destination is 375-acre **Bartholomew Park** (☎707-935-9511; www.bartholomewparkwinery.com; 1000 Vineyard Lane), off Castle Rd to the east of town, where you can picnic beneath giant oaks and hike 3 miles of trails, with hilltop vistas to San Francisco. There's also a good winery and small museum. The Palladian Villa, at the park's entrance, is a turn-of-the-20th-century replica of the original residence of Count Haraszthy, a pioneering Sonoma vintner. It's open noon to 3pm, Saturdays and Sundays, and operated by the **Bartholomew Foundation** (☎707-938-2244).

TRIP HIGHLIGHT

❼ Jack London State Historic Park

Napa has Robert Louis Stevenson, but Sonoma's got Jack London.
This 1400-acre **park** (☎707-938-5216; www.jacklondonpark.com; 2400 London Ranch Rd, Glen Ellen; parking $8; ◎10am-5pm Fri-Mon; 🚶) traces the last years of the author's life.

Changing occupations from Oakland fisherman to Alaska gold prospector to Pacific yachtsman – and novelist on the side – London (1876–1916) ultimately took up farming. He bought Beauty Ranch in 1905 and moved there in 1910. With his second wife, Charmian, he lived and wrote in a small cottage while his mansion, Wolf House, was under construction. On the

eve of its completion in 1913, it burned down. The disaster devastated London, and although he toyed with rebuilding, he died before construction got underway. His widow, Charmian, built the House of Happy Walls, which has been preserved as a museum. It's a half-mile walk from there to the remains of Wolf House, passing London's grave along the way. Other paths wind around the farm to the cottage where he lived and worked. Miles of hiking trails (some open to mountain bikes) weave through oak-dotted woodlands, between 600ft and 2300ft elevation.

The Drive » Drive east back to Hwy 12, and 3 miles north for the Wildwood Farm and Sculpture Garden.

❽ Kenwood

Gardeners shouldn't miss **Wildwood Farm and Sculpture Garden** (☎707-833-1161, 888-833-4181; www.wildwoodmaples.com; 10300 Sonoma Hwy; ◎10am-4pm Wed-Sun, 10am-3pm Tue), where abstract outdoor art sits between exotic plants and Japanese maples. Arachnophobes should probably overlook the creepy steel spiders.

Family-run **Figone's Olive Oil** (☎707-282-9092; www.figoneoliveoil.com; 9580 Sonoma Hwy; ◎10:30am-5:30pm) grows its own olives and presses extra-virgin olive oil. Take a break from wine tasting and sample the infused citrus oils (think Meyer lemons or blood oranges) and exquisite balsamics.

A cult favorite, supercool winery **Kaz** (☎707-833-2536; www.kazwinery.com; 233 Adobe Canyon Rd, Kenwood; tastings $5, bottles $20-48; ◎11am-5pm Fri-Mon; 🚶🍷) is about blends: whatever's in the organic vineyards goes into the wine – and they're blended at crush, not during fermentation. Expect lesser-known varietals like alicante bouchet and lenoir, and a worthwhile cabernet-merlot blend. Kids can sample grape juice, then run around the playground out back, while you sift through LPs and pop your favorites onto the turntable. Crazy fun.

Eating & Sleeping

Cornerstone Gardens ❶

✖ Fremont Diner   American $

(2698 Fremont Dr/Hwy 121; mains $8-11;
🕙8am-3pm Mon-Fri, 7am-4pm Sat & Sun; 👪)
Lines snake out the door weekends at this
order-at-the-counter, farm-to-table roadside
diner. Snag a table indoors or out and feast on
ricotta pancakes with real maple syrup, chicken
and waffles, oyster po' boys and finger-licking
barbecue. Arrive early to beat the line.

Sonoma ❹

✖ Café La Haye   Modern American $$

(📞707-935-5994; www.cafelahaye.com; 140 E
Napa St; mains $15-25; 🕙5:30-9pm Tue-Sat)
One of Sonoma's top tables for earthy New
American cooking, made with produce sourced
from within 60 miles, La Haye's tiny dining room
gets packed cheek-by-jowl and service can
border on perfunctory, but the clean simplicity
and flavor-packed cooking make it many
foodies' first choice. Reserve well ahead.

✖ Della Santina's   Italian $$

(www.dellasantinas.com; 135 E Napa St;
mains $11-17) The waiters have been
here forever, and the 'specials' never
change, but Della Santina's Italian-
American cooking – linguini pesto, veal
parmigiana, rotisserie chickens – is
consistently good. The brick courtyard
is charming on warm evenings.

▐▀ Sonoma Chalet   B&B, Cottages $$

(📞707-938-3129; www.sonomachalet.com;
18935 5th St W; r without bath $125, r with
bath $140-180, cottages $190-225; 🌼) An old
farmstead surrounded by rolling hills, Sonoma
Chalet has rooms in a Swiss chalet–style house
adorned with little balconies and country-style
bric-a-brac. We love the free-standing cottages;
Laura's has a wood-burning fireplace. Breakfast
is served on a deck overlooking a nature
preserve. No air-con in rooms with shared bath.
No phones, no internet.

▐▀ Sonoma Hotel   Historic Hotel $$

(📞707-996-2996; www.sonomahotel.com; 110
W Spain St; r incl breakfast $170-200, 🐾🔊)
Long on charm, this spiffy, 1880s-vintage hotel
is decked with Spanish Colonial and American-
country-crafts furnishings. No elevator or
parking lot.

Glen Ellen ❻

✖ fig café
& winebar   Californian, French $$

(📞707-938-2130; www.thefigcafe.com; 13690
Arnold Dr, Glen Ellen; mains $15-20; 🕙5:30-9pm
daily, 10am-2:30pm Sat & Sun) It's worth a trip
to Glen Ellen for the fig's earthy California-
Provençal comfort food, like flash-fried
calamari with spicy-lemon aioli, duck confit and
moules-frites (mussels and French fries). Good
wine prices and weekend brunch give reason
to return.

▐▀ Beltane Ranch   Inn $$

(📞707-996-6501; www.beltaneranch.com;
11775 Hwy 12; r incl breakfast $150-240; 🔊)
Surrounded by horse pastures, Beltane is
a throwback to 19th-century Sonoma. The
cheerful, lemon-yellow 1890s ranch house
occupies 100 acres and has double porches
lined with swinging chairs and white wicker.
Though technically a B&B, each unfussy,
country-Americana–style room has a private
entrance – nobody will make you pet the cat.
Breakfast in bed. No phones or TVs mean zero
distraction from pastoral bliss.

Jenner Rent kayaks .
Russian River's

Russian River & the Bohemian Highway

7

In western Sonoma County, tour organic wineries, stately redwood forests, ribbons of undulating road and the serene Russian River, then ogle seals and whales along the coast.

TRIP HIGHLIGHTS

36 miles

Jenner
Harbor seals frolic where the river meets the sea

Dry Creek Valley
FINISH

Healdsburg

50 miles

Guerneville
Splash and float in the Russian River

7

Monte Rio

5

Sebastopol
START

4

22 miles

Bodega Bay
Dramatic headland with great shoreside whale watching

**2 DAYS
112 MILES/180KM**

GREAT FOR...

BEST TIME TO GO

June to September for toasty days and idyllic river swimming.

ESSENTIAL PHOTO

Catch the Russian River as it barrels into the Pacific in Jenner.

BEST WHALE-WATCHING

Gray whales breach just offshore at Bodega Head.

99

Russian River & the Bohemian Highway

Lesser-known West Sonoma County was formerly famous for its apple farms and vacation cottages. Lately vineyards are replacing the orchards, and the Russian River has now taken its place among California's important wine appellations for superb pinot noir. 'The River,' as locals call it, has long been a summertime weekend destination for Northern Californians, who come to canoe, wander country lanes, taste wine, hike redwood forests and live at a lazy pace.

❶ Sebastopol

Grapes have replaced apples as the new cash crop, but Sebastopol's farm-town identity remains rooted in the apple – evidence the much-heralded summertime Gravenstein Apple Fair. The town center feels suburban because of traffic, but a hippie tinge and quirky shops such as a beekeeping store give it color.

Just north off Bodega Ave, prepare to giggle at the wacky **Patrick**

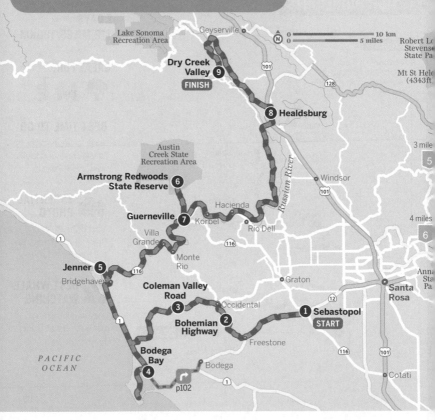

Amiot sculptures (www.patrickamiot.com; 🌐) grazing front yards along Florence Ave. Fashioned from recycled materials, a hot-rodding rat, hectic waitress and a witch in midflight are a few of the oversized and demented lawn ornaments parading along the street.

✕ p105

The Drive » From the central intersection of Hwys 116 and 12, head west on Bodega Ave (signed Bodega Bay) for 6 miles, passing apple orchards en route to tiny Freestone.

❷ Bohemian Highway

Running north from the town of **Freestone**, the pastoral 10-mile Bohemian Hwy tours

LINK YOUR TRIP

5 **Napa Valley**
In Dry Creek Valley, take Canyon Rd and then head east on Hwy 128 to visit the showcase wineries and destination restaurants of Napa Valley.

6 **Sonoma Valley**
From Sebastopol, head east on Hwy 12 for Sonoma Valley wine tasting and the historical sights around Sonoma Plaza.

past farmland and then constricts through stands of redwoods, ending at the Russian River in tiny Monte Rio. At the southern end, the crossroads of Freestone isn't much more than just that, though the former railway stop boasts a crazy-popular bakery, a cute country store and a Japanese-inspired spa specializing in unique cedar treatments. Stop by for a tasting at **Freestone Vineyards** (📞707-874-1010; www.freestonevineyards.com; cnr Bodega & Bohemian Hwys; tasting $10; ⏱11am-5pm), one of the rare spots in the area that produces excellent pinot noir, and with biodynamic farming methods to boot.

Just over 3 miles north, **Occidental** is a haven of artists, back-to-the-landers and counterculturalists. Historic 19th-century buildings line a single main street, easy to explore in an hour. On Fridays, meet the whole community at the detour-worthy **farmers market** (www.occidentalfarmersmarket.com; ⏱4pm-dusk Fri Jun-Oct), with musicians, craftspeople and – the star attraction – **Gerard's Paella** (www.gerardspaella.com) of TV-cooking-show fame.

✕ p105

The Drive » In the center of Occidental, turn west onto well-signed Coleman Valley Rd.

❸ Coleman Valley Road

Sonoma County's most scenic drive isn't through the grapes, but along these 10 miles of winding West County byway from Occidental to the sea. It's best in the late morning, after the fog has cleared and the sun's behind you. First you'll pass through redwood forests and lush valleys where Douglas firs stand draped in sphagnum moss – an eerie sight in the fog. The real beauty shots lie further ahead, when the road ascends 1000ft hills, dotted with gnarled oaks and craggy rock formations, with the vast blue Pacific unfurling below.

The Drive » The road ends at coastal Hwy 1 in the midst of Sonoma Coast State Beach, which stretches 17 miles from Bodega Head to just north of Jenner. From Hwy 1, head 2.5 miles south, then west onto Eastshore Rd. Go right at the stop sign onto Bay Flat Rd and along the harbor until road's end.

TRIP HIGHLIGHT

❹ Bodega Bay

The town of Bodega Bay sits at the southernmost section of the glorious **Sonoma Coast State Beach** (📞707-875-3483; www.parks.ca.gov), a series of beaches separated by several beautiful rocky headlands. Some beaches are tiny, hidden in little coves, while others stretch far and wide or are connected by vista-studded coastal hiking trails that wind along the bluffs. At the tip of a peninsula, the windy crown jewel of **Bodega Head** rises 265ft above sea level, with dreamy views out onto the open ocean and excellent whale watching and kite flying.

The Drive >> Return to Hwy 1 and trace the coastline 12 miles north to Goat Rock Rd in Jenner.

TRIP HIGHLIGHT

⑤ Jenner

In the small village of Jenner, the Russian River merges with the ocean and the confluence turns brackish. At the end of Goat Rock Rd, bear left for **Blind Beach**, where the mass of Goat Rock looms above and splendid Arched Rock seems to hover offshore. Then double back to **Goat Rock Beach**, where a harbor

seal colony sits at the river's mouth and pups are born from March to August. The best way to see the seals is by kayak, and most of the year you can rent them at the river's edge.

🍴 🛏 p105

The Drive >> After crossing the last bridge over the Russian River before it joins the sea, go east on Hwy 116/River Rd, a well-paved country road sandwiched between the river and abrupt hills speckled with weather-beaten wooden barns. In Guerneville, turn left at the sign for Armstrong Woods.

---

⑥ Armstrong Redwoods State Reserve

Soaring redwood trees and carpeted forest floor create a profound silence that spreads for 805 acres at **Armstrong Redwoods State Reserve** (📞707-869-2015; www.parks.ca.gov; 17000 Armstrong Woods Rd; day use per vehicle $8; ⏰day use

8am-1hr after sunset; 🚻 🎒). The *Return of the Jedi* Ewok-village chase scene was filmed here; speed-pods zoomed between

---

↱ **DETOUR:
BLOODTHIRSTY BIRDS OF BODEGA**

Start: ④ **Bodega Bay**

Bodega Bay has the enduring claim to fame as the setting for Alfred Hitchcock's *The Birds*. Although special effects radically altered the actual layout of the town, you still get a good feel for the supposed site of the farm owned by Mitch Brenner (played by Rod Taylor). The once-cozy Tides Restaurant, where much avian-caused havoc occurs in the movie, is still there, but since 1962 it has been transformed into a vast restaurant complex. Venture 5 miles inland (south on Hwy 1) to the tiny town of **Bodega** and you'll find two icons from the film: the schoolhouse and the church. Both stand just as they did in the movie – a crow overhead may make the hairs rise on your neck.

Bohemian Hwy Freestone Vineyards

the columnar trunks of these 265ft giants. The tranquil, disabled-accessible Discovery Trail passes Armstrong Tree, a 1400-year-old behemoth.

The Drive » Return 3 miles south to River Rd. Jog west one block to Church St and follow it one block south to the beach.

- - - - - - - - - - - -

TRIP HIGHLIGHT

⑦ Guerneville

The colorful, oddball main street of Guerneville bustles with life, as tourists and locals alike cruise the storefronts and galleries and dip in to the cafes, restaurants and bars.

There's nothing quite like floating in the cool river here on a scorching summer day. Head to **Johnson's Beach** (☎707-869-2022; www.johnsonsbeach.com; 16241 First St; admission free, kayak & canoe per hr/day $10/25; ☉10am-6pm, closed Oct-Apr; 🖈) to rent kayaks and canoes that you launch from and return to the beach.

About 2.5 miles east of central Guerneville, the ivy-draped brick winery at **Korbel Champagne Cellars** (☎707-824-7000; www.korbel.com; 13250 River Rd; tours & tastings free; ☉tours 11am-3pm, tasting room 10am-4:30pm) gets

jammed on weekends as folks come from all around to sip the champagnes it's been making since 1882. The fascinating 50-minute winery tour teaches you Champagne Making 101.

✕ p105

The Drive » Continue east on River Rd, forking left onto Westside Dr about 2.5 miles after Korbel. The two-lane road passes numerous wineries, and opens up to views of 4343ft-tall Mt St Helena to the northeast. Cross Dry Creek and Hwy 101 to reach Healdsburg in 12 miles.

RAINBOW FLAGS EVERYWHERE

You'll know it's Lazy Bear Weekend (August) because every establishment displays a hand-hewn bear statuette or a sign greeting the Bears. Who are the Bears, you may ask? Seven thousand gay men, prerequisite burly, coming to kick back *rio* style. Other gay gatherings like Women's Weekend (May) and Leather Weekend (November) maintain Guerneville's reputation as one of the most gay-friendly resorts in California.

8 Healdsburg

Once a sleepy agricultural town best known for its Future Farmers of America parade, Healdsburg has emerged as northern Sonoma County's culinary capital. Foodie-scenester restaurants and cafes, wine-tasting rooms and fancy boutiques line **Healdsburg Plaza**, the town's sun-dappled central square (bordered by Healdsburg Ave and Center, Matheson and Plaza Sts). Traffic grinds to a halt on summer weekends, when second-home-owners and tourists jam downtown. Old-timers aren't happy with the Napa-style gentrification, but at least Healdsburg retains its historic look, if not its once-quiet summers. It's best visited weekdays – stroll tree-lined streets, sample locavore cooking and soak up the NorCal flavor.

Tasting rooms surround the plaza and free summer concerts play Tuesday afternoons. And on a hot day, take a dip in the Russian River at **Healdsburg Veterans Memorial Beach** (📞707-433-1625; www.sonoma-county.org/parks; 13839 Healdsburg Ave; parking $7; 🚻), where lifeguards are on duty daily in summer.

✖ 🍴 p105

The Drive » From Healdsburg Plaza, drive 1 mile north on Healdsburg Ave and then west onto Dry Creek Rd, a fast-moving main thoroughfare; it's about 10 miles on to Truett-Hurst. To reach the wineries on West Dry Creek Rd, a parallel and undulating country lane, take Yoakim Bridge Rd.

9 Dry Creek Valley

A wine-growing region hemmed in by 2000ft-high mountains, Dry Creek Valley is relatively warm, ideal for sauvignon blanc and zinfandel, and in some places, cabernet sauvignon.

Dry Creek's newest biodynamic winery, **Truett-Hurst** (📞707-433-9545; www.truetthurst.com; 5610 Dry Creek Rd; tastings $5, refundable with purchase; 🕙10am-5pm; 🐾) has terrific old-vine zins, standout petite sirah and Russian River pinots at the handsome, contemporary tasting room, and you can meander to the creek where salmon spawn in autumn.

An early leader in organics, the 19th-century farm of **Preston Vineyards** (📞707-433-3372; www.prestonvineyards.com; 9282 W Dry Creek Rd; tasting $10, refundable with purchase, bottles $24-38; 🕙11am-4:30pm; 🐾) feels like old Sonoma County. Weathered picket fencing frames the 19th-century farmhouse-turned–tasting room with candy-colored walls. The signature is citrusy sauvignon blanc, but try the Rhône varietals and small-lot wines.

Atop the valley's north end, caves are built into the hillside at always-fun **Bella Vineyards** (📞707-473-9171; www.bellawinery.com; 9711 W Dry Creek Rd; tasting $5-10, bottles $25-40; 🕙11am-4:30pm; 🐾). The focus is on zin and syrah, but there's terrific rosé and late-harvest zin.

Eating & Sleeping

Sebastopol

✕ Hardcore Espresso
Cafe $

(1798 Gravenstein Hwy S; ☺6am-7pm; 📶) Meet local hippies and art freaks over smoothies at this classic NorCal off-the-grid, indoor-outdoor coffeehouse that's essentially a corrugated-metal-roofed shack surrounded by umbrella tables. The organic coffee is the town's best.

Bohemian Highway ②

✕ Wild Flour Bakery
Bakery $

(www.wildflourbread.com; 140 Bohemian Hwy, Freestone; ☺8:30am-6pm Fri-Mon) Hearty artisanal brick-oven breads, scones and coffee.

✕ Howard Station Cafe
Breakfast, Cafe $

(www.howardstationcafe.com; 3811 Bohemian Hwy, Occidental; mains $8-11; ☺7am-2:30pm Mon-Fri, 7am-3pm Sat & Sun; 📶🍴🐾) Makes big plates of comfort food, with organic eggs, ample burgers and fresh-squeezed juices. Pooches welcome on the patio.

Jenner ⑤

✕ River's End
Californian $$$

(☎707-865-2484; www.rivers-end.com; 11048 Hwy 1; lunch mains $13-26, dinner mains $25-39; ☺noon-3pm & 5-8:30pm Thu-Mon; 🍴) This picture-perfect restaurant is perched on a cliff overlooking the river's mouth and the grand sweep of the Pacific Ocean. It serves world-class meals at world-class prices, but the real reward is the view.

⊨ Jenner Inn & Cottages
Inn $$

(☎707-865-2377; www.jennerinn.com; 10400 Hwy 1; r incl breakfast creekside $118-178, ocean-view $178-278, cottages $228-278; @) It's difficult to sum up this collection of properties dispersed throughout Jenner – some are in fairly deluxe ocean-view cottages with kitchen and ready-to-light fireplaces, others are small and upland near a creek. All have the furnishings of a stylish auntie from the early 1990s.

Guerneville ⑦

✕ Coffee Bazaar
Cafe $

(14045 Armstrong Woods Rd; mains $5-9; ☺6am-8pm; 📶) Happening cafe with salads, sandwiches and all-day breakfasts; adjoins a good secondhand bookstore.

Healdsburg ⑧

✕ Downtown Bakery & Creamery
Bakery, Cafe $

(www.downtownbakery.net; 308a Center St; ☺7am-5:30pm) Healdsburg's finest bakery makes scrumptious pastries. Half-price goodies available from 4:30pm.

✕ Scopa
Italian $$

(☎707-433-5282; www.scopahealdsburg.com; 109a Plaza St; mains $12-26; ☺5:30-10pm Tue-Sun) Space is tight inside this converted barbershop, but it's worth cramming in for perfect thin-crust pizza and rustic Italian home cooking, like Nonna's slow-braised chicken, with sautéed greens, melting into toasty polenta. A lively crowd and good wine prices create a convivial atmosphere.

⊨ Best Western Dry Creek Inn
Motel $$

(☎707-433-0300; www.drycreekinn.com; 198 Dry Creek Rd; r Sun-Thu $59-129, Fri & Sat $199-259; ❄@📶♨) Town's top motel has good service and an outdoor hot tub. New rooms have jetted tubs and gas fireplaces. Check for weekday discounts.

⊨ Madrona Manor
Historic Hotel $$$

(☎707-433-4231, 800-258-4003; www.madronamanor.com; 1001 Westside Rd; r & ste $270-390; ❄📶♨) The first choice for lovers of country inns and stately manor homes, the regal 1881 Madrona Manor exudes Victorian elegance. Surrounded by 8 acres of woods and gorgeous century-old gardens, the hilltop mansion and restaurant is decked out with many original furnishings. A mile west of downtown, it's convenient to Westside Rd wineries.

Mendocino County Rolling coas
hills and jagged cliffs aw

Mendocino & Anderson Valley

8

The uninitiated might roll their eyes at 'Mendocino Magic,' but spend a few days here cruising two-lane blacktop and you'll discover the enchantment of this place is undeniable.

TRIP HIGHLIGHTS

60 miles

Mendocino
A seaside gem of historic buildings and excellent B&Bs

6

90 miles

Orr Hot Springs
Soak among redwoods at this magical getaway

8
FINISH

Philo

2

Hopland
START

Boonville
Learn to speak Boontling and sip excellent local brew

25 miles

3–4 DAYS
114 MILES/183KM

GREAT FOR...

BEST TIME TO GO

This trip is best in fall, when skies are clear and apples harvested.

ESSENTIAL PHOTO

Otters swimming alongside your canoe on the Big River.

BEST TWO DAYS

Spending a day hiking through pygmy forests in Van Damme State Park and canoeing up the Big River.

107

8

Mendocino & Anderson Valley

This trip is about family-operated vineyards, hushed stands of redwoods and a string of idiosyncratic villages perched in the border area between California's rolling coastal hills and the jagged cliffs of the Pacific. Just far enough out of the Bay Area orbit to move to its own relaxed rhythm, this makes an unforgettable weekend filled with low-key pampering, specialty pinot noir, sun-drenched days and romantic, foggy nights.

❶ Hopland

Tired of treading over the same ground with Napa and Sonoma? Make for adorable little Hopland, the wine hub of the Mendocino County. Less than 100 miles north of San Francisco, this unsung winemaking region offers rich Mediterranean reds and brawny, fruit-forward zinfandels. You can taste many of the family farms you'll approach en route at the downtown wine shop **Sip! Mendocino** (www.sipmendocino.com;

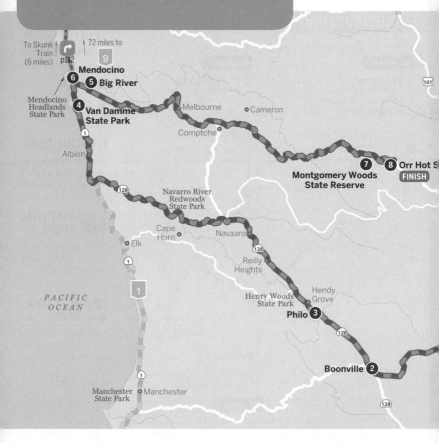

13420 S Hwy 101; tastings $5; ⏱11am-6pm). There the expert proprietor pours hand-picked flights that include rare vintages you might not even taste at the wineries themselves.

The Drive » Head north on Hwy 101 about 10 minutes before exiting on Hwy 253, a beautiful, serpentine route through the hills. Hwy 253 ends at Hwy 128, just south of Boonville.

TRIP HIGHLIGHT

❷ Boonville

Descending from the hills, visitors spill out into the sun-washed village of Boonville, a short main street with historical buildings, boutiques and artisanal ice cream. Still, the town's most famous taste is just a bit down the street at the **Anderson Valley Brewing Company** (www.avbc.com; 17700 Hwy 253; ⏱11am-7pm). The brewery sits on a big corner lot overlooking the valley, and the grounds are complete with a sparely furnished tasting room, a copper-clad brewery and beefy draft horses that graze the grounds. The place also includes a Frisbee golf course, where players can buy beer to drink as they play. The brewery's long-standing green credentials include a solar array that generates a sizeable amount of its power.

✖ 🛏 p113

The Drive » Drive just north out of town on Hwy 128, passing a number of family wineries

and fruit stands. The best fruit is ahead, in Philo, only 6 miles north of Boonville.

❸ Philo

The gorgeous **Philo Apple Farm** (www.philoapplefarm. com; 18501 Greenwood Rd; ⏱dawn-dusk) is a bit like something out of a storybook: a dreamy patch of green run by warm-hearted staff and scented with apple blossoms. It's worth skipping over the other farm stands on the way here for their organic preserves, chutneys, heirloom apples and pears. (If you get here after hours, you're likely to be able to leave a few dollars in a jar and take some goodies along for the ride.) Those who linger can take cooking classes with some of the Wine Country's best chefs. For a swim, the rocky, shallow waters of the Navarro River are just a short stroll up the road.

🛏 p113

hlin
Redwood Valley

Calpella ㉚

Lake Mendocino

10 km
5 miles

START
❶ Hopland

🔗 LINK YOUR TRIP

1 Pacific Coast Highways

Those who can't get enough beachcombing and breathtaking cliffs can link to California's most epic drive along Hwy 1.

9 Lost Coast & Southern Redwoods

The northern edge of this trip nears California's wildest shores, perfect for travelers with sturdy hiking boots and a thirst for untouched wilds. Continue up Hwy 101 to connect with this trip.

The Drive » Take the twisting drive west along Hwy 128 though majestic fog-shrouded stands of redwood and you'll eventually emerge at Hwy 1. Go north on Hwy 1 through the seaside town of Albion.

---

❹ Van Damme State Park

After emerging on one of California's most serene stretches of Hwy 1, a stroll along the waves seems mandatory. Three miles south of Mendocino, this sprawling 1831-acre **park** (✆707-937-5804; www.parks.ca.gov; day use $6) draws beachcombers, divers and kayakers to its easy-access beach, and hikers to its pygmy forest. The latter is a unique and precious place, where acidic soil and an impenetrable layer of hardpan have created a miniature forest of decades-old trees. You can reach the forest after moderate 3.5-mile Fern Canyon Scenic Trail, which

BLAINE HARRINGTON III / CORBIS ©

crosses back and forth over Little River and past the Cabbage Patch, a bog of skunk cabbage that's rich with wildlife. The **visitor center** (✆707-937-4016; ◷10am-3pm Fri-Sun) has nature exhibits and programs.

🛏 p113

The Drive » A short 2-mile drive north along Hwy 1 brings you to the bridge over the Big River. Just before the bridge, take a right on Comptche Ukiah Rd.

---

❺ Big River

A lazy paddle up the Big River is a chance to get an intimate look at the border between land and sea – a place where otters, sea lions and majestic blue herons keep you company as you drift silently by. Although the area near the mouth of the river is an excellent place to watch the waves or catch the sunset, more adventurous travelers can check in at **Catch**

A Canoe & Bicycles, Too! (www.stanfordinn.com; Comptche-Ukiah Rd & Hwy 1; ◷9am-5pm), a friendly riverside outfit that rents bikes, kayaks and stable outrigger canoes for trips

---

TOP ANDERSON VALLEY WINERIES

The valley's cool nights yield high-acid, fruit-forward, food-friendly wines. Pinot noir, chardonnay and dry gewürztraminer flourish. Most **Anderson Valley wineries** (www.avwines.com) sit outside Philo. Many are family-owned and offer tastings, some give tours. The following are particularly noteworthy.

Navarro (www.navarrowine.com; 5601 Hwy 128; ◷10am-6pm) The best option, and picnicking is encouraged.

Esterlina (www.esterlinavineyards.com; 1200 Holmes Ranch Rd) For big reds, pack a picnic and head high up the rolling hills; call ahead.

Husch (www.huschvineyards.com; 4400 Hwy 128; ◷10am-5pm) Husch serves exquisite tastings inside a rose-covered cottage.

Skunk Train The train at Willits

up the 8-mile Big River tidal estuary, the longest undeveloped estuary in Northern California. Years of conservation efforts have protected this area from highways or buildings. Bring a picnic and a camera to enjoy the marshes and empty, log-strewn beaches, wildlife and ramshackle remnants of century-old train trestles.

The Drive » The next stop, Mendocino, is just over the bridge from the Big River.

TRIP HIGHLIGHT

❻ Mendocino

Perched on a gorgeous headland, Mendocino is the North Coast's salt-washed gem, with B&Bs and rose gardens, white picket fences and New England–style redwood water towers. Bay Area weekenders walk along the headland among berry bramble and wildflowers, where cypress trees stand over dizzying cliffs. A stroll through this dreamy little village is a highlight of a trip through the region.

To get a sense for the village's thriving art scene, drop in at the **Mendocino Art Center** (☏707-937-5818; www.mendocinoartcenter.org; 45200 Little Lake St; ⏰10am-4pm), a hub for visual, musical and theatrical arts. The center is also home to the **Mendocino Theatre Company** (www.1mtc.org), which stages contemporary plays in the 81-seat Helen Schoeni Theatre.

The town itself is loaded with galleries, all of which host openings on the second Saturday of the month, when doors are thrown open

DETOUR: SKUNK TRAIN

Start: ❻ **Mendocino**

Go north to Mendocino's humble sister city, Fort Bragg, to board the **Skunk Train** (www.skunktrain.com; adult/child $49/24). The vintage narrow-gauge track got its nickname in 1925 for its stinky gas-powered steam engines, but today the historic steam and diesel locomotives are odorless. Passing through redwood-forested mountains, along rivers, over bridges and through deep mountain tunnels, the trains run from both Fort Bragg and Willits to the midway point of Northspur, where they turn around (if you want to go to Willits, plan to spend the night). The depot is downtown at the foot of Laurel St, one block west of Main St.

to strolling connoisseurs of art and wine, and Mendocino buzzes with life. Of course, the natural setting here is a work of art itself. The spectacular **Mendocino Headlands State Park** surrounds the village, with trails crisscrossing the bluffs and rocky coves. Ask at the visitor center about guided weekend walks, including spring wildflower walks and whale-watching.

✗ ⛺ p113

The Drive ❯❯ Just south of town, turn inland at Comptche Ukiah Rd. It will make a loop taking you back toward the trip's beginning. All the turns make the next 30 miles slow going, but the views are impressive.

---

❼ Montgomery Woods State Reserve

Two miles west of Orr, this 13,250-acre **reserve** (Orr Springs Rd) protects five old-growth redwood groves, and some of the best groves within a day's drive from San Francisco. A 2-mile loop trail crosses the creek, winding through the serene groves, starting near the picnic tables and toilets. It's out of the way, so visitors are likely to have it mostly to themselves. The trees here are impressive – some are up to 14ft in diameter – but remember to admire them from the trail, both to protect the

tree's root systems and to protect yourself from poison oak, which is all over the park.

The Drive ❯❯ From the park's parking area, continue 2 miles more on Comptche Ukiah Rd (which may be called Orr Springs Rd on some maps) to reach Orr Hot Springs.

TRIP HIGHLIGHT

❽ Orr Hot Springs

After all the hiking, canoeing and beachcombing, a soak in the thermal waters of this rustic resort is heavenly, the ultimate zen-out to end the journey. While it's not for the bashful, the clothing-optional resort is beloved by locals, back-to-the-land hipsters, backpackers and liberal-minded tourists. Still, you don't have to let it all hang out to enjoy **Orr Hot Springs** (⏰10am-10pm). The place has private tubs, a sauna, a spring-fed, rock-bottomed swimming pool, steam room, massage and lovely, slightly shaggy gardens. Day use costs $25, or $20 on Mondays. Soaking in the rooftop pools on a clear night is magical.

⛺ p113

Eating & Sleeping

Boonville 2

✖ Paysenne   Ice Cream $

(14111 Hwy 128; ice-cream cone $3; ⊙10am-3pm Thu-Mon) Boonville's new ice-cream shop serves the innovative flavors of Three Twins Ice Cream, whose delightful flavors include Lemon Cookie and Strawberry Je Ne Sais Quoi (which has a hint of balsamic vinegar).

✖ Table 128   Modern American $$$

(☎707-895-2210; www.boonvillehotel.com; 14040 Hwy 128; 3-/4-course prixe-fixe menu $40/50; ⊙5-9pm Thu-Mon) Food-savvy travelers love the constantly changing modern American menu here, featuring simple, well-executed dishes and a freewheeling, family-style service at big farm tables.

⊫ Boonville Hotel   Boutique Hotel $$

(☎707-895-2210; www.boonvillehotel.com; 14040 Hwy 128; r $125-200, ste $225) Decked out in a contemporary American-country style, this historic hotel's rooms are safe for urbanites who refuse to abandon style just because they've gone to the country.

Philo 3

⊫ Philo Apple Farm   Cottages $$$

(☎707-895-2333; www.philoapplefarm.com; 18501 Greenwood Rd; r Mon-Thu $175, Fri-Sun $250) Set within the orchard, four exquisite cottages are built with reclaimed materials and have bright, airy spaces. Red Door cottage is a favorite because of the bathroom – you can soak in a slipper tub, or shower on the private deck under the open sky.

Van Damme State Park 4

⊫ Van Damme
State Park Campgrounds   Campground $

(☎800-444-7275; www.reserveamerica.com; tent & RV sites $35; 🕾) Great for families, these two campgrounds have lots of space and hot showers. One is just off Hwy 1, the other is in a highland meadow. Nine **environmental campsites** (tent sites $25) lie just a 1.25-mile hike up Fern Canyon.

Mendocino 6

✖ Cafe Beaujolais   California $$$

(☎707-937-5614; www.cafebeaujolais.com; 961 Ukiah St; lunch mains $9-20, dinner mains $27-40; ⊙11:30am-2:30pm Wed-Sun, 5:45-9pm nightly) Mendocino's iconic, much-beloved country, Cal-French restaurant draws diners from San Francisco, who make this the centerpiece of their trip. The best of the best; you can't go wrong here. Reservations essential.

⊫ Andiron   Cottages $$

(☎800-955-6478; www.theandiorn.com; 6051 N Hwy 1; r $99-149; 🕾🛏🐾) Styled with hip vintage decor, this cluster of playfully themed 1950s roadside cottages is a refreshing option amid the stuffy cabbage-rose and lace aesthetic of Mendocino.

⊫ MacCallum House Inn   B&B $$$

(☎707-937-0289; www.maccallumhouse.com; 45020 Albion St; r from $204; @🕾🛏🐾) There are cheerful cottages and a modern luxury home, but the most memorable space here is within one of Mendocino's iconic historic water towers – where living quarters fill the ground floor, a sauna is on the 2nd floor, and there's a view of the coast from the top.

Orr Hot Springs 8

⊫ Orr Hot
Springs   Resort, Campground $$

(☎707-462-6277; tent sites $45-50, d $140-160, cottages $195-230) Elegantly rustic rooms are a good match for this earthy spa. Accommodations include use of the spa and communal kitchen; some cottages have their own kitchens.

Sinkyone Wilderness *A rugged mystifying stretch of coas*

Lost Coast & Southern Redwoods

9

Get lost along the empty shores of this pristine coastal area, then cruise under the ancient trees of the Avenue of the Giants. This trip puts the charms of the NorCal coast at center stage.

TRIP HIGHLIGHTS

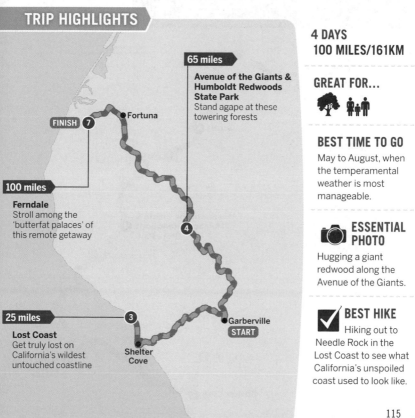

65 miles

Avenue of the Giants & Humboldt Redwoods State Park
Stand agape at these towering forests

● Fortuna

FINISH 7

100 miles

Ferndale
Stroll among the 'butterfat palaces' of this remote getaway

4

25 miles

Lost Coast
Get truly lost on California's wildest untouched coastline

3

Shelter Cove

● Garberville
START

4 DAYS
100 MILES/161KM

- - -

GREAT FOR...

- - -

BEST TIME TO GO
May to August, when the temperamental weather is most manageable.

- - -

ESSENTIAL PHOTO

Hugging a giant redwood along the Avenue of the Giants.

- - -

✔ BEST HIKE

Hiking out to Needle Rock in the Lost Coast to see what California's unspoiled coast used to look like.

Lost Coast & Southern Redwoods

With its secluded trails and pristine slice of coast, the gorgeous 'Lost Coast' is one of the state's most untouched coastal areas and most exciting hiking adventures. The region became 'lost' when the highway system bypassed it early in the 20th century and has developed around the outsider culture of political radicals, marijuana farmers and nature lovers.

❶ Garberville

The first stop on a Lost Coast romp is scrappy little Garberville, the first town beyond the so-called 'Redwood Curtain.' There's an uneasy relationship between the old-guard loggers and hippies, many of whom came in the 1970s to grow marijuana after the feds chased them out of Santa Cruz. A visit to the three-block downtown should include browsing at **Brown's Sporting Goods** (☎707-923-2533; 797 Redwood Dr; ⊙9am-6pm Mon-

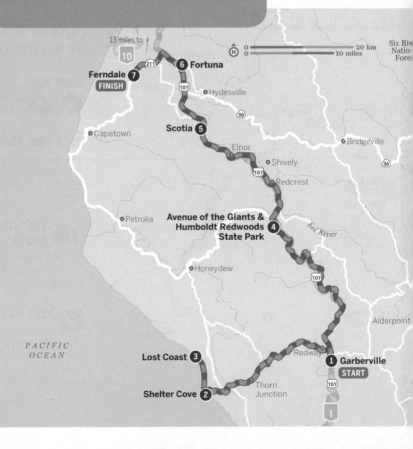

Fri, to 5pm Sat). The Brown family has run the place for a couple generations and has encyclopedic knowledge of activities in the area. The small-town service is ideal: owner Darren Brown delivers supplies to hotels for folks arriving late on Friday night. Those with extra time can spend the day south at the **Benbow Lake State Recreation Area** (☎ summer 707-923-3238, winter 707-923-3318; per car $8). The Eel River cuts through the park and is excellent for swimming and sunbathing.

✗ ⌂ p121

The Drive » Take it easy and in a low gear on the steep and twisting drive down Briceland Thorn Rd (which becomes Shelter Cove Rd eventually) – getting to Shelter Cove can be a

LINK YOUR TRIP

1 Pacific Coast Highways

See California's other iconic trees – swaying palms – by riding along the edge of California.

10 Northern Redwood Coast

Still don't have enough of the giant trees? Link this trip with a jaunt to the forests of the Redwood National Park by continuing north past Ferndale on Hwy 101.

challenge. Best to heed the 'No Trespassing' signs on this part of the drive. The weed farmers who take shelter under this misty canopy don't take kindly to strangers.

---

❷ Shelter Cove

At the end of the road – and what seems like the end of the earth! – is the isolated community of Shelter Cove, the gateway to the Lost Coast. The tiny encampment of restaurants and shops sometimes seems equally populated by humans and Roosevelt elk. Although primarily used as a launching point for the nearby wilds, it makes a relaxing destination in its own right. From town, scan the water for migrating whales (look for mothers and their calves in the spring), and explore tidepools teeming with crabs, snails, sea stars and sponges. (Locals even spot an octopus on occasion!).

✗ ⌂ p121

The Drive » There are trailheads for exploring the Lost Coast Trail both north and south of town. That's where the drive pauses; the trail has to be done on foot.

TRIP HIGHLIGHT

❸ Lost Coast

The North Coast's superlative backpacking destination is a rugged, mystifying stretch of coast with trails

crossing coastal peaks and volcanic black-sand beaches. The King Range boldly rises 4000ft within 3 miles of the coast, which became 'lost' when the state's highway system deemed the region impassable in the early 20th century.

Made up of the Sinkyone and Kings Range Wilderness areas, the best way to explore is on a multiday hike. Leaving from Shelter Cove, a three-day hike north on the **Lost Coast Trail** ends at the mouth of the Mattole River. Equally challenging and rewarding, it passes the abandoned **Punta Gorda Lighthouse** along the way. You can arrange a shuttle service back to your car through **Lost Coast Shuttle** (☎ 707-223-1547; www.lostcoastshuttle. com). Those who don't have as much time can take in a day hike at **Black Sand Beach**, or head to overnight at **Needle Rock**, about 9 miles south of the Hidden Valley Trailhead. The **visitor center** (www.parks. ca.gov; sites/Barn Room $15/20; ⏰ staffed 4 hr per day) there affords gorgeous views along the coast.

The Drive » Retrace the twisting drive back to Garberville, then continue north on Hwy 101. Exit Hwy 101 when you see the 'Avenue of the Giants' sign, 6 miles north of Garberville, near Phillipsville. This is the heart of the big tree country.

TRIP HIGHLIGHT

4 Avenue of the Giants & Humboldt Redwoods State Park

The incredible, 32-mile, two-lane stretch of highway known as the Avenue of the Giants is one of the most justifiably celebrated drives in California, and a place where travelers stand with jaws agape and necks craned upward at the canopy. The route connects a number of small towns with midcentury motels, diners serving 'Lumberjack' meals and pull-offs parked with Harleys. Visitors would be remiss to drive past the majestic groves along the Avenue: the **California Federation of Women's Clubs Grove**, which is home to an interesting four-sided hearth designed by renowned San Franciscan architect Julia Morgan and the **Founders Grove**, home to the 370ft **Dyerville Giant**, which was knocked down in 1991 by another falling tree.

Much of the Avenue of the Giants snakes in and out of **Humboldt Redwoods State Park** (www.humboldtredwoods.org). At 53,000 acres – 17,000 of which are old-growth – it boasts three-quarters of the world's tallest 100 trees. Tree huggers take note: these groves rival (and may surpass) those in Redwood National Park. The 100-plus miles of trails can be taken on foot, horse or bike and range in difficulty from the kid-friendly **Drury-Chaney Loop Trail** (with berry picking in summer) to the rugged **Grasshopper Peak Trail**, which climbs to the 3379ft fire lookout. The primeval **Rockefeller**

Avenue of the Giants, Humboldt Redwoods State Park

Forest, 4.5 miles west of the Avenue via Mattole Rd, is one of the park's most pristine stands. It's the world's largest contiguous old-growth redwood forest, containing about 20% of all such remaining trees.

✕ 🛏 p121

The Drive » From the Avenue of the Giants, follow signs to the groves in the park. You'll pass a number of small villages along the way, which are a ramshackle collection of midcentury tourist traps, woodsy lodges and huge stands of trees. Avenue of the Giants ends at Hwy 101. Drive 22 miles north to Scotia.

💬 LOCAL KNOWLEDGE: SCOTIA ARCHITECTURE

Scotia was the last lumber company town operating in California and perhaps the American West. Most company towns have a hard workin' look, but Scotia is handsome and well built, with green lawns and homes from the 1890s. It even has its own style of architecture – I call it Tyrolean Redwood style. Look at the columns, the porticos and the porches of the stores and shopping center; they're redwood logs with the bark still clinging to them. That bark is so deeply furrowed it looks like the flutes of Greek columns. The builders left the redwood unpainted so you can appreciate its beauty. It is said that walking into a grove of ancient redwoods is like walking into Nature's Cathedral. When it comes to redwood, the result is extremely beautiful whether built by the hand of God or the hand of Man.

Ray Hillman, historian, teacher and tour narrator

TOP TIP: ACCESSING THE LOST COAST

Hikers who wish to hike the entirety of the Lost Coast often go from north to south in order to avoid northerly winds. Many trailheads start at the Mattole Campground, just south of Petrolia, which is on the northern border of the Kings Range.

➎ Scotia

For years, Scotia was California's last 'company town,' entirely owned and operated by the Pacific Lumber Company, which built cookie-cut houses and had an open contempt for long-haired outsiders who liked to get between their saws and the big trees. The company went belly up in 2007, but the town is still in operation (feels a bit like a scene from *Twilight Zone*). A history of the town awaits visitors at the **Scotia Museum & Visitor Center** (www.townofscotia.com; cnr Main & Bridge Sts; ◷8am-4:30pm Mon-Fri Jun-Sep), at the town's south end. But the real highlight of a stop is the museum's **fisheries center** (admission free). Remarkably informative, the fishery houses the largest freshwater aquarium on the North Coast.

The Drive ›› Follow Hwy 101 for 9 miles north to exit 687 for Kenmar Rd.

➏ Fortuna

The penultimate stop is a cold, refreshing pint of beer at **Eel River Brewing Company** (www. eelriverbrewing.com; 1777 Alamar Way; ◷11am-11pm Mon-Sun) in Fortuna. This place is completely in step with its amazing natural surroundings – it was the first certified organic brewery in the world and uses 100% renewable energy (there's a bit of irony in the fact that most of their beer is brewed in a building that formerly belonged to the Pacific Lumber Company). The breezy beer garden and excellent burgers are an ideal pit stop.

The Drive ›› Go just 2 miles north and take exit 691. Follow Hwy 211 for 5 miles south past rolling dairy farms to Ferndale.

TRIP HIGHLIGHT

➐ Ferndale

The trip through the Lost Coast ends at one of the region's most charming towns, stuffed with impeccable Victorians – known locally as 'butterfat palaces' because of the dairy wealth that built them. The entire town is a state and federal historical landmark. Main St offers galleries, old-world emporiums and soda fountains and – of course – ice- cream parlors. The **Kinetic Sculpture Museum** (580 Main St; ◷10am-5pm Mon-Sat, noon-4pm Sun; ⛟) ends the trip with whimsy; it houses fanciful, astounding, human-powered contraptions used in the town's annual Kinetic Grand Championship. Shaped like giant fish and UFOs, these colorful piles of junk propel racers over roads, water and marsh in the May event.

✖ p121

Eating & Sleeping

Garberville ①

✗ Woodrose Café
Breakfast $

(www.woodrosecafe.com; 911 Redwood Dr; meals $7-11; ⊙7am-1pm; ✗ 👶) Garberville's beloved cafe serves organic omelets, veggie scrambles and buckwheat pancakes with *real* maple syrup in a cozy room.

⊨ Benbow Inn
Historic Hotel $$$

(✆707-923-2124, 800-355-3301; www.benbowinn.com; 445 Lake Benbow Dr; r $90-305, cottage $395-595; ✳ 🛜 🏊) A monument to 1920s rustic elegance; the Redwood Empire's first luxury resort is a Tudor-style national historic landmark. How elegant? Rooms come with a complimentary decanter of sherry.

Shelter Cove ②

✗ Cove Restaurant
American $

(✆707-986-1197; 10 Seal Ct; mains $8-25; ⊙10am-2pm & 5-9pm Thu-Sun) Sup on excellent salads and fresh fish at this oceanfront eatery. A treat after the trail.

⊨ Tides Inn
Hotel $$

(✆707-986-7900; www.sheltercovetidesinn.com; 59 Surf Pt; r $160, ste with kitchen $185) Charming place sits right above the crashing waves and has lots of good activities for kids.

Avenue of the Giants & Humboldt Redwoods State Park ④

✗ Groves
New American $$

(13065 Ave of the Giants, Myers Flat; ⊙5-9pm) This is the most refined eating option within miles, despite an aloof staff. The menu turns out simple, brick-oven pizzas, but spicy prawns and fresh salads are all artfully plated.

⊨ Humboldt Redwoods State Park Campgrounds
Campground $

(✆800-444-7275; www.reserveamerica.com; tent & RV sites $20-35) The park runs three campgrounds, with hot showers, two environmental camps, five trail camps, a hike-bike camp and an equestrian camp. Of the developed spots, Burlington Campground is open year-round beside the visitor center and near a number of trailheads.

⊨ Miranda Gardens Resort
Resort $$

(✆707-943-3011; www.mirandagardens.com; 6766 Ave of the Giants, Miranda; cottages with kitchen $165-275, without kitchen $115-175; 🏊 👶 🐾) Cozy, slightly rustic cottages have redwood paneling and fireplaces, and are spotlessly clean. The grounds – replete with ping pong, a playground and swaying redwoods – have wholesome appeal.

Ferndale ⑦

✗ Francis Creek Inn
Motel $

(✆707-786-9611; www.franciscreekinn.com; 577 Main St; r from $85; 🛜) White picket balconies stand in front of this sweet little downtown motel, which is family owned and operated (check in at the Red Front convenience store, around the corner). The value is outstanding.

✗ Lotus Asian Bistro & Tea Room
Fusion $

(www.lotusasianbistro.com; 619 Main St; mains $7-14; ⊙11:30am-9pm Tue, Sat & Sun, 4-9pm Mon & Fri summer, closed winter) Cherry-glazed beef, crispy scallion pancakes with pulled duck and udon bowls are offered at this excellent Asian fusion bistro.

✗ Sweetness & Light
Sweets $

(554 Main St; confections $2-3) The house-made, gooey Moo bars are the flagship at this antique candy shop. It also serves great ice cream and espresso.

STRETCH YOUR LEGS
ARCATA

Start/Finish Arcata Plaza

Distance 4 miles

Duration 4–5 hours

The North Coast's colorful college town offers a stroll on the most progressive edge of America, an artsy community – with visionary sustainability practices, excellent parks, amazing food and a wealth of historic buildings – that marches proudly to its own beat.

Take this walk on Trips

Arcata Plaza

The buzzing hub of Arcata is a place where 20-somethings toss Frisbees, farmers hawk crops (legal or otherwise) and bearded professors saunter by dreadlocked vagabonds. Lined by boutiques and bars, the centerpiece is a bronze of President William McKinley who sternly observes one festival after another. The 1915 **Hotel Arcata** (cnr G & 9th Sts) is a National Historic Landmark on the northeast corner.

The Walk >> Walk up G St past a number of excellent, cheap restaurants and take the pedestrian bridge over the highway at 17th St, which brings you to campus.

Humboldt State University

Humboldt State University is the secluded intellectual center of the North Coast. In addition to a clutch of leading environmentalists its alumni also include novelist Raymond Carver and Stephen Hillenburg, creator of SpongeBob SquarePants. The Campus Center for Appropriate Technology (CCAT) is a world leader in developing sustainable technologies; on Fridays at 2pm you can take a self-guided tour of the **CCAT House,** a converted residence that uses only 4% of the energy of a comparably sized dwelling.

The Walk >> Walk south through campus to reach 14th St. Take a left to enter Redwood Park.

Arcata Community Forest

Few city parks hold a candle to **Redwood Park**, where 700 acres of forest is crossed by trails for biking, hiking and horseback riding. Without the big stands of trees common to the area, it doesn't have an untamed feel, but trail No 1 is a half-mile loop that makes an enjoyable hike for kids. Despite a few scruffy, semipermanent residents, whose tents flout the 'no camping' ordinance, the place feels magical, particularly when there's a performance on the park's stage.

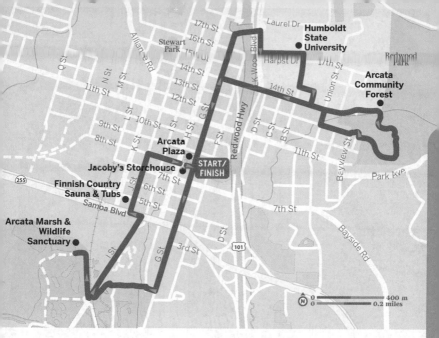

The Walk » Retrace your path on 14th St and continue, crossing over the highway. When you reach G St, take a left. Eventually, this will cross H St, where a right takes you to a trailhead of the Arcata Marsh.

Arcata Marsh & Wildlife Sanctuary

On the shores of Humboldt Bay, the **Arcata Marsh & Wildlife Sanctuary** has 5 miles of walking trails and outstanding bird-watching – during sunset it can be arrestingly beautiful – particularly when you consider that it was once the site of lumber mills and that the water originates at Arcata's water treatment system. Two organizations – **Redwood Region Audubon Society** (www.rras.org; donation welcome) and **Arcata Marsh Interpretive Center** (707-826-2359; 569 South G St; tours free; 9am-5pm) – offer guided walks.

The Walk » Trails through the marshes will bring you to a colorful array of migratory and shore birds. Exit the marsh on I St, take a quick left on Samoa Blvd and then a right on J St.

Finnish Country Sauna & Tubs

The private, open-air redwood tubs at the **Finnish Country Sauna & Tubs** (707-822-2228; www.cafemokkaarcata.com; cnr 5th & J Sts; noon-11pm Sun-Thu, to 1am Fri & Sat) make an ideal place to rest your legs. The tubs (half-hour/hour $9/17) and sauna are situated around a frog pond, and birds flutter in the redwood branches above. The attached coffee house has a mellow, old-world vibe.

The Walk » Continue north on J Street and take a right at 8th to reach the Plaza.

Jacoby's Storehouse

The final stop returns to another corner of Arcata Plaza and another National Historic Landmark, **Jacoby's Storehouse** (cnr H & 8th Sts). The creaking halls of this 1857 mercantile building have received a handsome upgrade and now lead to restaurants, some tasteful history displays and – importantly for any traveling stop – an ice-cream parlor.

Redwood National Park Towering, mystical, ancient redwoods

Northern Redwood Coast

10

Hug a 700-year-old tree, stroll moody coastal bluffs and drop in on roadside attractions of yesteryear on this trip through verdant redwood parks and personality-packed villages.

TRIP HIGHLIGHTS

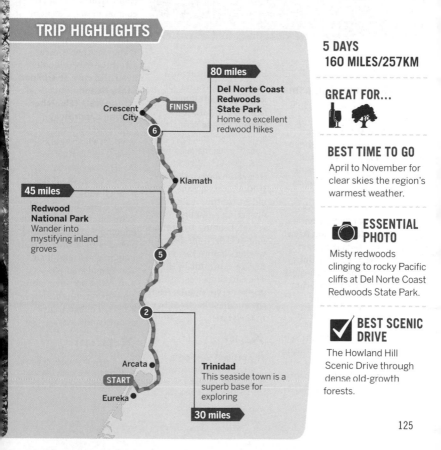

80 miles

Del Norte Coast Redwoods State Park
Home to excellent redwood hikes

Crescent City — **FINISH**

6

● Klamath

45 miles

Redwood National Park
Wander into mystifying inland groves

5

2

Arcata ●

START

Eureka ●

Trinidad
This seaside town is a superb base for exploring

30 miles

5 DAYS
160 MILES/257KM

GREAT FOR...

BEST TIME TO GO

April to November for clear skies the region's warmest weather.

ESSENTIAL PHOTO

Misty redwoods clinging to rocky Pacific cliffs at Del Norte Coast Redwoods State Park.

BEST SCENIC DRIVE

The Howland Hill Scenic Drive through dense old-growth forests.

125

10 Northern Redwood Coast

This trip may have been charted in the glory days of the midcentury American road trip – roadside attractions include giant Paul Bunyan statues, drive-through trees and greasy burger stands – but that might as well be yesterday in this land of towering, mystical, ancient redwood forests. Curving roads and misty trails bring visitors to lush, spectacular natural wonders that are unlike any other place on earth. Prepare to be impressed.

❶ Samoa Peninsula

Even though this trip is about misty primeval forest, the beginning is a study of opposites: the grassy dunes and windswept beaches of the 7-mile long **Samoa Peninsula**.

At the peninsula's south end is **Samoa Dunes Recreation Area** (☼sunrise-sunset), part of a 34-mile-long dune system that's the largest in Northern California. While it's great for picnicking or fishing, the wildlife viewing is excellent. You might see 200 species of migrating waterfowl in spring and fall, songbirds in spring and summer, shorebirds in fall and winter, and waders year-round. Or, leave the landlubbers behind and take a **Harbor Cruise** (www. humboldtbaymaritimemuseum. com; 75-minute narrated cruise adult/child $18/10, cocktail cruise $10) aboard the 1910 *Madaket,* America's oldest continuously operating passenger vessel. Leaving from the foot of C St, it ferried mill workers before the Samoa Bridge was built in 1972. The $10 sunset cocktail cruise serves drinks from the smallest licensed bar in the state.

✕ p131

The Drive » Head north on Hwy 101 passing myriad views of Humboldt Bay. Pass Arcata and take the exit to Trinidad.

Note that the corridor between Eureka and Arcata (p122) is a closely watched safety corridor (aka speed trap), so keep it slow.

Note that the corridor between Eureka and Arcata (p122)

TRIP HIGHLIGHT

❷ Trinidad

Perched on an ocean bluff, cheery Trinidad somehow manages an off-the-beaten-path feel despite a constant flow of visitors. The free town map at the information kiosk will help you navigate the town's cute little shops and several fantastic hiking trails, most notably the **Trinidad Head Trail** with superb coastal views; excellent for whale-watching (December to April). If the weather is nice, stroll the exceptionally beautiful cove at **Trinidad State Beach**; if not, make for the **HSU Telonicher Marine Laboratory** (☎707-826-3671; www. humboldt.edu/marinelab; Ewing St; ☼9am-4:30pm Mon-Fri, noon-4pm Sat Sep–mid-May; ♿). It has a touch tank, several aquariums (look for the giant Pacific octopus), an enormous whale jaw and a cool three-dimensional map of the ocean floor. You can also join a naturalist on tidepooling expeditions (90 minutes, $3); call ahead to ask about conditions.

✕ 🛏 p131

The Drive » Head back north on Patrick's Point drive to hug the shore for 6 miles.

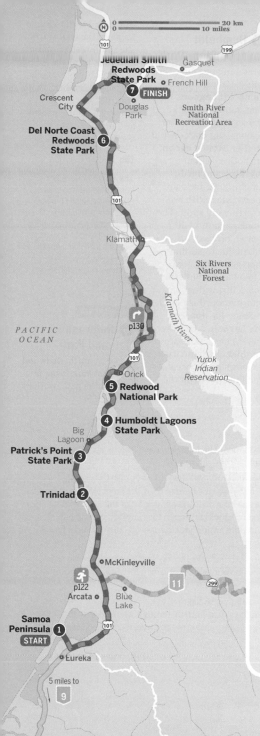

③ Patrick's Point State Park

Coastal bluffs jut out to sea at 640-acre **Patrick's Point State Park** (☏707-677-3570; 4150 Patrick's Point Dr; day use $8; 🚻), where sandy beaches abut rocky headlands. The super-easy access to dramatic coastal bluffs makes this a best bet for families, but any age will find a feast for the senses as they climb rock formations, search for breaching whales, carefully navigate tidepools and listen to barking sea lions and singing birds. The park also has **Sumêg**, an authentic reproduction of a Yurok village, with

LINK YOUR TRIP

9 Lost Coast & Southern Redwoods

Linking to the southern Redwood wonders and the untouched Lost Coast brings on the best hiking adventures on the north coast. These routes connect directly via Hwy 101.

11 Trinity Scenic Byway

Cut inland on Hwy 299 and get lost in the wild country of the California's northern mountains to channel the spirit of mountain men and gold hunters.

hand-hewn redwood buildings. In the native plant garden you'll find species for making traditional baskets and medicines. The 2-mile **Rim Trail,** a former Yurok trail around the bluffs, circles the point with access to huge rocky outcrops. Don't miss **Wedding Rock,** one of the park's most romantic spots, or **Agate Beach** where lucky visitors find bits of jade and sea-polished agate.

🛏️ p131

The Drive » Make your way back out to Hwy 101 through thick stands of redwoods. North another 5 minutes will bring you to the sudden clearing of Big Lagoon, part of Humboldt Lagoons State Park. Continue just a minute for the visitors center.

④ Humboldt Lagoons State Park

Stretching out for miles along the coast, **Humboldt Lagoons** has long, sandy beaches and a string of coastal lagoons. **Big Lagoon** and prettier **Stone Lagoon** are both excellent for kayaking and bird-watching. Sunsets are spectacular, with no structures in sight. The Stone Lagoon Visitor Center, on Hwy 101, has closed due to staffing shortages, but there's a toilet and a bulletin board displaying information. Just south of Stone Lagoon, tiny **Dry Lagoon** (a freshwater marsh) has a fantastic day hike. Park at Dry Lagoon's picnic area and hike north on the unmarked trail to Stone Lagoon; the trail skirts the southwestern shore and ends up at the ocean, passing through woods and marshland rich with wildlife. Mostly flat, it's about 2.5 miles one way – and nobody takes it because it's unmarked.

🛏️ p131

The Drive » Now, at last, you'll start to lose all perspective among the world's tallest trees. This is likely the most scenic part of the entire trip; you'll emerge from curvy two-lane roads through redwood groves to stunning mist-shrouded shores dotted with rocky islets.

TRIP HIGHLIGHT

⑤ Redwood National Park

Heading north, **Redwood National Park** is the first park in the patchwork of

GIANT TREES

With lots of kitsch mid-century appeal, the following destinations are a throwback to those bygone days of the great American road trip.

Trees of Mystery (www.treesofmystery.net; 15500 Hwy 101; adult/child & senior $14/7; ⏰8am-7pm Jun-Aug, 9am-4pm Sep-May; ♿) It's hard to miss the giant statues of Paul Bunyan and Babe the Blue Ox towering over the parking lot at this shameless, if lovable, tourist trap. It has gondola running through the redwood canopy and, if you come on summer weekends, the lumberjack giant even cracks wise at tourists wandering in from the parking lot.

Chandelier Drive Thru Tree (www.drivethrutree.com; 67402 Drive Thru Tree Road, Leggett; $5 per car, ⏰8:30am-9pm; ♿) Fold in your mirrors and inch forward, then cool off in the überkitsch gift shop.

Shrine Drive-Thru Tree ($3/6 walk/drive through; 13078 Avenue of the Giants, Myers Flat; ⏰sunrise-sunset; ♿) Look up to the sky as you roll through, on the Ave of the Giants in Myers Flat. Though it's the least impressive of the three, it's a necessary stop for the drive-through trifecta.

Tour-Thru Tree (430 Highway 169, Klamath; ⏰sunrise-sunset; ♿) Squeeze through a tree and check out an emu.

Trees of Mystery Statue of Paul Bunyan and Babe the Blue Ox

state and federally administered land under the umbrella of the Redwood National & State Parks. After picking up a map at the **Kuchel Visitor Center** (☏707-465-7765; www.nps.gov/redw; Hwy 101, Orick) you'll have a suite of choices for hiking, but the half-mile stroll to **Gold Bluffs Beach** will lead you to the best spot for a picnic. Take the easy trail about

another mile to **Fern Canyon**, whose 60ft, fern-covered, sheer rock walls are seen in *In the Lost World: Jurassic Park*. This is one of the most photographed spots on the North Coast – damp and lush, all emerald green – and totally worth getting your toes wet to see. Alternatively, a trip inland will get you lost in the secluded seren-

ity of **Tall Trees Grove**. To protect the grove, a limited number of cars per day are allowed access; get permits at the visitor center. This can be a half-day trip itself, but you're well rewarded after the challenging approach (a 30-minute rumble on an old logging road, then a moderately strenuous 1.3-mile hike).

🛏 p131

DETOUR: NEWTON B DRURY SCENIC PARKWAY

Start: 5 Redwood National Park

Just north of Orick is the turn-off for the 8-mile parkway, which runs parallel to Hwy 101 through untouched ancient redwood forests. It's worth the short detour off the freeway to view the magnificence of these trees. Numerous trails branch off from roadside pullouts, including family- and ADA (American Disabilities Act) -friendly trails Big Tree and Revelation Trail.

The Drive » Follow the winding road through beautiful inland forests with views of the east and its layers of ridges and valleys, until you reach Klamath with its bear bridge. Del Norte Coast Redwoods State Park is just a few minutes up the road.

TRIP HIGHLIGHT

6 Del Norte Coast Redwoods State Park

Marked by steep canyons and dense woods, half the 6400 acres of this **park** (vehicle day-use $8) are virgin redwood forest, crisscrossed by 15 miles of hiking trails. Even the most cynical of redwood-watchers can't help but be moved. Tall trees cling precipitously to canyon walls that drop to the rocky, timber-strewn coastline. It's almost impossible to get to the water, except via gorgeous but steep **Damnation Creek Trail** or **Footsteps Rock Trail**. The former may be only 4 miles long, but the 1100-ft elevation change and cliffside redwood makes it the park's best hike. The unmarked trailhead starts from a parking area off Hwy 101 at Mile 16.

The Drive » Leaving Del Norte Coast Redwoods State Park you'll enter dreary little Crescent City, a fine enough place to gas up or grab a bite, but not worth stopping long. North of town, Hwy 199 splits off. Take it to South Fork Rd; turn right after crossing two bridges.

7 Jedediah Smith Redwoods State Park

The final stop on the trip is loaded with worthy superlatives – the northernmost park has the densest population of redwood and the last natural undammed, free-flowing river in California, the sparkling Smith. All in all **Jedediah Smith Redwoods State Park** is a jewel. The redwood here is so dense few trails penetrate the park, so instead of hiking, drive the outstanding 11-mile **Howland Hill Scenic Drive**, which cuts through otherwise inaccessible areas. It's a rough, unpaved road, and it gets graded only once a year in spring and can close if there are fallen trees or washouts, but you'll feel as if you're visiting from Lilliput as you cruise under the gargantuan trunks. To spend the night, reserve at the park's fabulous campground tucked along the banks of the Smith.

🛏 ✕ p131

Eating & Sleeping

Samoa Peninsula ❶

✖ Lost Coast Brewery   Brewery $

(📞707-445-4480; 617 4th St, Eureka; meals $8-15; 🛜) After a few pints of Downtown Brown Ale, Great White or Lost Coast Pale Ale, the fried pub grub looks pretty tasty.

✖ Samoa Cookhouse   American $$

(📞707-442-1659; www.samoacookhouse.net; off Samoa Blvd; breakfast/lunch/dinner $12/13/16; 🚼) The last surviving lumber camp cookhouse in the West is a place to shovel down all-you-can-eat family meals at long red-checkered tables.

Trinidad ❷

✖ Larrupin Cafe   Californian $$$

(📞707-677-0230; www.larrupin.com; 1658 Patrick's Point Dr; mains $20-30; ⊘5-9pm Thu-Tue) Moroccan rugs, floral arrangements and deep-burgundy Oriental carpets create a moody atmosphere perfect for a lovers' tryst. The sumptuous menu has mesquite-grilled seafood and meats.

🛏 Trinidad Bay B&B   B&B $$$

(📞707-677-0840; www.trinidadbaybnb.com; 560 Edwards St; r incl breakfast from $200; 🛜) Opposite the lighthouse, this light-filled Cape Cod is scented with fresh baked cookies and overlooks Trinidad Head. Each room has a loaner iPad loaded with apps focused on local activities.

Patrick's Point State Park ❸

🛏 Patrick's Point State Park Campgrounds   Campground $

(📞reservations 800-444-7275; www.reserveamerica.com; tent & RV sites $35) Three well-tended campgrounds have hot showers and clean bathrooms. Penn Creek and Abalone campgrounds are more sheltered than Agate Beach.

Humboldt Lagoons State Park ❹

🛏 Humboldt County Parks Campgrounds   Campground $

(📞707-445-7651; tent sites $20) This campground beside Big Lagoon has first-come, first-served sites. Check in at Patrick's Point State Park, at least 30 minutes before sunset.

Redwood National Park ❺

🛏 Historic Requa Inn   Historic Hotel $$

(📞707-482-1425; www.requainn.com; 451 Requa Rd, Klamath; r $85-155; 🛜) A woodsy country lodge on bluffs overlooking the mouth of the Klamath, the 1914 Requa Inn is a North Coast favorite and it's carbon neutral.

Jedediah Smith Redwoods State Park ❼

✖ Beacon Burger   Burgers $

(160 Anchor Way, Crescent City; burgers $6-10; ⊘11:30am-8:30pm Mon-Sat) This scrappy one-room burger joint has been here forever, amid a parking lot overlooking the South Bay. It might invite a health inspector's scorn, but you'll quickly forgive it after ordering a burger – perfectly greasy and mysteriously wonderful.

🛏 Curly Redwood Lodge   Motel $

(📞707-464-2137; www.curlyredwoodlodge.com; 701 Hwy 101 S, Crescent City; r $68-73; ❄🛜) The Redwood Lodge is a marvel: it's entirely built and paneled from a single curly redwood tree that measured over 18-in thick in diameter. Progressively restored and polished into a gem of midcentury kitsch, the inn is a delight for retro junkies.

🛏 Jedediah Smith Redwoods State Park Campground   Campground $

(📞reservations 800-444-7275; www.reserveamerica.com; tent & RV sites $35) The popular campground has gorgeous sites tucked through the redwoods beside the Smith River.

Shasta Lake Bald eagles, hiking trails and great fishing

Trinity Scenic Byway

11

Cruising this secluded corner of California you'll pass majestic peaks, tranquil inland lakes and historic mountain towns, experiencing both rugged nature and plush hospitality.

TRIP HIGHLIGHTS

0 miles

Mt Shasta
Explore Northern California's volcanic beauty

START
1

McKinleyville
Arcata
FINISH

6

Shasta Lake

4

Redding

120 miles

Weaverville
This rugged little mountain town has a fascinating history

90 miles

Whiskeytown National Recreation Area
Camp on the shore of this scenic lake

3 DAYS
235 MILES/378KM

GREAT FOR...

BEST TIME TO GO

June through October, when the lakes and rivers are full and the air is crisp and clean.

 ESSENTIAL PHOTO

The space age futurism of Santiago Calatrava's Sundial Bridge.

✓ BEST FOR FAMILIES

Lake Shasta Caverns admission includes a boat ride, wildlife watching and a cave tour.

133

Trinity Scenic Byway

The back-to-landers, outdoor-types and new-age escapists in this remote corner of California proudly count the number of stoplights and fast-food joints in their counties on one hand. An epic cruise along the Trinity Scenic Byway takes visitors from California's most distinctive mountain to the Pacific shore, passing ample natural wonders and sophisticated small towns along the way.

TRIP HIGHLIGHT

❶ Mt Shasta

'When I first caught sight of it I was 50 miles away and afoot, alone and weary. Yet all my blood turned to wine, and I have not been weary since,' wrote naturalist John Muir of Mt Shasta in 1874. Though not California's highest (at 14,179ft it ranks fifth), the sight of this solitary peak is truly intoxicating. Start this trip at the top: you can drive almost all the way up via the Everitt

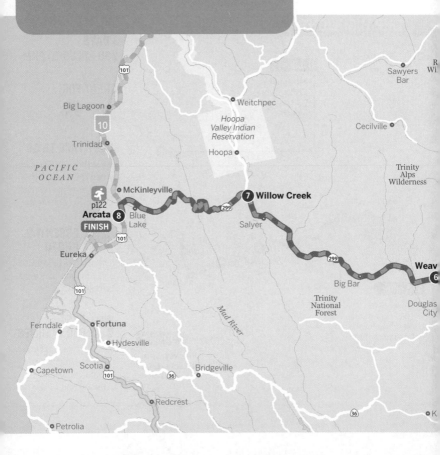

Memorial Hwy (Hwy A10) to enjoy exquisite views any time of year. By the time you reach **Bunny Flat** (6860ft) you'll be gasping at the sights (and the thin air), but if the road is clear of snow continue the ascent for more amazing views. You'll see Lassen Peak to the south. Look west for a bird's-eye preview of the rest of this trip, towards Mt Eddy and Marble Mountains and the green hills along the scenic Trinity Byway. For information about hikes, contact the **Mt**

Shasta ranger station (☎530-926-4511; 204 W Alma St; ⏲8am-4:30pm), which issues permits and good advice.

✕ ⬛ p139

The Drive ≫ Follow Everitt Memorial Hwy back down the hill. It'll take about 30 minutes to get down to Mt Shasta Village, a new-agey village that's worth a look. Go south 8 miles on I-5 and exit at Dunsmuir.

- - - - - - - - - - - - -

❷ **Shasta Lake**

The largest reservoir in California, **Shasta Lake** (www.shastalake.com) has the state's biggest population of bald eagles, an endless network of hiking trails, and great fishing. On the north side, stop to tour the crystalline caves of the **Lake Shasta Caverns** (www.lakeshastacaverns. com; adult/child 3-11 $22/13; ⏲tours 9am-4pm; 🚗). Tours include a boat ride that's great for families (bring a sweater – it's chilly down there!). The **Shasta Dam visitors center** (⏲8:30am-4:30pm) to the south has maps of hiking trails and a picture-window view of the monstrous **Shasta Dam**. The colossal, 15-million-ton dam is second only in size to Hoover Dam in Nevada; its 487ft spillway is as high as a 60-story building. Woody Guthrie wrote 'This Land is Your

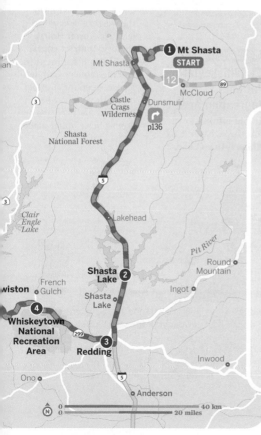

LINK YOUR TRIP

10 Northern Redwood Coast

Turn south on Hwy 101 at Arcata and link this epic mountain journey with a visit to the proud redwood stands of the far North Coast.

12 Volcanic Legacy Scenic Byway

Skirt Shasta's volcanic sister for a through trip around California's untouched north by going east of Red Bluff on Hwy 39.

Land' while working here. At the visitor center you can arrange for a fascinating free guided tour of the structure's rumbling interior.

🛏 p139

The Drive ≫ Retrace your path back to I-5 and head south 10 minutes to Redding.

- - - - - - - - - - - -

❸ Redding

Redding's sprawl – malls, big-box stores and large housing developments – might be discordant with the north's natural wonders, but it's the launching point for the Trinity Scenic Byway, which starts west of town. Still, it's worth a stop for the **Turtle Bay Exploration Park** (www.turtlebay.org; 840 Auditorium Dr; adult/child 4-12 $14/10; ☺9am-5pm May-Sep, shorter in winter; 👪). Situated on 300 acres, the complex of art and natural-science museums has interactive exhibits for kids, extensive

gardens, a butterfly house and a 22,000-gallon, walk-through river aquarium with regional aquatic life. Don't leave without a photo of the starkly futuristic **Sundial Bridge** that connects the Park to the north bank of the Sacramento River and was designed by renowned Spanish architect Santiago Calatrava.

🍴 p139

The Drive ≫ The banner stretch of the trip starts here: the Trinity Scenic Byway (Hwy 299) starts west of Redding and traces a winding path through the mountains to the Pacific Coast. Forests, mountain lakes, crumbling cabins and rushing rivers accompany the drive.

- - - - - - - - - - - -

TRIP HIGHLIGHT

❹ Whiskeytown National Recreation Area

An old mining town lent the rich name to **Whiskeytown Lake**, a

lovely, multiuse reservoir that was dedicated by John F Kennedy less than two months before his assassination. Today folks descend on the lake's serene 36 miles of forested shoreline to0. The **visitors center** (☎530-246-1225; ☺9am-6pm May-Sep, 10am-4pm Oct-Apr), on the northeast point of the lake, just off Hwy 299, provides information, free maps and leads guided walks. The hike from the visitors center to roaring **Whiskeytown Falls** (3.4 miles round trip) follows a former logging road and is a quick trip. On the western side of the lake, the **Tower House Historic District** contains the El Dorado mine ruins and the pioneer Camden House, open for summer tours. In winter, when the trees are bare, it's an atmospheric, quiet place to explore.

↱ DETOUR: DUNSMUIR

Start: ❶ Mt Shasta

Built by Central Pacific Railroad, Dunsmuir (population 1650) was originally named Pusher, for the auxiliary 'pusher' engines that muscled the heavy steam engines up the steep mountain grade. The town's reputation is still inseparable from the trains, making the stop essential for rail buffs. You can also stop there to quench your thirst; it could easily be – as locals claim – 'the best water on earth.' Maybe that water is what makes the beer at **Dunsmuir Brewery Works** (www.dunsmuirbreweryworks.info; 5701 Dunsmuir Ave; mains $11-20; ☺11am-9pm Tue-Sun; 🛜) so damn good. The crisp ales and chocolate porter are perfectly balanced. The IPA is apparently pretty good too, because patrons are always drinking it dry. Go south from Mt Shasta on I-5 for 9 miles and take exit 730 for central Dunsmuir.

Redding Sundial Bridge

The Drive » Leaving Whiskeytown Lake, Hwy 299 enters more remote country – say goodbye to that cell service. About 10 miles west of the lake the road is steep with white-knuckled turns and excellent lake vistas. Cut north on Trinity Dam Blvd.

⑤ Lewiston

Blink and you might miss **Lewiston** (www. lewistonca.com), a collection of buildings beside a rushing stretch of the Trinity River known for fishing. If you're passing through town, stop at the **Country Peddler** (4 Deadwood Rd), a drafty old barn filled with antiques that seem as if they have been plucked from some long-lost uncle's hunting cabin. The owners, avid outdoor enthusiasts, know the area like the backs of their hands. **Lewiston Lake** is about 1.5 miles north of town and is a serene alternative to the other area lakes. Early in the evening you may see ospreys and bald eagles diving for fish. Still, the best natural sights are deeper afield – particularly the **Trinity Alps Wilderness**, west of Hwy 3. Look no further for rugged adventure: it hosts excellent hiking and backcountry camping, and 600 miles of trails that cross granite peaks and skirt deep alpine lakes.

🛏 p139

The Drive » Take Lewiston Lake Rd back south for about 15 minutes and you'll enter Weaverville, the final village of the trip.

TRIP HIGHLIGHT

⑥ Weaverville

Of all California's historic parks, the walls of the **Joss House State Historic Park** (cnr Hwy 299 & Oregon St; admission $3; ☺10am-5pm Sat winter, Wed-Sun rest of yr) actually talk – they're papered inside with 150-year-old donation ledgers from the once-thriving Chinese community, a testament to the rich culture of immigrants who built Northern California's infrastructure and all but disappeared. The rich blue-and-gold Taoist shrine contains an ornate 3000-year-old altar, which was brought here from China. Sadly, state budget issues have made the future of this park uncertain, but it still makes a surprising gem within this far-flung mountain community.

✗ 🛏 p139

The Drive » Gas up and get ready for awe-inspiring views of the granite mountains, the Wild-and-Scenic-designated Trinity and sun-dappled forest are in every direction. There are

137

TRINITY BYWAY BEVVIES

Something about hiking though pine-scented forests can really work up a thirst for a hoppy IPA. Here are some favorite watering holes along the Trinity Scenic Byway.

Dunsmuir Brewery Works (www.dunsmuirbreweryworks.info; 5701 Dunsmuir Ave, Dunsmuir; ☺11am-9pm Tue-Sun;🛜) The best microbrew in the Northern Mountains.

Goats Tavern (www.thegoatmountshasta.com; 107 Chestnut St, Mt Shasta City; ☺7am-6pm; 🛜) Twelve taps rotating some of the best microbrewed beer in the country.

Alehouse Pub (www.reddingalehouse.com; 2181 Hilltop Dr, Redding; ☺3pm-midnight Mon-Thu, to 1:30am Fri & Sat) Get highly hopped beers on tap and T-shirts emblazoned with 'No Crap on Tap.'

Six Rivers Brewery (www.sixriversbrewery.com; 1300 Central Ave, McKinleyville; mains $11-18; ☺11:30am-midnight Tue-Sun, from 4pm Mon) End the byway trip with a sip at this 'brew with a view.'

no turns; simply continue west on Hwy 299.

❼ Willow Creek

Stay sharp as you navigate the road to Willow Creek – this remote little community was the sight of some of the most convincing homemade footage ever captured of a Sasquatch. This makes an obligatory stop of the **Willow Creek–China Flat Museum** (www.bigfootcountry.net; ☺10am-4pm Wed-Sun May-Sep, noon-4pm Fri-Sun Oct, closed winter) for the fun, constantly changing Big Foot Exhibit that includes casts of very large footprints and some provocative (if blurry) photos. The 25ft-tall redwood sculpture of the hairy beast in the parking lot is hard to miss. Willow Creek is also the beginning of the Bigfoot Scenic Byway – a route that takes you through the region with the most Bigfoot sightings in the country; see http://byways.org/explore/byways/62352 for more information.

The Drive » About 10 miles west of Willow Creek, you'll cross the Berry Summit Vista Point (Mile 28.4) and then start to drop in elevation toward the Pacific. Continue 31 twisting miles on Hwy 299 to Arcata.

❽ Arcata

Congratulations, road warrior, you've finally arrived in Arcata, an idiosyncratic college town on the sparkling shores of the Pacific and smack dab in the middle of California's majestic Redwood country. Park the car at **Arcata Plaza** and stroll around the historic downtown to find a bite to eat (the restaurants in Arcata are top-notch) or explore the campus of **Humboldt State University**, home to a world-class environmental sustainability program. Also try our self-guided walking tour (p122).

🍴 🛏 p139

Eating & Sleeping

Mt Shasta ❶

✖ Trinity Café
Californian $$

(☎530-926-6200; 622 N Mt Shasta Blvd; mains $17-28; ⏱5-9pm Tue-Sat) Trinity has long rivaled the Bay Area's best with an extensive, excellent wine selection and organic menu.

☐ Historic Lookout & Cabin Rentals
Cabin $

(☎530-994-2184; www.fs.fed.us/r5/shastatrinity; up to 4 people from $35) These restored fire lookouts on the slopes of Little Mt Hoffman or Girard Ridge were built from the 1920s to '40s and can accommodate four people.

☐ Shasta MountInn
B&B $$

(☎530-926-1810; www.shastamountinn.com; 203 Birch St; r without/with fireplace $130/175; @ 🛜) Only antique on the outside, inside this bright Victorian farmhouse is all relaxed minimalism, bold colors and graceful decor. Need to relax more? Try porch swings and on-site massage.

Shasta Lake ❷

☐ US Forest Service (USFS) Campgrounds
Campgrounds $

(☎877 444 6777; www.reserveusa.com; tent sites $6-26) The lake has a range of camping, with lake and mountain views. Camping outside organized campgrounds requires campfire permits from May to October, available free from any USFS office.

Redding ❸

✖ Carnegie's
Californian $$

(1600 Oregon St; meals $12; ⏱10am-3pm Mon & Tue, to 11pm Wed-Fri; 🖋) This hip and homey, split-level cafe serves up healthy food – big fresh salads, garlicky prawns and pasta and homemade tomato soup.

✖ Jack's Grill
Steakhouse $$$

(www.jacksgrillredding.com; 1743 California St; mains $15-31; ⏱5-11pm, bar from 4pm Mon-Sat) This funky old-time place doesn't look so inviting – the windows are blacked out and it's dark as a crypt inside – but the thick, charbroiled decadence keeps 'em coming back.

Lewiston ❺

☐ Lewiston Hotel
Historic Hotel $

(☎530-778-3823; www.lewistonhotel.net; 125 Deadwood Rd; r $69-89; 🛜) This 1862 hotel was recently reopened to guests, and the rooms – with river views – have tons of character.

Weaverville ❻

✖ La Grange Café
Californian $$

(☎530-623-5325; 315 N Main St; mains $15-30; ⏱11:30am-9pm Mon-Thu, to 10pm Fri-Sun, with seasonal variations) This celebrated multistar restaurant serves satisfying fare without a whiff of pretension: apple-stuffed red cabbage in the fall and chicken enchiladas in the summer.

☐ Weaverville Hotel
Historic Hotel $$

(☎800-750-8957; www.weavervillehotel.com; 203 Main St; r $100-260; ❄🛜) Play like you're in the Old West at this upscale hotel and historic landmark, refurbished in grand Victorian style.

Arcata ❽

✖ Folie Douce
Modern American $$$

(☎707-822-1042; www.holyfolie.com; 1551 G St; dinner mains $27-36; ⏱5:30-9pm Tue-Thu, to 10pm Fri & Sat; 🖋) Just a slip of a place, but the short, inventive menu features seasonally inspired bistro cooking.

☐ Hotel Arcata
Historic Hotel $$

(☎707-826-0217; www.hotelarcata.com; 708 9th St; r $96-156; 🛜) Anchoring the plaza, the renovated 1915 brick landmark is an excellent perch for people-watching on the square, but the quietest rooms face the back.

Lassen Volcanic National Park Bump
Hell, an active geothermal a

Volcanic Legacy Scenic Byway

12

Even in the peak of summer, the byways of Northern California's wilderness are largely empty. This loop skirts the edge of Lassen Peak, one of the largest dormant volcanoes on the planet.

TRIP HIGHLIGHTS

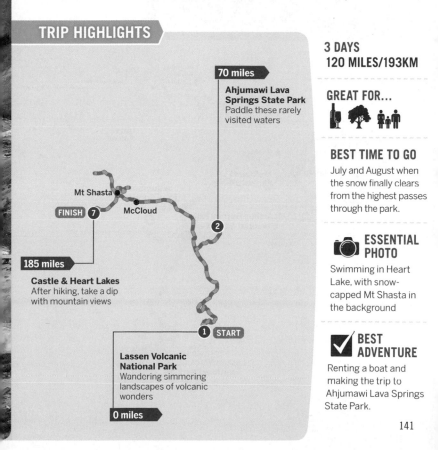

70 miles

Ahjumawi Lava Springs State Park
Paddle these rarely visited waters

Mt Shasta

FINISH 7

McCloud

2

185 miles

Castle & Heart Lakes
After hiking, take a dip with mountain views

1 START

Lassen Volcanic National Park
Wandering simmering landscapes of volcanic wonders

0 miles

3 DAYS
120 MILES/193KM

GREAT FOR...

BEST TIME TO GO

July and August when the snow finally clears from the highest passes through the park.

ESSENTIAL PHOTO

Swimming in Heart Lake, with snow-capped Mt Shasta in the background

BEST ADVENTURE

Renting a boat and making the trip to Ahjumawi Lava Springs State Park.

141

12 Volcanic Legacy Scenic Byway

Looping the big, green patches of the map: perfect for hiking, fishing, camping or just getting lost. This is a place where few people venture, but those who do come back with stories. The settlements in this neck of the woods are mostly just places to gas up and buy some jerky, but adventurers are drawn to this place for just that reason. This is the deeply satisfying final frontier of California wilderness.

TRIP HIGHLIGHT

❶ Lassen Volcanic National Park

Driving through the surrounding fields studded with volcanic boulders, **Lassen Volcanic National Park** (☎530-595-4444; www.nps.gov/lavo; park entrance $10; ⏰9am-6pm Jun-Sep, with seasonal variations; 👪) glowers in the distance. Lassen rises 2000 dramatic feet over the surrounding landscape to 10,457ft above sea level. Lassen's dome has a volume of half a cubic mile, making

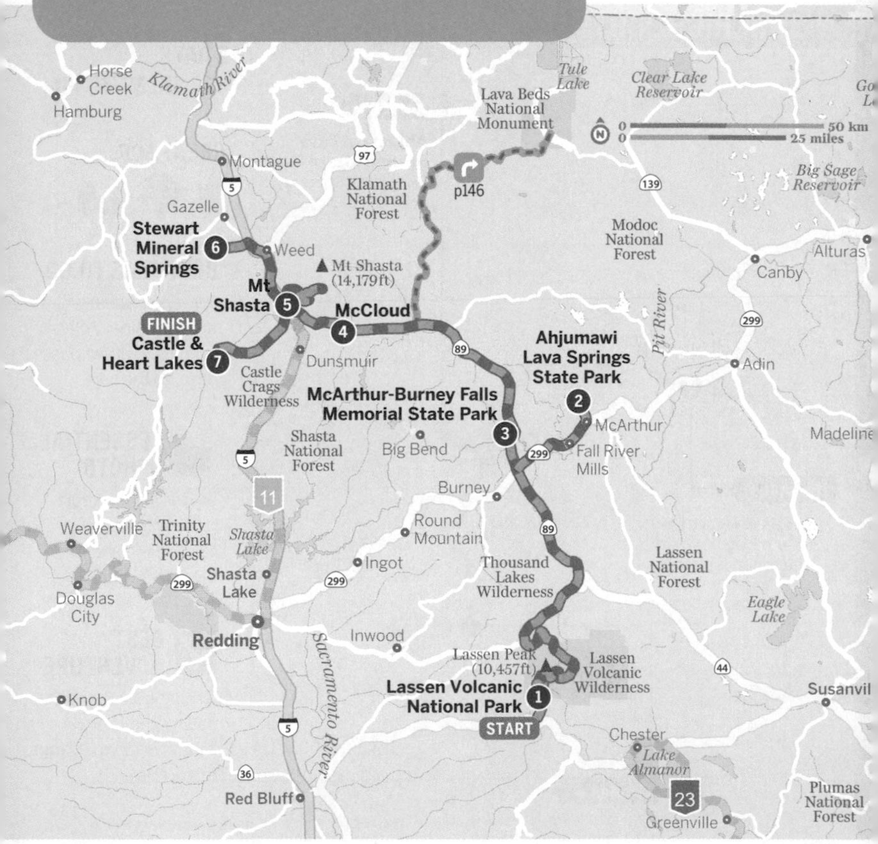

Horse Creek
Hamburg
Klamath River
Tule Lake
Clear Lake Reservoir
Lava Beds National Monument
0 50 km
0 25 miles
Montague
97
5
Klamath National Forest
p146
139
Big Sage Reservoir
Gazelle
Stewart Mineral Springs
6
Weed
Mt Shasta (14,179ft)
Modoc National Forest
Alturas
Canby
Mt Shasta
5
McCloud
4
Pit River
FINISH
Castle & Heart Lakes
7
Dunsmuir
89
Ahjumawi Lava Springs State Park
299
Adin
Castle Crags Wilderness
McArthur-Burney Falls Memorial State Park
2
3
McArthur
Shasta National Forest
Big Bend
Fall River Mills
Madeline
11
Burney
Round Mountain
Weaverville
Trinity National Forest
Shasta Lake
Ingot
Thousand Lakes Wilderness
Lassen National Forest
Douglas City
Shasta Lake
Eagle Lake
Redding
Inwood
Sacramento River
Lassen Peak (10,457ft)
Lassen Volcanic Wilderness
44
Lassen Volcanic National Park
1
Susanvil
Knob
START
Chester
Lake Almanor
36
Red Bluff
23
Plumas National Forest
Greenville

it one of the world's largest plug-dome volcanoes – its most recent eruption took place in 1915, when it blew a giant billow of smoke, steam and ash 7 miles into the atmosphere.

Approaching the peaks, the road begins to climb, entering corridors of dense forest and emerging at the green-certified **Kohm Yah-mah-nee Visitor Facility**. Stop in to pick up maps and the handy newspaper, which outlines campsites and includes maps of the 150 miles of hiking trails. Heading north, you can roam through the tawny stone slopes of burbling **Sulfur Works** – you'll know it by the ripe scent in the air and the gaseous bursts hissing

LINK YOUR TRIP

23 **Feather River Scenic Byway**

Link this epic mountain journey just south in Chester, with a trip through inland wilderness along Hwy 70 and the Feather River.

11 **Trinity Scenic Byway**

Go from the rugged Trinity Alps to the sparkling sea, following this route of pristine wilderness along Hwy 299.

over the roadway. The moderate 1.5-mile hike to **Bumpass Hell** traverses an active geothermal area festooned with otherworldly colored pools and billowing clouds of steam.

🛌 p147

Follow Hwy 89 27 miles through the park, circling east of Lassen. At the intersection of Hwy 299, go right for the little town of Fall River Mills, where you can rent a kayak or canoe. Then, enter McArthur and continue past the Intermountain Fairgrounds, crossing a canal and continuing to the boat launch.

TRIP HIGHLIGHT

❷ Ahjumawi Lava Springs State Park

Of all the stops along this trip, none is more remote and more rewarding than the **Ahjumawi Lava Springs State Park** (☎530-336-5535; www.parks.ca.gov). A visit here comes with serious bragging rights as the abundant springs, aquamarine bays and islets, and jagged flows of black basalt lava are truly off the beaten path, and can be reached only by boat. You can make arrangements for boat rental and primitive camping through McArthur-Burney Falls Memorial State Park, but the best way to visit is to silently glide across these waters on a canoe or kayak. These can be rented in nearby Fall

River Mills at **Fall River Boat Rentals** (☎530-336-6085; www.fallriverboatrentals.com; 42079 Riverbank Rd; canoe $40 per day). After you push out, the hikes are glorious: there are basalt outcroppings, lava tubes, cold springs bubbling and all kinds of volcanic features.

The Drive » Get back to Hwy 89 and take it north to McCloud.

❸ McArthur-Burney Falls Memorial State Park

After all the volcanic rock and sulfur fields, there's a soothing stop up the road in **McArthur-Burney Falls Memorial State Park** (☎530-335-2777; summer reservations ☎800-444-7275; www.parks.ca.gov; day-use/campsites $8/25; 👪📶). Fed by a spring, the splashing 129ft-waterfalls flow at the same temperature, 42°F, year-round. Rangers are quick to point out that it might not be California's highest waterfall, but it may be the most beautiful (Teddy Roosevelt called it the 'eighth wonder of the world.') Clear, lava-filtered water surges over the top and also from springs in the waterfall's face. Hiking trails include a portion of the Pacific Crest Trail, which continues north to Castle Crags State Park. The 1.3-mile **Burney Falls Trail**

KEN BROWN / PICTURELAKE / ISTOCKPHOTO ©

is the one you shouldn't miss. Recently upgraded with guardrails, it's an easy loop for families and allows close-up views of water rushing right out of the rock.

🛏 p147

The Drive » Go west on Hwy 299 and turn north on 89.

---

❹ McCloud

The old logging town McCloud sits serenely on the southern slopes of Mt Shasta, with the peak looming in the distance. It is a mellow, comfortable place from which to explore the pristine wilderness that surrounds it. Bump along the tiny, partially paved McCloud River Loop, which begins off Hwy 89 about 11 miles east of McCloud, to find the lovely trail at **Three Falls** on the lower reaches of Mt Shasta. The easy, 1.5-mile trail passes gorgeous, secluded falls, and you'll discover a lovely habitat for bird-watching in the Bigelow Meadow. Other good hiking trails include the **Squaw Valley Creek Trail** (not to be confused with the ski area near Lake Tahoe), an easy 5-mile loop trail south of town, with options for

VOLCANOES GALORE

This trip is but a smidgen of the entirety of the Volcanic Legacy Scenic Byway – a route that stretches some 500 miles north into Oregon. The northern terminus of the byway is the stupendous Crater Lake National Park in Oregon.

McArthur-Burney Falls Memorial State Park Burney Falls

swimming, fishing and
picnicking.

🛏 p147

The Drive » Hwy 89 climbs
steeply to reach the city of Mt
Shasta. Along the way you'll
pass Mt Shasta Board & Ski
Park, which has ski trails that
are converted into awesome
mountain biking runs in the
summer.

- - - - - - - - - - - - -

⑤ Mt Shasta

Still classified as an
active volcano, **Mt
Shasta** (☎530-926-
4511; www.fs.fed.us/r5/
shastatrinity; 204 W Alma
St, Mt Shasta City; ☺8am-
4:30pm) remains a mecca
for mystics. Seekers

are attracted to the
peak's reported cosmic
properties, but this
reverence for the great
mountain is nothing
new: for centuries
Native Americans have
honored it as sacred,
considering it to be
no less than the Great
Spirit's wigwam. Reach
its highest drivable point
by heading through Mt
Shasta City to Everitt
Memorial Hwy, which
leads to **Bunny Flat,** one
of the lower access points
on the mountain for
excellent hikes. An amble
around the town at the
base of the mountain
will provide you with an

opportunity to duck into
book shops and excellent
eateries. Visitors can also
fill their water bottles
at the **Sacramento
River Headwaters** off
Mt Shasta Blvd, about a
mile north of downtown.
Pure water gurgles up
from the ground in a
large, cool spring amid
a city park with walking
trails, picnic spots and a
children's playground.

✕ 🛏 p147

The Drive » From Mt Shasta
City go 10 miles north on I-5,
past Weed to the Edgewood exit,
then turn left at Stewart Springs
Rd and follow the signs.

DETOUR: LAVA BEDS NATIONAL MONUMENT

Start: 4 McCloud

Lava Beds National Monument (www.nps.gov/labe), perched on yet another crater, is a truly remarkable 72-sq-mile landscape of volcanic features – lava flows, craters, cinder cones, spatter cones, shield volcanoes and amazing lava tubes. Nearly 750 caves have been found in the monument and they remain a comfortable 55°F no matter what the outside temperature. Spy Native American petroglyphs throughout the park too. From McCloud, go southeast several miles on Hwy 89, then take Harris Springs Rd north. The whole trip should take about two hours.

6 Stewart Mineral Springs

Make all the jokes you want about the name of the little town of Weed, but a visit to **Stewart Mineral Springs** (☎530-938-2222; www. stewartmineralsprings.com; 4617 Stewart Springs Rd; mineral baths $28, sauna $18; ☺10am-6pm Sun-Wed, to 7pm Thu-Sat) will only inspire a satisfied sigh. At this popular alternative (read clothing optional) hangout on the banks of a clear mountain stream guests soak in a private claw-foot tub or cook in the dry-wood sauna. There's also massage, body wraps, a Native American sweat lodge and a riverside sunbathing deck. You'll want to call ahead to be sure there is space in the steam and soaking rooms, especially on busy weekends. While in the area, tickle your other senses at **Mt Shasta Lavender Farms** (www. mtshastalavenderfarms.com). 16 miles northwest of Weed, off Hwy A12, on Harry Cash Rd. You can harvest your own sweet French lavender in the June and July blooming season.

✖ ⌖ p147

The Drive » The lake can be reached by driving south on I-5 and taking exit 736. Go under the highway and the service road to the north on the west side of the highway to connect with Crater Lake Rd. The lake is approximately 7 miles beyond Lake Siskiyou. Along the way you'll pass Ney Springs and Faery Falls, both fun places to pull over for a photo.

TRIP HIGHLIGHT

7 Castle & Heart Lakes

Castle Lake is an easily accessible yet pristine mountain pool surrounded by granite formations and pine forest. In the distance you'll see two of Northern California's most recognizable rocks: Castle Crags and Mt Shasta. After you park, orient yourself with the signboards and put on that swimsuit for the half-hour hike to **Heart Lake** – considered one of the most rewarding easy hikes in the region. Heading east along the shore, a trail crosses a wildflower-lined creek before coming to saddle about 100 feet before a small pond. Go right at the saddle and follow an unsigned trail southwest for a half-mile to reach Heart Lake. In the summer months, this is a dream come true, as Heart Lake's shallow waters offer excellent for swimming and a spectacular view of Mt Shasta.

⌖ p147

Eating & Sleeping

Lassen Volcanic National Park ❶

🛏 Manzanita Lake Camping Cabins
Cabins, Campground $

(winter ☎530-200-4578, summer ☎530-335-7557; www.lassenrecreation.com; Hwy 89, near Manzanita Lake; tent & RV sites $18, r $57-81; 🛜📶) These freshly built log cabins come in one- and two-bedroom options and slightly more basic bunk configurations, which are a bargain for groups.

🛏 National Park Campgrounds
Campground $

(☎877-444-6777; www.recreation.gov; tent & RV sites $10-18) The park has eight developed campgrounds that are open from late May to late October, depending on snow conditions. Manzanita Lake is the only one with hot showers.

McArthur-Burney Falls Memorial State Park ❸

🛏 McArthur-Burney Falls Memorial State Park Campground
Campground $

(☎530-335-2777, summer reservations ☎800-444-7275; www.parks.ca.gov; day-use/campsites $6/20; 📶) The park's campgrounds have hot showers and are open year-round, even when there's snow on the ground.

McCloud ❹

🛏 McCloud River Mercantile Hotel
Boutique Hotel $$

(☎530-964-2330; www.mccloudmercantile.com; 241 Main St; r $129-250; 🛜) The rooms have antique furnishings and open floor plans. Guests are greeted with fresh flowers and can drift to sleep on feather beds after soaking in claw-foot tubs. Certainly the best hotel in the northern mountains, with a perfect marriage of preservationist class and modern panache.

Mt Shasta ❼

🍴 Mount Shasta Pastry
Bakery $

(610 S Mt Shasta Blvd; mains $17-28; ⏱6am-2:30pm Mon-Sat, 7am-1pm Sun) Walk in hungry and you'll be plagued with an existential breakfast crisis: the potato and egg frittata topped with red peppers, ham and melted cheese, or the smoky breakfast burrito? The flaky croissants or peach cobbler?

🛏 Woodsman Cabins & Lodge
Motel $

(☎530-926-3411; 1121 S Mt Shasta Blvd; r $89-139; ❄🛜) Owned by the same folks who have the Strawberry Valley Inn across the street, the cluster of renovated mid-century buildings that make up the Woodsman is the mannish alternative. Taxidermy looks over the reception area, where a fire keeps things warm in the winter.

Stewart Mineral Springs ❻

🍴 Weed Mt Shasta Brewing Company
Brewery $

(www.weedales.com; 360 College Ave, Weed) Try a tasty porter or the rich, amber-colored Mountain High IPA. The latter is delicious, but watch out – at 7% alcohol it has real kick.

🛏 Stewart Mineral Springs
Camping $

(tent & RV sites $35, tepees $45, r $65-85) There are a number of basic accommodations available, including a rough-cut lodge and some tepees.

Castle & Heart Lakes ❼

🛏 Castle Lake Campground
Campground $

(☎530-926-4511; Mt Shasta Ranger Station; free) There are six primitive sites about a quarter mile below the lake with tables and fire pits.

Central California Trips

THE FAIRYTALE STRETCH OF COAST BETWEEN SAN FRANCISCO AND LA is too often dismissed as 'flyover country.' But it's packed with beaches, historic lighthouses and tall redwoods hiding forest waterfalls.

Get acquainted with central California's agricultural heartland while driving along inland highways. Roll past vineyards and farms where you can taste the goodness of the land, from juicy strawberries to wines to artichokes.

Further east rises the Sierra Nevada, uplifted along faultlines and weathered by glaciers, wind and rain. Soothe your soul with natural wonders, from Yosemite Valley to Lake Tahoe. Then drop into the foothills to trace California's Gold Rush history and take a dip in summertime swimming holes or crystal lakes.

Lake Tahoe (Trip 18)
MICK ROESSLER / CORBIS ©

Central California Trips

13 Big Sur 2 Days
Get lost at wild beaches and bohemian camps along coastal Hwy 1. (p153)

14 Along Highway 1 to Santa Cruz 2–3 Days
Cruise south from San Francisco past lighthouses, tidepools and monster surf. (p161)

15 Around Monterey & Carmel 2–3 Days
Putter around the idyllic peninsula fronting wildlife-rich Monterey Bay. (p169)

16 Around San Luis Obispo 2–3 Days
Laid-back beach towns and outdoor adventures mix with break-out wineries. (p179)

17 Santa Barbara Wine Country 2–3 Days
Spend a weekend in pastoral Foxen Canyon and the Santa Rita Hills. (p187)

18 Lake Tahoe Loop 2–3 Days
Drive round 'Big Blue' to reach mountain-framed beaches and bays. (p197)

Classic Trip

19 Yosemite, Sequoia & Kings Canyon National Parks 5–7 Days
Be awed by Sierra Nevada peaks, wildflower meadows, sequoias and waterfalls. (p205)

20 Eastern Sierra Scenic Byway 3–5 Days
A rugged wilderness gateway to hot springs, hikes and ghost towns. (p217)

Classic Trip

21 Highway 49 Through Gold Country
3–4 Days
Head for the hills and California's historic pioneer mining towns. (p227)

22 Ebbetts Pass Scenic Byway 2 Days
Cross the Sierra Nevada at heady elevations on hidden Hwy 4. (p237)

23 Feather River Scenic Byway 3–4 Days
Cool off with a swim or paddle around sunny lakes and rivers. (p245)

24 Lazy Delta Dawdle 2 Days
Ride the Sacramento River Delta on lazy backcountry explorations. (p253)

25 Highway 99 Through Central Valley
3 Days
Country-and-western music, cow towns and farms fill California's sun-baked flatland. (p261)

DON'T MISS

Pfeiffer Beach

Catch sunset shining through a sea arch and dig down into the purple-tinged sand on Trip 13

Kings Canyon Scenic Byway

Wind down into the USA's deepest river canyon carved by glaciers to Road's End in Cedar Grove on Trip 19

Alabama Hills

Where famous Western movies and TV shows were filmed outside of Lone Pine, just below Mt Whitney, on Trip 20

South Yuba River State Park

Swim, hike and photograph the USA's longest covered wooden bridge, west of the 19th-century mining town of Nevada City, on Trip 21

Kingsburg

A global melting pot of immigrants have farmed California's Central Valley, including the Swedes of Kingsburg, a whistle-stop on Trip 25

Big Sur Ocean vistas beckon along Hwy 1

Big Sur

13

Nestled up against mossy redwood forests, the rocky Big Sur coast is a secretive place. On this overnight trip, get to know it like locals do, visiting wild beaches, waterfalls and hot springs.

TRIP HIGHLIGHTS

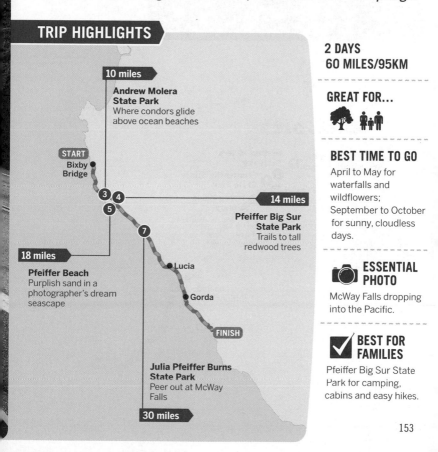

10 miles

Andrew Molera State Park
Where condors glide above ocean beaches

START
Bixby Bridge

3 4
5
7

14 miles

Pfeiffer Big Sur State Park
Trails to tall redwood trees

18 miles

Pfeiffer Beach
Purplish sand in a photographer's dream seascape

Lucia

Gorda

FINISH

Julia Pfeiffer Burns State Park
Peer out at McWay Falls

30 miles

2 DAYS
60 MILES/95KM

GREAT FOR...

BEST TIME TO GO

April to May for waterfalls and wildflowers; September to October for sunny, cloudless days.

ESSENTIAL PHOTO

McWay Falls dropping into the Pacific.

BEST FOR FAMILIES

Pfeiffer Big Sur State Park for camping, cabins and easy hikes.

13 Big Sur

Much ink has been spilled extolling the raw beauty of this craggy land shoehorned between the Santa Lucia Mountains and the Pacific. Yet nothing quite prepares you for that first glimpse through the windshield of Big Sur's wild, unspoiled coastline. There are no traffic lights, banks or strip malls, and when the sun goes down, the moon and the stars are the only streetlights – if coastal fog hasn't extinguished them.

❶ Bixby Bridge

To tell the truth, Big Sur is more a state of mind than a place you can pinpoint on a map. But the photogenic **Bixby Bridge** lets you know you've finally arrived. Arching above Rainbow Canyon, this landmark is one of the world's highest single-span bridges, completed in 1932 by prisoners eager to lop time off their sentences. Stop on the north side of the bridge for an irresistible photo op.

The Drive » From Bixby Bridge, it's about 6 miles south along Hwy 1, rolling beside pasture lands, to Point Sur State Historic Park. Like everywhere else along Big Sur's coast, watch out for cyclists and use signposted roadside pullouts to let fast-moving traffic pass by.

❷ Point Sur State Historic Park

Rising like a velvety green fortress out of the sea, **Point Sur State Historic Park** (☏831-625-4419; www.pointsur.org, www.parks.ca.gov; adult/child $10/5; ☺tours usually 1pm Wed, 10am Sat & Sun Nov-Mar, 10am & 2pm Wed & Sat, 10am Sun Apr-Oct) looks like an island, but is actually connected to the mainland by a sandbar. On the volcanic rock sits California's

LINK YOUR TRIP

1 Pacific Coast Highways

Big Sur is just one famous stretch of Hwy 1 along the California coast, which you can drive from Mexico to Oregon.

15 Around Monterey & Carmel

From Bixby Bridge, drive about 20 miles north on Hwy 1 to Monterey for maritime history lessons and California's top-ranked aquarium.

only turn-of-the-20th-century lightstation that's still open to the public. Ocean views and tales of the lighthouse-keepers' family lives are engrossing, especially during spooky moonlight tours. Call ahead to confirm schedules; arrive early because space is limited (no reservations).

The Drive » Lighthouse tours meet at the locked farm gate a quarter-mile north of Point Sur Naval Facility. Afterwards, drive south on Hwy 1 another 2 miles along the coast to Andrew Molera State Park.

TRIP HIGHLIGHT

❸ Andrew Molera State Park

With ocean vistas beckoning along Hwy 1, you'll be eager to put your feet on a beach by now. Named after the farmer who first planted artichokes in California, **Andrew Molera State Park** (☏831-667-2315; www.parks.ca.gov; Hwy 1; per car $10; ☺30min before sunrise-30min after sunset; 🚹) is a trail-laced pastiche of grassy meadows, ocean bluffs and sandy beaches, all offering excellent wildlife watching. Hike for about a mile out to where the Big Sur River meets the rocky driftwood-strewn beach, whipped by strong winds and the surf. Back at the parking lot, walk south to the **Big Sur Discovery Center** (☏831-620-0702; www.

ventanaws.org; admission free; ☺usually 9am-4pm Sat & Sun late May-early Sep) to learn all about endangered California condors that sometimes soar overhead.

The Drive » Speeds rarely top 35mph along Hwy 1, which narrows and becomes curvier the further south you go. Slow down a few miles beyond the state park and watch for pedestrians in 'the village,' Big Sur's hub for shops, services, motels and cafes (see p159). About 5 miles south of Andrew Molera State Park, you'll see the entrance for Pfeiffer Big Sur State Park on the inland side of the highway.

TRIP HIGHLIGHT

❹ Pfeiffer Big Sur State Park

The biggest all-natural draw on the Big Sur coast is **Pfeiffer Big Sur State Park** (☏831-667-2315; www.parks.ca.gov; 47225 Hwy 1; per car $10; ☺30min before sunrise-30min after sunset; 🚹). Named after Big Sur's first European settlers, who arrived here in 1869, it's also the largest state park along this coast. Hiking trails loop through tall redwood groves and run uphill to 60ft-high **Pfeiffer Falls**, a delicate cascade hidden in the forest that usually flows between December and May. Near the park entrance, inside a rustic lodge built in the 1930s by the Civilian Conservation Corps (CCC), you'll find a

LARRY DALE GORDON / CORBIS ©

convenient general store selling cold drinks, ice cream, snacks, camping supplies and road trip souvenirs.

🛏 p159

The Drive » Just 2 miles south of Pfeiffer Big Sur State Park, about half a mile past ranger-staffed Big Sur Station, make a sharp right turn off Hwy 1 onto Sycamore Canyon Rd, marked only by a small yellow sign saying 'Narrow Rd.' Partly unpaved, this road (RVs and trailers prohibited) corkscrews down for over 2 miles to Pfeiffer Beach.

<hr />

TRIP HIGHLIGHT

❺ Pfeiffer Beach

Hidden down a side road to the sea, **Pfeiffer Beach** (☎831-667-2315; www.fs.fed.us/r5/lospadres; Sycamore Canyon Rd; per car $5; ☉9am-8pm; 🚻👶)

is worth the trouble it takes to reach it. This phenomenal, crescent-shaped strand is known for its huge double rock formation, through which waves crash with life-affirming power. It's often windy, and the surf is too dangerous for swimming. But dig down into the wet sand – it's purple! That's because manganese garnet

Pfeiffer Beach

washes down from the craggy hillsides above.

The Drive » Backtrack up narrow, winding Sycamore Canyon Rd for more than 2 miles, then turn right onto Hwy 1 southbound. After two more twisting, slow-moving miles, look for Nepenthe restaurant on your right. The Henry Miller Library is another 0.4 miles south, at a hairpin turn on your left.

6 Henry Miller Library

'It was here in Big Sur I first learned to say Amen!' wrote Henry Miller, a surrealist novelist and local resident from 1944 to 1962. More of a beatnik memorial, alt-cultural venue and bookshop, the **Henry Miller Library** (☏831-667-2574; www. henrymiller.org; 48603 Hwy 1; admission by donation; ⏰11am-6pm Wed-Mon; @ 📶) was never actually the writer's home. The house belonged to Miller's friend, painter Emil White. Inside are copies of all of Miller's published books, many of his paintings and a collection of Big Sur and Beat Generation material.

DETOUR: ESALEN HOT SPRINGS

Start: ❼ Julia Pfeiffer Burns State Park

Ocean beaches and waterfalls aren't the only places to get wet in Big Sur. At private **Esalen Institute** (☎831-667-3047; 55000 Hwy 1; hot-springs entry $20, credit cards only; ☼public access 1am-3am, by reservation only), clothing-optional baths fed by a natural hot spring sit on a ledge above the ocean. Dollars to donuts you'll never take another dip that compares scenery-wise, especially on stormy winter nights. Only two small outdoor pools perch directly over the waves, so once you've stripped and taken a quick shower, head outside immediately. Advance telephone reservations are required. The signposted entrance is on Hwy 1, about 3 miles south of Julia Pfeiffer Burns State Park.

Stop by to browse and hang out on the front deck with coffee, or join the bohemian carnival of live music, open-mic nights and independent film screenings.

✖ 🛏 p159

The Drive » You'll leave most of the traffic behind as Hwy 1 continues southbound, curving slowly along the vertiginous cliffs, occasionally opening up for ocean panoramas. It's fewer than 8 miles to Julia Pfeiffer Burns State Park; the entrance is on the inland side of Hwy 1.

TRIP HIGHLIGHT

❼ Julia Pfeiffer Burns State Park

If you've got an appetite for chasing waterfalls, swing into **Julia Pfeiffer Burns State Park** (☎831-667-2315; www.parks.ca.gov; Hwy 1; per car $10; ☼30min before sunrise-30min after sunset; 🚻). From the parking lot, the short Overlook Trail rushes downhill towards the sea, passing through a

tunnel underneath Hwy 1. Everyone is in a hurry to see **McWay Falls**, which tumbles year-round over granite cliffs and free-falls into the ocean – or the beach, depending on the tide. This is the classic Big Sur postcard shot, with tree-topped rocks jutting above a golden beach next to swirling blue pools and crashing white surf. During winter, watch for migrating whales offshore.

The Drive » The tortuously winding stretch of Hwy 1 southbound is sparsely populated, rugged and remote, running through national forest. Make sure you've got enough fuel in the tank to at least reach the expensive gas station at Gorda, over 20 miles south of Julia Pfeiffer Burns State Park.

❽ Los Padres National Forest

About 5 miles south of Nacimiento-Fergusson Rd, **Sand Dollar Beach Picnic Area** (www.fs.usda.gov; per vehicle $5; ☼9am-

8pm) faces southern Big Sur's longest sandy beach, protected by high bluffs. Once you pass Plaskett Creek Campground, look for trails down to **Jade Cove** from roadside pull-offs along Hwy 1. In 1971, local divers recovered a 9000lb jade boulder here that measured 8ft long and was valued at $180,000!

If you have any slivers of sunlight left, keep trucking down Hwy 1 approximately 8 miles past Gorda to **Salmon Creek Falls** (www.fs.fed.us/r5/lospadres; Hwy 1; admission free; 🚻🐕), which usually runs from December through May. Take a short hike to splash around in the pools at the base of this double-drop waterfall, tucked uphill in a forested canyon. In a hairpin turn of Hwy 1, the roadside turnoff is marked only by a small brown trailhead sign.

🛏 p159

Eating & Sleeping

Big Sur Village

✗ Habanero Burrito Bar
Deli, Supermarket $

(46840 Hwy 1; mains $4-6; ⊘11am-7pm; 🕱📶) Something about the salty sea air will make you ravenous. Order a San Francisco–sized burrito or a healthier wrap sandwich with a real-fruit smoothie from the back of the Big Sur River Inn's well-stocked general store.

🛏 Glen Oaks Motel
Motel $$$

(☎831-667-2105; www.glenoaksbigsur.com; Hwy 1; d $175-350; 🕱) Snug romantic rooms and a woodsy cottage out back each come with a gas-burning fireplace at this 1950s redwood-and-adobe motor lodge, dramatically transformed by chic ecodesign.

Pfeiffer Big Sur State Park ④

🛏 Big Sur Lodge
Cottages $$

(☎831-667-3100, 800-424-4787; www.bigsurlodge.com; 47225 Hwy 1; restaurant mains $10-27, d $159-339; 📶📶) Inside peaceful Pfeiffer Big Sur State Park, well-worn duplexes have decks or balconies looking out into the redwoods, while family-sized rooms may have kitchens and/or wood-burning fireplaces. Past the lobby, the rustic restaurant serves three square locally sourced, sustainable meals a day.

🛏 Pfeiffer Big Sur State Park
Campground $

(☎800-444-2725; www.reserveamerica.com; 47225 Hwy 1; tent & RV sites $35-50; 📶) Over 150 family campsites inside the park are shaded by redwoods; facilities include hot showers and laundry, but no RV hookups.

Henry Miller Library ⑥

✗ Nepenthe
Californian $$$

(☎831-667-2345; www.nepenthebigsur.com; 48510 Hwy 1; mains $16-39; ⊘11:30am-10pm; 📶) Nepenthe comes from a Greek word meaning 'isle of no sorrow,' and it's hard to feel blue while sitting on this clifftop terrace with a bottle of California wine cracked. Just-OK bistro cuisine takes a backseat to ocean views.

✗ Restaurant at Ventana
Californian $$$

(☎831-667-4242; www.ventanainn.com; Ventana Inn & Spa, 48123 Hwy 1; dinner mains $31-50; ⊘11:30am-9pm; 🕱) The old truism about the better the views, the worse the food does not apply at this terrace restaurant and bar. Fork into bison steaks with truffled mac 'n' cheese or roasted-vegetable pasta flavored with herbs grown in their own garden.

🛏 Post Ranch Inn
Resort $$$

(☎831-667-2200; www.postranchinn.com; 47900 Hwy 1; d from $595; 🕱📶) The last word in Big Sur luxury, ocean-view rooms with fireplaces and private decks celebrate the sea, while tree houses have an unnerving bit of sway. Paddle around the infinity pool after a shamanic healing session in the spa.

Los Padres National Forest ⑧

🛏 Treebones Resort
Yurt $$

(☎877-424-4787; www.treebonesresort.com; 71895 Hwy 1; d incl breakfast $189-249; 📶) Don't let the word 'resort' throw you. Canvas-sided yurts with polished pine floors, quilt-covered beds and redwood decks are more like 'glamping.' Shared bathrooms and showers and a cliffside swimming pool and hot tub are all a short walk away.

Pigeon Point One of West Coast's tallest lighthouses

Along Highway 1 to Santa Cruz

14

South of San Francisco to Santa Cruz, you'll travel one of the most jaw-dropping stretches of scenic highway on California's coast, passing family farmstands, lighthouses and beaches.

TRIP HIGHLIGHTS

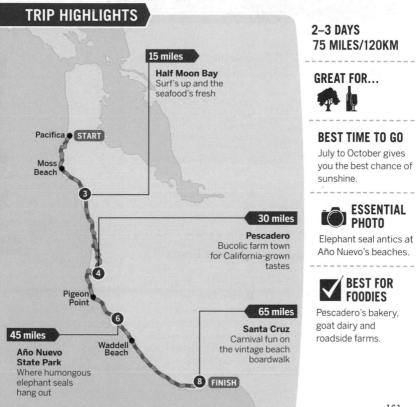

15 miles

Half Moon Bay
Surf's up and the seafood's fresh

Pacifica ● START

Moss Beach ●

3

30 miles

Pescadero
Bucolic farm town for California-grown tastes

Pigeon Point

6

45 miles

Año Nuevo State Park
Where humongous elephant seals hang out

4

Waddell Beach

65 miles

Santa Cruz
Carnival fun on the vintage beach boardwalk

8 FINISH

2–3 DAYS
75 MILES/120KM

GREAT FOR...

BEST TIME TO GO

July to October gives you the best chance of sunshine.

ESSENTIAL PHOTO

Elephant seal antics at Año Nuevo's beaches.

BEST FOR FOODIES

Pescadero's bakery, goat dairy and roadside farms.

14

Along Highway 1 to Santa Cruz

A lazily flowing river of tourism, serpentine Hwy 1 is most celebrated for its scenic charms along the Big Sur coast. But some locals says that the most enchanting stretch of this iconic road starts just south of San Francisco, winding its way slowly down to Santa Cruz. Most beaches are buffeted by wild and unpredictable surf, making them better for tidepooling than swimming or sunbathing. But oh, the views!

❶ Pacifica

In often fog-bound Pacifica, the divided four-lane highway from San Francisco peters out at an intersection overlooking pounding waves, a portent of things to come. Narrowing to two lanes, Hwy 1 jogs inland through thick eucalyptus groves before turning back to the coast. Downhill at **Pacifica State Beach**, stretch your legs or surf, and breath the sea-salted air. Then swerve up to **Devil's Slide**. Highly unstable, these rocky hillsides are crumbling in slow motion. Heavy winter storms regularly

close Hwy 1 as parts drop into the ocean below.

The Drive » Hwy 1 stabilizes heading south, which is good, as you'd probably rather be enjoying the views than watching out for a yawning chasm of doom. In the next 6 miles, you'll pass Gray Whale Cove and Montara State Beaches. In Moss Beach, turn right onto Vermont Ave, then follow Lake St to its end.

❷ Moss Beach

South of Point Montara Lightstation, **Fitzgerald Marine Reserve** (http://fitzgeraldreserve.org; admission free; ☀ sunrise-sunset; 👬) is a thriving habitat for harbor seals and natural tidepools. Walk out among the

pools at low tide to observe (but never pick up) myriad crabs, sea stars, mollusks and rainbow-colored sea anemones. Note it's illegal to remove any creatures, shells or even rocks.

Back on Hwy 1 southbound, take the next right onto Cypress Ave, turning left onto Beach Way to find **Moss Beach Distillery** (www. mossbeachdistillery.com; 140 Beach Way; ☺noon-9pm Sun-Thu, noon-9:30pm Fri & Sat; 🐾). Overlooking the cove where bootleggers used to unload Prohibition-era liquor, the heated ocean-view deck is perfectly positioned for sunset cocktails. Head elsewhere for a meal if you're hungry.

LINK YOUR TRIP

3 **Earthquake Trail**
As the coast defines California, so does the rattling San Andreas Fault. Find it off Hwy 1, starting in San Francisco or Santa Cruz.

15 **Around Monterey & Carmel**
From Santa Cruz, Hwy 1 winds 40 miles south to Monterey, passing more beaches, fishing ports and farms.

163

The Drive » Continue south on Hwy 1 past the airport. Pillar Point Harbor is on the right after 2 miles. For downtown Half Moon Bay, go four more miles south on Hwy 1, turn left onto Hwy 92, then right onto Main St.

TRIP HIGHLIGHT

❸ Half Moon Bay

Offshore from the western end of Pillar Point Harbor lies **Mavericks** (www.maverickssurf.com), a serious surf break, where an annual contest attracts the world's pro big-wave riders to battle huge, steep wintertime swells over 50ft high. Not feeling that brave? Paddle in calmer waters with **Half Moon Bay Kayak** (☎650-773-6101; www.hmbkayak.com), which rents kayaks and guides tours. Further south down Hwy 1, detour inland to amble down this Victorian-era seaside resort's quaint Main St, its tree-lined blocks overstuffed with knick-knackeries, bookstores, antiques shops and cafes.

✕ ⌂ p167

The Drive » For the next 11 miles heading south, Hwy 1 gently follows the contours of the coast. Vistas of pounding surf, unspoiled shores and dramatic rock outcrops seem boundless. Turn inland onto Hwy 84 at San Gregorio, then right after less than a mile onto Stage Rd, which narrowly winds through the hills for 7 miles south to Pescadero.

TRIP HIGHLIGHT

❹ Pescadero

With its long coastline, mild weather and abundant fresh water, Pescadero has always been prime real estate. Spanish for 'fishmonger,' Pescadero was formally established in 1856, when it was mostly a farming and dairy settlement with a key location along the stagecoach route. Munch on a fresh-baked, pull-apart loaf of Italian garlic-and-herb bread stuffed with juicy artichokes from **Arcangeli Grocery Co** (www.normsmakert.com; 287 Stage Rd; ☺10am-6pm) before traipsing around downtown's art galleries and antiques shops. At the north end of the main drag, turn right onto North St and drive a mile to steal-your-heart **Harley Farms Goat Dairy** (www.harleyfarms.com; 205 North St; ☺11am-5pm; ⊞). The farm shop sells creamy artisanal goat cheeses festooned with fruit, nuts and a rainbow of edible flowers. Call ahead for a sustainable-farm tour or just pat the heads of the goats in the pens out back.

✕ ⌂ p167

The Drive » Continue driving past the goat farm on North St to Pescadero Rd. Turn right and head west 2 miles to Pescadero State Beach, passing marshlands where

bird-watchers spot waterfowl. Turn left back onto Hwy 1, driving south beside pocket beaches and coves for 5.5 miles to the Pigeon Point turnoff on your right.

❺ Pigeon Point

One of West Coast's tallest lighthouses stands in **Pigeon Point Light Station State Historic Park** (www.parks.ca.gov; ☺8am-sunset). The 1872 landmark had to close access to its Fresnel lens when chunks of its cornice began to rain from the sky, but the beam still flashes brightly and the bluff is a prime though

Half Moon Bay Mavericks surf break

blustery spot to scan for breaching gray whales.

📖 p167

The Drive » Back at Hwy 1, turn right and cruise south along the coastline, curving slightly inland as the wind howls all around you, for about 5 miles to Año Nuevo State Park's main entrance.

- - - - - - - - - - - -

TRIP HIGHLIGHT

❻ Año Nuevo State Park

During winter and early spring, thousands of enormous northern elephant seals noisily mate, give birth, learn to swim, battle for dominance or just laze around on the sands at **Año Nuevo State Park** (📞650-879-0227, tour reservations 800-444-4445; http://anonuevo. reserveamerica.com; entry per car $10, tour per person $7; ⊙public entry 8:30am-3:30pm daily Apr-Nov, guided tours only mid-Dec–Mar; 🚹). Join park rangers for a guided hike (reservations required) through the sand dunes for up-close views of the huge pinnipeds – a mature male weighs twice as much as your car!

The Drive » Over the next 6 miles, Hwy 1 southbound traces the coast. As you descend a long hill bordered by a sheer cliff face that recalls Devil's Slide, look for Waddell Beach on your right.

- - - - - - - - - - - -

❼ Waddell Beach

These thrilling breaks are usually alive with windsurfers, kitesurfers and other daredevils. Wander the chilly sands, get blasted by the winds and you'll quickly understand that without a wet suit, you won't be hankering to swim here. Across Hwy 1 is the end of the popular Skyline-to-the-Sea Trail that descends from the redwoods of Big Basin State Park. Just inland, **Rancho Del Oso Nature**

DETOUR:
SANTA CRUZ MOUNTAINS

Start: ⑧ Santa Cruz

Hwy 9 is a sun-dappled backwoods byway into the Santa Cruz Mountains, passing towering redwood forests and a few fog-blessed vineyards (estate-bottled Pinot Noir is a specialty). Seven miles north of Santa Cruz, **Henry Cowell Redwoods State Park** (www.parks.ca.gov; 101 N Big Trees Park Rd; per car $10; ☼sunrise-sunset) has hiking trails through old-growth redwood trees. Nearby in Felton, **Roaring Camp Railroads** (☏831-335-4484; www.roaringcamp.com; 5401 Graham Hill Rd; adult/child from $24/17, parking $8; ☼call for schedules) operates narrow-gauge steam trains up into the redwoods. It's another 7 miles up to Boulder Creek, a tiny mountain town with a brewpub. Take Hwy 236 northwest for 10 more twisty miles to **Big Basin Redwoods State Park** (www.bigbasin.org, www.parks.ca.gov; 21600 Big Basin Way; per car $10), where misty nature trails loop past skyscraping redwoods.

and History Center
(☏831-427-2288; 3600 Hwy 1, Davenport; admission free; ☼noon-4pm Sat & Sun; ⊞) has two kid-friendly nature trails, both open daily, through the marshlands behind the beach.

The Drive ≫ Hwy 1 begins slowly moving away from the rocky shoreline as the coast's limestone and sandstone cliffs regularly shed chunks into the white-capped waters below. Motor past roadside farmstands and barns and more pocket beaches before rolling into Santa Cruz after 15 miles.

- - - - - - - - - - - - -

TRIP HIGHLIGHT

⑧ Santa Cruz
SoCal beach culture meets NorCal counterculture in Santa Cruz. Witness the old-school radical and freak-show weirdness along

Pacific Ave, downtown's main drag. Tumble downhill to the West Coast's oldest oceanfront amusement park, **Santa Cruz Beach Boardwalk** (☏831-423-5590; www.beachboardwalk.com; 400 Beach St; admission free, rides $3-5; ☼seasonal hr vary; ⊞), where the smell of cotton candy mixes with the salt air. Continue up W Cliff Dr, which winds for a mile to Lighthouse Point. Join the gawkers on the cliffs peering down at the floating kelp beds, hulking sea lions, playful sea otters and black wet-suit-clad surfers riding **Steamers Lane** surf break. Inside the 1960s-era lighthouse is the memorabilia-packed **Surfing Museum** (www.santacruzsurfingmuseum.org; 701 W Cliff Dr; admission

by donation; ☼noon-4pm Thu-Mon early Sep-early Jul, 10am-5pm Wed-Mon early Jul-early Sep). Almost 2 miles further west, W Cliff Dr dead-ends at **Natural Bridges State Beach** (www.parks.ca.gov; per car $10; ☼8am-sunset; ⊞), named for its sea arches. Starfish, anemones, crabs and more inhabit myriad tidepools carved into the limestone rocks. Find out about sea creatures both great (look at that blue-whale skeleton!) and small at the nearby **Seymour Marine Discovery Center** (http://seymourcenter.ucsc.edu; 100 Shaffer Rd; adult/child $6/4; ☼10am-5pm Tue-Sat, noon-5pm Sun; ⊞).

 p167

Eating & Sleeping

Half Moon Bay ❸

✖ Flying Fish Grill   Seafood, Mexican $$

(www.flyingfishgrill.net; 211 San Mateo Rd/Hwy 92; dishes $5-16; ⏱11am-8:30pm Wed-Mon) The tastiest seafood shack around is actually inland from the ocean: duck inside this colorful hacienda for fish tacos, crabby, cheesy bread and grilled fresh catch.

✖ Half Moon Bay
Brewing Company   Brewpub $$

(www.hmbbrewingco.com; 390 Capistrano Rd, off Hwy 1; mains $11-21; ⏱11:30am-9pm Mon-Thu, to 10pm Fri & Sat, 11am-9pm Sun) At Pillar Point Harbor, kick back with dynamite local brews and just-OK seafood and burgers on a heated outdoor bay view patio.

⇌ Beach House at
Half Moon Bay   Hotel $$$

(☎650-712-0220; www.beach-house.com; 4100 N Cabrillo Hwy/Hwy 1; r $185-385; 🛜🏊) Overlooking the bay from the oceanfront bluffs near Pillar Point Harbor, all of these loft-style suites have down comforters and gas fireplaces to keep you toasty in the fog.

Pescadero ❹

✖ Duarte's Tavern   American $$

(☎650-879-0464; www.duartestavern.com; 202 Stage Rd; mains $11-40; ⏱7am-9pm) Some of the coast's freshest seafood, along with artichoke and green-chili cream soups and olallieberry pie, grace the menu at this 1894 tavern. It gets jammed on weekends, so make reservations.

⇌ Costanoa Lodge   Cabin, Hotel $$

(☎650-879-1100; www.costanoa.com; 2001 Rossi Rd, off Hwy 1; cabins $89-219, r $179-279; ♿🛜) Down bedding warms up canvas-tent cabins, while communal 'comfort stations' offer 24-hour dry saunas, fireside patio seating and hot showers. Lodge rooms with fireplaces are not as Spartan. It's 9 miles south of Pescadero State Beach.

Pigeon Point ❺

⇌ Pigeon Point
Lighthouse Hostel   Hostel $

(☎650-879-0633; www.norcalhostels.org/pigeon; 210 Pigeon Point Rd, off Hwy 1; dm $25-30, r $73-177; @🛜) On a quiet windswept coastal perch, this 'green' hostel inhabits the historic lightkeeper's quarters. It's popular (especially for its clifftop hot tub), so book ahead.

Santa Cruz ❽

✖ Picnic Basket   Deli, Bakery $

(http://thepicnicbasketsc.com; 125 Beach St; menu items $4-10; ⏱7am-9pm Sun-Thu, to midnight Fri & Sat; ♿) Locavarian kitchen across the street from the beach boardwalk makes creative sandwiches, soups and baked goodies from scratch. Zany artisanal ice-cream flavors like avocado, cherry balsamic or sea-salt olive oil are addictive.

⇌ Dream Inn   Hotel $$$

(☎831-426-4330; www.dreaminnsantacruz. com; 175 W Cliff Dr; r $200-380; ❄@🛜🏊) Peering down on the wharf, this retro-chic boutique hotel is as stylish as Santa Cruz gets. Hilltop rooms have all mod cons. Drop by ocean-view Aquarius restaurant (dinner mains cost $15 to $30) and lounge for happy hour.

⇌ Pacific Blue Inn   B&B $$

(☎831-600-8880; http://pacificblueinn.com; 636 Pacific Ave; r incl breakfast $189-239; 🛜) Downtown courtyard B&B is truly ecoconscious. Refreshingly clean-lined rooms have pillowtop beds, fireplaces and flat-screen TVs with DVD players. Free bikes to borrow.

Monterey Bay Aquarium From sea
stars to sea slugs to sea otters

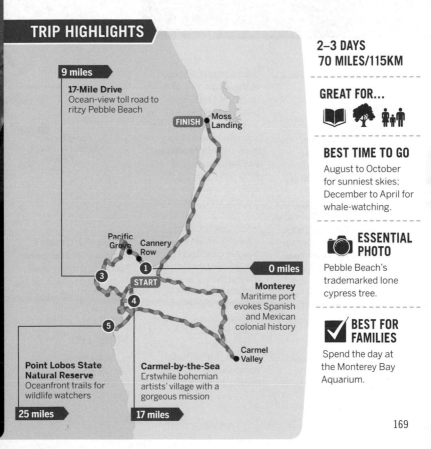

Around Monterey & Carmel

15

Briny sea air and drifting fog define Monterey, a fishing village that holds relics of California's Spanish and Mexican past. As you explore, witness the scenery lauded by artists and writers.

TRIP HIGHLIGHTS

9 miles

17-Mile Drive
Ocean-view toll road to ritzy Pebble Beach

FINISH Moss Landing

2–3 DAYS
70 MILES/115KM

GREAT FOR...

BEST TIME TO GO
August to October for sunniest skies; December to April for whale-watching.

Pacific Grove Cannery Row

3 **1**
START

4

0 miles

Monterey
Maritime port evokes Spanish and Mexican colonial history

ESSENTIAL PHOTO
Pebble Beach's trademarked lone cypress tree.

5

Carmel Valley

BEST FOR FAMILIES
Spend the day at the Monterey Bay Aquarium.

Point Lobos State Natural Reserve
Oceanfront trails for wildlife watchers

25 miles

Carmel-by-the-Sea
Erstwhile bohemian artists' village with a gorgeous mission

17 miles

Around Monterey & Carmel

Tourist-choked Cannery Row isn't actually the star attraction on the Monterey Peninsula. Much more memorable are ocean panoramas caught from roadside pull-offs on the edge of the bay, on the hiking trails of Point Lobos or from the open-air decks of a winter whale-watching boat. Historical roots show all along this drive, from well-preserved Spanish Colonial adobe buildings in downtown Monterey to Carmel's jewel-box Catholic mission.

PACIFIC OCEAN

Pac
Gro
2
Cannery Row

17-Mile Drive **3**
Pebble Beach

Monter

4
Carmel-by-the-Sea

5
Point Lobos State Natural Reserve

7 miles to

13

TRIP HIGHLIGHT

① Monterey

Working-class Monterey is all about the sea. Start exploring by taking our walking tour (see p176) of **Old Monterey**, downtown's historic quarter, which preserves California's Mexican and Spanish Colonial roots. It's just inland from the salt-sprayed **Municipal Wharf II**, overlooking Monterey Bay National Marine Sanctuary, which protects kelp forests, seals, sea lions, dolphins and whales.

Less than 2 miles northwest of downtown via Lighthouse Ave, **Cannery Row** was the hectic, smelly epicenter of the sardine-canning industry, Monterey's lifeblood till the 1950s, as immortalized by novelist John Steinbeck. Today the ecoconscious **Monterey Bay Aquarium** (☎831-648-4800, tickets 866-963-9645; www.montereybayaquarium.org; 886 Cannery Row; adult/child $33/20; ⏰10am-5pm or 6pm daily, extended summer hr; 🛜♿) puts aquatic creatures on educational display, from touch-tolerant sea stars and slimy sea slugs to animated sea otters.

Walking south along Cannery Row, take a few steps up Bruce Ariss Way to peek into the one-room shacks of former cannery workers. Further south along Cannery Row, stop at **Steinbeck Plaza** (cnr Cannery Row & Prescott Ave) to soak up bay views and snap a photo of yourself with a bronze bust of the famous writer.

✗ 🛏 p175

The Drive ❯❯ From Cannery Row, Ocean View Blvd slowly traces the bayfront coastline for 2.5 miles west to Point Pinos,

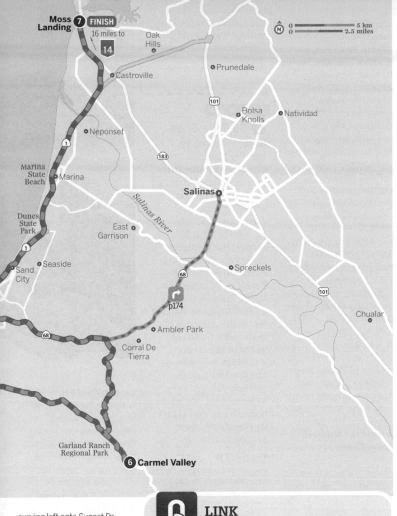

curving left onto Sunset Dr.
Watch out for cyclists along
this route.

2 Pacific Grove

Founded as a tranquil
Methodist retreat in
1875, Pacific Grove was
where John Steinbeck's
family once had a
summer cottage. Aptly

LINK YOUR TRIP

13 Big Sur

Big Sur's
vertiginous coastal cliffs,
hippie-beatnik retreats
and redwood forests
alongside Hwy 1 start 15
miles south of Carmel-
by-the-Sea.

14 Along Highway 1 to Santa Cruz

Santa Cruz's 'Surf City'
beaches are about 25
miles north of Moss
Landing via Hwy 1, which
curves around Monterey
Bay.

named Ocean View Blvd runs from Lover's Point west to Point Pinos, where it becomes Sunset Dr heading south to Asilomar State Beach. There are plenty of tempting turnoffs along this route where you can walk past pounding surf, rocky outcrops and teeming tidepools.

Point Pinos Lighthouse (www.ci.pg. ca.us/lighthouse/default.htm; enter off Asilomar Ave; adult/child $2/1; ☺1-4pm Thu-Mon) has been warning ships off this peninsula's hazardous point since 1855. Next to the lighthouse, golfers crowd the windy **Pacific Grove Golf Links** (☏831-648-5775; www.pggolflinks.com; 77 Asilomar Blvd; greens fees $42-65), a penny-pincher's version of Pebble Beach.

Follow Lighthouse Ave east, turning right onto Ridge Rd after half a mile. Park to stroll around the **Monarch Grove Sanctuary** (www. pgmuseum.org; Ridge Rd; ☺dawn-dusk) between October and February or March, when over 25,000 migratory monarch butterflies cluster in this thicket of tall eucalyptus trees – watch out for falling branches!

✕ ⊨ p175

The Drive » Drive back north on Ridge Rd to Lighthouse Ave, which heads east toward leafy downtown Pacific Grove, with its shops, cafes and a natural-history museum for kids. To

bypass downtown PG, take the next right after Ridge Rd onto 17-Mile Drive. Drive another mile southwest, crossing Sunset Dr/Hwy 68, to the Pacific Grove toll gate.

- - - - - - - - - - -

TRIP HIGHLIGHT

❸ 17-Mile Drive

Once promoted as 'Mother Nature's Drive-Thru,' the **17-Mile Drive** (www.pebblebeach.com; entry $10) is a spectacularly scenic private toll road (motorcyclists prohibited) that loops around the Monterey Peninsula, connecting Pacific Grove with Pebble Beach and Carmel-by-the-Sea. Using the self-guided tour map handed out at the toll gates, motor past postcard vistas of the ocean and Monterey cypress trees, world-famous golf courses, a luxury lodge and the bay where Spanish explorer Gaspar de Portolá dropped anchor in 1769.

The Drive » If you follow the coastal road heading south, then wrap around back east again, the 17-Mile Drive is only 9 miles long between the Pacific Grove and Carmel toll gates. After exiting the toll road, continue south to Ocean Ave, then turn right for downtown Carmel-by-the-Sea.

- - - - - - - - - - -

TRIP HIGHLIGHT

❹ Carmel-by-the-Sea

Once an artists' beach colony, this quaint village now has the well-manicured feel of a country club. Watch

BLAINE HARRINGTON III / CORBIS ©

the parade of behatted ladies toting fancy-label shopping bags, and dapper gents driving top-down convertibles along **Ocean Ave**, the slow-mo main drag.

On the south side of town, **Carmel River State Beach** (www.parks. ca.gov; end of Carmelo St; admission free; ☺sunrise-sunset; 🐾) is a gorgeous white-sand crescent, where pampered pups excitedly run off-leash. Just inland, 20th-century poet Robinson Jeffers' **Tor House** (☏831-624-1813; www.torhouse.org; 26304 Ocean View Ave; adult/child $10/5; ☺tours by reservation

Mission San Carlos de Borroméo de Carmelo

Fri & Sat only) **offers fascinating insights into bohemian Old Carmel.**

Farther east off Rio Rd, take another leap back in time. Established in 1769, the arched basilica and flowering garden courtyard of **Mission San Carlos de Borroméo de Carmelo** (www.carmelmission.org; 3080 Rio Rd; adult/child $6.50/2; 9:30am-5pm Mon-Sat, 10:30am-5pm Sun) make you feel as if you've landed in old Spain. The second-oldest California mission, this is where Padre Junípero Serra lies buried.

 p175

The Drive » From the mission, continue southeast down Rio Rd to the intersection with Hwy 1. Turn right and drive about 2 miles south to the turn-off for Point Lobos State Natural Reserve on your right.

TRIP HIGHLIGHT

⑤ Point Lobos State Natural Reserve

They bark, they bathe and they're fun to watch – sea lions are the stars here at Punta de los Lobos Marinos (Point of the Sea Wolves), where a dramatically rocky coastline offers excellent tidepooling. Short walks around **Point Lobos State Natural Reserve**

(www.parks.ca.gov, www.pointlobos.org; per car $10; 8am-30min after sunset;) take in wild scenery and wildlife watching, including on Bird Island, shady Piney Woods, the historic Whaler's Cabin and Devil's Cauldron, a whirlpool that gets splashy at high tide.

The Drive » Back at the park entrance, turn left onto Hwy 1 northbound. Wind 2.5 miles uphill away from the coast to the stoplight intersection with Carmel Valley Rd. Turn right and drive east through farmlands and vineyards toward Carmel Valley village, about 11.5 miles away.

DETOUR: SALINAS

Start: ❻ **Carmel Valley**

From Salinas farmhands to Monterey cannery workers, the sun-baked Central Valley hills to the fishing coastline, Nobel Prize–winning author John Steinbeck drew a perfect picture of the landscapes and communities he knew. See the land and people of his hometown Salinas, a 25-minute drive east of Monterey on Hwy 68.

Downtown, the **National Steinbeck Center** (☎831-775-4721; www.steinbeck.org; 1 Main St; adult/child/youth/senior $11/6/8/9; ☺10am-5pm; 🚼) brings his novels to life with interactive exhibits and short movie clips. Look for Rocinante, the camper Steinbeck drove across America while writing *Travels with Charley*. An adjunct agriculture museum showcases the local economy, incorporating historical labor struggles, water politics and the stories of immigrant farmworkers.

A few blocks west, **Steinbeck House** (☎831-424-2735; www.steinbeckhouse.com; 132 Central Ave; ☺restaurant 11:30am-2pm Tue-Sat, gift shop 11am-3pm) is the author's childhood home. A classic Queen Anne Victorian with dainty bird-patterned lace curtains, it's both a minimuseum and a twee restaurant, where waitstaff in quasi-period dress serve lunch and high tea.

Two miles southeast of downtown, Steinbeck pilgrims can pay their last respects at **Garden of Memories Memorial Park** (850 Abbott St). An iron sign points the way to the Hamilton family plot, where a simple grave marker identifies where some of Steinbeck's ashes were buried.

❻ Carmel Valley

Where sun-kissed vineyards and farm fields rustle beside one another, Carmel Valley is a peaceful side trip. At organic **Earthbound Farm** (www.ebfarm.com; 7250 Carmel Valley Rd; ☺8am-6:30pm Mon-Sat, 9am-6pm Sun; 🚼), sample the fresh-fruit smoothies and homemade soups, or cut your own herbs in the garden. Several wineries further east offer tastings – don't miss the pinot noir bottled by **Boekenoogen** (www.boekenoogenwines.com; 24 W Carmel Valley Rd; tasting fees $5-10; ☺11am-5pm). Afterwards, stretch your legs in Carmel Valley village, chock-a-block with genteel cafes and whimsical shops.

The Drive › Backtrack 2 miles west of the village along Carmel Valley Rd, then turn right onto Laureles Grade. After 6 miles, turn left on Hwy 68, driving west to join Hwy 1 northbound. After passing sand dunes, suburbs and artichoke and strawberry fields, Hwy 1 swings back towards the coast. Turn left onto Moss Landing Rd.

❼ Moss Landing

Here's your last chance to get out of the car and meet the local wildlife. Rent a kayak from outfitters on Hwy 1 and paddle past harbor seals into **Elkhorn Slough National Estuarine Research Reserve** (☎831-728-2822; www.elkhornslough.org; 1700 Elkhorn Rd, Watsonville; adult/child $2.50/free; ☺9am-5pm Wed-Sun), or take a guided weekend hike and go bird-watching. From the fishing harbor at the ocean end of Moss Landing Rd, **Sanctuary Cruises** (☎831-917-1042; www.sanctuarycruises.com; Moss Landing Harbor Dock A; adult/child $50/40) operates year-round whale-watching and dolphin-spotting cruises aboard biodiesel-fueled boats (make advance reservations).

✕ p175

Eating & Sleeping

Monterey ❶

✖ Cannery Row Brewing Co
American $$

(www.canneryrowbrewingcompany.com; 95 Prescott Ave; ⊙11:30am-11pm, bar till midnight Sun-Thu, 2am Fri & Sat) Dozens of craft beers from around the world bring crowds to Cannery Row's bar-and-grill, and so does the outdoor deck with roaring fire pits. Decent menu of burgers, barbeque, salads and garlic fries.

🛏 Casa Munras
Boutique Hotel $$

(☎831-375-2411; www.hotelcasamunras.com; 700 Munras Ave; r $150-280; @ 🛜 🛰 🐕) Built around an adobe hacienda once owned by a 19th-century Spanish Colonial don, small but chic contemporary rooms inhabit two-story motel-esque buildings. Unwind with a sea-salt scrub in the spa.

🛏 InterContinental – The Clement
Hotel $$$

(☎831-375-4500; www.intercontinental.com; 750 Cannery Row; r $200-455; ✳ @ 🛜 🛰 🛗) Like a New England millionaire's seaside clapboard house, this four-star resort presides over Cannery Row. For utmost luxury, book an ocean-view suite with a private balcony and fireplace, then dine in bayfront C Restaurant.

Pacific Grove ❷

✖ Passionfish
Seafood $$$

(☎831-655-3311; www.passionfish.net; 701 Lighthouse Ave; mains $16-28; ⊙5-9pm Sun-Thu, to 10pm Fri & Sat) Eureka! Sustainable seafood is dock-fresh, every preparation fully flavored and the global wine list priced almost at retail. Tables are squeezed together, though. Reservations recommended.

🛏 Sunset Inn
Motel $$

(☎831-375-3529; www.gosunsetinn.com; 133 Asilomar Blvd; r $110-300; 🛜) At this small motor lodge near the beach, attentive staff check you into crisply redesigned rooms that have hardwood floors, king-sized beds and, for romance, a hot tub and gas-burning fireplace.

Carmel-by-the-Sea ❹

✖ La Bicyclette
French, Italian $$$

(☎831-622-9899; www.labicycletterestaurant. com; Dolores St at 7th Ave; lunch mains $7-16, 3-course prix-fixe dinner $30; ⊙8-11am & 11:30am-10pm) Rustic European and California country fare, along with a wood-burning pizza oven, packs canoodling couples into this bistro. Excellent local wines too.

✖ Mundaka
Tapas $$$

(☎831-624-7400; www.mundakacarmel.com; San Carlos St btwn Ocean & 7th Aves; small plates $6-20; ⊙5:30-10pm Sun-Wed, to 11pm Thu-Sat) Stone courtyard hideaway is a svelte escape from Carmel's 'newly wed and nearly dead' crowd. Share Spanish tapas and sip house-made sangria while DJs or flamenco guitarists play.

🛏 Cypress Inn
Boutique Hotel $$$

(☎831-624-3871; www.cypress-inn.com; Lincoln St & 7th Ave; r $185-325; 🛜🐕) Done up in Spanish Colonial style, this 1929 inn is co-owned by movie star Doris Day. Airy terra-cotta hallways with colorful tiles give it a Mediterranean feel, and rooms facing the courtyard dazzle with light.

Moss Landing ❼

✖ Phil's Fish Market
Seafood $$

(www.philsfishmarket.com; 7600 Sandholdt Rd; mains $10-20; ⊙10am-8pm Sun-Thu, to 9pm Fri & Sat; 🛗) Devour buckets of crab, mussels, squid, scallops and prawns covered in San Francisco–style cioppino sauce at this warehouse-sized eatery right by the harbor.

STRETCH YOUR LEGS MONTEREY

Start/Finish Municipal Wharf II

Distance 2.2 miles

Duration 2–4 hours

Old Monterey holds California's most extraordinary collection of 19th-century brick and adobe buildings, all located along the self-guided Path of History. Museums and hidden gardens are also within a fishing line's cast of Monterey Bay.

Take this walk on Trips

Municipal Wharf II

For an authentic look at seaside life in Monterey, start by walking out onto **Municipal Wharf II**. There, fishing boats bob and sway, plein-air landscape painters work on their canvases and seafood purveyors hawk fresh catches.

The Walk » From the foot of the wharf, walk south and join the paved recreational trail heading west. Before Fisherman's Wharf, turn south toward Custom House Plaza.

Museum of Monterey

On the plaza's east side, the **Museum of Monterey** (☎831-372-2608; http://museumofmonterey.org; 5 Custom House Plaza; adult/child $10/5; ☺10am-5pm Tue-Sat, noon-5pm Sun) illuminates Monterey's salty past, from early Spanish colonial life to the roller-coaster rise and fall of the sardine industry that brought Cannery Row to life.

The Walk » It's a quick stroll across the plaza to Pacific House.

Pacific House

Inside a beautifully preserved 1847 adobe, **Pacific House** (☎831-649-7118; www.parks.ca.gov, www.montereystatehistoricpark association.org; 20 Custom House Plaza; admission $3; ☺10am-4pm Fri-Sun) has in-depth exhibits on California's complex multicultural history. Grab a free Path of History map, find out what other historical houses are currently open, and buy guided-tour tickets here. Just north, peek into the 1827 **Custom House**.

The Walk » Head south through Portola Plaza onto Alvarado St, passing the historical Monterey Hotel, theaters, shops, bars and cafes. Continue to Munras Ave and across the street.

Cooper-Molera Adobe

A stately 19th-century home, the **Cooper-Molera Adobe** (☎831-649-7172; 525 Polk St; tours $5; ☺tours usually 10:30am & 1:30pm Fri-Sun) was built by John Rogers Cooper, a New England sea captain. Over time, bountiful gardens were added. The **museum shop** (☺10am-4pm)

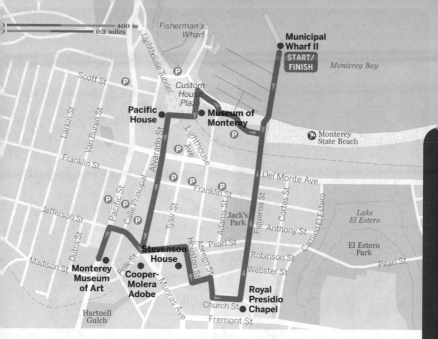

sells nostalgic toys, household goods, artisan crafts and books.

The Walk » Head west on Jefferson St, then turn left onto Pacific St. Ahead on your right is Colton Hall, where California's first constitutional convention took place in 1849, nearby the old jail. Further down on your left is the art museum.

Monterey Museum of Art

Downtown's **MMA Pacific Street** (☎831-372-5477; www.montereyart.org; 559 Pacific St; adult/child $10/free; ◷11am-5pm Wed-Sat, 1-4pm Sun) is small, but particularly strong in California contemporary art and modern landscape painters and photographers, including famous names such as Ansel Adams and Edward Weston.

The Walk » Retrace your steps up Pacific St, turning right onto Jefferson St back to the Cooper-Molera Adobe at Munras Ave. Follow Pearl St one block east, the turn right onto Houston St.

Stevenson House

Writer Robert Louis Stevenson came to Monterey in 1879 to court his wife-to-be, Fanny Osbourne. **Stevenson House**

(530 Houston St; admission free; ◷1-4pm every Sat & 4th Sun of the month), then called the French Hotel, was where he stayed while reputedly devising the novel *Treasure Island*. The restored interior is filled with memorabilia, including from the writer's later years in Polynesia.

The Walk » Continue down Houston St, then zigzag southeast by turning left on Webster St, right on Abrego St and finally left on Church St.

Royal Presidio Chapel

Today known as San Carlos Cathedral, graceful **Royal Presidio Chapel** (☎831-373-2628; www.sancarloscathedral.net; 500 Church St; admission by donation; ◷call for hr) is California's oldest continuously functioning church. As Monterey expanded under Mexican rule in the 1820s, older buildings were destroyed, leaving behind this national landmark as the strongest reminder of the defeated Spanish colonial presence.

The Walk » Head north up Figueroa St for eight blocks back to the foot of Municipal Wharf II.

Paso Robles Wine Country Sniff out boutique winemakers

Around San Luis Obispo

16

It's nothing but all-natural fun in SLO County, with sunny beaches and rolling vineyard roads. Slow down — this idyllic coast deserves to be savored, not gulped.

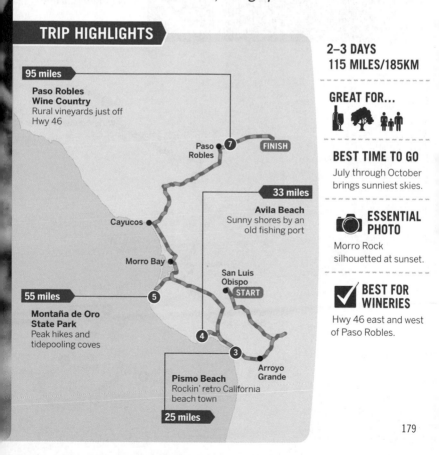

TRIP HIGHLIGHTS

95 miles

Paso Robles Wine Country
Rural vineyards just off Hwy 46

Paso Robles ● 7 FINISH

33 miles

Avila Beach
Sunny shores by an old fishing port

Cayucos ●

Morro Bay ●

San Luis Obispo ● START

55 miles

5

Montaña de Oro State Park
Peak hikes and tidepooling coves

4

3

Arroyo Grande

Pismo Beach
Rockin' retro California beach town

25 miles

2–3 DAYS
115 MILES/185KM

GREAT FOR...

BEST TIME TO GO
July through October brings sunniest skies.

ESSENTIAL PHOTO
Morro Rock silhouetted at sunset.

BEST FOR WINERIES
Hwy 46 east and west of Paso Robles.

179

MACDUFF EVERTON / ©RBIS ©

Around San Luis Obispo

Halfway between San Francisco and LA, the laid-back college town of San Luis Obispo (aka 'SLO') is a gateway to coastal adventures. Beach towns and fishing villages offer a bucketful of outdoor pursuits, both on land and at sea – and wherever there's natural beauty, it's never too far from Hwy 1. Farm-to-table locavarian restaurants and vineyards abound, especially in Paso Robles' wine country, ideal for lazy weekend or weekday drives.

❶ San Luis Obispo

Oprah called it 'the happiest place in America,' and once you spend a few hours downtown, you might agree. CalPoly university students inject a healthy dose of hubbub into the streets, shops, pubs and cafes, especially during the weekly **farmers market** (⏱6-9pm Thu), which turns downtown's Higuera St into a street festival with live music and sidewalk food stalls. Like many other California towns,

SLO grew up around a Spanish Catholic **mission** (www.missionsanluisobispo. org; 751 Palm St; donation $2; ⏰9am-4pm Sep-May, to 5pm Jun-Aug), founded in 1772 by missionary Junípero Serra. The creek once used to irrigate mission orchards still flows through downtown, beside tranquil, shaded walking paths.

 p185

The Drive » From downtown SLO, follow Broad St/Hwy 227 for 2.5 stop-and-go miles southeast, turning left before the airport onto Tank Farm Rd. After a mile, curve right and continue onto Orcutt Rd, which rolls up and down past vineyards into Edna Valley.

❷ Edna Valley

Cradled by the rich volcanic soil of the Santa Lucia foothills,

LINK YOUR TRIP

17 Santa Barbara Wine Country

Want more good grapes? Follow Hwy 101 south of Pismo Beach for 45 miles to the Santa Ynez Valley.

13 Big Sur

From Cayucos, cruise Hwy 1 north to the southern Big Sur coast, passing Hearst Castle (see p39) halfway along.

thriving **Edna Valley wineries** (www.slowine. com) are known for their crisp, often unoaked chardonnays and some subtle syrahs and pinot noirs. Pick up a free map from any tasting room. All are signposted along Orcutt Rd and Edna Rd/Hwy 227, which run parallel through the peaceful valley that is cooled by drifting coastal fog in the morning before being brightened by afternoon sunshine. **Niven Family Wine Estates** (www. baileyana.com; 5828 Orcutt Rd; ⏰10am-5pm) pours inside a 20th-century wooden schoolhouse, while **Edna Valley Vineyard** (www. ednavalleyvineyard.com; 2585 Biddle Ranch Rd; ⏰10am-5pm) has panoramic windows, which overlook vineyards. Further southeast, **Talley Vineyards** (www. talleyvineyards.com; 3031 Lopez Dr; ⏰10:30am-4:30pm) offers winery tours daily.

The Drive » From Talley Vineyards, Lopez Rd winds west toward Arroyo Grande, just over 6 miles away. Turn left onto Branch St, then merge onto Hwy 101 north to Pismo Beach. Exit at Price St, which enters downtown Pismo Beach. Turn left onto Pomeroy Ave and roll downhill to the ocean.

TRIP HIGHLIGHT

❸ Pismo Beach

By a wooden pier that stretches towards the setting sun, here James

Dean once trysted with Pier Angeli. Today this classic California beach town feels like somewhere straight out of a 1950s hot-rod dream. Pismo likes to call itself the 'Clam Capital of the World,' but these days the wide, sandy beach is pretty much clammed out. You'll have better luck catching something fishy off the pier. To ride the waves, rent a wet suit and board from any surf shop. After dark, go bar hopping or knock down pins at the retro bowling alley. The next day, drive a mile south of downtown to the **Monarch Butterfly Grove** (www.monarchbutterfly.org; North Beach Campground, Pismo State Beach, Hwy 1; admission free; ⏰sunrise-sunset; 🚻), where migratory monarchs roost by the thousands in eucalyptus trees, usually from late October through February.

 p185

The Drive » Follow Hwy 1 north through downtown Pismo Beach, then follow the signs to rejoin Hwy 101 northbound for almost 4 miles to exit 195 for Avila Beach Dr. Keep left at the fork, then wind slowly west downhill to Avila Beach, about 3 miles away.

TRIP HIGHLIGHT

❹ Avila Beach

For a perfectly lazy summer day at the beach, rent beach chairs and umbrellas underneath

Avila Pier, off downtown's sparkling new waterfront promenade. Two miles further west, the coastal road dead-ends at Port San Luis. The barking of sea lions echoes as you stroll leisurely past seafood markets and shacks to the end of creaky weather-worn **Harford Pier**, where you while away time gazing out over the choppy waters. If you'd like to visit 1890 **Point San Luis Lighthouse** (☎trolley tours 805-540-5771, hiking tours 805-541-8735; www. sanluislighthouse.org; adult/ child $5/free, trolley tour $20; ☉guided hikes 9am Wed & Sat, trolley tours noon, 1pm & 2pm Sat), guided tour reservations are required.

Back uphill near Hwy 101, you can pick your own fruit and feed the goats at **Avila Valley Barn** (http://avilavalleybarn. com; 560 Avila Beach Dr; ☉10am-6:30pm mid-Mar–late Dec; ⊞) farmstand, or do some stargazing from a private redwood hot tub at **Sycamore Mineral Springs** (☎805-595-7302; www.sycamoresprings.com; 1215 Avila Beach Dr; per hr per person $13.50-17.50; ☉8am-

Morro Bay Kayaks in the bay

midnight, last reservation 10:45pm).

The Drive » Take Hwy 101 back northbound toward San Luis Obispo. Exit after 4.5 miles at Los Osos Valley Rd, which leaves behind stop-and-go strip-mall traffic to slowly roll past rural farmlands for about 11 miles. After passing through downtown Los Osos, curve left onto Pecho Valley Rd, which enters Montaña de Oro State Park a few miles later.

TRIP HIGHLIGHT

❺ Montaña de Oro State Park

In spring, the hillsides of **Montaña de Oro State Park** (www.parks. ca.gov; end of Pecho Rd, Los Osos; admission free; ☉sunrise-sunset; 🚹) are blanketed by bright California native poppies, wild mustard and other wildflowers, giving this park its Spanish name, meaning 'mountain of gold.' Along the winding access road, sand dunes and the wind-tossed bluffs of the Pacific appear. Pull over at Spooner's Cove, a postcard-perfect sandy beach once used by smugglers. Here the grinding of the Pacific

DETOUR: JAMES DEAN MEMORIAL

Start: ❼ Paso Robles Wine Country

On Hwy 46 about 25 miles east of Paso Robles, there's a monument near the spot where *Rebel Without a Cause* star James Dean fatally crashed his Porsche on September 30, 1955, at the age of 24. Ironically, the actor had recently filmed a public-safety campaign TV spot against drag racing and speeding on US highways, in which he advised, 'Take it easy driving. The next life you save might be mine.' Look for the shiny brushed-steel memorial wrapped around an oak tree outside the Jack Ranch Cafe truck stop, which has a few old photographs and some dusty movie-star memorabilia inside.

and North American plates has uplifted and tilted sedimentary layers of submarine rock, visible from shore. Hike along the beach and the park's grassy ocean bluffs, or drive uphill past the visitor center to tackle the 4-mile round-trip trail up rocky Valencia Peak – the summit views are exhilarating.

The Drive » Backtrack on Pecho Rd out of the park, curving right onto Los Osos Valley Rd. East of Los Osos, turn left onto Bay Blvd, curving north alongside Morro Bay's estuary. Before reaching Hwy 101, turn left onto Morro Bay State Park Rd, continuing on Main St into downtown Morro Bay. Turn left on Marina St and drive downhill to the Embarcadero.

- - - - - - - -

❻ Morro Bay

This fishing village is home to **Morro Rock**, a volcanic peak jutting up from the ocean floor. (Too bad about those power-plant smokestacks obscuring the views, though.) You're likely to spot harbor seals and sea otters as you paddle around the bay in a kayak rented from the waterfront Embarcadero, crowded with seafood shacks. Or drive a mile north of the marina to walk partway around the base of the landmark rock. West of downtown in **Morro Bay State Park** (www.parks.ca.gov; admission free; ☺sunrise-sunset; 🚻) at the **Museum of Natural History** (Morro Bay State Park Rd; adult/child $3/free; ☺10am-5pm; 🚻), kids can touch interactive models of the bay's ecosystem and stuffed wildlife mounts.

✕ 🛏 p185

The Drive » Follow Main St north to Hwy 1. For 4 miles, Hwy 1 northbound rides above wild ocean beaches. In Cayucos, turn right onto Old Creek Rd, a winding, narrow two-lane back road, passing citrus farms and cattle ranches. Turn right after 9 miles onto Hwy 46, which heads east through wine country for 11 miles to Paso Robles.

- - - - - - - - - -

TRIP HIGHLIGHT

❼ Paso Robles Wine Country

Franciscan missionaries brought the first grapes to this region in the late 18th century, but it wasn't until the 1920s that the now-famous zinfandel vines took root in Paso Robles. Coasting through golden-brown hills and grassy pasture lands, Hwy 46 passes family-owned vineyards, olive orchards and rustic farmstands. Pick up a free **winery tour map** (www.pasowine.com) from any tasting room and sniff out boutique winemakers such as Kenneth Volk, Adelaida, Linne Calodo and Zenaida, as well as established big-name producers like Justin, Eberle and Tobin James. Or trust serendipity and follow rural side roads to discover the region's next break-out winery. After a long afternoon spent in sun-drenched vineyards, retreat to leafy downtown Paso Robles. Just off the central park square, you'll find dozens more wine-tasting rooms and bars, restaurants and urbane boutiques.

✕ 🛏 p185

Eating & Sleeping

San Luis Obispo ❶

✖ Big Sky Cafe   Californian $$
(www.bigskycafe.com; 1121 Broad St; mains $6-22; ⏱7am-9pm Mon-Thu, 7am-10pm Fri, 8am-10pm Sat, 8am-9pm Sun; 🖋) With the tagline 'analog food for a digital world,' this big-hearted locavarian cafe gets top marks for market-fresh breakfasts (served until 1pm daily). Vegetarians have almost as many big-plate dinner options as omnivores.

🛏 Peach Tree Inn   Motel $$
(📞805-543-3170; www.peachtreeinn.com; 2001 Monterey St; r $79-200; @ 🛜) Folksy, nothing-fancy motel has inviting rooms creekside and rocking chairs on wooden porches overlooking a tree swing. Continental breakfast includes homemade breads.

Pismo Beach ❸

✖ Cracked Crab   Seafood $$$
(www.crackedcrab.com; 751 Price St; mains $9-48; ⏱11am-9pm Sun-Thu, to 10pm Fri & Sat; 🖐) When the famous bucket o' seafood gets dumped on your butcher paper–covered table, with flying bits of shellfish, Cajun sausage, red potatoes and corn cobs, make sure you're wearing one of the plastic bibs and have a wooden mallet in hand.

🛏 Pismo Lighthouse Suites   Hotel $$
(📞805-773-2411; www.pismolighthousesuites.com; 2411 Price St; ste incl breakfast $149-389; ✳ @ 🛜 🏊 🖐) Contemporary all-suites beach hotel offers everything a family beach vacation needs, from kitchenettes to a life-sized outdoor chessboard. Second location in Avila Beach.

Morro Bay ❻

✖ Giovanni's Fish Market & Galley   Seafood $$
(www.giovannisfishmarket.com; 1001 Front St; mains $7-13; ⏱9am-6pm; 🖐) Folks line up at this family-run joint for batter-fried fish-and-chips and killer garlic fries. Enjoy the harbor views from the outdoor deck, but guard your meal from aggro pigeons.

✖ Taco Temple   Californian $$
(2680 Main St; mains $8-15; ⏱11am-9pm Mon & Wed-Sat, noon-8:30pm Sun; 🖐) Off Hwy 1, stop in for huge helpings of Cal-Mex fusion. At the next table might be fishers talking about the old days or starving surfer buddies. Daily specials deserve the name. Cash only.

🛏 Beach Bungalow Inn & Suites   Motel $$
(📞805-772-9700; www.beachbungalowmorrobay.com; 1050 Morro Ave; d $135-250; 🛜🏊) Uphill from the harbor, this butter-yellow motor court's chic, contemporary rooms painted in ocean hues have all mod cons, some with gas fireplaces to ward off coastal fog.

Paso Robles Wine Country ❼

✖ Artisan   Californian $$$
(📞805-237-8084, www.artisanpasorobles.com; 1401 Park St; dinner mains $26-31; ⏱11am-2:30pm Mon-Sat, 10am-2pm Sun, plus 5-10pm daily) Chef Kobayashi ducks out of the kitchen to make sure you're loving his New American cuisine, featuring sustainably farmed meats, wild-caught seafood and artisanal California cheeses.

🛏 Zenaida Cellars   B&B $$$
(📞866-936-5638; www.zenaidacellars.com; 3775 Adelaida Rd; ste $250-375; 🛜) Steal yourself away among the pastoral vineyards of Paso Robles' west side. The winemaker's loft above the tasting room has a full kitchen; the cellar master's suite is comfy for couples.

Santa Ynez Valley *Rhône-st[yle]*
grapes do best he[re]

Santa Barbara Wine Country

17

Oak-dotted hillsides, winding country roads, rows of sweetly heavy grapevines stretching into the distance – let yourself be seduced sideways by the Santa Maria and Santa Ynez Valleys.

TRIP HIGHLIGHTS

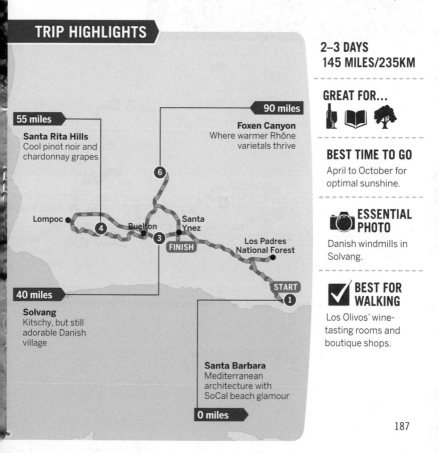

90 miles

Foxen Canyon
Where warmer Rhône varietals thrive

55 miles

Santa Rita Hills
Cool pinot noir and chardonnay grapes

6

Lompoc

4

Buelton

Santa Ynez

3

FINISH

Los Padres National Forest

START

1

40 miles

Solvang
Kitschy, but still adorable Danish village

Santa Barbara
Mediterranean architecture with SoCal beach glamour

0 miles

2–3 DAYS
145 MILES/235KM

GREAT FOR...

BEST TIME TO GO
April to October for optimal sunshine.

ESSENTIAL PHOTO
Danish windmills in Solvang.

BEST FOR WALKING
Los Olivos' wine-tasting rooms and boutique shops.

187

17 Santa Barbara Wine Country

The 2004 Oscar-winning film *Sideways*, an ode to wine-country living as seen through the misadventures of middle-aged buddies Miles and Jack, may have gotten the party started. But passionate vintners, ecominded entrepreneurs and gorgeous wine trails are what's keeping Santa Barbara in the juice. More than 100 wineries spread out across the pastoral landscape, with five small towns all clustered prettily within a 10-mile drive of one another.

TRIP HIGHLIGHT

1 Santa Barbara

Start pretending to live the luxe life in Santa Barbara, a coastal Shangri-la where the air is redolent of citrus, and flowery bougainvillea drapes whitewashed buildings with Spanish Colonial-style red-tiled roofs, all cradled by pearly beaches. Before heading out of town into the wine country for the day or the weekend, make time to visit landmark **Mission Santa Barbara**

(http://santabarbaramission.org; 2201 Laguna St; adult/child $5/1; ⏰9am-5pm), California's 'Queen of the Missions.' Then take our self-guided walking tour of downtown's historical buildings and museums (see p194), all on or just off **State St**, which leads downhill to the ocean and splintered wooden **Stearns Wharf**, the West Coast's oldest continuously operating pier. A few blocks inland from the beach, follow Santa Barbara's **Urban Wine Trail** (www.urbanwinetrailsb.com), where boutique wine-tasting rooms are typically open from noon to 6pm daily (tasting fees $5 to $10).

✕ 🛏 p193

The Drive » In the morning, take a short drive north on Hwy 101, then follow winding, narrow Hwy 154 up into the Santa Ynez Mountains and over San Marcos Pass. About 9 miles from Hwy 101, turn left onto Stagecoach Rd, passing the 1860s Cold Springs Tavern. After 2 miles, turn right on Paradise Rd.

- - - - - - - - - - - - - -

② Los Padres National Forest

Off Paradise Rd, the tall-treed **Los Padres National Forest** (www.fs.usda.gov/lpnf; 🚻) contains several good hiking trails for all ages, all easily accessed off Hwy 154. Starting beyond the family campgrounds and river crossing on Paradise Rd, the creekside Red Rock Trail leads for a mile to rocky pools and waterfalls where you can sunbathe or swim.

The Drive » Backtrack along Paradise Rd, then turn right and follow Hwy 154 northbound past Lake Cachuma and the rolling hillsides for over 13 miles. Turn left onto Hwy 246 and keep motoring five more flat miles through the Santa Ynez Valley west to Solvang.

- - - - - - - - - - - - - -

TRIP HIGHLIGHT

③ Solvang

Loosely translated as 'Sunny Fields,' this touristy Danish village was founded in 1911 on what was once a Mexican *rancho* land grant. Filled with knick-knack stores and storybook-esque motels, the town is almost as sticky-sweet as the Scandinavian bakery pastries gobbled by day-trippers. Wine-tasting rooms and windmills decorate the village's pedestrian-friendly streets. Where locals gather for after-work drinks, **Tocatta Tasting Room** (www.llwine.com; 1665 Copenhagen Dr; tasting fee $8-12; ⏰11am-5:30pm) specializes in Italian varietals and robust Tuscan blends. On a residential side street, the tiny **Elverhøj Museum** (www.elverhoj.org; 1624 Elverhoy Way;

0 ▭▭▭▭ 10 km
0 ▭▭▭▭ 5 miles

Rafael erness

Los Padres National Forest
②

154

Goleta
01

p194
START ①
Santa Barbara

LINK YOUR TRIP

16 Around San Luis Obispo
Want more wine, but beaches too? Drive Hwy 101 north of Santa Ynez Valley for 45 miles to Pismo Beach.

28 Mission Trail
Trace the path of Spanish colonial history at La Purísima Mission, 18 miles west of Solvang via Hwy 246.

189

suggested donation $3; ☺1-4pm Wed & Thu, noon-4pm Fri-Sun) uncovers the real roots of Danish life in Solvang. Tranquil today, **Mission Santa Inés** (www.missionsantaines.org; 1760 Mission Dr; adult/child $5/free; ☺9am-4:30pm) witnessed an 1824 Chumash revolt against Spanish colonial cruelty.

✕ 🛏 p193

The Drive ≫ Continue west on Hwy 246 past equestrian ranches and the famous ostrich farm (as seen during Jack's predawn run in *Sideways*) for just a few miles to Buellton. Continue across Hwy 101 and drive west toward Lompoc.

TRIP HIGHLIGHT

❹ Santa Rita Hills

When it comes to rolling scenery, ecoconscious farming practices and top-notch pinot noirs and chardonnays kissed by coastal fog, the **Santa Rita Hills** (www.staritahills.com) undoubtedly hold their own. Almost a dozen tasting rooms open their doors daily along this 36-mile scenic loop west of Hwy 101. Be prepared to share these slow-moving roads with sweaty cyclists, Harley Davidson bikers and an occasional John Deere tractor. Heading west of Buellton into the countryside, **Babcock Winery** (www.babcockwinery.com; 5175 E Hwy 146, Lompoc; tasting fee $10-15; ☺10:30am-4pm Nov-Feb, to

5pm Mar-Oct) and **Melville Vineyards and Winery** (www.melvillewinery.com; 5185 E Hwy 146, Lompoc; tasting fee $10; ☺11am-4pm) are neighboring small-lot estate winemakers who talk about pounds per plant, not tons per acre. Turn left onto Hwy 1 south, then left again on Santa Rosa Rd. Follow the cacti and cobblestones into organic-certified **Alma Rosa Winery & Vineyards** (www.almarosawinery.com; 7250 Santa Rosa Rd, Buellton; tastings fee $10-15; ☺11am-4:30pm), whose tasting room cameoed in *Sideways*.

The Drive ≫ At the eastern end of Santa Rosa Rd, merge onto fast-tracked Hwy 101 northbound. After 6 miles, take the Hwy 154 exit for Los Olivos, driving another 3 miles further east past more rolling vineyards.

---

❺ Los Olivos

Strutting in cowboy hats and high heels, the ranching town of 'The Olives' has a four-block-long main street lined with wine bars and restaurants, art galleries, cafes and fashionable shops seemingly airlifted straight out of Napa Valley. To make it all the more perfect, you can easily walk between downtown's inviting wine-tasting rooms on a long, lazy afternoon. **Qupé Wines** (www.qupe.com; 2963 Grand Ave; tastings $10; ☺11am-5pm)

ranks among the most respected syrah and chardonnay producers on California's Central Coast. Or chat with the family winemakers inside the wooden-shack tasting room at **Carhartt Vineyard** (www.carharttvineyard.com; 2990A Grand Ave; tasting fee $10; ☺11am-5pm). For a break from the grapes, the pint-sized **Wildling Art Museum** (www.wildlingmuseum.org; 2928 San Marcos Ave; admission by donation; ☺11am-5pm Wed-Sun) exhibits nature-themed California and American Western art.

✕ p193

The Drive ≫ From Los Olivos, drive west on Hwy 154 for 3 miles. Before reaching Hwy 101, turn right onto Zaca Station Rd, then follow it for 3 winding miles northwest onto Foxen Canyon Rd.

TRIP HIGHLIGHT

❻ Foxen Canyon

On the celebrated wine trail through **Foxen Canyon** (www.foxencanyonwinetrail.com), tidy rows of grapevines border some of Santa Barbara County's prettiest wineries. This country lane meanders north all the way to the Santa Maria Valley before finally reaching the 1875 **San Ramon Chapel** (www.sanramonchapelorg), a good turnaround point after 13 miles.

Mission Santa Inés Statue of St Agnes

LOCAL KNOWLEDGE: TASTING ROOM TIPS

To make the most of your wine tour, Chris Burroughs, the tasting room manager at Alma Rosa Winery & Vineyards, recommends small groups and an itinerary focused on just a handful of wineries. Keep an open mind: don't tell the staff you never drink chardonnay – who knows, the wine you try that day may change your mind. Picnicking on-site is always welcome, and you'll be considered especially cool if you complement your lunch with just-purchased wine. Not so cool? Heavy perfume and smoking. Otherwise, enjoy yourself and don't be afraid to ask questions – most winemakers welcome novices.

Furthest south, tour buses crowd **Firestone Vineyard** (www.firestonewine.com; 5017 Zaca Station Rd, Santa Maria; tasting fee $10-15; ⊘ tasting room 10am-5pm, tours usually 11:15am, 1:15pm & 3:15pm), Santa Barbara's oldest estate winery (it's where Miles, Jack and their dates sneak into the barrel room in *Sideways*). At hidden **Demetria Estate** (☎805-686-2345; www. demetriaestate.com; 6701 Foxen Canyon Rd, Santa Maria; tasting fee $15; ⊘ by appointment only) Rhône varietals and pinot grapes are farmed biodynamically. On a former cattle ranch, sustainable **Foxen Winery** (www.foxenvineyard.com; 7200 & 7600 Foxen Canyon Rd, Santa Maria; tastings $10;

⊘11am-4pm) cracks open steel-cut chardonnays and full-fruited pinot noirs in a solar-powered tasting room. Up the road, Foxen's old 'shack' – with a corrugated-metal roof and funky decor – pours Bordeaux-style and Cal-Ital varietals that are award-winning.

The Drive » Backtrack just over 17 miles along Foxen Canyon Rd, keeping left at the intersection with Zaca Station Rd to return to Los Olivos. Turn left onto Hwy 154 southbound for 2 miles, then turn right onto Roblar Ave for Ontiveros Rd.

- - - - - - - - - - - - -

❼ Santa Ynez Valley

Further inland in the warm Santa Ynez Valley, Rhône-style grapes do best, including syrah and viognier. Some of the most popular tasting

rooms cluster between Los Olivos, Solvang and Santa Ynez, but noisy tour groups, harried staff and stingy pours too often disappoint.

Thankfully that's not the case at **Beckmen Vineyards** (www. beckmenvineyards.com; 2670 Ontiveros Rd, Solvang; tasting fee $10-15; ⊘11am-5pm), where biodynamically farmed, estate-grown varietals flourish on the unique terroir of Purisima Mountain. For more natural beauty, backtrack east on Roblar Ave to family-owned **Clairmont Farms** (2480 Roblar Ave; ⊘ usually 10am-4pm), where purple lavender fields bloom like a Monet masterpiece in early summer.

Turn right onto Refugio Rd, which flows south past more vineyards, fruit orchards and farms and straight across Hwy 154 to **Kalyra Winery** (www.kalyrawinery. com; 343 N Refugio Rd, Santa Ynez; tasting fee $10; ⊘11am-5pm Mon-Fri, 10am-5pm Sat & Sun), where an Australian traveled halfway around the world to combine two loves: surfing and wine making. Try his unique Cashmere blend made with imported Australian grapes or locally grown varietals, all in bottles with Aboriginal art–inspired labels.

Eating & Sleeping

Santa Barbara ❶

✖ Olio Pizzeria   Italian $$

(www.oliopizzeria.com; 11 W Victoria St; shared plates $3-24; ⏱11:30am-2pm Mon-Sat, 5-10pm Sun-Thu, to 11pm Fri & Sat) Cozy, high-ceilinged pizzeria and enoteca has a happening wine bar and a satisfying selection of crispy pizzas, imported cheeses and meats, traditional antipasti and *dolci* (desserts).

🛏 Agave Inn   Motel $$

(☎805-687-6009; www.agaveinnsb.com; 3222 State St; r $99-189; ❇🛜) North of downtown, a 'Mexican pop meets modern' motif livens things up with a color palette out of a Frieda Kahlo painting. A few of the bigger family-sized rooms each have a kitchenette and pull-out sofa bed.

🛏 Harbor House Inn   Motel $$

(☎805-962-9745; www.harborhouseinn.com; 104 Bath St; r $130-335; 🛜🛁) All of these brightly lit studios inside a converted motel come with hardwood floors, small kitchens and a cheery design scheme. Fall in love with the welcome basket of breakfast goodies, DVD library and bikes to borrow.

Solvang ❸

✖ El Rancho Marketplace   Supermarket $$

(www.elranchomarket.com; 2886 Mission Dr/ Hwy 246; ⏱6am-10pm) Before that first sip of wine, pick your designated driver and load up on picnic fixings and barbeque take-out from the deli inside this grocery store, which has a bargain wine room and espresso bar.

🛏 Hadsten House   Boutique Hotel $$

(☎805-688-3210; www.hadstenhouse.com; 1450 Mission Dr; r incl breakfast $150-255; ❇🛜🏊) Revamped motel has glammed up just

about everything except its uninspiring exterior. Inside rooms are surprisingly plush, with luxury mattresses and L'Occitane bath products.

🛏 Hamlet Inn   Motel $$

(☎805-688-4413; http://thehamletinn.com; 1532 Mission Dr; r $70-200; ❇🛜) This motel is to wine-country lodging what IKEA is to interior design: a budget-friendly, trendy alternative. Crisp, modern rooms have panache, with art-splashed walls. Free loaner bicycles and a bocce-ball court for guests.

Los Olivos ❺

✖ Los Olivos Café   Californian, Mediterranean $$

(☎805-688-7265; www.losolivoscafe.com; 2879 Grand Ave; mains $13-28; ⏱11:30am-9pm) With white canopies and a wisteria-covered trellis, this bistro swirls up a casual-chic ambience. Stick with antipasto platters, hearty salads or rustic pizzas and wine flights at the bar. Reservations recommended.

✖ Petros   Greek $$$

(☎805-686-5455; www.petrosrestaurant.com; Fess Parker Wine Country Inn & Spa, 2860 Grand Ave; shared plates $7-16, dinner mains $22-38; ⏱7am-10pm Sun-Thu, to 11pm Fri & Sat) In a sunny dining room, sophisticated Greek cuisine makes a refreshing change from Italianate wine-country kitsch. Housemade meze (appetizers) will satisfy even picky foodies.

✖ Sides Hardware & Shoes   Californian $$$

(☎805-688-4820; www.brothersrestaurant. com; 2375 Alamo Pintado Ave; breakfast & lunch $8-16, dinner $18-28; ⏱7am-2:30pm & 5-9pm Tue-Sun) Inside a historic storefront, this farm-fresh cafe puts upscale twists on country classics like 'hammered pig' pork tenderloin, fried chicken, buttermilk cornmeal pancakes and roasted poblano-pepper omelets.

STRETCH YOUR LEGS
SANTA BARBARA

Start/Finish Santa Barbara County Courthouse

Distance 1.6 miles

Duration 2–4 hours

Frankly put, this chic SoCal city is damn pleasant to putter around. Low-slung between lofty mountains and the sparkling Pacific, downtown's red-tiled roofs, white stucco buildings and Mediterranean vibe make this an irresistible ramble on any sunny afternoon.

Take this walk on Trips

Santa Barbara County Courthouse

Built in Spanish-Moorish Revival style, the **county courthouse** (www.santabarbaracourthouse.org; 1100 Anacapa St; admission free; ☺8:30am-4:30pm Mon-Fri, 10am-4:30pm Sat & Sun) is an absurdly beautiful place to stand trial. The magnificent 1929 courthouse features hand-painted ceilings, wrought-iron chandeliers and Tunisian and Spanish tiles. Step into the 2nd-floor mural room, then climb the *Vertigo*-esque clocktower for arch-framed panoramas.

The Walk » Exit the courthouse and head southwest along Anapamu St, passing the striking Italianate 1924 Santa Barbara Public Library. Turn left onto State St, downtown's main drag.

Santa Barbara Museum of Art

This petite **museum** (☎805-963-4364; www.sbma.net; 1130 State St; adult/child $9/6; ☺11am-5pm Tue-Sun; ⊞) holds a nevertheless impressive collection of contemporary California artists, modern European and American masters like Matisse and O'Keeffe, 20th-century photography and classical antiquities. Traipse up to the 2nd floor, where Asian art exhibits include an intricate Tibetan sand mandala and the armor of a Japanese samurai.

The Walk » Walk three blocks southeast on State St, jam-packed with cafes, restaurants and boutiques. Turn left on Cañon Perdido St, passing the 1873 Lobero Theatre, then cross Anacapa St.

El Presidio de Santa Barbara State Historic Park

Built to defend Santa Barbara's mission, this 18th-century **fort** (☎805-965-0093; www.sbthp.org; 123 E Cañon Perdido St; adult/child $5/free; ☺10:30am-4:30pm) was colonial Spain's last military stronghold in Alta California. Today this small park encloses several reconstructed adobe buildings. Be sure to peek inside the chapel, its interior radiant with gold and scarlet.

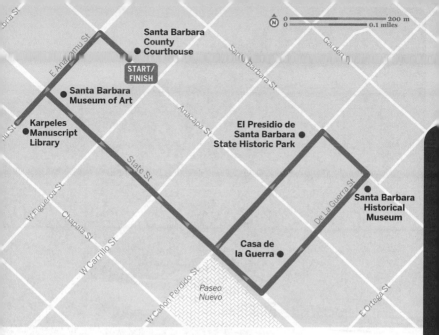

**The Walk ›› **Farther northeast along Cañon Perdido St are Handlebar Coffee Roasters and Sojourner Cafe for refueling. Otherwise walk one block southeast, turning right onto De La Guerra St.

Santa Barbara Historical Museum

Embracing a romantic cloistered Spanish-style adobe courtyard, this peaceful little **museum** (📞805-966-1601; www.santabarbaramuseum.com; 136 E De La Guerra St; admission by donation; ⊙10am-5pm Tue-Sat, noon-5pm Sun) has an interesting collection of local memorabilia, ranging from the simply beautiful, such as Chumash woven baskets and colonial-era textiles, to the simply odd, like an intricately carved coffer that belonged to missionary Junípero Serra.

**The Walk ›› **Keep walking southwest on De La Guerra St, crossing Anacapa St. Casa de la Guerra stands on the northwest side of the block.

Casa de la Guerra

Your admission ticket to El Presidio de Santa Barbara also includes entry to

Casa de la Guerra (📞805-965-0093; www.sbthp.org; 15 E De La Guerra St; adult/child $5/free; ⊙noon-4pm Sat & Sun), a grand 18th-century colonial home with Spanish, Mexican and American heritage exhibits. Authentically restored, this whitewashed adobe with red-tiled roofs was an architectural model for rebuilding all of downtown after a devastating 1925 earthquake.

**The Walk ›› **Continue walking southwest, crossing State St over to the Paseo Nuevo shopping mall. Head northwest four blocks to Anapamu St and turn left.

Karpeles Manuscript Library

Stuffed with historical written artifacts, this **museum** (📞805-962-5322; www.rain.org/~karpeles; 21 W Anapamu St; ⊙noon-4pm Wed-Sun) is an embarrassment of riches for history nerds, science geeks, and literary and music lovers. Traveling exhibits often spotlight literary masterworks, from Shakespeare's to Sherlock Holmes.

**The Walk ›› **Head northeast on Anapamu St. Turn right onto Anacapa St to return to the courthouse.

Lake Tahoe During summer h
mountain-bike forest trai

Lake Tahoe Loop **18**

Shimmering in myriad blues and greens, Lake Tahoe is the USA's second-deepest lake, astounding in its clarity. Drive around its spellbinding 72-mile shoreline.

TRIP HIGHLIGHTS

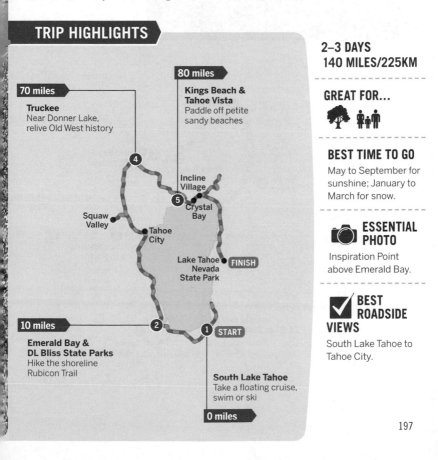

80 miles

Kings Beach & Tahoe Vista
Paddle off petite sandy beaches

70 miles

Truckee
Near Donner Lake, relive Old West history

④

Incline
Village

⑤ Crystal
Bay

Squaw
Valley

Tahoe
City

Lake Tahoe **FINISH**
Nevada
State Park

10 miles

Emerald Bay & DL Bliss State Parks
Hike the shoreline Rubicon Trail

②

① START

South Lake Tahoe
Take a floating cruise, swim or ski

0 miles

2–3 DAYS
140 MILES/225KM

GREAT FOR...

BEST TIME TO GO

May to September for sunshine; January to March for snow.

ESSENTIAL PHOTO

Inspiration Point above Emerald Bay.

BEST ROADSIDE VIEWS

South Lake Tahoe to Tahoe City.

18 Lake Tahoe Loop

The horned peaks surrounding Lake Tahoe, straddling the California–Nevada state line, are four-seasons playgrounds. During summer hit the cool sapphire waters by sandy beaches or trek and mountain-bike forest trails. In wintertime, Lake Tahoe woos powder-hungry skiers and boarders with scores of slopes. Year-round, the north shore is quiet and upscale; the west shore, rugged and old-timey; the east shore, blissfully undeveloped; and the south shore, always busy.

TRIP HIGHLIGHT

① South Lake Tahoe

South Lake Tahoe is a chock-a-block commercial strip bordering the lake framed by postcard-perfect mountains. In winter, go swooshing down the double-black diamond runs and monster vertical drops of **Heavenly** (☎775-586-7000; www.skiheavenly.com; 3860 Saddle Rd; adult/child lift ticket $88/50, gondola $34/20; 👪), a behemoth ski resort. From the top, you're on the spine of the

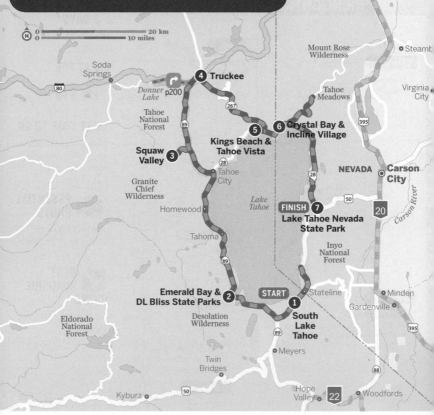

Sierra Nevada between mountains and desert flatlands. For killer lake views in summer, ascend the gondola from Heavenly Village, or board the paddle wheelers of **Lake Tahoe Cruises** (800-238-2463; www.zephyrcove.com; adult/child from $39/15;) that ply the 'Big Blue.' Survey the azure expanse of the lake at eye level from in-town beaches or aboard a kayak launched from **Zephyr Cove** (775-589-4906; www.zephyrcove.com; 760 Hwy 50; entry per car $8;), which also has sandy swimming beaches. It's about 3 miles north of Stateline, NV, where you can bet a stack of chips at the hulking casinos, all buzzing with bars, nightclubs and 24-hour restaurants.

p203

Eastern Sierra Scenic Byway
20

Downtown Reno's casinos are just over 30 miles northeast of Truckee via the I-80.

Ebbetts Pass Scenic Byway
22

From South Lake Tahoe, it's 20 miles south along Hwy 89 to Hope Valley, although Ebbetts Pass is closed during winter and spring.

The Drive » Unless the road has been closed by heavy snowfall, set a course heading northwest from South Lake Tahoe's 'The Y' intersection onto scenic lakeside Hwy 89. You'll pass USFS Tallac Historic Site and Taylor Creek Visitor Center, both of which have nature trails and educational exhibits, before reaching Inspiration Point and, further along, Vikingsholm Castle's parking lot.

- - - - - - - - - - - - -

TRIP HIGHLIGHT

❷ Emerald Bay & DL Bliss State Parks

Sheer granite cliffs and a jagged shoreline mark glacier-carved **Emerald Bay** (530-541-3030; www.parks.ca.gov; per car $8-10; ⏰usually late May–early Sep;), a teardrop cove that will get you digging for your camera. Panoramic pullouts all along Hwy 89 peer over the uninhabited granite speck of **Fanette Island**, which harbors the vandalized remains of a 1920s teahouse once belonging to heiress Lora Knight. She also built **Vikingsholm Castle** (tour adult/child $8/5; ⏰10:30am or 11am–4:30pm late May–early Sep), a Scandinavian-style mansion on the bay that's reached via a steep 2-mile round-trip hiking trail. Heading north, the 4.5-mile **Rubicon Trail** ribbons along the lakeshore past hidden coves to **DL Bliss State Park** (530-525-7277; www.parks.ca.gov; per car $10; ⏰usually mid-Jun–early Sep), with its old lighthouse and sandy beaches. In

summer, the **Nifty Fifty Trolley** (530-541-7149; www.bluego.org; rides $2) shuttles between the parks.

p203

The Drive » Head north on Hwy 89 past the sandy beach at Meeks Bay, forested Ed Z'berg Sugar Pine Point State Park and the lakeshore hamlets of Tahoma and Homewood. At the intersection with N Lake Blvd/Hwy 28, Tahoe City's commercial strip, turn left to stay on Hwy 89 another 5 miles northwest to Squaw Valley Rd.

- - - - - - - - - - - - -

❸ Squaw Valley

After stopping in Tahoe City for supplies and to refuel your stomach and the car, it's a short drive up to **Squaw Valley USA** (800-403-0206; www.squaw.com; 1960 Squaw Valley Rd, Olympic Valley; adult/child ski-lift ticket $92/41, aerial-tram ride $29/10, all-access summer activity pass $63/30;), a megasized ski resort that hosted the 1960 Winter Olympics. You could spend a whole winter weekend here and not ski the same run twice. Hold on tight as the aerial tram rises over granite ledges to High Camp at a lofty 8200ft, where you can take a spin around the ice rink while being mesmerized by vistas of the lake so very far below. In summer, families crowd the outdoor swimming lagoon, disc-golf course, zip-line and the hiking and mountain-biking

MARTYN GODDARD / CORBIS ©

DETOUR:
DONNER LAKE

Start: ④ Truckee

Donner Summit is where the infamous Donner Party became trapped during the fierce winter of 1846–47. Their grisly tale of survival – and cannibalism – is chronicled at the **museum** (🕙10am-5pm, closed Tue & Wed Sep-May) inside **Donner Memorial State Park** (📞530-582-7892; www.parks.ca.gov; 12593 Donner Pass Rd; per car $8; 🚻), where tree-lined **Donner Lake** offers sandy beaches. Further west, popular municipal **West End Beach** (📞530-582-7777; www.tdrpd.com; adult/child $4/3; 🚻) has a roped-off swimming area for kids, and kayak, paddleboat and stand-up paddle boarding (SUP) rentals. The state park and lakeshore are just a few miles east of Truckee via Donner Pass Rd.

trails radiating out from High Camp.

The Drive » Backtrack out of Squaw Valley, turning left onto Hwy 89 and driving north for about 8 miles. Before reaching I-80, turn right onto W River St for another mile to downtown Truckee.

TRIP HIGHLIGHT

④ Truckee

Cradled by mountains and forests, this speck of a town is steeped in Old West history. Truckee was put on the map by the railroad, grew rich on logging and ice harvesting, and found Hollywood fame with the

Emerald Bay Motorcyclist on Hwy 89

1924 filming of Charlie Chaplin's *The Gold Rush*. Its well-preserved historical downtown is close to a dozen downhill and cross-country ski resorts, most famously **Northstar-at-Tahoe** (☎800-466-6784; www.northstarattahoe.com; 5001 Northstar Dr, off Hwy 267; adult/child lift ticket winter $91/53, summer $10/free; 👪), where ski lifts also transport summer hikers and mountain-bikers into the highlands.

✗ 🛏 p203

The Drive » In downtown Truckee, cross over the railroad tracks and the river, following Brockway Rd southeast for 1.5 miles. Turn right onto Hwy 267 back toward Lake Tahoe, passing Northstar-at-Tahoe ski resort before cruising downhill to the lakeshore town of Kings Beach, 10 miles away.

- - - - - - - - - - - - - -

TRIP HIGHLIGHT

❺ Kings Beach & Tahoe Vista

On summer weekends, picturesque **Kings Beach State Recreation Area** (www.parks.ca.gov; admission free; ☯dawn-10pm; 👪🐾) gets deluged with sun-seekers, especially the picnic tables, barbecue grills and boat rentals. **Adrift Tahoe** (☎530-546-1112; www.standuppaddletahoe.com; 8338 N Lake Blvd; ☯seasonal hr vary) handles kayak, outrigger canoe and stand-up paddle boaring (SUP) rentals and paddling lessons, and tours, as well as yoga classes on the beach. Just inland, the 1920s **Old Brockway Golf Course** (☎530-546-9909; www.oldbrockway.com; 7900 N Lake Blvd; greens fee $25-70, club rental $20-30) runs along pine-bordered fairways where Hollywood celebs once hobnobbed. Spread southeast along Hwy 28, **Tahoe Vista** has more public beaches than any other lakeshore town.

TAHOE RIM TRAIL

The 165-mile **Tahoe Rim Trail** (http://tahoerimtrail.org) treks the lofty ridges of the Lake Tahoe Basin. Day hikers, equestrians and – in some sections – mountain-bikers are rewarded by high-altitude views of the lake and Sierra Nevada peaks while tracing the footsteps of early pioneers, Basque shepherds and Washoe tribespeople.

Lose the crowds on the hiking and mountain-biking trails or disc-golf course at **North Tahoe Regional Park** (http://northtahoeparks.com; 6600 Donner Rd, off National Ave; per car $3; 🚻), which also has a snow-sledding hill.

🍴 🛏 p203

The Drive » East of Kings Beach, Hwy 28 barrels uphill across the California–Nevada border past the small-potatoes casinos of Crystal Bay before reaching Incline Village just a few miles later.

- - - - - - - - - - - - -

❻ Crystal Bay & Incline Village

Crossing into Nevada, the neon starts to flash and old-school gambling palaces appear. You can try your luck at the gambling tables or catch a live-music show at the **Crystal Bay Club Casino** (📞775-833-6333; www.crystalbaycasino.com; 14 Hwy 28). Straddling the state border, **Cal-Neva Resort** (📞800-233-5551; www.calnevaresort.com; 2 Stateline Rd; admission free, tour $10; 🕐call for tour schedules) evokes a colorful history of ghosts, mobsters and ex-owner Frank Sinatra on guided tours of its 'secret' underground tunnels.

One of Lake Tahoe's ritziest communities, **Incline Village** is a gateway to wintertime ski resorts. During summer, you can tour the eccentric **Thunderbird Lodge** (📞800-468-2463; http://thunderbirdtahoe.org; tour adult/child from $39/19; 🕐tours usually Tue-Sat Jun-Sep, reservations required), a historical mansion only accessible by bus, boat or kayak. Or drive northeast up Hwy 431 into the Mt Rose Wilderness, a gateway to miles of unspoiled terrain, including easy wildflower walks at **Tahoe Meadows**.

The Drive » Beyond the stop-and-go traffic of Incline Village, Hwy 28 winds south, staying high above Lake Tahoe's east shore, offering peekaboo lake views and roadside pull-offs, from where locals scramble down the cliffs to hidden beaches. It's a slow-moving 13 miles south to Spooner Lake.

- - - - - - - - - - - - -

❼ Lake Tahoe Nevada State Park

With pristine beaches and miles of wilderness trails for hikers, mountain-bikers, skiers and snowshoers, **Lake Tahoe Nevada State Park** (📞775-831-0494; http://parks.nv.gov; Hwy 28; per car $7-12; 🚻) is the east shore's big draw. Summer crowds splash in the turquoise waters of **Sand Harbor**, a few miles south of Incline Village. The 13-mile **Flume Trail** (📞775-749-5349; www.theflumetrail.com; trailhead bike rental $45-65, shuttle $10-15), a mountain-biker's holy grail, starts further south at **Spooner Lake**, where anglers fish along the shore (no swimming – too many leeches!). It's just north of the Hwy 50 junction.

Eating & Sleeping

South Lake Tahoe ❶

✖ Burger Lounge   Fast Food $

(717 Emerald Bay Rd; menu items $3-6; ⏱11am-8pm, to 9pm Jun-Aug; 👪) Look for a giant beer mug propped above a shingled cabin. Step right up for tasty burgers, including 'Just a Jiffy' (with peanut butter, bacon and cheddar cheese), and zingy fries.

✖ Ernie's Coffee Shop   Diner $

(www.erniescoffeeshop.com; 1207 Hwy 50; mains $7-11; ⏱6am-2pm; 👪) A sun-filled local institution, Ernie's dishes out filling four-egg omelets, hearty biscuits with gravy, fruity and nutty waffles and bottomless cups of locally roasted coffee.

⛨ 968 Park Hotel   Motel $$

(☎530-544-0968; www.968parkhotel.com; 968 Park Ave; r $139-289; @🛜🏊). Recycled, rescued and re-envisioned building materials have made this LEED-certified motel a hip ecohaven within easy walking distance of Heavenly Village.

⛨ Alder Inn   B&B $$

(☎530-544-4485; www.thealderinn.com; 1072 Ski Run Blvd; r $89-229; 🛜🏊) Even better than staying at your best friend's house by the lake, this hospitable inn is painted in color schemes that really pop, plus pillow-top mattresses and organic bath goodies in your room.

Emerald Bay & DL Bliss State Parks ❷

⛨ Tahoma Meadows B&B Cottages   Cabin $$

(☎530-525-1553; www.tahomameadows.com; 6821 W Lake Blvd, Tahoma; cabin incl breakfast $95-199; 🛜👪🏊) Cute but not too kitschy, these country cabins with fireplaces and claw-foot tubs dot a pine grove, 8 miles north of DL Bliss State Park.

Truckee ❹

✖ Coffeebar   Cafe $

(www.coffeebartruckee.com; 10120 Jiboom St; items $2-8; ⏱6am-8pm; 🛜) Acid-orange molded chairs are scattered around this beatnik, industrial-chic coffee shop on a backstreet.

⛨ Cedar Sport House Hotel   Boutique Hotel $$$

(☎530-582-5655; www.cedarhousesporthotel.com; 10918 Brockway Rd; r incl breakfast $160-290; ❄@🛜🏊) Environmentally conscious, design-savvy contemporary lodge will get you back to nature, but also doesn't skimp on plush robes or the outdoor hot tub. Stella bistro serves seasonal California fusion dinners (restaurant mains from $25 to $35).

⛨ Larkspur Hotel Truckee-Tahoe   Hotel $$

(☎530-587-4525; www.larkspurhotels.com; 11331 Brockway Rd; r incl breakfast $159-249; ❄@🛜🏊👪🏊) You'll forget about retro ski-lodge kitsch when you're inside these crisp, earth-toned hotel rooms where you can sink back after sunset into feather-topped mattresses.

Kings Beach & Tahoe Vista ❺

✖ Old Post Office Cafe   American $

(5245 N Lake Blvd, Tahoe Vista; mains $6-12; ⏱6:30am-2pm) Head west to Carnelian Bay, where this always-packed wooden shack serves scrumptious breakfasts – buttery potatoes, crab-cake eggs Benedict and fresh-fruit smoothies. Waits can be long.

⛨ Franciscan Lakeside Lodge   Cottage, Cabin $$

(☎530-546-6300; http://franciscanlodge.com; 6944 N Lake Blvd, Tahoe Vista; d $90-275; 🛜🏊👪) Spend the day on a private sandy beach or in the outdoor pool, then light the barbeque grill after sunset. Simple cabins, cottages and suites have kitchenettes.

Yosemite Falls *Triple-tiered, t*
waterfall is North America's tall

Yosemite, Sequoia & Kings Canyon National Parks

19

Drive up into the lofty Sierra Nevada, where glacial valley and ancient forests overfill the windshield scenery. Go climb a rock, pitch a tent or photograph wildflowers and wildlife.

TRIP HIGHLIGHTS

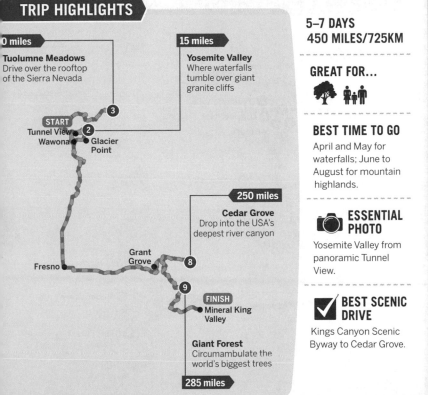

0 miles

Tuolumne Meadows
Drive over the rooftop of the Sierra Nevada

15 miles

Yosemite Valley
Where waterfalls tumble over giant granite cliffs

START
Tunnel View
Wawona
Glacier Point

250 miles

Cedar Grove
Drop into the USA's deepest river canyon

Grant Grove

Fresno

FINISH
Mineral King Valley

Giant Forest
Circumambulate the world's biggest trees

285 miles

**5–7 DAYS
450 MILES/725KM**

GREAT FOR...

BEST TIME TO GO

April and May for waterfalls; June to August for mountain highlands.

ESSENTIAL PHOTO

Yosemite Valley from panoramic Tunnel View.

BEST SCENIC DRIVE

Kings Canyon Scenic Byway to Cedar Grove.

205

19

Yosemite, Sequoia & Kings Canyon National Parks

Glacier-carved valleys resting below dramatic peaks make Yosemite an all-ages playground. Here you can witness earth-shaking waterfalls, clamber up granite domes and camp out in high-country meadows where wildflowers bloom in summer. Home to the USA's deepest canyon and the biggest tree on the planet, Sequoia & Kings Canyon National Park justify detouring further south into the Sierra Nevada, which conservationist John Muir called 'The Range of Light.'

❶ Tunnel View

Arriving in **Yosemite National Park** (📞20 9-372-0200; www.nps. gov/yose; 7-day pass per car $20; 🚻) at the Arch Rock entrance station, follow Hwy 140 east. Pull over at **Tunnel View** for your first look into Yosemite Valley, which has inspired painters, poets, naturalists and adventurers for centuries. On the right, Bridalveil Fall swells with snowmelt in late spring, but by late summer, it's a mere whisper, often lifted and blown aloft by the wind. Spread below you are the pine forests and meadows of the valley

LINK YOUR TRIP

20 Eastern Sierra Scenic Byway

From Yosemite's Tuolumne Meadows, roll over high-elevation Tioga Pass and downhill towards Mono Lake, a 20-mile trip.

25 Highway 99 Through Central Valley

En route between Yosemite and Kings Canyon National Parks, you'll intersect sun-baked historic Hwy 99, just northwest of Reedley.

floor, with the sheer face of El Capitan rising on the left, and in the distance straight ahead, iconic granite Half Dome.

The Drive » Merge carefully onto Wawona Rd, which continues downhill into Yosemite Valley, full of confusingly intersecting one way roads. Drive east along the Merced River on Southside Dr past the Bridalveil Fall turnoff. Almost 6 miles from Tunnel View, turn left and drive across Sentinel Bridge to Yosemite Village's day-use parking lots. Ride free shuttle buses that circle the valley.

TRIP HIGHLIGHT

❷ Yosemite Valley

From the bottom looking up, this dramatic valley cut by the meandering Merced River is song-inspiring, and not just for birds: rippling meadow grasses; tall pines; cool, impassive pools reflecting granite monoliths; and cascading, glacier-cold whitewater ribbons. At busy **Yosemite Village**, start inside the **Yosemite Valley Visitor Center** (🕘9am-6pm late Jun-early Sep, shorter off-peak hr; 🚻), with its thought-provoking history and nature displays and free *Spirit of Yosemite* film screenings. At the nearby **Yosemite Museum** (🕘9am-5pm), Western landscape paintings are hung beside Native American baskets and beaded clothing.

The valley's famous waterfalls are thunderous

cataracts in May, but mere trickles by late July. Triple-tiered **Yosemite Falls** is North America's tallest, while **Bridalveil Fall** is hardly less impressive. A strenuous, often slippery staircase beside **Vernal Fall** leads you, gasping, right to the top edge of the waterfall, where rainbows pop in clouds of mist. Keep hiking up the same Mist Trail to the top of **Nevada Fall** for a heady 5.5-mile round-trip trek.

In midsummer, you can rent a raft at Curry Village and float down the **Merced River**. The serene stretch between Stoneman Bridge and Sentinel Beach is gentle enough for kids. Or take the whole family to see the stuffed wildlife mounts at the hands-on **Nature Center at Happy Isles** (🕘10am-4pm late May-Sep; 🚻), east of Curry Village.

🍴 📖 p214

The Drive » From Yosemite Village, drive west on Northside Dr, passing Yosemite Falls and El Capitan. After 6 miles, turn right onto Big Oak Flat Rd/Hwy 120. For almost 10 miles, the road curves above the valley into the forest. Near Crane Flat gas station, turn right to follow Tioga Rd/Hwy 120 east (open summer and fall only). Continuing straight ahead, Big Oak Flat Rd/ Hwy 120 west exits the park, leading past the turnoff to Hetch Hetchy (p214) and Evergreen Lodge.

Classic Trip

TRIP HIGHLIGHT

❸ Tuolumne Meadows

Leave the crushing crowds of Yosemite Valley behind and escape to the Sierra Nevada high country along Tioga Rd, which follows a 19th-century wagon road and Native American trading route. **Warning!** Completely closed by snow in winter, Tioga Rd is usually open *only* from May or June through October.

About 45 miles from Yosemite Valley, stop at **Olmsted Point**. Overlooking a lunar-type landscape of glaciated granite, gaze deeply down Tenaya Canyon to the backside of Half Dome. A few miles further east, a sandy half-moon beach wraps around **Tenaya Lake**, tempting you to brave some of the coldest swimming in the park. Sunbathers lie upon the rocks that rim the lake's northern shore.

About a 90-minute drive from Yosemite Valley, **Tuolumne Meadows** is the Sierra Nevada's largest subalpine meadow, with fields of wildflowers, bubbling streams, ragged granite peaks and cooler temperatures at an elevation of 8600ft. Hikers and climbers find a paradise of trails and granite domes to tackle, or unpack a picnic basket by the stream-fed meadows.

🍴 🛏 p214

**The Drive ›› ** From Tuolumne Meadows, backtrack 50 miles to Yosemite Valley, turning left on El Portal Rd, then right on Northside Dr and right again on Wawona Rd. Follow narrow Wawona Rd/Hwy 41 up out of the valley. After 9 miles, turn

---

HIKING HALF DOME & AROUND YOSEMITE VALLEY

Over 800 miles of hiking trails in Yosemite National Park fit hikers of all abilities. Take an easy half-mile stroll on the valley floor or underneath giant sequoia trees, or venture out all day on a quest for viewpoints, waterfalls and lakes in the mountainous high country.

Some of the park's most popular hikes start right in Yosemite Valley, including to the top of **Half Dome** (17-mile round-trip), the most famous of all. It follows a section of the John Muir Trail and is strenuous, difficult and best tackled in two days with an overnight in Little Yosemite Valley. Reaching the top can only be done in summer after park rangers have installed fixed cables; depending on snow conditions, this may occur as early as late May or as late as July and the cables usually come down in October. To limit the cables' notorious human logjams, the park now requires permits for day hikers, but the route is still nerve-wracking as hikers must share the cables. **Advance permits** (☎877-444-6777; www.recreation.gov) go on sale by lottery in early spring, with a limited number available via another lottery two days in advance. Permit regulations and prices keep changing; check the park website (http://www.nps.gov/yose) for current details.

The less ambitious or physically fit will still have a ball following the **Mist Trail** as far as Vernal Fall (3-mile round-trip), the top of Nevada Fall (6-mile round-trip) or idyllic Little Yosemite Valley (8-mile round-trip). The **Four Mile Trail** (9-mile round-trip) up to Glacier Point is a strenuous but satisfying climb to a glorious viewpoint. If you've got the kids in tow, nice and easy **valley walks** include to Mirror Lake (2-mile round-trip) and viewpoints at the base of thundering Yosemite Falls (1-mile round-trip) and lacy Bridalveil Fall (0.5-mile round-trip).

WINTER WONDERLANDS

When the temperature drops and the white stuff falls, there are still tons of fun outdoor activities around the Sierra Nevada's national parks. In Yosemite, strap on some skis or a snowboard and go tubing downhill at Badger Pass; plod around Yosemite Valley or to Dewey Point on a ranger-led snowshoe tour; or just try to stay upright on ice skates at Curry Village. Further south in Sequoia & Kings Canyon National Park, the whole family can go snowshoeing or cross-country skiing among groves of giant sequoias. Before embarking on a winter trip to the parks, check road conditions on the official park websites or by calling ahead. Don't forget to put snow tires on your car, and always carry tire chains too.

left onto Glacier Point Rd at the Chinquapin intersection, driving 15 more miles to Glacier Point.

- - - - - - - - - - - - -

④ Glacier Point

In only an hour, you can zip from Yosemite Valley up to head-spinning Glacier Point. **Warning!** Glacier Point is closed by snow in winter, usually not opening again until May. Between November and April, the road remains open as far as Badger Pass ski area, but snow tires and tire chains may be required.

Rising over 3000ft above the valley floor, dramatic **Glacier Point** (7214ft) practically puts you at eye level with Half Dome. Glimpse what John Muir and US President Teddy Roosevelt saw when they camped here in 1903: the waterfall-strewn Yosemite Valley below and the distant peaks ringing Tuolumne Meadows. To get away from the crowds, hike a little way down the Panorama Trail, just

south of the crowded main viewpoint.

On your way back from Glacier Point, take time out for a 2-mile hike up **Sentinel Dome** or out to **Taft Point** for incredible 360-degree valley views.

🛏 p215

The Drive » Drive back downhill past Badger Pass, turning left at the Chinquapin intersection and winding south through thick forest on Wawona Rd/Hwy 41. After almost 13 curvy miles, you'll reach Wawona, with its hotel, visitor center, general store and gas station, all on your left.

- - - - - - - - - - - - -

⑤ Wawona

At Wawona, a 45-minute drive south of the valley, drop by the **Pioneer Yosemite History Center**, with its covered bridge, pioneer-era buildings and historic Wells Fargo office. In summer you can take a short, bumpy stagecoach ride and really feel like you're living in the past. Peek inside the **Wawona Visitor Center** (☉8:30am-5pm mid-May–late Nov)

at 19th-century artist Thomas Hill's recreated studio, hung with romantic Sierra Nevada landscape paintings. On summer evenings, imbibe a civilized cocktail in the lobby lounge of the Wawona Hotel, where pianist Tom Bopp plays tunes from Yosemite's bygone days.

🛏 p215

The Drive » In summer, leave your car at Wawona and take a free shuttle bus to Mariposa Grove. By car, follow Wawona Rd/Hwy 41 south for 4.5 miles to the four-way stop by the park's south entrance. Continue straight ahead on Mariposa Rd (closed in winter) for 3.5 miles to the parking lot – when it's full, drivers are turned away.

- - - - - - - - - - - - -

⑥ Mariposa Grove

Wander giddily around the Mariposa Grove, home of the 1800-year-old Grizzly Giant and 500 other giant sequoias that tower above your head. Nature trails wind through this popular grove, but you can only hear yourself think above

GALEN ROWELL / CORBIS ©

GALEN ROWELL / CORBIS ©

LOCAL KNOWLEDGE
SCHUYLER
GREENLEAF

Director of Projects
for Yosemite Conservancy

For a family-friendly hike (no little kids, though) off Tioga Rd, take the recently rehabilitated trail up Mt Hoffman. About 2.5 miles long, the trail takes you past May Lake, where you can take a dip either before or after your hike. When you're standing on top of Mt Hoffman, you're at the geographical center of Yosemite National Park with spectacular views all around, including of the Tuolumne River canyon.

Top: John Muir Trail, Yosemite Valley
Left: Tuolumne Meadows
Right: Woman standing in sequoia trunk, Sequoia National Park

the noise of vacationing crowds and motorized tram tours during the early morning or evening. Notwithstanding a cruel hack job back in 1895, the walk-through California Tunnel Tree continues to survive, so pose your family in front and snap away. If you've got the energy for a 5-mile round-trip hike to the upper grove, the **Mariposa Grove Museum** (⊘10am-4pm May-Sep) has displays about sequoia ecology inside a pioneer cabin.

The Drive » From Yosemite's south entrance station, it's a 120-mile, three-hour trip to Kings Canyon National Park. Follow Hwy 41 south 60 miles to Fresno, then slingshot east on Hwy 180 for another 50 miles, climbing out of the Central Valley back into the mountains. Keep left at the Hwy 198 intersection, staying on Hwy 180 towards Grant Grove.

- - - - - - - - - - - -

❼ Grant Grove

Through **Sequoia & Kings Canyon National Park** (☏559-565-3341; www.nps.gov/seki; 7-day pass per car $20; ♿), roads seem barely to scratch the surface of the twin parks' beauty. To see real treasures, you'll need to get out and stretch your legs. North of Big Stump entrance station in Grant Grove Village, turn left and wind downhill to **General Grant Grove**, where you'll see some of the park's landmark

giant sequoia trees along a paved path. You can walk right through the Fallen Monarch, a massive, fire-hollowed trunk that's done duty as a cabin, hotel, saloon and horse stable. For views of Kings Canyon and the peaks of the Great Western Divide, follow a narrow, winding side road (closed in winter, no RVs or trailers) starting behind John Muir Lodge up to **Panoramic Point**.

🛏 p215

The Drive » Kings Canyon National Park's main visitor areas, Grant Grove and Cedar Grove, are linked by narrow, twisting Hwy 180, which dramatically descends into Kings Canyon. Expect spectacular views all along this outstandingly scenic 30-mile drive. **Warning!** Hwy 180 from the Hume Lake turnoff to Cedar Grove is closed during winter (usually mid-November through mid-April).

- - - - - - - - - - - -

TRIP HIGHLIGHT

❽ Cedar Grove

Serpentining past chiseled rock walls laced with waterfalls, Hwy 180 plunges down to the Kings River, where roaring whitewater ricochets off the granite cliffs of North America's deepest canyon, technically speaking. Pull over partway down at **Junction View overlook** for an eyeful, then keep rolling along the river to **Cedar Grove Village**. East of the village, **Zumwalt Meadow** is the place for spotting birds, mule deer and black bears. If the day is hot and your suit is handy, stroll from Road's End to **Muir Rock**, a large flat-top river boulder where John Muir once gave outdoor talks, now a popular summer swimming hole. Starting from Road's End, a very popular day hike climbs 4 miles each way to roaring **Mist Falls**.

🛏 p215

The Drive » Backtrack from Road's End nearly 30 miles up Hwy 180. Turn left onto Hume Lake Rd. Curve around the lake past swimming beaches, turning right onto 10 Mile Rd, which runs by US Forest Service (USFS) campgrounds. At Hwy 198, turn left and follow the Generals Hwy (sometimes closed in winter) south for about 23 miles to the Wolverton Rd turn-off on your left.

- - - - - - - - - - - -

TRIP HIGHLIGHT

❾ Giant Forest

We dare you to try hugging the trees in **Giant Forest**, a 3-sq-mile grove protecting the park's most gargantuan specimens. Park off Wolverton Rd and walk downhill to reach the world's biggest living tree, the **General Sherman Tree**, which towers 275ft into the sky. With sore arms and sticky sap fingers, you can lose the crowds on any of many forested trails nearby. The trail network stretches all the way south to Crescent Meadow, a 5-mile one-way ramble.

By car, drive 2.5 miles south along the Generals Hwy to get schooled on

---

➡ DETOUR: BUCK ROCK LOOKOUT

Start: ❽ **Cedar Grove**

To climb one of California's most evocative fire lookouts, drive east of the Generals Hwy on Big Meadows Rd into the Sequoia National Forest between between Grant Grove and the Giant Forest. Follow the signs to staffed **Buck Rock Lookout** (www.buckrock.org; Forest Rd 13S04; admission free; ☺ usually 9:30am-6pm Jul-Oct). Constructed in 1923, this active fire lookout allows panoramic views from a dollhouse-sized cab lording over the horizon from 8500ft atop a granite rise, reached by 172 spindly stairs. It's not for anyone with vertigo!

sequoia ecology and fire cycles at the **Giant Forest Museum** (⊙ usually 9am–5pm or 6pm mid-May–mid-Oct; 🅿). Across the highway, **Beetle Rock Education Center** (⊙ call for hr, usually open Jun-Aug; 🅿) lets kids ogle bugs, taxidermied wildlife and (fake) animal poop.

Starting outside the museum, Crescent Meadow Rd makes a 6-mile loop out through Giant Forest, passing right through the **Tunnel Log**. For 360-degree views of the Great Western Divide, climb the steep quarter-mile staircase up **Moro Rock**. **Warning!** Crescent Meadow Rd is closed to traffic by winter snow; during summer, ride the free shuttle buses around the loop road rather than driving yourself.

✕ 🛏 p215

The Drive ›› Narrowing, the Generals Hwy drops for almost 20 miles into the Sierra Nevada foothills, passing Amphitheatre Point and exiting the park beyond Foothills Visitor Center. Before reaching the town of Three Rivers, turn left on Mineral King Rd, a dizzyingly scenic 25-mile road (partly unpaved, no trailers or RVs allowed) that switchbacks up to Mineral King Valley.

DETOUR: CRYSTAL CAVE

Start: ❾ Giant Forest

Off the Generals Hwy, about 2 miles south of the Giant Forest Museum, turn right onto twisting 6.5-mile-long Crystal Cave Rd for a fantastical walk inside 10,000-year-old **Crystal Cave** (www.sequoiahistory.org; tours adult/child from $13/7; ⊙ usually 10:30am-4:30pm mid-May–Oct; 🅿), carved by an underground river. Stalactites hang like daggers from the ceiling, and 10,000-year-old milky-white marble formations take the shape of ethereal curtains, domes, columns and shields. Bring a light jacket – it's 50°F inside the cave. You must buy tour tickets in advance from the Lodgepole or Foothills Visitor Centers.

---

❿ Mineral King Valley

Navigating over 700 hairpin turns, it's a winding 1½-hour drive up to the glacially sculpted **Mineral King Valley** (7500ft), a 19th-century silver-mining camp and lumber settlement, and later a mountain retreat. Trailheads into the high country begin at the end of Mineral King Rd, where historic private cabins dot the valley floor flanked by massive mountains. Your final destination is just over a mile past the ranger station, where the valley unfolds all of its hidden beauty, and hikes to granite peaks and alpine lakes beckon.

Warning! Mineral King Rd is typically open only from late May through late October. In early summer, marmots like to chew on parked cars, so wrap the undercarriage of your vehicle with a tarp or stake chicken-wire fencing (which can be rented from Silver City Resort) around the outside.

Eating & Sleeping

Yosemite Valley ②

✖ Degnan's Deli   Deli $

(www.yosemitepark.com; Yosemite Village; mains $6-10; ⊘7am-5pm; ⬤) Grab a custom-made deli sandwich and bag of chips before hitting the trail. Not far away, the Village Store sells groceries, snacks and camping supplies until 8pm or later.

✖ Mountain Room Restaurant   American $$

(www.yosemitepark.com; Yosemite Lodge at the Falls; mains $18-35; ⊘5:30-9:30pm; ⬤) Cut into grass-fed steaks, river trout and organic veggies at this no-reservations dining room with waterfall views. A few steps away, the fireplace lounge serves microbrews and snacks.

🛏 Ahwahnee   Historic Hotel $$$

(☏209-372-1407, reservations 801-559-4884; www.yosemitepark.com; Ahwahnee Rd; r from $445; ❄@🛜🏊⬤) Charlie Chaplin, Eleanor Roosevelt and JFK have each slept at this 1927 National Historic Landmark. Sit a spell by the roaring fireplace beneath sugar-pine timbers. Skip the formal dining room (except at Sunday brunch) for cocktails in the lobby.

🛏 Curry Village & Housekeeping Camp   Cabin, Cottage $$

(☏reservations 801-559-4884; www.yosemitepark.com; off Southside Dr; tent cabins $100-125, hard-sided cabins & r $160-220; 🏊⬤) With a noisy summer-camp ambience, hundreds of helter-skelter tent cabins scatter beneath evergreens and beside the valley's Merced River.

🛏 Yosemite Bug Rustic Mountain Resort   Cabin, Hostel $

(☏209-966-6666; www.yosemitebug.com; 6979 Hwy 140; dm $22-25, tent cabins $55-75, r $85-195; @🛜🔑⬤🐾) In the forest about 25 miles

west of Yosemite Valley, this mountain hostelry hosts globetrotters who dig the clean rooms, yoga studio, hot-tub spa, shared kitchen and vegetarian-friendly cafe (mains from $5 to $18).

🛏 Yosemite Valley Campgrounds   Campground $

(☏reservations 877-444-6777; www.recreation.gov; campsites $20; ⊘most Apr-Sep, some year-round; ⬤🐾) Comparatively quieter North Pines Campground offers some riverside sites, while Upper and Lower Pines Campgrounds are busy and crammed. Reserve campsites online up to five months in advance.

Hetch Hetchy

🛏 Evergreen Lodge   Cabin, Camping $$

(☏209-379-2606, 800-935-6343; www.evergreenlodge.com; 33160 Evergreen Rd; tents $75-100, cabins $170-370; @🛜🏊⬤) Outside Yosemite's northwest entrance near Hetch Hetchy Reservoir, this classic mountain resort foregoes roughing it for deluxe cabins and tents. Outdoor recreational activities abound. There's a general store, a tavern with a pool table and a restaurant (mains from $10 to $28) serving three hearty meals a day.

Tuolumne Meadows ③

✖ Tuolumne Meadows Grill   American $

(Tioga Rd; mains $4-9; ⊘8am-5pm mid-Jun–mid-Sep) Scarf down burgers and grill items, breakfast sammiches and soft-serve ice cream at the picnic tables outside this summertime tent-topped eatery. The general store stays open till 8pm.

🛏 Tuolumne Meadows & White Wolf Lodges   Cabin $$

(☏reservations 801-559-4884; www.yosemitepark.com; Tioga Rd; tent cabins

$100-130; ⊙mid-Jun–mid-Sep; ♿) In the high country away from the hubbub of the valley, these canvas tent cabins without electricity (bring a flashlight!) are always in demand. Both camps offer breakfast, boxed lunches and dinner by reservation.

🛏 Tuolumne Meadows Campground
Campground $

(📞reservations 877-444-6777; www.recreation. gov; Tioga Rd; campsites $20; ⊙mid-Jul–late Sep; ♿🚻) At the park's biggest campground, 300-plus sites are decently spaced through the shady forest. Good news if you didn't book ahead: half are first-come, first-serve.

Glacier Point ❹

🛏 Bridalveil Creek Campground
Campground $

(www.nps.gov/yose; Glacier Point Rd; campsites $14; ⊙mid-Jul–mid-Sep; ♿🚻) When the day ends, retreat to your own tent at this no-reservations campground shaded by pine forest. At 7200ft, nights can be chilly.

Wawona ❺

🛏 Wawona Hotel
Historic Hotel $$

(📞209-375-6556, reservations 801-559-4884; www.yosemitepark.com; Wawona Rd; r shared/ private bath incl breakfast from $155/225; ⊙Apr-late Nov & mid-Dec–Jan 1; 🛜🎱♿) Full of character, this Victorian-era throwback has wide porches with Adirondack chairs, manicured lawns and a golf course. Some of the thin-walled rooms, none of which have phones or TVs, share baths. A lamp-lit dining room serves classic American cooking (mains $12 to $30).

Grant Grove ❼

🛏 Grant Grove Campgrounds
Campground $

(www.nps.gov/seki; Hwy 180; campsites $10-18; ⊙most May-Sep, some year-round; ♿🚻) All of Grant Grove's no-reservations campgrounds are shaded by evergreens. Crystal Springs is quieter than Sunset; Azalea stays open during winter.

🛏 John Muir Lodge & Grant Grove Cabins
Hotel, Cabin $$

(📞559-335-5500; www.sequoia-kingscanyon. com; Hwy 180; d $70-195; 🛜) This woodsy lodge has a cozy fireplace lobby with board games and wi-fi. Oddly assorted cabins range from thin-walled canvas tents to historical cottages. The back-porch pizza parlor and general store nearby will keep you from starving.

Cedar Grove ❽

🛏 Cedar Grove Campgrounds
Campground $

(www.nps.gov/seki; Hwy 180; campsites $18; ⊙usually late Apr–mid-Nov; ♿🚻) Slumber creekside at Sheep Creek Campground or at Sentinel Campground next to the ranger station. Sunny campsites are found further east at Moraine and tent-only Canyon View.

🛏 Cedar Grove Lodge
Motel $$

(📞559-335-5500; www.sequoia-kingscanyon. com; Hwy 180; r $120-140; ⊙mid-May–mid-Oct; ❄🛜) This riverside lodge offers 21 rooms (no TVs), some with air-con, shady patios and kitchenettes. Check in downstairs at the market, next to the snack bar and grill (mains $6 to $12).

Giant Forest ❾

🍴 Lodgepole Market
Self-Catering, Deli $

(www.visitsequoia.com; Lodgepole Village; mains $6-10; ⊙mid-Apr–mid-Oct, seasonal hr vary) Inside the general store selling groceries and camping supplies, a fast-food deli sells picnic fare like focaccia sandwiches and salads.

🛏 Lodgepole Campground
Campground $

(📞877-444-6777; www.recreation.gov; Lodgepole Village; campsites $10-20; ⊙May-Nov; ♿🚻) On the Kaweah River, Sequoia's biggest and busiest campground shoehorns in tents and RVs.

🛏 Wuksachi Lodge
Hotel $$$

(📞559-565-4070; www.visitsequoia.com; 64740 Wuksachi Way, off Generals Hwy; r $215-350; 🛜) Sequoia's most upscale lodging and dining option. The dining room (mains $12 to $40) has an inviting stone fireplace and forest views, but the motel-style rooms are charmless.

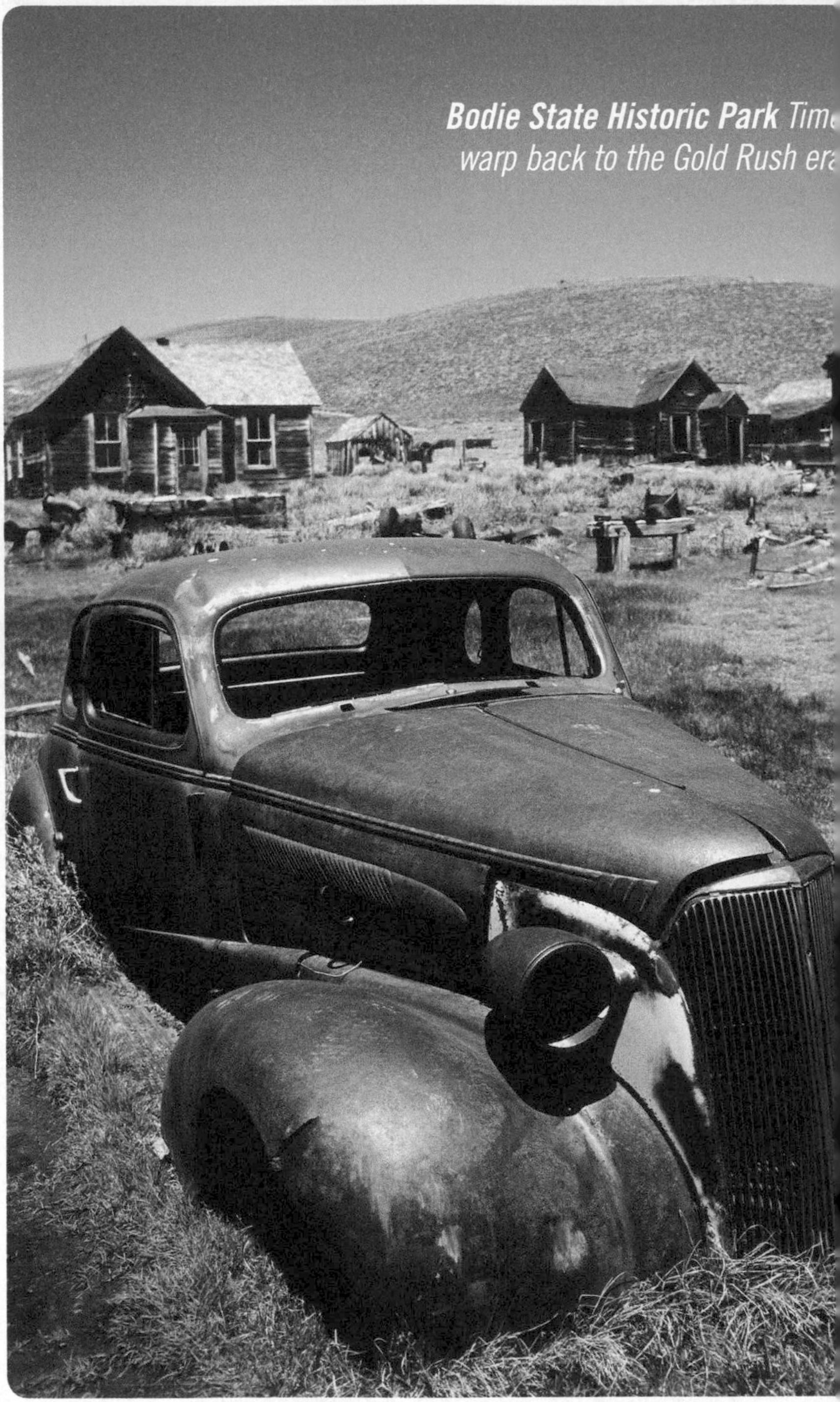

Bodie State Historic Park *Tim*
warp back to the Gold Rush er

Eastern Sierra Scenic Byway

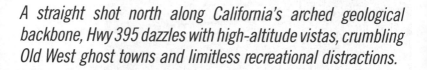

20

A straight shot north along California's arched geological backbone, Hwy 395 dazzles with high-altitude vistas, crumbling Old West ghost towns and limitless recreational distractions.

TRIP HIGHLIGHTS

FINISH Reno

Carson City

Bridgeport **10**

170 miles **9**

Mono Lake
An eerie blue desert basin sprouting towers of tufa

7 **6**

Bishop

130 miles

Reds Meadow
Shuttle to an ancient volcanic formation and a splendid waterfall

Lone Pine
START

195 miles

Bodie State Historic Park
A haunting and solitary Wild West ghost town

115 miles

Mammoth Lakes
A snow-sports resort with summertime mountain biking

3–5 DAYS
360 MILES/580KM

GREAT FOR...

BEST TIME TO GO
June to September for warm days and (mostly) snow-free mountain ramblings.

 ESSENTIAL PHOTO

Sunrise or sunset at Alabama Hills, framed by the snowy Sierra Nevada.

✓ BEST FOR OUTDOORS

Hike tranquil mountain trails and camp in Mammoth Lakes.

217

20 Eastern Sierra Scenic Byway

The gateway to California's largest expanse of wilderness, Hwy 395 – also called the Eastern Sierra Scenic Byway – borders towering mountain vistas, glistening blue lakes and the seemingly endless forests of the Eastern Sierra. A lifetime of outdoor activities beckon beyond the asphalt, and desolate ghost towns, unique geological formations and burbling natural hot springs await exploration.

❶ Lone Pine

The diminutive town of Lone Pine stands as the southern gateway to the craggy jewels of the Eastern Sierra. In the southern end of town, drop by the **Museum of Lone Pine Film History** (☎760-876-9909; www.lonepinefilmhistorymuseum.org; 701 S Main St; admission $5; ⏱10am-6pm Mon-Sat, to 4pm Sun), which contains exhibits of paraphernalia from the over 450 movies shot in the area. Don't miss the 7pm screenings in its theater every Thursday and Friday or the tricked-out Cadillac convertible in its foyer.

Just outside the center of town on the Whitney Portal Rd, an orange otherworldly alpenglow makes the **Alabama Hills** a must for watching a slow-motion sunset. A frequent backdrop for movie Westerns and the *Lone Ranger* TV series, the rounded earthen-colored mounds stand out against the steely gray foothills and jagged pinnacles of the Sierra range, and a number of graceful rock arches are within easy hiking distance of the roads.

✗ p225

The Drive » From Lone Pine, the jagged incisors of the Sierra surge skyward in all their raw and fierce glory. Continue west past the Alabama Hills – a total of 13 miles from Hwy 395 – and then brace yourself for the

dizzying ascent to road's end. The White Mountains soar to the east, and the dramatic Owens Valley spreads below.

---

❷ Whitney Portal

At 14,505ft, the celestial granite giant of **Mt Whitney** (www.fs.usda. gov/inyo) stands as the loftiest peak in the Lower 48 and the obsession of thousands of high-country hikers every summer. Desperately coveted permits (assigned by advance lottery) are your only passport to the summit, though drop-in day-trippers can swan up the mountain as far as Lone Pine Lake – about 6 miles round-trip – to kick up some dust on the iconic Whitney Trail. Near the trailhead, stop by

🔗 LINK YOUR TRIP

19 Yosemite, Sequoia & Kings Canyon National Parks

In Lee Vining, go west on Hwy 120 to enter Yosemite National Park via the 9945ft Tioga Pass.

32 Life in Death Valley

From Lone Pine, head southeast on Hwys 136 and 190 to reach Panamint Springs, a western access point to the desiccated landscapes of Death Valley.

the cafe at the **Whitney Portal Store** (www. whitneyportalstore.com) for enormous burgers and plate-sized pancakes fit for ravenous hikers.

As you get a fix on this majestic megalith cradled by scores of smaller pinnacles, remember that the country's lowest point is only 80 miles (as the crow flies) east of here: Badwater (p333) in Death Valley.

The Drive » Double back to Lone Pine and drive 9 miles north on divided Hwy 395. Scrub brush and tumbleweed desert occupy the valley between the copper-colored foothills of the Sierra Nevada and the White Mountain range. Well-signed Manzanar sits along the west side of the highway.

❸ Manzanar National Historic Site

A monument to one of the darkest chapters in US history, the Manzanar unfolds across a barren and windy sweep of land cradled by snow-dipped peaks. During the height of WWII, the federal government interned more than 10,000 people of Japanese ancestry here following the attack on Pearl Harbor. Though little remains of the infamous war concentration camp, the camp's former high-school auditorium houses a superb **interpretive center** (760-878-2194; www.nps.gov/manz; admission

free; ⏱9am-4:30pm Nov-Mar, to 5:30pm Apr-Oct). Watch the 20-minute documentary, then explore the thought-provoking exhibits chronicling the stories of the families that languished here yet built a vibrant community. Afterwards, take a self-guided, 3.2-mile driving tour around the grounds, which includes a recreated mess hall and barracks, vestiges of buildings and gardens, as well as the haunting camp cemetery.

Often mistaken for Mt Whitney, 14,375ft Mt Williamson looms above this flat, dusty plain, a lonely expanse that bursts with yellow wildflowers in spring.

The Drive » Continue north 6 miles on Hwy 395 to the small town of Independence. In the center of town, look for the columned Inyo County Courthouse and turn left onto W Center St. Drive six blocks through a residential area to the end of the road.

❹ Independence

This sleepy highway town has been a county seat since 1866 and is home to the **Eastern California Museum** (760-878-0364; www. inyocounty.us/ecmuseum; 155 N Grant St; donation requested; ⏱10am-5pm). An excellent archive of Eastern Sierra history and culture, it contains one of the most complete collections of

Paiute and Shoshone baskets in the country, as well as historic photographs of local rock climbers scaling Sierra peaks – including Mt Whitney – with huge packs and no harnesses. Other highlights include artifacts from Manzanar and an exhibit about the fight to keep the region's water supply from being diverted to Los Angeles.

Fans of Mary Austin (1868–1934), renowned author of *The Land of Little Rain* and vocal foe of the desertification of the Owens Valley, can follow signs leading to her former house at **253 Market St**.

The Drive » Depart north along Hwy 395 as civilization again recedes amid a buffer of dreamy granite mountains, midsized foothills and (most of the year) an expanse of bright blue sky. Tuffs of blackened volcanic rock occasionally appear roadside. Pass through the blink-and-you-missed-it town of Big Pine, and enter Bishop approximately 40 miles from your starting point.

❺ Bishop

The second-largest town in the Eastern Sierra and about a third of the way north from Lone Pine to Reno, Bishop is a major hub for hikers, cyclists, anglers and climbers. To see what draws them here, visit the **Mountain Light Gallery** (760-873-7700; 106 S Main St; admission free; ⏱10am-6pm),

Mammoth Lakes Woman in hot springs

featuring the stunning outdoor photography of the late Galen Rowell, whose High Sierra images are some of the best in existence.

Where Hwy 395 swings west, continue north for 4.5 miles on Hwy 6 to reach the **Laws Railroad Museum & Historical Site** (☎760-873-5950; www. lawsmuseum.org; Silver Canyon Rd, Laws; donation $5; ☻10am-4pm; 🚻), a remnant of the narrow-gauge Carson and Colorado rail line that closed in 1960. Train buffs will hyperventilate over the collection of antique railcars, and kids love exploring the

1883 depot and clanging the brass bell. Dozens of historic buildings from the region reassembled with period artifacts to create a time-capsule village.

The Drive » Back on Hwy 395, continue 35 miles north to Hwy 203, passing Crowley Lake and the southern reaches of the Long Valley Caldera seismic hot spot. On Hwy 203 before the center of town, stop in at the Mammoth Lakes Welcome Center for excellent local and regional information.

- - - - - - - - - - -

TRIP HIGHLIGHT

❻ Mammoth Lakes

Splendidly situated at a breathless 8000ft,

Mammoth Lakes is an active year-round outdoor-recreation town buffered by alpine wilderness and punctuated by its signature 10,000ft peak, **Mammoth Mountain** (☎800-626-6684; www. mammothmountain.com; winter lift ticket adult $96, child 7-12 $30, child 13-18 $75, 1-day bike pass adult/child $43/22; 🚻). This ever-burgeoning resort complex has 3100 vertical feet – enough to whet any snow-sports appetite – and an enviably long season that often lasts from November to June.

When the snow finally melts, the ski and snowboard resort does a quick costume change and becomes the massive Mammoth Mountain Bike Park, and with a slew of mountainbikers decked out in body armor, it could be mistaken for a movie set of an apocalyptic *Mad Max* sequel. With more than 100 miles of well-tended single-track trails and a crazy terrain park, it draws those who know their knobby tires.

Year-round, a vertiginous **gondola** (adult $24, child 7-12 $8, child 13-18 $19) whisks sightseers to the apex for breathless views of snow-speckled mountaintops.

 p225

The Drive » Keep the car parked at Mammoth Mountain and catch the mandatory Reds Meadow shuttle bus from the Gondola Building. However, you may want to drive up 1.5 miles west and back on Hwy 203 as far as Minaret Vista to contemplate eye-popping views of the Ritter Range, the serrated Minarets and the remote reaches of Yosemite National Park.

TRIP HIGHLIGHT

❼ Reds Meadow

One of the most beautiful and varied landscapes near Mammoth is the Reds Meadow Valley, west of Mammoth Mountain. The most fascinating attraction in Reds Meadow is the surreal 10,000-year-old volcanic formation of **Devils Postpile National Monument**. The 60ft curtains of near-vertical, six-sided basalt columns formed when rivers of molten lava slowed, cooled and cracked with perplexing symmetry. This honeycomb design is best appreciated from atop the columns, reached by a short trail. The columns are an easy, half-mile hike from the **Devils Postpile Ranger Station** ([📞]760-934-2289; www.nps.gov/depo; ☺9am-5pm summer).

From the monument, a 2.5-mile hike passing through fire-scarred forest leads to the spectacular **Rainbow Falls**, where the San Joaquin River gushes over a 101ft basalt cliff. Chances of actually seeing a rainbow forming in the billowing mist are greatest at midday. The falls can also be reached via an easy 1.5-mile walk from the Reds Meadow shuttle stop.

The Drive » Back on Hwy 395, continue north to Hwy 158

DETOUR:
ANCIENT BRISTLECONE PINE FOREST

Start: ❹ Independence

For encounters with some of the earth's oldest living things, plan at least a half-day trip to the Ancient Bristlecone Pine Forest. These gnarled, otherworldly looking trees thrive above 10,000ft on the slopes of the seemingly inhospitable White Mountains, a parched and stark range that once stood even higher than the Sierra. The oldest tree – called Methuselah – is estimated to be over 4700 years old, beating even the Great Sphinx of Giza by about two centuries.

To reach the groves, take Hwy 168 east 12 miles from Big Pine to White Mountain Rd, then turn left (north) and climb the curvy road 10 miles to **Schulman Grove**, named for the scientist who first discovered the trees' biblical age in the 1950s. The entire trip takes about one hour one-way from Independence. There's access to self-guided trails, and a new solar-powered **visitors center** ([📞]760-873-2500; www.fs.usda.gov/inyo; per vehicle $5; ☺late May-Oct). White Mountain Rd is usually closed from November to April.

and pull out the camera for the alpine lake and peak vistas of the June Lake Loop.

- - - - - - - - - -

8 June Lake Loop

Under the shadow of massive Carson Peak (10,909ft), the stunning 14-mile June Lake Loop (Hwy 158) meanders through a picture-perfect horseshoe canyon, past the relaxed resort town of June Lake and four sparkling, fish-rich lakes: Grant, Silver, Gull and June. It's especially scenic in fall when the basin is ablaze with golden aspens, and hardy ice climbers scale its frozen waterfalls in winter.

June Lake is backed by the Ansel Adams Wilderness, which runs into Yosemite National Park. From Silver Lake, Gem and Agnew Lakes make spectacular day hikes, and boat rentals and horseback rides are available.

The Drive » Rejoin the highway, where the rounded Mono Craters dot the dry and scrubby eastern landscape and the Mono Lake Basin unfolds into view.

- - - - - - - - -

TRIP HIGHLIGHT

9 Mono Lake

North America's second-oldest lake is a quiet and mysterious expanse of deep blue water, whose glassy surface reflects jagged Sierra peaks, young volcanic cones and the unearthly tufa (too-fah) towers that make the lake so distinctive. Protruding from the water like drip sand castles, tufas form when calcium bubbles up from subterranean springs and combines with carbonate in the alkaline lake waters.

The salinity and alkaline levels are unfortunately too high for a pleasant swim. Instead, paddle a kayak or canoe around the weathered towers of tufa, drink in wide-open views of the Mono Craters volcanic field, and discreetly spy on the ospreys and water birds that live in this unique habitat.

For area information, the **Mono Basin Scenic Area Visitors Center** (📞760-647-3044; www.fs.usda.gov/inyo; Hwy 395, 🕐8am-5pm mid-Apr–Nov), a half a mile north of Lee Vining, has interpretive displays, a bookstore and a 20-minute movie about Mono Lake.

 p225

The Drive » Ten miles north of Lee Vining, Hwy 395 arrives at its highest point, Conway Summit (8148ft). Pull off at the vista point for awe-inspiring panoramas of Mono Lake, backed by the Mono Craters and June and Mammoth Mountains. Continue approximately 8 miles north, and go 13 miles east on high desert Hwy 270; the last 3 miles are unpaved.

- - - - - - - - - -

TRIP HIGHLIGHT

10 Bodie State Historic Park

For a time warp back to the Gold Rush era, swing by **Bodie** (📞760-647-6445; www.parks.ca.gov/bodie; Hwy 270; adult/child $7/5; 🕐9am-6pm Jun-Aug, to 3pm Sep-May), one of the West's most authentic and best-preserved ghost towns. Gold was discovered here in 1859, and the place grew from a bare-bones mining camp to a lawless boomtown of 10,000.

HOT SPRINGS

Nestled between the White Mountains and the Sierra Nevada near Mammoth is a tantalizing slew of natural pools with snow-capped panoramic views. When the high-altitude summer nights turn chilly and the coyotes cry, you'll never want to towel off. About 9 miles south of town, Benton Crossing Rd juts east off Hwy 395, accessing a delicious bounty of hot springs. For detailed directions and maps, pick up Matt Bischoff's excellent *Touring California and Nevada Hot Springs* or see www.mammothweb.com/recreation/hottubbing.cfm for directions to a few.

DETOUR: VIRGINIA CITY

Start: ⑩ Bodie State Historic Park

During the 1860s gold rush, Virginia City was a high-flying, rip-roaring Wild West boomtown. It was the site of the legendary Comstock Lode, a massive silver bonanza that began in 1859 and stands as one of the world's richest strikes. Some of the silver barons went on to become major players in California history, and much of San Francisco was built with the treasure dug up from the soil beneath the town. Mark Twain spent time in this raucous place during its heyday, and his eyewitness descriptions of mining life were published in *Roughing It*.

The high-elevation town is a National Historic Landmark, with a main street of Victorian buildings, wooden sidewalks, wacky saloons and small museums ranging from hokey to intriguing. On the main drag, C street, you'll find the **visitors center** (www.visitvirginiacitynv.com; 86 South C St; ☺10am-4pm). To see how the mining elite lived, stop by the **Mackay Mansion** (D St) and the **Castle** (B St).

From Carson City, go east on Hwy 50, and then another 7 miles via Hwy 341 and Hwy 342. Continuing on to Reno, wind through a spectacular 13 miles of high desert along Hwy 341 to rejoin Hwy 395, with another 7 miles to reach Reno.

Fights and murders occurred almost daily, fueled by liquor from 65 saloons, some of which doubled as brothels, gambling halls or opium dens.

The hills disgorged some $35 million worth of gold and silver in the 1870s and '80s, but when production plummeted, Bodie was abandoned, and about 200 weather-beaten buildings now sit frozen in time in this cold, barren and windswept valley. Peering through dusty windows you'll see stocked stores, furnished homes, a schoolhouse with desks and books, the jail and many other buildings. The former Miners' Union Hall now houses a **museum** and **visitors center** (☺9am-1hr before park closes), and rangers conduct free general tours.

The Drive » Retrace your way back to Hwy 395, where you'll soon come to the big sky settlement of Bridgeport. From there, it's approximately two hours to Reno along a lovely two-lane section of the highway that traces the bank of the snaking Walker River.

- - - - - - - - - - - -

⑪ Reno

Nevada's second-largest city has steadily carved a noncasino niche as an all-season outdoor-recreation spot. The Truckee River bisects the heart of the high mountain-ringed city, and in the heat of summer, the **Truckee River Whitewater Park** teems with urban kayakers and swimmers bobbing along on inner tubes. Two kayak courses wrap around Wingfield Park, a small river island that hosts free concerts in summertime. **Tahoe Whitewater Tours** (☎775-787-5000; www.gowhitewater.com) and **Sierra Adventures** (☎866-323-8928; www.wildsierra.com) offer kayak trips and lessons.

 p225

Eating & Sleeping

Lone Pine ❶

✖ Alabama Hills Café & Bakery Diner $

(111 W Post St; mains $8-12; ⊙6am-2pm Mon-Fri, 7am-2pm Sat & Sun; ♪) Swing by early in the morning to line up for lumberjack-sized breakfasts (think eggs with corned-beef hash, or whole-grain pancakes), then grab a deli sandwich stacked on home-baked bread for a trailside lunch or linger for the hearty soups and scratch-made fruit pies.

Mammoth Lakes ❻

⊨ Tamarack Lodge & Resort Resort $$

(☎760-934-2442, 800-626-6684; www.tamaracklodge.com; lodge r $99-169, cabins $169-599; @🗢🐾) A charming year-round hideaway on the forested shore of Lower Twin Lake, its 1924 lodge building sports a dozen cozy homespun rooms with creaky floors, and the wood-beamed lobby is a spiffy setting for a nighttime book by the fireplace. Privacy-seekers can choose between cabins ranging from the very simple to simply deluxe.

⊨ USFS campgrounds Campground $

(☎877-444-6777; www.recreation.gov; tent & RV sites $21; 🐾; ⊙mid-Jun–mid-Sep) Sleep under the twinkling stars at one of the dozen or so 15 US Forest Service (USFS) campgrounds (see 'Recreation' at www.fs.usda.gov/inyo) scattered in and around Mammoth Lakes. Many sites are available on a first-come, first-served basis, and some are reservable, and all have flush toilets but no showers.

Mono Lake ❾

✖ Whoa Nellie Deli Deli $$

(www.whoanelliedeli.com; near junction of Hwys 120W & 395, Lee Vining; mains $8-19; ⊙7am-9pm mid-Apr–Oct) Great food in a gas station? Come on… No, really, you gotta try this amazing kitchen where chef Matt 'Tioga' Toomey feeds delicious fish tacos, wild-buffalo meatloaf and other tasty morsels to locals and clued-in passersby. Portions are huge and the views from the outdoor patio are as great as the food.

⊨ Yosemite Gateway Motel Motel $$

(☎760-647-6467; www.yosemitegatewaymotel.com; Hwy 395, Lee Vining; r $169; 🗢) Think vistas. This is the only motel on the east side of the highway, and the views from some of the rooms are phenomenal.

Reno ⓫

✖ Silver Peak Restaurant & Brewery Pub $$

(www.silverpeakbrewery.com; 124 Wonder St; mains lunch $8-10, dinner $9-21; ⊙11am-midnight) Casual and pretense-free, this place hums with the chatter of happy locals settling in for a night of microbrews and great food, from pizza with roasted chicken to shrimp pasta and filet mignon.

⊨ Peppermill Casino Hotel $$

(☎775-826-2121; www.peppermillreno.com; 2707 S Virginia St; r Sun-Thu $50-140, Fri & Sat $70-200; 🎴@🗢🏊) Awash in Vegas-style opulence, the popular Peppermill boasts Tuscan-themed rooms in its newest 600-room tower, and is completing a plush remodel of its older rooms. The three sparkling pools (one indoor) are dreamy, with a full spa on hand. Geothermal energy powers the resort's hot water and heat.

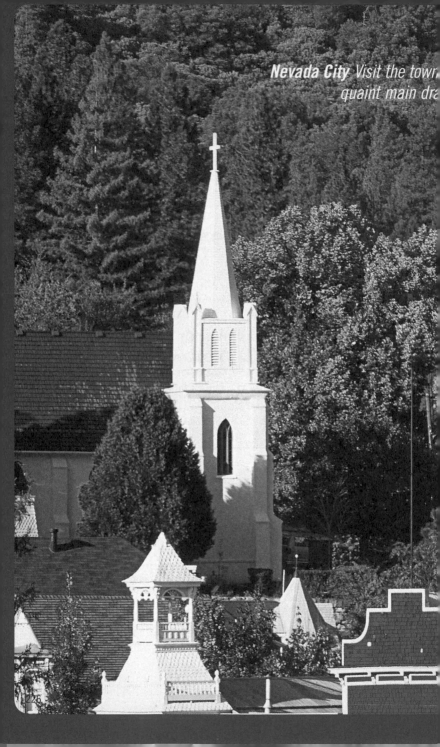

Nevada City *Visit the town*
quaint main dra

Classic Trip

Highway 49 Through Gold Country

21

There's plenty to see on winding Hwy 49; a trip through Gold Country shows off California's early days, when hell-raising prospectors and ruffians rushed helter-skelter into the West.

TRIP HIGHLIGHTS

FINISH ⑨ ━━━ **160 miles**

Around Nevada City
Explore Empire Mine, then take a dip

Auburn

⑧ **115 miles**

Placerville

Coloma
Eureka! Discover gold on the American River

miles

⑥

mador County Wine ountry
un-loving red wines om old vines

Sutter Creek
Jackson

miles

olumbia
rip back in time to the old Rush's heyday

② Sonora
START

3–4 DAYS
200 MILES/325KM

GREAT FOR..:

BEST TIME TO GO
April to October for sunny skies.

ESSENTIAL PHOTO
Sutter's Mill, California's original gold discovery site.

BEST FOR SWIMMING
South Yuba River State Park.

Classic Trip

Highway 49 Through Gold Country

21

When you roll into Gold Country on a sunny afternoon, the promise of adventure recalls the days when headlines screamed about gold discoveries and the Golden State was born. Today this rural region offers different cultural riches: exploring crumbling false-front saloons, rusting machines that once moved mountains and an endless parade of patinaed bronze historical markers along Hwy 49, one of California's most enchantingly scenic byways.

① Sonora

Settled in 1848 by Mexican miners, Sonora soon became a cosmopolitan center with ornate saloons for gamblers, drunkards and gold diggers. Its downtown district is so well preserved that it's frequently a location for Hollywood films such as Clint Eastwood's *Unforgiven*. Likewise, **Railtown 1897 State Historic Park** (☏209-984-3953; www.railtown1897.org, www.parks.ca.gov; 18115 5th Ave, Jamestown; museum adult/child $5/3, incl train ride $13/6; ☺9:30am-4:30pm Thu-Mon Apr-Oct, 10am-3pm Thu-Mon Nov-Mar, train rides 11am-3pm Sat & Sun Apr-Oct; ♠) and the surrounding hills of **Jamestown**, about 4 miles southeast of Sonora along Hwy 49, have been a backdrop for over 200 Western films and TV shows including *High Noon*. There's a lyrical romance to the historical railway yard, where orange poppies bloom among the rusting shells of steel goliaths and you can board the

narrow-gauge railroad that once transported ore, lumber and miners.

 p235

The Drive » Follow Hwy 49 just over 2 miles north of Sonora, then turn right onto Parrots Ferry Rd at the sign for Columbia. The state historic park is 2 miles further along this two-lane country road.

- - - - - - - - - - -

TRIP HIGHLIGHT

2 Columbia

Grab some suspenders and a floppy hat for **Columbia State Historic Park** (☏209-588-9128; www. parks.ca.gov/columbia; 11255 Jackson St; admission free; ☉museum 10am-4pm, most businesses till 5pm; 👭👪), near the so-called 'Gem of the Southern Mines.' It's like a miniature Gold-Rush Disneyland, but with more authenticity and heart. Four blocks

LINK YOUR TRIP

22 Ebbetts Pass Scenic Byway

From Columbia, take a winding 13-mile drive northeast via Parrots Ferry Rd and Hwy 4 to Murphys' wine country.

24 Lazy Delta Dawdle

Sacramento is an hour's drive or less from Gold Country towns such as Placerville via Hwy 50 and Auburn via I-80.

Classic Trip

of town have been preserved, where volunteers perambulate in 19th-century dress and demonstrate gold panning. The blacksmith's shop, theater, hotels and saloon are all carefully framed windows into California's past. The yesteryear illusion of Main St is shaken only a bit by fudge shops and the occasional banjo-picker whose cell phone rings.

🛏 p235

The Drive » Backtrack south on Parrots Ferry Rd, veering right and then turning right to stay on Springfield Rd for just over a mile. Rejoin Hwy 49 northbound, which crosses a long bridge over an artificial reservoir. After a dozen miles or so, Hwy 49 becomes Main St through Angels Camp.

❸ Angels Camp

On the southern stretch of Hwy 49, one literary giant looms over all other Western tall-tale tellers: Samuel Clemens, aka Mark Twain, who got his first big break with the short story *The Celebrated Jumping Frog of Calaveras County*, written and set in Angels Camp. With a mix of Victorian and art-deco buildings that shelter antiques shops and cafes, this 19th-century mining camp makes the most of its Twain connection, hosting the **Jumping Frog Jubilee & Calaveras County Fair** (www.frogtown. org; Gun Club Rd; adult/child $10/6) on the third weekend in May. You could score $5000 if your frog beats the world-record jump (over 21ft) set by 'Rosie the Ribeter' back in 1986.

The Drive » Hwy 49 heads north of Angels Camp through hillsides of farms and ranches. Past San Andreas, make a short detour through Mokelumne Hill, another historic mining town. In Jackson, turn right onto Hwy 88 east. After 9 miles, turn left on Pine Grove-Volcano Rd to reach Indian Grinding Rock State Historic Park.

❹ Volcano

Although the village of Volcano once yielded tons of gold and saw Civil War intrigue, today it slumbers away in solitude. Huge sandstone rocks lining Sutter Creek were blasted from the surrounding hills using a hydraulic process before being scraped clean of gold-bearing dirt. Hydraulic mining had dire environmental consequences, but at its peak, miners raked in nearly $100 a day. Under a mile southeast of town, **Black Chasm** (📞888-762-2837; www.caverntours.com;

DETOUR: CALIFORNIA CAVERN

Start: ❸ Angels Camp

A 25-minute drive east of San Andreas via Mountain Ranch Rd, off Hwy 49 about 12 miles north of Angels Camp, **California Cavern State Historical Landmark** (📞209-736-2708; www.caverntours.com; 9565 Cave City Rd, Mountain Ranch; tour adult/child from $15/8; ⏲10am-4pm Apr-Oct, hr vary Nov-Mar; 🚻) has the mother lode's most extensive system of natural underground caverns. John Muir described them as 'graceful flowing folds deeply placketed like stiff silken drapery.' Regular tours take 60 to 90 minutes, or reserve ahead for a five-hour 'Middle Earth Expedition' ($130), which includes some serious spelunking (no children under age 16 allowed). The Trail of Lakes walking tour, available only during the wet season, is magical.

15701 Pioneer Volcano Rd;
tours adult/child from $15/8;
⊙9am-5pm Jun-Aug, 10am-
4pm Sep-May) has the whiff
of a tourist trap, but
one look at the helictite
crystals – sparkling white
formations resembling
giant snowflakes – makes
the crowds bearable. Two
miles southwest of town
at **Indian Grinding Rock
State Historic Park** (☎20
9-296-7488; www.parks.ca.gov;
14881 Pine Grove-Volcano Rd;
per car $8; ⊙sunrise-sunset
daily, museum 11am-2:30pm
Fri-Mon; ♿), a limestone
outcrop is covered with
petroglyphs and over
1000 mortar holes called
chaw'se used for grinding
acorns into meal. Learn
more about the Sierra
Nevada's indigenous
tribes inside the park's
museum shaped like a
Native American *hun'ge*
(roundhouse).

🛏 p235

The Drive » Backtrack along
Pine Grove-Volcano Rd, turning
right onto Hwy 88 for about
half a mile, then turn right
onto Ridge Rd, which winds
through forests and past rural
homesteads for 8 miles back
to Hwy 49. Turn right and head
north about a mile to Sutter
Creek.

- - - - - - - - - - - -

⑤ Sutter Creek

Perch on the balcony
of one of Main St's
gracefully restored
buildings and view this
gem of a Gold Country
town, boasting raised,
arcaded sidewalks and
high-balconied, false-

fronted buildings that
exemplify California's
19th-century frontier
architecture. At the
visitor center (☎209-267-
1344; www.suttercreek.org; 71a
Main St; ⊙daily, hr vary) pick
up self-guided walking
and driving tour maps.
Nearby **Monteverde
General Store Museum**
(⊙209-267-0493; 11a
Randolph St; admission free;
⊙by appointment only) is a
trip back in time, as is
Sutter Creek Theatre
(☎916-425-0077; www.
suttercreektheater.com; 44
Main St), an 1860s saloon
and billiards hall, now
hosting live music, plays,
films and cultural events.

🛏 p235

The Drive » Follow Main
St north of Sutter Creek for 3
miles through quaint Amador
City. Back at Hwy 49, turn right
and continue north another few
miles to Drytown Cellars, south
of the Hwy 16 junction.

- - - - - - - - - - - -

TRIP HIGHLIGHT

**⑥ Amador County
Wine Country**

Amador County might
be something of an

underdog among
California's winemaking
regions, but a welcoming
circuit of family-owned
wineries and local
characters make for
great sipping without
any pretension. Planted
with California's oldest
surviving zinfandel
vines, the countryside
has a lot in common with
its most celebrated grape
varietal – bold, richly
colored and earthy. North
of tiny Amador City,
Drytown Cellars (www.
drytowncellars.com; 16030
Hwy 49; ⊙11am-5pm) has a
gregarious host and an
array of rich red blends
and single-varietal wines.
Drive further north to
the one-horse town of
Plymouth, then head east
on Plymouth Shenandoah
Rd, where rolling hills
are covered with rocky
rows of neatly pruned
vines, soaking up gallons
of sunshine. Turn left
onto Steiner Rd towards
Renwood Winery (www.
renwoodwinery.com; 12225
Steiner Rd; ⊙10:30am-5pm)
and **Deaver Vineyards**
(www.deavervineyards.com;
12455 Steiner Rd; ⊙10:30am-

Classic Trip

RICHARD CUMMINS / GETTY IMAGES ©

LOCAL KNOWLEDGE
JOHN SCOTT LAMB

Columbia Resident & Former Cavern Guide

South of Vallecito and Hwy 49, there's a very short but memorable hike called Natural Bridges. The area has been a magnet for gold explorers and locals since the 1850s and it features two prominent caves where Coyote Creek flows through. In summertime, you can swim right through the upper cave – amazing! Look for the signed turnoff about 3 miles south of Moaning Cavern on Parrots Ferry Rd.

Top: Tepees, Marshall Gold Discovery State Historic Park
Left: Museum, Marshall Gold Discovery State Historic Park
Right: Main St, Jamestown

5pm), both crafting outstanding zinfandels. Backtrack and continue straight across Plymouth Shenandoah Rd, bending south towards hilltop estate **Wilderotter Vineyard** (www.wildrottervineyard. com; 19890 Shenandoah School Rd; ⊙10:30am-5pm Wed-Mon), which pours dry, minerally whites and smoothly balanced reds.

✕ p235

The Drive ≫ Follow Shenandoah School Rd another mile west until it ends. Turn left back onto Plymouth Shenandoah Rd for 1.5 miles, then turn right onto Hwy 49 northbound. Less then 20 miles later, after up-and-down roller-coaster stretches, you'll arrive in downtown Placerville, south of Hwy 50.

---

❼ Placerville

Things get livelier in 'Old Hangtown,' a nickname Placerville earned for the vigilante-justice hangings that happened here in 1849. Most buildings along Placerville's Main St date from the 1850s. Poke around antiques shops and **Placerville Hardware** (441 Main St; ⊙8am-6pm Mon-Sat, 9am-5pm Sun), the oldest continuously operating hardware store west of the Mississippi River. Downtown dive bars open in the early morning, get an annual cleaning at Christmas and are great for knocking elbows with odd birds. Marked by a vintage neon sign

Classic Trip

and a dummy hanging in a noose outside, the **Hangman's Tree** (305 Main St) bar is built over the stump of the eponymous tree. For family-friendly shenanigans, head 1 mile north of town via Bedford Ave to **Gold Bug Park** (☎530-642-5207; www.goldbugpark.org; 2635 Gold Bug Lane; mine adult/child $5/3, gold panning per hr $2; ☺10am-4pm daily Apr-Oct, noon-4pm Sat & Sun Nov-Mar; 👪), where hard-hatted visitors can descend into a 19th-century mine shaft, or try gold panning.

✕ p235

The Drive >> Back on Hwy 49 northbound, you'll ride along one of the most scenic stretches of the Golden Country's historic route. Patched with shade from oak and pine trees, Hwy 49 drifts beside Sierra Nevada foothills for the next 9 miles to Coloma.

TRIP HIGHLIGHT

⑧ Coloma

At pastoral, low-key **Marshall Gold Discovery State Historic Park** (☎530-622-3470; www.parks.ca.gov, www.marshallgold.org; 310 Back St; per car $8; ☺8am-5pm, to 7pm late May-early Sep, museum 10am-3pm Nov-Mar, to 4pm Apr-Oct; 👪🐾), a simple dirt path leads to the place along the banks

of the American River where James Marshall made his famous discovery of gold flecks below Sutter's Mill on January 24, 1848. Today, several reconstructed and restored historical buildings are all within a short stroll along grassy trails that pass mining artifacts, a blacksmith's shop, pioneer emigrant houses and a historical museum. Panning for gold is always popular at **Bekeart's Gun Shop** (329 Hwy 49; per person $7; ☺10am-3pm Tue-Sun Apr-Oct). Opposite the pioneer cemetery, you can walk or drive up California's shortest state highway, Hwy 153, to where the **James Marshall Monument** marks Marshall's final resting place. Ironically, he died bankrupt, penniless and a ward of the state.

The Drive >> Rolling northbound, Hwy 49 unfolds more of the region's historical beauty over the next 15 miles. In Auburn, drive across I-80 and stay on Hwy 49 north for another 22 miles, gaining elevation while heading toward Grass Valley. Exit onto Empire St, turning right to follow the signs for Empire Mine State Historic Park's visitor center.

TRIP HIGHLIGHT

⑨ Around Nevada City

You've hit the biggest bonanza of the mother lode: **Empire Mine State Historic Park** (☎530-273-

8522; www.empiremine.com, www.parks.ca.gov; 10791 E Empire St, Grass Valley; adult/child $7/3, guided cottage tour $2; ☺10am-5pm; 👪), where California's richest hard-rock mine produced 5.8 million ounces of gold between 1850 and 1956. The mine yard is littered with the massive mining equipment and buildings constructed from waste rock.

Backtrack west, then follow the Golden Chain Hwy (Hwy 49) four more miles north to Nevada City. On the town's quaint main drag, hilly Broad St, the **National Hotel** (211 Broad St) purports to be the oldest continuously operating hotel west of the Rockies. Mosey around the block to **Historic Firehouse No 1 Museum** (www.nevadacountyhistory.org; 214 Main St; admission free; ☺1-4pm Fri-Sun May-Oct), where Native American artifacts join displays about Chinese laborers and creepy Donner Party relics.

Last, cool off with a dip at **South Yuba River State Park** (☎530-432-2546; www.parks.ca.gov; 17660 Pleasant Valley Rd, Penn Valley; admission free; ☺sunrise-sunset; 👪🐾), with hiking trails and swimming holes near the USA's longest covered wooden bridge. It's a 30-minute drive northwest of Nevada City or Grass Valley.

✕ 🛏 p235

Eating & Sleeping

Sonora ❶

✖ Diamondback Grill & Wine Bar
Californian $$

(☎209-532-6661; www.thediamondbackgrill.com; 93 S Washington St; mains $9-12; ⏰11am-9pm Mon-Thu, to 9:30pm Fri & Sat, to 8pm Sun) With exposed-brick walls and a long wooden bar, this contemporary cafe crafts sandwiches, salads, burgers and six daily specials.

🛏 Gunn House
B&B $

(☎209-532-3421; www.gunnhousehotel.com; 286 S Washington St; r incl breakfast $79-115; ❄🛜🏊🅿) A frilly, floral alternative to cookie-cutter chain hotels, with cozy rooms that feature period decor. Rocking chairs on wide porches overlook downtown's historic main drag.

Columbia ❷

🛏 City & Fallon Hotels
Historic Hotel $$

(☎209-532-1470/1472; www.briggshospitalityllc.com; 22768 Main St & 11175 Washington St; r incl breakfast $80-150; ❄🛜) Hunt Gold Rush–era ghosts at these restored, but still rustic hotels (some shared bathrooms). City Hotel's atmospheric What Cheer saloon, hung with oil paintings of 'soiled doves' and striped wallpaper, serves casual pub-grub dinners.

Volcano ❹

🛏 Volcano Union Inn
Historic Hotel $$

(☎209-296-7711; www.volcanounion.com; 21375 Consolation St; r incl breakfast $109-139; ❄@🛜) Of four lovingly updated rooms with crooked floors and flat-screen TVs, two come with street-facing balconies. Open Friday through Monday, the Union Pub has a wine-country menu, (mains $12 to $23) dartboards and live music.

Sutter Creek ❺

🛏 Hanford House Inn
B&B $$

(☎209-267-0747; www.hanfordhouse.com; 61 Hanford St; d incl breakfast $99-259; @🛜🏊🅿) Nod off on platform beds in contemporary rooms or fireplace cottage suites. Chef-prepared breakfasts are harvested from the inn's garden, while evening brings out cheese-and-wine pairings.

Amador County Wine Country ❻

✖ Taste
Californian $$$

(☎209-245-3463; www.restauranttaste.com; 9402 Main St, Plymouth; shared plates $8-16, mains $21-42; ⏰11:30am-2pm Sat & Sun, plus 5pm-9pm Thu-Mon; 🅿) Top-notch wines meld with artfully presented California fusion cooking. Pull on the oversized fork-shaped door handle and step inside the wine bar. Reservations recommended.

Placerville ❼

✖ Cozmic Cafe
Cafe $

(www.ourcoz.com; 594 Main St; mains $6-10; ⏰7am-6pm Tue & Wed, to 8pm or later Thu-Sun; 🛜🍴🅿) With tables set in an underground mine shaft, this hippie-dippy spot's healthy menu is backed by fresh-fruit smoothies, organic coffee and tea. Live music most weekends.

Around Nevada City ❾

✖ Ike's Quarter Cafe
Creole, Californian $$

(www.ikesquartercafe.com; 401 Commercial St, Nevada City; mains $8-22; ⏰8am-3pm Mon, Wed & Thu, to 8pm Fri & Sat; 🅿) Gigantic brunch plates are dished up on a N'awlins-style garden patio. Try the miners' classic 'Hangtown Fry' – cornmeal-crusted oysters, bacon, caramelized onions and spinach.

🛏 Broad Street Inn
Inn $$

(☎530-265-2239; www.broadstreetinn.com; 517 E Broad St, Nevada City; r $110-120; ❄🛜) Forget about fussy B&Bs. This refreshingly simple, six-room Victorian inn has modern, brightly furnished rooms and sociable garden patios with fire pits and porch swings.

Ebbetts Pass Scenic Byway For outd
fanatics, it's a road trip through parad

Ebbetts Pass Scenic Byway

22

Follow this winding road over the rooftop of the Sierra Nevada, crossing from Gold Country to Lake Tahoe, passing lakes, sequoia groves, hot springs and all-seasons resorts.

TRIP HIGHLIGHTS

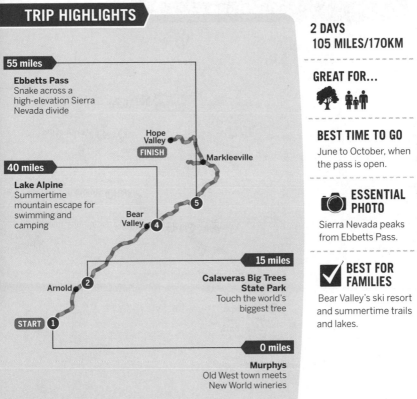

55 miles

Ebbetts Pass
Snake across a high-elevation Sierra Nevada divide

40 miles

Lake Alpine
Summertime mountain escape for swimming and camping

Hope Valley
FINISH

Markleeville

5

Bear Valley **4**

Arnold **2**

START 1

15 miles

Calaveras Big Trees State Park
Touch the world's biggest tree

0 miles

Murphys
Old West town meets New World wineries

**2 DAYS
105 MILES/170KM**

GREAT FOR...

BEST TIME TO GO
June to October, when the pass is open.

ESSENTIAL PHOTO
Sierra Nevada peaks from Ebbetts Pass.

BEST FOR FAMILIES
Bear Valley's ski resort and summertime trails and lakes.

237

22 Ebbetts Pass Scenic Byway

Stretched along a Gold Rush–era mining route, Hwy 4 jogs through a handful of mountain hamlets and forests before crossing Ebbetts Pass, only open in summer and fall. For outdoor fanatics, it's practically a road trip through paradise. Go hiking among giant sequoias and on the Sierra Crest, paddle tranquil lakes, climb granite boulders, splash in summer swimming holes, or strap on skis or snowshoes in winter.

TRIP HIGHLIGHT

❶ Murphys

With its white-picket fences, the 19th-century 'Queen of the Sierra' is one of the most picturesque towns along the southern stretch of California's Gold Country. Amble along Main St, which shows off plenty of historical charm alongside its wine-tasting rooms, art galleries, boutiques and cafes. These rocky, volcanic Sierra Nevada foothills are known

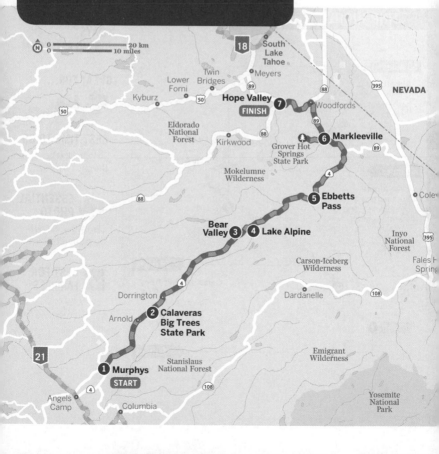

for making brambly zinfandels and spicy syrahs, which you can sample at a dozen wineries all crowded together on a four-block stretch downtown. It's best to arrive early if you're visiting on the weekend. Start at **Tanner** (www.tannervineyards.com; 202 Main St; ☺1-5pm Mon & Thu-Fri, noon-5:30pm Sat, noon-5pm Sun), whose family was the first to plant grapes and pay an alcohol tax in Calaveras County in the 1860s. Don't miss the 'Train Wreck' red blend at **Newsome Harlowe** (www.nhvino.com; 403 Main St; ☺noon-5pm Mon-Thu, 11am-5:30pm Fri-Sun) or the '%£&@' (rhymes with 'duck') Rhône red

LINK YOUR TRIP

18 Lake Tahoe Loop

From Hope Valley, it's a 20-mile drive northwest on Hwy 89 past stream-fed meadows to South Lake Tahoe's beaches and ski resorts.

21 Highway 49 Through Gold Country

From Murphys, mosey 13 miles along Hwy 4 and Parrots Ferry Rd to old-time Columbia State Historic Park.

blend at tongue-in-cheek **Twisted Oak** (www.twistedoak.com; 363 Main St; ☺11:30am-5:30pm Sun-Fri, 10:30am-5:30pm Sat).

✕ 🏠 p243

The Drive » Hwy 4 ascends through the workaday small town of Arnold, which has a few cafes and motels strung along the roadside 12 miles east of Murphys. After motoring another 2.5 miles uphill, turn right into Calaveras Big Trees State Park.

- - - - - - - - - - - -

TRIP HIGHLIGHT

❷ Calaveras Big Trees State Park

Truthfully named **Calaveras Big Trees State Park** (☎209-795-2334; www.parks.ca.gov; entry per car $8; ☺sunrise-sunset; ♿) is home to giant sequoias. The most massive trees on earth, they grow only in the western Sierra Nevada range. Reaching over 300ft tall and with trunk diameters over 55ft, these leftovers from the Mesozoic era are thought to weigh upwards of 3000 tons, or more than 20 blue whales. Close to the park entrance, the **North Grove Big Trees Trail** is a 1.5-mile self-guided loop, where the air is scented with fresh pine, fir and incense cedar. To escape some of the crowds, drive 8.5 miles along the curving park road to the start of the **South Grove Trail.** This 3.5-mile loop

ascends to a peaceful grove that protects 10 times as many giant sequoias; a 1.5-mile round-trip spur trail leads to the Agassiz Tree, the big daddy of them all. Afterward, cool off with a summertime dip in Beaver Creek below the trail's footbridge or in the Stanislaus River along the main park road.

🏠 p243

The Drive » Back at Hwy 4, turn right and drive uphill past Dorrington, a 19th-century stagecoach stop and toll-road station, stopping at Hell's Kitchen Vista Point for panoramas of the glaciated volcanic landscape. About 22 miles northeast of the state park lies Bear Valley.

- - - - - - - - - - - -

❸ Bear Valley

It's all about outdoor family fun here. Sniff out anything from rock climbing to mountain biking and hiking all within a short distance of Bear Valley Village, which has a gas station, shops and casual restaurants. In winter, **Bear Valley Mountain** (☎209-753-2301; www.bearvalley.com; lift ticket adult/child $67/49; ☺usually Dec-Mar) ski area will get your brain buzzing with 2000ft of vertical rise and 12 lifts. The resort's somewhat off-the-beaten-track location gives it a beginner-friendly, locals-only feel. On your left as you pull into Bear Valley Village, **Bear Valley Adventure Company** (209-753-2834; www.bearvalleyxc.com) is a one-stop shop for outdoor gear and supplies – kayak, stand-up paddle boarding (SUP), mountain bike and cross-country ski rentals – plus insider information on just about everything there is to do in the area. Staff also arrange mountain bike shuttles and sell helpful maps.

The Drive » From the Bear Valley Village turnoff, it's just 4 miles up Hwy 4 to Lake Alpine's beaches, campgrounds and day-use parking lots.

TRIP HIGHLIGHT

❹ Lake Alpine

Suddenly Hwy 4 reaches the shores of a gasp-worthy alpine reservoir, skirted by slabs of granite and offering several sandy beaches and a handful of rustic US Forest Service (USFS) campgrounds. Paddling, swimming and fishing opportunities abound, which mean that it's always jammed with people on summer weekends. No matter how many folks descend upon the lake (and there are far fewer midweek), it's still hard to beat the gorgeous Sierra Nevada setting, 7350ft above sea level. Of several nearby hiking trailheads, the scramble to Inspiration Point gets you spectacular views of

lakes and the Dardanelles; this 3-mile round-trip hike starts from the Lakeshore Trail near Pine Marten Campground. Next to the boat ramp on the lake's northern shore, the Lake Alpine Resort's summertime kiosk rents DIY rowboats, paddleboats, kayaks and canoes.

🛏 p243

The Drive » Make sure you've got plenty of gas in the tank before embarking on the 33-mile drive over Ebbetts Pass downhill to Markleeville. There are campgrounds, but no services, gas stations, motels or places to eat along this high-elevation, twisting mountain road, which is only open seasonally during summer and fall (see the boxed text on p242).

Ebbetts Pass

⑤ Ebbetts Pass

Ebbetts Pass National Scenic Byway officially runs from Arnold to Markleeville, yet it's the dramatic stretch east of Lake Alpine that really gets drivers' hearts pumping. Narrowing, the highway continues 4 miles past **Cape Horn** **Vista** to **Mosquito Lake** and over Pacific Grade Summit before slaloming through historic **Hermit Valley**, where the Molokume River meadow blooms with summer wildflowers. Finally, Hwy 4 winds up and over the actual summit of **Ebbetts Pass** (elevation 8730ft), where the top-of-the-world scenery encompasses snaggletoothed granite peaks rising above the tree line. About 0.4 miles east of the signposted pass, the highway crosses the **Pacific Crest Trail** (PCT), which zigzags from Mexico to Canada. For wildflowers, volcanic cliffs and granite canyon views, take an 8-mile round-trip hike to Nobel Lake. Or park the car and have a picnic beside

CROSSING EBBETTS PASS

Hwy 4 is usually plowed from the west as far as Bear Valley year-round, but Ebbetts Pass closes completely after the first major snowfall in October, November or December. The pass typically doesn't open again until mid-May, sometimes June. Check current road conditions with the **California Department of Transportation** (📞800-427-7623; www.dot.ca.gov).

Kinney Reservoir, just over another mile east.

The Drive » With a maximum 24% grade (no vehicles with trailers or over 25ft long), Hwy 4 loses elevation via dozens of steep hairpin turns, crossing multiple creek and river bridges as forested valley views open up below bald granite peaks. After 13 miles, turn left onto Hwy 89 and drive 4.5 miles northwest to Markleeville.

❻ Markleeville

Breathlessly coming down from Ebbetts Pass, Hwy 4 winds past remnants of old mining communities long gone bust, including a pioneer cemetery, ghost towns and cattle ranches. From Monitor Junction, Hwy 89 runs gently north alongside the Carson River, where anglers fish for trout from pebble-washed beaches that kids love. Crossing Hangman's Bridge, Hwy 89 threads through **Markleeville**, a historic toll-road

outpost that boomed with silver mining in the 1860s. Today it's a quiet spot to refuel and relax. Downtown, turn left onto Hot Springs Rd, then head up School St to **Alpine County Historical Complex** (📞530-694-2317; www.alpinecountyca. gov; School St; ⏰ usually late May-Oct), with its one-room 1882 schoolhouse, log-cabin jail and tiny museum displaying Native American baskets and pioneer-era artifacts. Back on Hot Springs Rd, drive 4 miles west through pine forests to **Grover Hot Springs State Park** (📞530-694-2248/2249; www.parks.ca.gov; Hot Springs Rd; ⏰ usually 11am-7pm Thu-Tue Sep-May, daily Jun-Aug; 👶), which has a shady picnic area, campground and natural spring-fed swimming pool. Carry tire chains in winter.

✕ 🛏 p243

The Drive » Drive north out of Markleeville for 6 miles to the unremarkable junction of Hwys 88 and 89 at Woodfords. Turn left and continue lazily west another 6 miles, crossing the bridge over the Carson River to Hope Valley, where Hwys 88 and 89 split at Picketts Junction.

❼ Hope Valley

After all the fantastical scenery leading up to and over Ebbetts Pass, what's left? **Hope Valley**, where wildflowers, grassy meadows and burbling streams are bordered by evergreen pines and aspen trees that turn brilliant yellow in fall. This panoramic valley is ringed by Sierra Nevada peaks, which remain dusted with snow even in early summer. Incidentally, the historic Pony Express route once ran through this way. Today, whether you want to dangle a fishing pole or splash around in the chilly mountain waters, or just take a bird-watching stroll or trek on snowshoes in winter around the meadows, Hope Valley can feel like the most magical place in Alpine County. Start exploring on the nature trails of **Hope Valley Wildlife Area** (www.drg. ca.gov).

🛏 p243

Eating & Sleeping

Murphys ❶

✕ Fire Wood   Californian $$
(☏209-728-3248; www.firewoodeats.com;
420 Main St; mains $6-14; ⊙11am-9pm; ▥)
When the weather's sunny, this lofty minimalist
kitchen has a casual *alfresco* atmosphere, with
wines by the glass, pub grub and toasty wood-
fired pizzas.

✕ Mineral   Modern American $$$
(☏209-728-9743; www.mineralrestaurant.
com; 419 Main St; mains $10-30; noon-3pm &
5-8:30pm Thu, noon-8:30pm Fri & Sat, 10am-
3pm Sun) Creative lunches and brunches, with
chef-made dishes like avocado-agave pudding
or shiitake pâté, make this mod restaurant
stand out from the pack. Reservations advised.

▣ Murphys Historic
Hotel & Lodge   B&B, Lodge $$
(☏209-728-3444, 800-532-7684; www.
murphyshotel.com; 457 Main St; d $89-179) This
1850s hostelry where Mark Twain once slept
anchors Main St. The original structure is rough
around the edges, with shared baths, a bar
and an old-school dining room. The adjoining
building has bland but contemporary rooms
with private baths.

▣ Victoria Inn   B&B $$
(☏209-728-8933; www.victoriainn-murphys.
com; 402 Main St; r $125-350; ❄ @ 🛜) This
downtown D&D is free of dusty antique clutter,
but thankfully still has claw-foot tubs, sleigh
beds and balconies. Enjoy tapas and Calaveras
County wines on the verandah of the next-door
bar and restaurant.

Calaveras Big Trees State Park ❷

▣ Calaveras Big Trees
State Park Campgrounds   Campground $
(reservations ☏800-444-7275; www.
reserveamerica.com; off Hwy 4; campsites
$20-35; ⊙usually mid-May–mid-Sep; ▥ 🐾)

At the park entrance is busy North Grove
Campground. Less crowded, hillside Oak Hollow
Campground is about 4 miles further along the
park's main road.

Lake Alpine ❹

▣ Lake Alpine Resort   Lodge $$
(☏209-753-6350; www.lakealpineresort.com;
4000 Hwy 4, Bear Valley; tent cabins $60-65,
cabins with kitchenette $130-275; ⊙usually
May-Oct; ▥🐾) If you're not ready to rough it at
rustic lakeshore campgrounds, this lodge with
a general store, bar and lake-view restaurant
has a handful of wooden and canvas-tent cabins
for families.

Markleeville ❻

✕ Stone Fly   Californian $$
(☏530-694-9999; www.stoneflyrestaurant.
com; 14821 Hwy 89; mains $15-24; ⊙usually
5-9pm Fri & Sat) Seasonal meaty mains like pork
loin with cranberry chutney take a back seat
to wood-fired pizzas and stomach-warming
antipasto, all delivered to an open-air patio in
summer. Reservations helpful.

▣ Creekside Lodge   Inn $
(☏866-802-7335; www.markleevilleusa.com;
14820 Hwy 89; r $85-115) Beside busy Wolf
Creek restaurant, this quaint white-shingled
inn has a dozen tidy little rooms with pedestal
sinks, high-end mattresses and country quilts
covering the beds.

Hope Valley ❼

▣ Sorenson's   Cottages, Cabins $$
(☏530-694-2203, 800-423-9949; www.
sorensonsresort.com; 14255 Hwy 88; r $135-325;
▥🐾) A year-round outdoor-adventure base
camp with a country cafe, Sorenson's rents
charming cabins with kitchenettes and cottages
in the woods, not far from the Carson River.

Feather River Rushing streams,
daunting volcanic peaks
and quiet forest lakes

Feather River Scenic Byway

23

Get ready for an icy plunge into a Feather River swimming hole. This trip visits unexplored forests, and is rich with wildlife, awesome hiking and views of volcanic peaks.

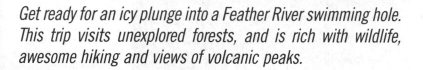

TRIP HIGHLIGHTS

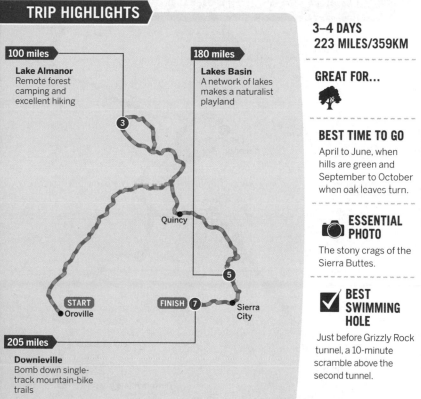

100 miles

Lake Almanor
Remote forest camping and excellent hiking

180 miles

Lakes Basin
A network of lakes makes a naturalist playland

Quincy

START
Oroville

FINISH 7

Sierra City

205 miles

Downieville
Bomb down single-track mountain-bike trails

3–4 DAYS
223 MILES/359KM

GREAT FOR...

BEST TIME TO GO
April to June, when hills are green and September to October when oak leaves turn.

ESSENTIAL PHOTO
The stony crags of the Sierra Buttes.

BEST SWIMMING HOLE
Just before Grizzly Rock tunnel, a 10-minute scramble above the second tunnel.

23 Feather River Scenic Byway

As you cruise the remote two-lane blacktop of the Feather River Scenic Byway you're surrounded by California's northern natural wonders — rushing streams, daunting volcanic peaks and quiet forest lakes. Eventually, the route leads to character-filled small towns, where hikers shovel down hearty fare and stock up on supplies. The best way to soak up the sights is by camping; a number of cheap (or free) federal campgrounds line the route.

1 Oroville

This journey begins in Oroville, a little town that shares a name with the nearby lake that's filled by the Feather River. There's not much to see in Oroville, save the stunning **Chinese Temple** (📞530-538-2496; 1500 Broderick St; adult/child $2/free; 🕑 noon-4pm), a quiet monument to the 10,000 Chinese people who once lived here. During the 19th century, theater troupes from China toured a circuit of Chinatowns in California and Oroville was the end

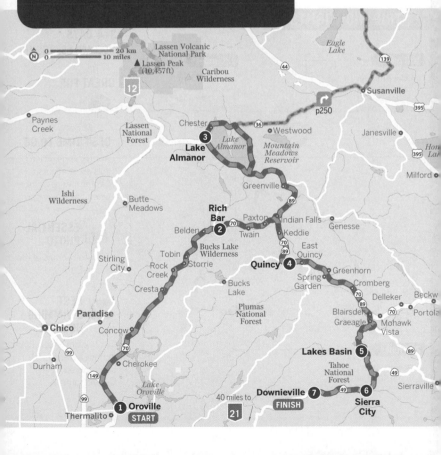

of the line, which explains the unrivaled collection of 19th-century Chinese stage finery. The **Feather River Ranger District** (☎530-534 6500; 875 Mitchell Ave; ⊙8am-4:30pm Mon-Fri) is also in town; they issue permits and have a handout detailing historic stops along the Byway. The nearby **Lake Oroville Recreation Area** is an excellent place to hike, camp and hook bass. Climb the 47ft-observation tower and look west at smallest mountain range in the world, the Sutter Buttes.

✕ ⨋ p251

LINK YOUR TRIP

21 Highway 49 Through Gold Country

More swimming holes, wild history lessons and winding byways await for those who connect to the 'Golden Chain.' Link to Hwy 49 in Downieville.

12 Volcanic Legacy Scenic Byway

Find the headwaters of some of California's other scenic waterways and skirt the volcanic domes of Shasta and Lassen. Follow signs in Chester for Lassen Volcanic National Park, the first stop of that trip.

The Drive » Take Hwy 70 into the granite gorge passing hydroelectric plants, mountain tunnels and historic bridges, including the Pulga Bridge. Four miles past the red bridge to Belden turn off Hwy 70 onto Rich Bar Rd, on your right.

❷ Rich Bar

Although the so-called Golden Chain, Hwy 49, is still further up the road, the Feather River area was dotted with its own rough-and-ready encampments of fortune hunters. One of the most successful of these was the aptly named **Rich Bar**, where little remains today except a crumbling graveyard and a historic marker. The quiet place wasn't so tame in the 1850s, when a resident named Dame Shirley chronicled life at Rich Bar as a part of her fascinating diary of life in California gold towns. Published as *The Shirley Letters,* her letters paint Rich Bar as a chaotic place of bloody accidents, a couple of murders, mob rule enforced by horsewhipping and hanging, an attempted suicide and a fatal duel. And she was only here a single month!

The Drive » Continue the lovely drive on Hwy 70, catching quick views of Lassen and Shasta peaks in the rearview mirror. Go north on Hwy 89 to reach the south shore of Lake Almanor. Follow the shore around the lake clockwise (left).

❸ Lake Almanor

This artificial lake is a crystalline example of California's beautiful, if sometimes awkward, conservation and land-management policy: the lake was created by the now-defunct Great Western Power Company and is now ostensibly owned by the Pacific Gas & Electric Company. The lake is surrounded by lush meadows and tall pines, most of it is the **Lassen National Forest** and **Caribou Wilderness** area. Both offer quiet camping with a free permit from the **Lassen National Forest Almanor Ranger Station** (☎530-258-2141; 900 E Hwy 36; ⊙8am-4:30pm Mon-Fri). The main town near the lake is **Chester**, and though you could whiz right by and dismiss it as a few blocks of nondescript roadside storefronts, don't – it's not. This robust little community has a fledgling art scene, decent restaurants and some comfy places to stay. You can rent bicycles for a cruise along the lake at **Bodfish Bicycles & Quiet Mountain Sports** (☎530-258-2338; 152 Main St; bike hire per hour/day $10/33).

✕ ⨋ p251

The Drive » Continue around the lake and retrace the route south on Hwy 89, which will bring you back to the Feather River Scenic Byway. You'll hit Quincy when the road makes a T-junction.

❹ Quincy

Idyllic Quincy (population 1738) is one of the Northern Mountains three mountain communities, which teeter on the edge of becoming an incorporated town. It's no metropolis, but after the route along the Feather it may feel like one: it boasts a large grocery and two of the three fast-food franchises in the entirety of Plumas County. Three streets make up Quincy's low-key commercial district. Pick up free walking and driving tour pamphlets from the visitors center to guide you through the gorgeous surrounding **American Valley**. One of the nicest community museums in the state is also located here, the **Plumas County Museum** (☎530-283-6320; www. plumasmuseum.org; 500 Jackson St, at Coburn St; adult/ child $1/50¢; ⏰8am-5pm Mon-Sat, also 10am-4pm Sun May-Sep), amid flowering gardens. Visit the museum and you'll find that the building houses hundreds of historical photos and relics from the county's pioneer and Maidu days, early mining

and timber industries, and construction of the Western Pacific Railroad.

✖ p251

The Drive » Continue down Hwy 70/89 passing horse pastures and distant mountain views. At Graeagle, take a fork in the road following Hwy 89, then after about 2 miles take a right on Gold Lake Hwy and start climbing.

TRIP HIGHLIGHT

❺ Lakes Basin

Haven Lake, Gold Lake, Rock Lake, Deer Lake: dotted with crystal alpine waters, this area is a secluded corner of paradise. Over a dozen of these gems can be reached only on foot and great trails are virtually endless – you can even

Feather River area

connect to the Pacific Crest Trail. The most scenic hike in the area is the **Haskell Peak Trail**, which affords views of both Lassen and Shasta and, on a clear day, Mt Rose in Nevada. To reach the trailhead, turn right from Gold Lake Hwy at Haskell Peak Rd (Forest Rd 9) and follow it for 8.5 miles. The hike is only 3 miles, but it's not for the faint of heart – you'll climb some 1000ft through dense forest before it opens on an expansive view. From here you can see the rugged Sierra Buttes, distinguished from their surrounding mountains by jagged peaks, which look like a miniature version of the Alps.

🛏 p251

The Drive » Gold Lake Hwy will now descend and connect to Hwy 49 in Bassetts (a town that consists of little more than a gas station). Go right on Hwy 49 for five minutes to reach Sierra City.

⑥ Sierra City

Sierra City is the primary supply station for people headed to the **Sierra Buttes**, which offers

DETOUR:
EAGLE LAKE

Start: ❸ Lake Almanor

Those who have the time to get all the way out to Eagle Lake, California's second-largest natural lake, are rewarded with one of the most striking sights in the region: a stunningly blue jewel on the high plateau. From early June until October this lovely lake, about 15 miles northwest of Susanville, attracts a smattering of visitors who come to cool off, swim, fish, boat and camp. On the south shore, you'll find a pristine 5-mile **recreational trail** and several busy **campgrounds** (reservations ☏877-444-6777; www.recreation.gov; tent sites $20, RV sites $29-33) administered by Lassen National Forest and the **Bureau of Land Management** (BLM; ☏530-257-5381). Nearby **Eagle Lake Marina** (www.eaglelakerecreationarea.com) offers hot showers, laundry and boat rentals. It also can help you get out onto the lake with a fishing license. To get to Eagle Lake, take Hwy 36 north of Lake Almanor to reach Susanville. Then, continue north on Hwy 139 to the shore of Eagle Lake.

another chance at an amazing short hike to the summit. From the **Sierra Country Store** (☏530-862-1181; Hwy 49; ⊙9am-7pm; 🛜), there's a vast network of trails that is ideal for backpacking and casual hikes. They are listed in the *Lakes Basin, Downieville – Sierra City* map ($2), which is on sale at the store. Sierra City's local museum, the **Kentucky Mine** (☏530-862-1310; adult/child $7/3.50; ⊙10am-4pm Wed-Sun Jun-Aug), is a worthy stop that ably introduces the famed 'Golden Chain Highway.' Its gold mine and stamp mill are just north of town.

✕ 🛏 p251

The Drive » Head west on Hwy 49 along the North Yuba River to Downieville.

- - - - - - - - - -

TRIP HIGHLIGHT

❼ Downieville

Even with a population smaller than 400, Downieville is the biggest town in the remote Sierra County, located at the junction of the North Yuba and Downie Rivers. With a reputation that quietly rivals Moab, Utah (before it got big), the town is the premiere place for trail riding in the state, and a staging area for true wilderness adventures. Brave souls bomb down the **Downieville Downhill**, a molar-rattling 5000ft vertical descent, which is rated among the best mountain-bike routes in the USA. **Downieville Outfitters** (☏530-289-3010; www.downievilleoutfitters.com; 114 Main St; bike rentals from $60, shuttles $20; ⊙shuttles 10am, 2pm weekdays, every 2hr weekends) is a good place to rent a bike and the shuttle to make the trip, and a thrilling end to the journey.

🛏 p251

Eating & Sleeping

Oroville ❶

✗ Luceddies American & Italian Restaurant
American $

(☎530-533-1722; 2053 Montgomery St; mains $6-15; ⊘Mon-Sat) This new Oroville eatery dishes out pasta and burgers in the afternoon but locals rave over its breakfasts. The Big Boy Scramble is a delicious heartstopper.

🛏 Lake Oroville State Recreation Area
Camping $

(☎530-538-2219, 800-444-7275; www.parks. ca.gov; 917 Kelly Ridge Rd; tent/RV sites $15/35; 🛜) Not the most rustic choice, but there are good primitive sites if you're willing to hike, and floating campsites accessible only by boat.

Lake Almanor ❸

✗ Red Onion Grill
New American $$

(www.redoniongrill.com; 384 Main St, Chester; meals $10-25; ⊘11am-9pm) Hands down the finest in Chester, the upscale New American cuisine has generous Italian influences (like the simply prepared rock shrimp and crab Alfredo) and there's bar food with panache. The setting is cozy with wall lanterns and a crackling fire.

🛏 Feather Bed B&B
B&B $$

(☎530-283-0102; www.featherbed-inn.com; 542 Jackson St, at Court St, Chester; d from $150, cottages $179-190; 🐾) This frilly pink 1893 Queen Anne home is all antiques and cuteness. A teddy bear adorns every quilted bed.

Quincy ❹

✗ Café Le Coq
French $$

(☎530-283-0114; www.cafelecoq.biz; 189 Main St; prix fixe menu lunch/dinner $17/32; ⊘11:30am-1:30pm Mon-Wed & 5-8pm Tue-Sat) The French chef and owner Michel LeCoq ambles out to explain the specials (the prix fixe lunch is a steal), including house-cured meats.

Lakes Basin ❺

🛏 Salmon Creek Campground
Campground $

(☎530-993-1410; tent & RV sites without hookups $18) One of nicest US Forest Service (USFS) campgrounds in the area is 2 miles north of Bassetts on Gold Lake Hwy. It has vault toilets, running water and first-come, first-served sites.

Sierra City ❻

✗ Big Springs Gardens
Brunch $$$

(☎530-862-1333; 32163 Hwy 49; mains incl price of admission $35-37; ⊘lunch Fri-Sun summer, reservations required) This private botanical garden makes for an enjoyable stroll when the weather is warm, but the best time to visit is for their special brunch. Dine on berries from the surrounding hills and trout fresh from the pond, served *alfresco*. Trails pass a waterfall-laced natural area.

🛏 Buttes Resort
Cabin $

(☎530-862-1170, 800-991-1170; www.sierracity. com; 230 Main St; cabins $55-145) In the heart of Sierra City, the small cluster of cabins occupies a lovely spot overlooking the river and is a favorite with hikers. Most cabins have a private deck and barbecue; some have full kitchens.

🛏 Wild Plum Campground
Campground $

(☎530-993-1410; tent sites $18) Of the handful of camping areas east of Sierra City, this is the most scenic, along a rushing stretch of the river. The facilities – vault toilets and first-come, first-served sites – are basic but clean.

Downieville ❺

🛏 Riverside Inn
Hotel $

(☎530-289-1000; www.downieville.us; 206 Commercial St; r $75-155) Rooms have TVs and bathrooms, and a screen door lets you keep the main door open to listen to the river run by.

Sacramento *The California State Capitol is an impressive stop*

Lazy Delta Dawdle

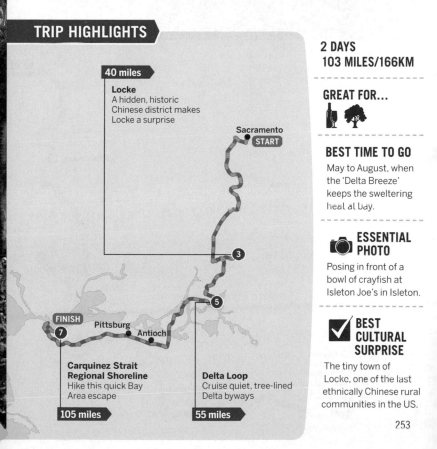

24

Slipping along the shady levy roads of the Sacramento-San Joaquin River Delta brings you to an eccentric string of one-horse towns, where surprises are around every bend.

40 miles

Locke
A hidden, historic
Chinese district makes
Locke a surprise

Sacramento
START

3

5

FINISH
7
Pittsburg
Antioch

**Carquinez Strait
Regional Shoreline**
Hike this quick Bay
Area escape

105 miles

Delta Loop
Cruise quiet, tree-lined
Delta byways

55 miles

**2 DAYS
103 MILES/166KM**

GREAT FOR...

BEST TIME TO GO

May to August, when
the 'Delta Breeze'
keeps the sweltering
heat at bay.

**ESSENTIAL
PHOTO**

Posing in front of a
bowl of crayfish at
Isleton Joe's in Isleton.

**BEST
CULTURAL
SURPRISE**

The tiny town of
Locke, one of the last
ethnically Chinese rural
communities in the US.

253

24 Lazy Delta Dawdle

When exploring the network of channels and back roads of the 750,000-acre Sacramento-San Joaquin River Delta, you'll take gently sweeping levy roads along a maze of endless channels. Although this region of California is between the crowded urban spaces of the Bay Area and Sacramento and the busy I-5 corridor, it feels like a million miles away.

❶ Sacramento

At the confluence of two of California's most powerful waterways – the American and Sacramento Rivers – lies the tidy grid of streets that make up the state capital. This is an excellent launching point to enter the Delta. In recent years Sacramento's cultural life along the midtown grid – an area along J St between 15th and 26th – has been revived and if you find yourself here on a Second Saturday

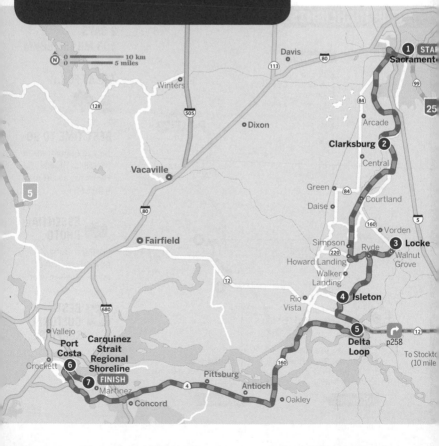

art crawl, be ready to party. Otherwise, the cool marble corridors of the **California State Capitol** is a mandatory and impressive stop as is the 40-acre garden surrounding the dome, **Capitol Park**. There are exotic trees from around the world, stern-looking statues of missionaries and a powerful Vietnam Memorial. A quieter war commemoration is the Civil War Memorial Grove, which was planted in 1897 with saplings from famous battlefields.

✖ ⊫ p259

The Drive » Point the car west from the state capital

LINK YOUR TRIP

25 Highway 99 Through Central Valley

Gassed up and ready for more unexpected regions of California? Link this trip to Hwy 99 just south of Sacramento and make the long ramble down south through the valley.

5 Napa Valley

For an elegant counterweight to the Delta's scrappy charm, tour Northern California's celebrated wine circuit, just next door via Hwy 12, which runs west from Rio Vista.

at the golden Tower Bridge, a landmark crossing of the Sacramento River. Cross it and then head south on Hwy 84, following Gregory Ave until it connects with S River Rd.

- - - - - - - - - -

❷ Clarksburg

The fields and arid heat surrounding West Sacramento offer little clue that the 'Thousand Miles of Waterways' is near. But as you enter Clarksburg the delta breeze begins to blow and travelers can't miss the **Old Sugar Mill** (www. oldsugarmill.com; 35265 Willow Ave, Clarksburg; admission free; ⊙11am-5pm Wed-Sun; 🖼), the hub of a thriving community of local winemakers. A jazz combo echoes through space to complement wines of the Carvalho family, who own this custom crushing facility. The wines of the region have developed a lot over the last decade, benefitting from the blazing sun and cool breeze. You can cruise past the vines on the seat of a bicycle, with the fun and informative tour from **Fast Eddy Bicycle Tours** (☎916-812-2712; www.fasteddiebiketours.com). His Upper Delta Rd tour makes an in-depth trip along the Delta towns and wine region and the more casual Delta Leisure Tour is a flat 10-mile trip that is easy for kids.

✖ p259

The Drive » Just south of the ferry stop, turn east on Hwy 220 to return to S River Rd, which has now joined Hwy 160 at the edge of a wide stretch of the Sacramento River. After five minutes south on Hwy 160, you'll pass Walnut Grove on the way to its sister city, Locke.

- - - - - - - - - -

TRIP HIGHLIGHT

❸ Locke

Declared a National Historic Landmark, Locke was founded by Chinese laborers, who built the levies that line nearly every inch of this trip. In its heyday, Locke had a fairly wild reputation; during Prohibition (1920–33) the town's lack of a police force and quiet nearby waterways made it a hotbed of boozing and gambling. As you drop down off the main road to the shadowy main street that parallels the river, the sight is unlike anywhere else in America: tightly packed rows of wooden structures with creaking balconies and architecture that blends Western and Asian details. Locke's wild days are evident in the **Dai Loy Museum** (5 Main St, Locke; admission $1.75; ⊙noon-3pm Sat & Sun; 🖼), a former gambling house with exhibits on regional history. Its humble exhibits are worth a peek, but the best part is the atmospheric building itself.

✖ p259

The Drive » Fifteen minutes south on the gently curving turns of Hwy 160, running parallel to the Sacramento River. As you approach Isleton, look for the yellow swing bridge, which turns on a pivot so that large ships can pass.

- - - - - - - - -

④ Isleton

Isleton, 'Crawdad Town, USA,' seems more like the Mississippi Delta than California and once it also boasted a thriving Chinese community, which is evident in the historic storefronts that line its main drag. The town is a regular stop for weekend Harley cruisers and Delta boaters, who lend the streets an amiably scruffy atmosphere as well as ensuring that the bars are always busy. **Isleton Joe's** (212 Second St; mains $5-17; 🕗8am-9pm) is the nerve center of town, a place where yuppie wine tourers and bikers suck down the crayfish on a breezy patio, which often hosts live bands. On hot weekends, the patio at Isleton Joe's is misted with water and this provides a welcome reprieve from the sun. Fishermen should drop in to **Bob's Bait Shop** (302 2nd St, 🕗7am-5pm) for advice from the self-described, ahem, 'Master Baiter.' As well as dispensing expert information on fishing in the area, he sells live

RICHARD CUMMINS / GETTY IMAGES ©

crayfish that you can take along for a picnic

✖ p259

The Drive » Take Jackson Slough Rd south out of town and go left on Hwy 12. Just before the bridge, go right on Brannan Island Rd and follow it along the Delta Loop for views of the bird-filled skies and marshy lowlands. At the junction of Hwy 12 you'll see Rio Vista across the river – a good stop to grab a bite and cool the engine (p259).

- - - - - - - - -

TRIP HIGHLIGHT

⑤ Delta Loop

The drive along the Delta Loop is best taken at an unhurried pace – proof that sometimes the journey itself is as important as the destination. This is the heart of the Delta: marinas line the southern stretch where you can

Brannan Island Houseboat

charter anything that floats, migratory birds fill the skies and cruisers meander the uncrowded roads. The loop ends at the **Brannan Island State Recreation Area** (www. parks.ca.gov; 17645 State Highway 160, Rio Vista; sites $11-25; 🚻 🐾), where sandy picnic areas and grassy barbecue areas draw hard-partying campers. It's also a great spot for families: there's lots of space to run around and a beach where a lifeguard watches little ones wade into the reeds. The park hosts some good wildlife watching at **Frank's Tract**, a protected wetland marsh, where keen-eyed visitors might spot mink, beaver or river otter. It also has loads of birds. Note that budgetary restrictions have recently limited park hours to the weekends.

The Drive » Take Hwy 160 south to connect with Hwy 4. Drive west for 30 minutes before reaching Port Costa, on the expansive San Pablo Bay. This drive is particularly nice as the sun is setting over the water.

257

DETOUR: STOCKTON

Start: ⑤ Delta Loop

When you find **Stockton** on a map, it hardly seems possible to reach it by the back roads of the Delta but you can detail a route that makes a highway-free shortcut – just continue east on Hwy 12 for 10 miles and take a right on Davis Rd, which will bring you to the city in 5 miles. Pull in at Rough and Ready Island, a WWII naval supply base that was decommissioned in 1995, and stroll to the historic downtown. You'll know you've reached the good part of town when you see the modern white edifice of the **Weber Point Events Center** (221 Center St), standing in the middle of a grassy park looking rather like a pile of sailboats. The events center holds the huge Asparagus Festival in April, a series of open-air concerts, and fountains where squealing children cool off during summer. Nearby is the beautiful new **Banner Island Ballpark** (www. stocktonports.com; 404 W Freemont St), where the minor-league Stockton Seals play baseball (April to September). Also near is the **Haggin Museum** (www.hagginmuseum. org; 1201 N Pershing Ave; tickets $5; ⊙1:30am-5pm Wed-Fri, noon-5pm Sat-Sun), which has an excellent collection of American landscape paintings and an Egyptian mummy.

⑥ Port Costa

The dazzling Suisun Bay greets travelers who make it to Port Costa, founded in 1879 as a landing for the Central Pacific Railroad ferry – this made the humble little spot a stop on the celebrated Transcontinental Railroad. Although the Amtrak still rumbles by, the ramshackle village seemed to all but freeze after the 1930s, when the Martinez bridge ended its *raison d'être* and the railroads changed route. The town's tiny downtown draws two fairly different demographics these days: antique hunters and motorcycle clubs, but its quiet charms give it a special air. If not for the approach, you'd never guess this early 20th century place was so close to the edge of the urban Bay Area sprawl.

✕ 🛏 p259

The Drive ≫ Head east out of town on Snake Rd, which becomes Carquinez Scenic Drive. The parking lot with access to the Carquinez Strait Regional Shoreline is well marked.

TRIP HIGHLIGHT

⑦ Carquinez Strait Regional Shoreline

After staying along the flat lands of the Delta for so long, it feels good to climb the gentle hills of the Carquinez Strait Regional Shoreline, a patch of green that includes several excellent, well-marked trails that afford views of the Delta.

Get the blood pumping by climbing up for views atop Franklin Ridge, the park's 420ft-highpoint where red-tailed hawks and the occasional golden eagle can be spotted. The **Franklin Ridge Loop Trail** is a 2.8-mile hike that overlooks the Carquinez Strait as well as the shimmering waters that the trip has followed from the beginning. At dusk this hike is best, with the fiery glow behind the distant silhouette of Mt Tamaulipas and the twinkling lights of the Benicia Bridge.

Eating & Sleeping

Sacramento ❶

✕ Pizza Rock
Pizza $$

(www.pizzarocksacramento.com; 1020 K St; pizzas $14-17; ⊙11am-midnight; ✳ @ 📶) This is the loud and raucous hub of the newly renovated K Street corridor. The chef here was the first American to win an Italian pizza-making prize.

🛏 Sacramento HI Hostel
Hostel $

(📞916-443-1691; www.norcalhostels.org/sac; 925 H St; dm $20-23, r $45-100; ⊙reception 7:30-9:30am & 5-10pm; ✳ @ 📶) This hostel, housed in a grand Victorian mansion, offers impressive trimmings at rock-bottom prices.

Clarksburg ❷

✕ Historic Grand Island Mansion
Brunch $$$

(📞916-775-1705; www.grandislandmansion. com; 13415 Grand Island Rd, Walnut Grove; brunch $22-26; ⊙10:30am-2pm Sun, Mon-Sat by appointment) This surprising Italian Renaissance building was built in 1917 for an orchard baron and hosts a Sunday champagne brunch.

Locke ❸

✕ Al the Wop's
Bar & Grill $

(13943 Main St, Locke; mains $8-15; ⊙11am-9pm) Al the Wop's is a magnet for amiable Harley crews. The draw isn't the food (the special is a peanut butter-slathered hamburger) so much as the ambience. Above the creaking floorboards, the ceiling's covered in crusty dollar bills and more than one pair of erstwhile undies.

Isleton ❹

✕ Isleton Joe's
Bar & Grill $

(www.isletonjoes.com; 212 Second St, Isleton; mains $5-17; ⊙8am-9pm) Wipe your chin after sucking down the crayfish on the breezy patio, which often hosts live bands.

Rio Vista

✕ Foster's Bighorn
Bar & Grill $$

(www.fostersbighorn.com; 143 Main St, Rio Vista; mains $8-25; ⊙11am-9pm) A veritable museum of taxidermy – with beer. Frozen snarls abound: 300 trophies include Kodak bears, rhinos and big cats of every stripe. The centerpiece is a full-grown African elephant, whose trunk extends 13ft from the wall. The menu? It's appropriately carnal, with steaks and big burgers.

🛏 Brannan Island State Recreation Area
Camping $

(📞916-777-7701; www.parks.ca.gov; 17645 State Highway 160, Rio Vista; sites $11-25; 🚻🐕) Reach campsites by boat or car, but the hike-in sites at the water are best. Note that due to budgetary cutbacks the camping area for the park is open only on weekends.

Port Costa ❻

✕ Warehouse Café
Bar & Grill $$

(📞510-787-1827; 5 Canyon Lake Dr; meals $8-15; ⊙11am-1am; 🐕) Bikers and boaters mingle over microbrews. Inside, there's plenty on tap and an enormous stuffed polar bear encased behind glass. The food – boozy staples like burgers and fried stuff with fancy additions like shrimp scampi – is excellent.

🛏 Burlington Hotel
Hotel $

(📞510-787-1827; 5 Canyon Lake Dr, Port Costa; r $24-54) The weather-beaten lodgings have loads of musty charm but belie its history as a five-star Victorian brothel. It caps the voyage with aptly surreal details.

Kingsburg Sample fresh-pr
fruit at family-operated st.

Highway 99 Through Central Valley

25

Tripping down Hwy 99 offers a tour of what some call the real California. You'll find fresh-picked fruit, midcentury roadside cafes and the twang of Bakersfield's country music kings.

TRIP HIGHLIGHTS

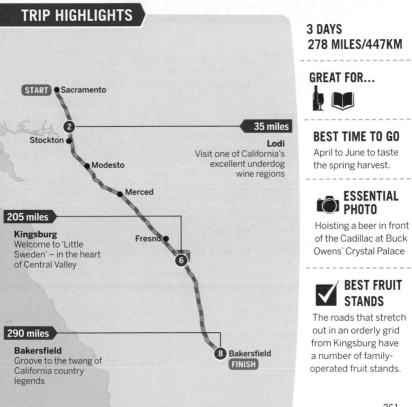

3 DAYS
278 MILES/447KM

GREAT FOR...

BEST TIME TO GO

April to June to taste the spring harvest.

ESSENTIAL PHOTO

Hoisting a beer in front of the Cadillac at Buck Owens' Crystal Palace

BEST FRUIT STANDS

The roads that stretch out in an orderly grid from Kingsburg have a number of family-operated fruit stands.

START ● Sacramento

2

Stockton ●

● Modesto

● Merced

35 miles

Lodi
Visit one of California's excellent underdog wine regions

205 miles

Kingsburg
Welcome to 'Little Sweden' – in the heart of Central Valley

Fresno ●

6

290 miles

Bakersfield
Groove to the twang of California country legends

8 ● Bakersfield
FINISH

25

Highway 99 Through Central Valley

With the AC off and the windows down, the rush of heat through the open window smells of tilled earth, pollen and, somehow, even sunshine. Once known as 'California's Main Street,' the byway between Sacramento and Bakersfield reveals a part of California that few slow down to enjoy – birthplace of a raucous brand of country music and two-stoplight farm towns that fade under 300-plus annual days of squint-bright sunshine.

---

❶ Sacramento

Taste the goods of the valley first at the sprawling **Sacramento Central Farmers Market** (www.california-grown.com; cnr 8th & W St, under Hwy 80 overpass; admission free; ☺8am-noon Sun; 🚻). In summer, Sacramento has a market every day of the week, but the biggest and best is on Sunday mornings year-round. It's held conveniently near the on-ramp to Hwy 99, under the elevated freeway at 8th and W St. Throughout summer it sells many of the 300-odd crops from the valley, a colorful riot of fruits and veggies that left the vine hours earlier: corn, stone fruit, strawberries and leafy greens. With a trunk full of vitals, start the voyage south, creeping out of the oft-jammed lanes of Elk Grove's suburban sprawl and into the sprawling valley. Soon, the air takes on the inimitable smell of the region, a mix of sweet pollen and pungent cattle.

🛏 p267

The Drive » As you leave Sacramento and head south on Hwy 99 the clogged traffic of the suburbs slowly give way to agricultural fields and large vineyards. If traffic is moving, you will arrive at Lodi in 45 minutes.

TRIP HIGHLIGHT

2 Lodi

Although Lodi used to be the 'Watermelon Capital of the World,' today, wine rules this patch of the valley. Breezes from the Sacramento River Delta soothe the area's hot vineyards, where more zinfandel grapes are grown than anywhere else in the world. Some particularly old vines have been tended by the same families for a century. Lodi's diverse soil is a sometimes rocky, sometimes sandy loam, giving its zinfandels a range of characteristics. Get your first taste of Lodi's powerful,

LINK YOUR TRIP

21 Highway 49 Through Gold Country

Connect to this northern trip through the towns that hosted California's gold rush. In Sacramento, take I-80 east to Auburn to connect with Hwy 49.

24 Lazy Delta Dawdle

Follow the same water that rushes out of the Sierra to flood these fields on a trip down the Sacramento River Delta, just east of Sacramento along the American River.

sun-soaked zins at the **Lodi Wine & Visitor Center** (www.lodiwine.com; 2545 W Turner Rd; tastings $5; ⏰10am-5pm), where 100 local vintages are sold by the glass at the tasting bar. Another stop, where you can sip the region's boutique wines and sample experimental labels by more famous names, is the Italian-style **Vino Piazza**. Park the car, order a bistro lunch and amble between tasting rooms.

✕ ⍞ p267

The Drive » Before leaving Lodi, make a circuit of its small but developing wine region – there's a map available at the visitor center. Follow Hwy 99 south through the valley, passing Stockton along the way. You'll reach Turlock in one hour.

---

❸ Turlock

Turlock is a city that's become a kind of Grand Central Station of Central Valley's cattle trade. Turlock is tiny, so it isn't hard to spot the stockyards near the center of town, where livestock options happen daily. A quick jog south on Rte 165 approaches the **Hilmar Cheese Factory** (www.hilmarcheese.com; 9001 North Lander Avenue, Hilmar; admission free; ⏰7am-7pm Mon-Sun; ♿). Aptly on scale with the agri-industry of the valley, it is the largest cheese-manufacturing site in the world, processing a million pounds of cheese a day. The product isn't gourmet (many of those million pounds

are simple varieties of cheddar or jack); the stars of the expansive visitors center are 'Squeakers,' young curds of cheese with a texture that squeaks as you chew them. A robotic cheese-making exhibit led by an animated Jersey cow, Daisy, is likely to thrill kids and creep out their parents.

The Drive » Leaving Turlock you'll get a glimpse of the California Aquaduct, which diverts the Sierra snowmelt to these farms. You'll also pass Chowchilla, which translates as 'murderers' in native Chauchila. Appropriate, since the town is the site of two correctional facilities. The drive to Selma is about one hour and 20 minutes.

---

❹ Selma

To taste more fresh goods, travel another hour and a half down Hwy 99 to Selma (the 'Raisin Capital of the World'), where you'll find the **Circle K Ranch** (www.circlekranch.com; 8640 E Manning Ave, Selma; ⏰8am-6pm Mon-Sat; ♿) just east of the highway amid orchards of peaches, plums and nectarines. The store has seasonal fruits and nuts from May to November, but the best deals are in the adjacent packing house, where, aided by some passable Spanish, it's possible to barter for a few bushels of freshly picked goods for a fraction of supermarket price.

KINGS OF BAKERSFIELD SOUND

Driving down Hwy 99 requires getting on a first-name basis with Bakersfield's two drawling titans: Merle and Buck. Masters of twanging Telecasters and hayseed heartbreak, they're the country kings of the Central Valley.

» *I'm Gonna Break Every Heart I Can* – Merle Haggard

» *I've Got a Tiger by the Tail* – Buck Owens

» *Okie from Muskogee* – Merle Haggard

» *Second Fiddle* – Buck Owens

» *The Bottle Let Me Down* – Merle Haggard

» *Under Your Spell Again* – Buck Owens

» *Swinging Doors* – Merle Haggard

» *The Streets of Bakersfield* – Buck Owens and Dwight Yoakam

Buck Owens' Crystal Palace Statue of Hank Williams (left) by Bill Rains

The Drive >> Orchards, orchards, everywhere! Go north east on S McCall Ave and take a right on E Manning Ave to enter Reedley, an easy 10-minute drive.

⑤ Reedley

Just east of Selma's sleepy downtown is the downright comatose Reedley ('the World's Fruit Basket'). Reedley was the wheat transport hub during the late 19th century and hasn't changed much since. Strolling one end of the sun-beaten downtown to the other, past the remodeled 1903 opera house in the shadow of the water tower, takes a few minutes. Reedley is the hub of the surprising Japanese American farm community, many of whom moved here after being interned during WWII. Visit www.reedley.com for an interactive **walking tour**.

The Drive >> Go south on County Rd J31 and then back toward Hwy 99 on Ave 400. This part of the drive – about 15 minutes – will pass one amazing orchard after the next.

TRIP HIGHLIGHT

⑥ Kingsburg

When you see the giant Scandinavian teapot water tower you'll know you've arrived in Little Sweden. Kingsburg's adorable downtown is done up in Swedish-inspired architecture, a testament to the Swedish farmers who settled here in the 1870s. By the 1920s some 94% of the population within a 3-mile radius had Swedish ancestry. Drop into the **Svensk Butik** (www.svenskbutik. net, 1465 Draper; ☺9am-5pm

LOCAL KNOWLEDGE: THE BAKERSFIELD SOUND

Some of the best places for music were surrounding towns like Farmersville – little places with no air-conditioning, no TV. Folks would come outside and drink beer and play guitar, and kids would play in the yard. You'd hear twangs from Texas, Oklahoma and Arkansas. That became the 'Bakersfield Sound.'

Gerald Haslam, Oildale, CA

Mon-Sat) to get all kinds of imported Swedish food and gifts (yes, they have Viking hats). Kingsburg also produces raisins...*a lot* of raisins. Heading just north of town on Golden State Blvd, you'll find the **Sun Maid Raisin Store** (13525 S. Bethel Ave; ⊙9:30-5pm Mon-Fri), where you can get all kinds of dried fruit and snap classic road-trip photos in front of the giant raisin box.

✕ p267

The Drive » Back out to Hwy 99 and 30 minutes further south is Tulare.

- - - - - - - - - - - - -

❼ Tulare

Tulare is another small agricultural hub and one-time headquarters of Southern Pacific railroad. Now the biggest news in town is the **International Agri-Center** (☎559-688-1751; www.farmshow.org; 4450 S Laspina St, Tulare; half-/full-day farm tours $15/$25; ⊙by appointment; ♿) and its annual World Ag Expo, held in February.

Native son David Watte offers half-day tours of local farms through the Agri-Center year around. Want to wander through fields of black-eyed beans or under shady almond trees? Watte is your man. He hosts groups of growers from other parts of the world and any city slickers looking to, in his own words, 'stop and kick the tires a little bit.' His own family farm – all 4000 acres of it – grows dairy feed and cotton.

✕ p267

The Drive » In the hour that it takes to drive to Bakersfield, the landscape is dotted by evidence of California's *other* gold rush: rusting rigs alongside the route that continue to burrow into Southern California's vast oil fields.

- - - - - - - - - - - - -

TRIP HIGHLIGHT

❽ Bakersfield

The children of tough-as-nails 'Okies' (people from Oklahoma) arrived in Bakersfield to work the derricks and minted the 'Bakersfield Sound' in

the mid-1950s. The poorly mannered child of western swing, Bakersfield's brand of country waved a defiant middle finger to the silky country of Nashville. Its heroes Buck Owens and Merle Haggard have streets named after them. Learn about them at the musty **Kern County Museum** (☎661-852-5000; www.kcmuseum.org; 3801 Chester Ave, Bakersfield; adult/child $8/5; ⊙10am-5pm Mon-Sat, noon-5pm Sun; ♿). The music memorabilia on the second floor includes the gold lamé stage gear of Bonnie Owens, the first lady of Bakersfield. She chalked up marriages to Buck (who supplied her surname *and* Merle Haggard.

At night, check out **Buck Owens' Crystal Palace** (☎661-328-7560; www.buckowens.com; 2800 Buck Owens Blvd, Bakersfield; mains $8-25; ⊙restaurant 5pm-midnight Mon-Sat, 9:30am-2pm Sun). Part music museum, part honky-tonk, part steakhouse, the Palace has a top-drawer country act every night. Check out the 1974 Pontiac convertible mounted behind the bar. Designed by rhinestone cowboy clothier Nudie Cohn, it's decorated with six-shooter door handles and a hand-tooled leather interior and is studded with silver dollars. According to lore, Buck won it off Elvis Presley in a poker game.

✕ 🛏 p267

Eating & Sleeping

Sacramento ❶

🛏 Citizen Hotel   Boutique Hotel $$
(📞916-492-4460; 926 J St; r $159, ste from $215; 📶) This ultrahip, recently remodeled hotel is stylish, whimsically decorated and the sleekest place to stay in Sacramento. They also have bikes to borrow: perfect for cruising the American River Trail.

🛏 Grange Restaurant   Modern American $$
(📞916-492-4460; 926 J St; mains from $25; ⏰6:30am-10pm; 📶) On the first floor of the Citizen Hotel, this upscale, locally sourced, hyper-seasonal restaurant will introduce you to the flavors of the Sacramento Valley.

Lodi ❷

🍴 Crush Kitchen & Bar   Italian $$
(www.crushkitchen.com; 115 S School St; mains $17-25; ⏰11:30am-9:30pm Sun, Mon, Thu, to 11:30pm Fri-Sat) Several levels of sophistication above anything else in town, the simple, rustic dishes – gnocchi with truffle oil, tomato salad, duck confit – are perfectly paired with the region's bold zinfandel .

🛏 Wine & Roses   B&B $$$
(📞209-334-6988; www.winerose.com; 2505 W Turner Rd; r $169-269📶) Surrounded by a rose garden and deep green lawn, this luxurious offering has tasteful, modern, romantic rooms with slate baths and fine linens. The nicer rooms come with private decks where you can soak up the sun.

Kingsburg ❻

🍴 Stockholm Bakery   Bakery $
(📞559-897-3377; www.stockholmbakery.com; 1448 Draper St; meals $5-9; ⏰9am-6pm Mon-Sat) You can butter up on all kinds of delectable Swedish baked goods at this cute bakery. They serve Swedish pancakes (in the morning) and traditional Scandinavian sandwiches with smoked salmon, cucumbers and dill.

Tulare ❼

🍴 Hazel's Kitchen   Sandwiches $
(www.thehazelskitchen.com; 237 N L Street; meals $10; ⏰9am-2pm Mon-Fri) This cute cafe occupies an the first floor of an early 1900s farmhouse and delivers amazing sandwiches. The teriyaki chicken comes on a soft Portuguese roll and the hot pastrami is pure perfection!

Bakersfield ❽

🍴 Dewar's Candy Shop   Ice Cream $
(📞661-322-0933; 1120 Eye St; mains $3-10; ⏰11am-9pm Mon-Thu, to 10pm Fri & Sat; 👶) A classic, pastel-painted soda fountain with fresh-made ice cream and candies. Flavors, which change seasonally, include lemon flake and cotton candy and they're all made from ingredients from surrounding farms.

🍴 Noriega Hotel   Basque $$
(📞661-322-8419; 525 Sumner St; lunch $14, dinner $20; ⏰Tue-Sun) Surly Basque gentlemen pat their ample stomachs over communal bottles of wine at this family-style institution, which recently won a James Beard award (a big deal in the elite American culinary world). Oxtail, pork chops and veal – it's all delicious. Dining hours are strict (breakfast is from 7am to 9am, lunch is noon, dinner is 7pm).

🛏 Padre Hotel   Boutique Hotel $$
(📞661-427-4900; www.thepadrehotel.com; 1702 8th St; r $89-199, ste from $500) This historic tower came roaring back to life and is looking sharp after a blindingly stylish retrofit. The standard rooms have cool details, foam beds, thick sheets and designer furniture. The suites (like the 'Oil Baron') are whimsical, decadent and out of this world.

Southern California Trips

SURF, SAND AND SEX WILL ALWAYS SELL SOCAL, especially in Hollywood's star-studded dreamscapes. The reality won't disappoint: the swimsuits are smaller, the water warmer, summers less foggy.

You'll find more adventure inland. Turn up the heat in SoCal's deserts. Start with the chic resorts of Palm Springs, then dig deep into the backcountry beauty of Death Valley and Joshua Tree, where dusty 4WD roads lead to ghost towns and hidden springs.

Escape to cool mountain climes around Big Bear Lake, or to artistic Idyllwild. Then leave the crowds behind on SoCal's most iconic road trips: the Spanish Mission Trail or Route 66, the USA's much-celebrated 'Mother Road'.

Coronado (Trip 27)
SLOBO MITIC / ISTOCKPHOTOS ©

Southern California Trips

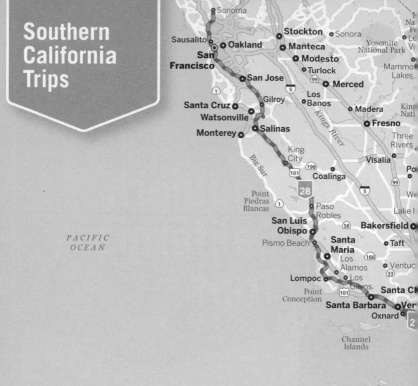

Classic Trip

26 Disneyland & Orange County Beaches 2–4 Days
Meet Mickey Mouse, then surf the sun-bronzed 'OC' coast. (p273)

27 Fun on the San Diego Coast 2–4 Days
Surf's up and the sun (almost) always shines, from Coronado to Carlsbad. (p283)

28 Mission Trail 4–5 Days
Follow in the historic footsteps of Spanish colonial soldiers and Catholic priests. (p295)

29 SoCal Pop Culture 3 Days
Where film and TV stars, new-age hippies and surfer punks collide. (p303)

Classic Trip

30 Route 66 3–4 Days
Dillydally through the desert, then zoom past retro icons into LA. (p313)

31 Big Bear & Rim of the World Scenic Byway 2–3 Days
Ride high in the forested San Bernardino Mountains to Big Bear Lake. (p323)

Classic Trip

32 Life in Death Valley 3 Days
Old West mining ghost towns, strange geology and inspiring panoramic views. (p331)

33 Palm Springs & Joshua Tree Oases 2–3 Days
Where palm trees shade hot springs and watering holes for wildlife. (p341)

34 Palms to Pines Scenic Byway 2 Days
Beat the desert heat in the mountain hamlet of Idyllwild. (p349)

35 Temecula, Julian & Anza-Borrego 3 Days
Vineyards and apple farms, then off-roading in California's biggest state park. (p357)

☑ DON'T MISS

Seal Beach
Slow way down for this old-fashioned beach town, squeezed between LA and the OC, where you can learn to surf by the weather-beaten wooden pier on Trip 26

Sunny Jim Cave
North of San Diego in La Jolla, walk down spooky steps through a tunnel into California's only sea cave accessible to landlubbers on Trip 27

Amboy
Watch desert tumbleweeds blow by on Route 66 outside classic Roy's Cafe, with its giant-sized landmark neon sign, on Trip 30

Valley of the Falls
Tumble down the Rim of the World Scenic Byway to SoCal's pint-sized version of Yosemite Valley on Trip 31

Tecopa
Soak in hot-springs pools where Native Americans once camped, then grab a snack at China Ranch Date Farm on Trip 32

Laguna Beach Dozens of beaches sprawl along a few miles of coastline

Classic Trip

Disneyland & Orange County Beaches

26

Let the kids loose at the 'Happiest Place on Earth,' then strike out for sunny SoCal beaches – as seen on TV and the silver screen. It's impossible not to have fun on this coastal getaway.

TRIP HIGHLIGHTS

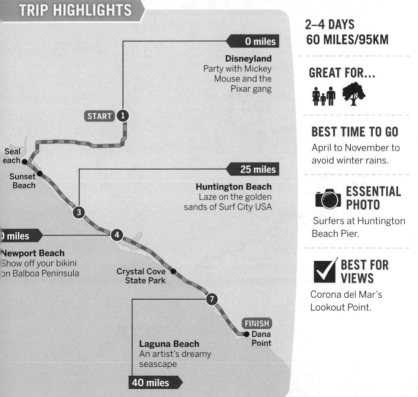

0 miles

Disneyland
Party with Mickey Mouse and the Pixar gang

START 1

Seal Beach

Sunset Beach

3

25 miles

Huntington Beach
Laze on the golden sands of Surf City USA

0 miles

4

Newport Beach
Show off your bikini on Balboa Peninsula

Crystal Cove State Park

7

FINISH
Dana Point

Laguna Beach
An artist's dreamy seascape

40 miles

**2–4 DAYS
60 MILES/95KM**

GREAT FOR...

BEST TIME TO GO
April to November to avoid winter rains.

ESSENTIAL PHOTO
Surfers at Huntington Beach Pier.

BEST FOR VIEWS
Corona del Mar's Lookout Point.

273

Classic Trip

26 Disneyland & Orange County Beaches

It's true you'll find gorgeous sunsets, prime surfing breaks and just-off-the-boat seafood when road tripping down the OC's sun-kissed coastal Hwy 1. Yet it's the unexpected and serendipitous discoveries you'll remember long after you've left this blissful 42 miles of surf and sand behind. Top it all off with a day or two at Disneyland's theme parks, and let's call it a wrap for the perfect SoCal family vacation.

TRIP HIGHLIGHT

❶ Disneyland

No SoCal theme park welcomes more millions of visitors every year than **Disneyland** (☎714-781-4636; www.disneyland.com; 1313 S Harbor Blvd; 1-day single-park admission adult/child $87/81, 2-park day pass $125/119; 🚹). From the ghostly skeletons of Pirates of the Caribbean to the screeching monkeys of the Indiana Jones Adventure, there's magical detail everywhere. Retro-futuristic Tomorrowland is where the Finding Nemo Submarine Voyage and *Star Wars*–themed Star Tours and Jedi Training Academy

LINK YOUR TRIP

1 **Pacific Coast Highways**

Orange County is California's official section of the Pacific Coast Hwy (PCH), running along Hwy 1 between laidback Seal Beach and Dana Point.

27 **Fun on the San Diego Coast**

It's just a 30-mile drive south of Dana Point along I-5 to Carlsbad in San Diego's family-friendly North County.

await. Use the Fastpass system and you'll be hurtling through Space Mountain – still the park's best adrenaline pumper – in no time. After dark, watch fireworks explode over Sleeping Beauty's Castle.

Any fear of heights? Then ditch the Twilight Zone Tower of Terror at **Disney's California Adventure** (DCA), Disneyland's newer neighbor. DCA's lightheartedly themed areas highlight the best of the Golden State, while plenty of adventures like Route 66–themed Cars Land don't involve losing your lunch. An exception is rockin' California Screamin' at Paradise Pier: this whip-fast coaster looks like an old-school carnival ride, but from the moment it blasts forward with a cannon-shot whoosh, this monster never lets go. Catch the enthusiasm of the Pixar Play Parade by day and World of Color special-effects show at night.

Just outside the parks, **Downtown Disney** pedestrian mall is packed with souvenir shops, family restaurants, after-dark bars and entertainment venues and, in summer, live musicians playing for the crowds.

✖ 🛏 p281

The Drive Follow Harbor Blvd south for 3 not-very-scenic miles, then take Hwy 22 west through inland Orange County, merging onto the I-405 north. After another mile or so, exit onto Seal Beach Blvd, which crawls 3 miles toward the coast. Turn right onto Hwy 1, also known as the Pacific Coast Hwy (PCH) throughout Orange County, then take a left onto Main St in Seal Beach.

❷ Seal Beach

In the SoCal beauty pageant for pint-sized beach towns, Seal Beach is the winner of the crown. Stop here and you'll discover it's a refreshingly unhurried alternative to the more crowded Orange County coast further south. Its three-block **Main St** is a stoplight-free zone that bustles with mom-and-pop restaurants and indie shops that are low on 'tude and high on nostalgia. Follow the path of barefoot surfers as they trot toward the beach to where Main St ends, then walk out onto **Seal Beach Pier**. The 1906 original first fell victim to winter storms in the 1930s, and since then it has been rebuilt three times with a splintery, wooden boardwalk. Down on the **beach**, you'll find families spread out on blankets, building sandcastles and playing in the water – all of them ignoring that hideous oil derrick offshore.

LEIGHSMITHIMAGES / ALAMY ©

LOCAL KNOWLEDGE
VERONICA HILL

'California Travel Tips' YouTube host

Want to get the most bang for your buck at Disneyland or Disney's California Adventure? If your kids are too young to ride, ask for the rider-switch pass. Grab it from a cast member as you enter the ride (while your partner watches the kids). Afterward, give the pass to your partner so they can whisk through the FastPass line. If you have an impatient teenager, send them through the single-rider line instead.

Top: Oceanfront homes, Newport Beach
Left: Restaurant, Newport Beach
Right: Competitor at US Open of Surfing, Huntington Beach Pier

The gentle waves make Seal Beach a great place to learn to surf. **M&M Surfing School** (☎714-846-7873; www.surfingschool. com; 1hr/3hr group lesson \$45/65, wetsuit/surfboard rental \$15/25; 🚗) parks their van in the lot just north of the pier, off Ocean Ave at 8th St.

The Drive » Past a short bridge farther south along Hwy 1, drivers drop onto a mile-long spit of land known as Sunset Beach, with its biker bars and harborside kayak and stand-up paddle boarding (SUP) rental shops. Keep cruising Hwy 1 south another 6 miles past Bolsa Chica State Beach and Ecological Reserve to Huntington Beach Pier.

TRIP HIGHLIGHT

❸ Huntington Beach

In 'Surf City USA,' SoCal obsession's with wave riding hits its frenzied peak. There's a statue of Hawaiian surfer Duke Kahanamoku at the intersection of Main St and PCH, and if you look down, you'll see names of legendary surfers in the sidewalk **Surfers' Hall of Fame** (www.hsssurf.com/ shof/). A few blocks east, the **International Surfing Museum** (☎714-960-3483; www.surfingmuseum.org; 411 Olive Ave; suggested donation \$2; ☺noon-5pm Mon & Wed-Fri, noon-9pm Tue, 11am-6pm Sat & Sun) honors those same legends. Then join the crowds on the **Huntington Beach Pier**, where you

277

Classic Trip

can catch up-close views of daredevils barreling through tubes. The surf here may not be the ideal place to test your newbie skills, however – locals can be territorial. In summer, the US Open of Surfing draws more than 600 world-class surfers and 400,000 spectators with a minivillage of concerts, motocross demos and skater jams. As for **Huntington City Beach** itself, it's wide and flat – a perfect place to snooze on the sand on a giant beach towel. Snag a fire pit just south of the pier to build an evening bonfire with friends.

✕ ⬛ p281

The Drive » From the Huntington Beach Pier at the intersection of Main St, drive south on Hwy 1 (PCH) alongside the ocean for another 4 miles to Newport Beach. Turn right onto W Balboa Blvd, leading onto the Balboa Peninsula, squeezed between the ocean and Balboa Island, off Newport Harbor.

TRIP HIGHLIGHT

❹ Newport Beach

As seen on Bravo's *Real Housewives of Orange County* and Fox's *The OC* and *Arrested Development,* in glitzy Newport Beach wealthy socialites, glamorous teens and gorgeous beaches all share the spotlight. Bikini vixens strut down the sandy beach stretching between the peninsula's twin piers, while boogie boarders brave human-eating waves at the **Wedge** and the ballet of yachts in the harbor makes you dream of being rich and famous. From the harbor, hop aboard a ferry over to old-fashioned **Balboa Island** or climb aboard the carousel by the landmark 1905 **Balboa Pavilion**. The Ferris wheel still spins at pint-sized **Balboa Fun Zone** (www.thebalboafunzone.com; per ride $3; ⏰11am-8pm Sun-Thu, to 9pm Fri, to 10pm Sat; 🚼), nearby the **Newport Harbor Nautical Museum** (📞949-675-8915; http://explorocean.org; 600 E Bay Ave; adult/child $4/2; ⏰11am-3pm Mon-Thu, to 6pm Fri & Sat, to 5pm Sun; 🚼). Just inland, visit the cutting-edge contemporary **Orange County Museum of Art** (📞949-759-1122; www.ocma.net; 850 San Clemente Dr; adult/child $12/free; ⏰11am-5pm Wed-Sun, to 8pm Thu) to escape SoCal's vainglorious pop culture.

✕ ⬛ p281

↱ ## DETOUR: KNOTT'S BERRY FARM

Start: ❶ **Disneyland**

Hear the screams? Got teens? Hello, **Knott's Berry Farm** (📞714-220-5200; www.knotts.com; 8039 Beach Blvd, Buena Park; adult/child $58/29; ⏰open daily from 10am, closing times vary; 🚼), America's first theme park, which opened in 1940. Today high-scream coasters lure fast-track fanatics. Look up as you enter to see the bare feet of riders who've removed their flip-flops for the Silver Bullet, the suspended coaster careening past overhead, famed for its corkscrew, double spiral and outside loop. In October, Knott's hosts SoCal's scariest after-dark Halloween party. Year-round, the *Peanuts* gang keeps moppets happy in Camp Snoopy, while the next-door water park **Knott's Soak City USA** (📞714-220-5200; www.soakcityoc.com; adult/child $26/23; ⏰open mid-May–Sep, hr vary; 🚼) keeps you cool on blazing-hot summer days. Knott's is a 20-minute drive from Disneyland via I-5 north to La Palma Ave west.

The Drive >> South of Newport Beach, prime-time ocean views are just a short detour off Hwy 1. First drive south across the bridge over Newport Channel, then after 3 miles turn right onto Marguerite Ave in Corona del Mar. Once you reach the coast, take another right onto Ocean Blvd.

Disneyland Jolly Trolley at Mickey's Toontown

5 Corona del Mar

Savor some of SoCal's most celebrated ocean views from the bluffs of Corona del Mar, a chichi bedroom community south of Newport Channel. Several postcard beaches, rocky coves and child-friendly tidepools beckon along this idyllic stretch of coast. One of the best viewpoints is at breezy **Lookout Point** on Ocean Blvd near Heliotrope Ave. Below the rocky cliffs to the east is half-mile long Main Beach, officially **Corona del Mar State Beach** (☎949-644-3151; www. parks.ca.gov; entry per vehicle $15; ⏰6am-10pm), with fire rings and volleyball courts (arrive early on weekends to get a parking spot). Stairs lead down to Pirates Cove which has a great, waveless pocket beach for families – scenes from *Gilligan's Island* were shot here. Head east on Ocean Blvd to **Inspiration Point**, near the corner of Orchid Ave, for more vistas of surf, sand and sea.

The Drive >> Follow Orchid Ave back north to Hwy 1, then turn right and drive southbound. Traffic thins out as ocean views become more wild and uncluttered by housing developments that head up into the hills on your left. It's just a couple of miles to the entrance of Crystal Cove State Park.

6 Crystal Cove State Park

With 3.5 miles of open beach and over 2300 acres of undeveloped woodland, **Crystal Cove State Park** (☎949-494-3539; www.parks.ca.gov, www.crystalcovestatepark. com; entry per vehicle $15; ⏰6am-sunset) lets you almost forget that you're in a crowded metro area. That is, once you get past the parking lot and stake out a place on the sand. Many visitors don't know it, but it's also an underwater park where scuba enthusiasts can check out the wreck of

a Navy Corsair fighter plane that went down in 1949. Or just go tidepooling, fishing, kayaking and surfing along Crystal Cove's exhilaratingly wild, windy shoreline. On the inland side of Hwy 1, miles of hiking and mountain biking trails wait for landlubbers.

✗ ⏹ p281

The Drive >> Drive south on Hwy 1 for another 4 miles or so. As shops, restaurants, art galleries, motels and hotels start to crowd the highway once again, you've arrived in Laguna Beach. Downtown is a maze of one-way streets just east of the Laguna Canyon Rd (Hwy 133) intersection.

TRIP HIGHLIGHT

7 Laguna Beach

This early 20th-century artist colony's secluded coves, romantic-looking cliffs and Arts and

Classic Trip

Crafts bungalows come as a relief after miles of suburban beige-box architecture. With joie de vivre, Laguna celebrates its bohemian roots with summer arts festivals, dozens of galleries and the acclaimed **Laguna Art Museum** (☎949-494-8971; www.lagunaartmuseum.org; 307 Cliff Dr; adult/child $7/free; ☺11am-5pm Fri-Tue, to 9pm Thu). In downtown's village, it's easy to while away an afternoon browsing the chic boutiques. Down on the shore, **Main Beach** is crowded with volleyball players and sunbathers. Just north atop the bluffs, **Heisler Park** winds past public art, palm trees, picnic tables and grand views of rocky shores and tidepools. Drop down to Divers Cove, a deep, protected inlet. Heading south, dozens of public beaches sprawl along just a few miles of coastline. Keep a sharp eye out for 'beach access' signs off Hwy 1, or pull into locals' favorite **Aliso Beach County Park** (www.ocparks.com/alisobeach; 31131 S Pacific Coast Hwy; parking per hr $1; ☺6am-10pm).

❌ 🍴 p281

The Drive » Keep driving south of downtown Laguna Beach on Hwy 1 (PCH) for about 3 miles to Aliso Beach County Park, then another 4 miles into the town of Dana Point. Turn right onto Green Lantern St, then left onto Cove Rd, which winds past the state beach and Ocean Institute onto Dana Point Harbor Dr.

- - - - - - - - - - - - - -

❽ Dana Point

Last up is marina-flanked Dana Point, the namesake of 19th-century adventurer Richard Dana, who famously called the area 'the only romantic spot on the coast.' These days it's more about family fun and sportfishing

DETOUR: PACIFIC MARINE MAMMAL CENTER

Start: ❼ Laguna Beach

About 3 miles northeast of Laguna Beach is the heart-warming **Pacific Marine Mammal Center** (☎949-494-3050; www.pacificmmc.org; 20612 Laguna Canyon Rd; admission by donation; ☺10am-4pm; 👶), dedicated to rescuing and rehabilitating injured or ill marine mammals. This nonprofit center has a small staff and many volunteers who help nurse rescued pinnipeds (mostly sea lions and seals) back to health before releasing them into the wild. Stop by and take a self-guided facility tour to learn more about these marine mammals and to visit the 'patients' out back.

boats at **Dana Point Harbor**. Designed for kids, the **Ocean Institute** (☎949-496-2274; www.ocean-institute.org; 24200 Dana Pt Harbor Dr; adult/child $6.50/4.50; ☺10am-3pm Sat & Sun; 👶) owns replicas of historic tall ships, maritime-related exhibits and a floating research lab. East of the harbor, **Doheny State Beach** (☎949-496-6172; www.parks.ca.gov, www.dohenystatebeach.org; entry per vehicle $15; ☺6am-10pm, to 8pm Nov-Feb; 👶) is where you'll find picnic tables, volleyball courts, an oceanfront bike path and a sandy beach for swimming, surfing, tidepooling and scuba diving.

Eating & Sleeping

Disneyland ❶

🛏 Candy Cane Inn   Motel $$

(📞714-774-5284, 800-345-7057; www.
candycaneinn.net; 1747 S Harbor Blvd; r $95-179;
❄ 🖥 🏊 👪) Bright bursts of flowers, tidy
grounds and a cobblestone drive welcome
guests to this cute motel within walking
distance of Disneyland.

🛏 Disney's Grand
Californian Hotel   Hotel $$$

(📞714-635-2300; www.disneyland.com; 1600
S Disneyland Dr; r from $385; ❄ @ 🖥 🏊 👪)
Timber beams soar above the fireplace lobby
of this six-story homage to the Golden State's
Arts and Crafts architectural movement. Rooms
have cushy amenities.

Huntington Beach ❸

🍴 Sugar Shack   Cafe $

(www.hbsugarshack.com; 213 Main St; mains
$6-10; ⏰6am-4pm Mon-Tue & Thu, to 8pm Wed,
to 5pm Fri-Sun; 👪) Expect a wait at this HB
institution with a bustling outdoor patio, or get
here early when surfer dudes don their wetsuits.
Breakfast served all day.

🛏 Shorebreak
Hotel   Boutique Hotel $$$

(📞714-861-4470; www.shorebreakhotel.com;
500 Pacific Coast Hwy; r $205-475; ❄ @ 🖥 🏊)
This hip hotel livens things up with a surf
concierge, yoga studio, beanbag chairs in the
lobby and geometric-patterned rooms. Knock
back sunset cocktails on the upstairs deck.

Newport Beach ❹

🍴 Bear Flag Fish Company   Seafood $$

(📞949-673-3434; www.bearflagfishco.com;
407 31st St; dishes $4-15; ⏰11am-9pm Tue-Sat,
to 8pm Mon & Sun; 👪) Seafood market that's
the place for spankin' fresh oysters, fish tacos,
Hawaiian-style *poke* and more. Pick what you
want from the ice-cold display cases.

Bay Shores
Peninsula Hotel   Hotel $$$

(📞949-675-3463, 800-222-6675; www.
thebestinn.com; 1800 W Balboa Blvd; r incl
breakfast $190-300; ❄ @ 🖥 👪) This three-
story hotel's beachy hospitality, surf murals,
fresh-baked cookies, and boogie boards and
beach chairs to borrow make up for its steep
rates.

Crystal Cove State Park ❻

🍴 Ruby's Shake Shack   Fast Food $

(www.rubys.com; 7703 E Coast Hwy; menu items
$5-10; ⏰7am-7pm Mon-Thu, to 8pm Fri & Sat;
🖥 👪 🐾) At this easy-to-miss roadside wooden
shack, recently bought by the Ruby's Diner
chain, the milkshakes and ocean views are as
good as ever.

🛏 Crystal Cove
Beach Cottages   Cottage $$

(reservations 📞800-444-7275; www.crystalcove
beachcottages.com, www.reserveamerica.com;
r with shared bath $35-170, cottages $125-360;
👪) To snag these historic oceanfront cottages,
book on the first day of the month six months
before your intended stay – or pray for last-
minute cancellations.

Laguna Beach ❼

🍴 The Stand   Health Food $

(238 Thalia St; mains $5-10; ⏰7am-7pm; 🌱 👪)
Tiny barn-shaped kitchen with a wooden patio
reflects what's best about Laguna living. A long
vegan-friendly menu includes veggie tamales,
sunflower-sprout salads and banana-date
shakes.

🛏 Laguna Cliffs Inn   Hotel $$$

(📞949-497-6645, 800-297-0007; www.
lagunacliffsinn.com; 475 N Coast Hwy; r
$165-325; ❄ 🖥 🏊) Be it feng shui, friendly
staff, comfy beds or proximity to the beach,
something just feels right at this 36-room inn.
Hit the outdoor hot tub as the sun drops over
the ocean.

Legoland *A fun fantasy park of rides, shows and attractions*

Fun on the San Diego Coast

27

With 70 miles of coastline and a near-perfect climate, it's tough to know where to start. So just do as the locals do: grab a fish taco and a surfboard and head for the beaches.

TRIP HIGHLIGHTS

**2–4 DAYS
85 MILES/135KM**

GREAT FOR...

BEST TIME TO GO

May to September for prime-time beach weather.

ESSENTIAL PHOTO

The red-turreted Hotel del Coronado.

BEST FOR OUTDOORS

La Jolla's coves, beaches and nature preserves.

Carlsbad
FINISH

Encinitas

Del Mar

42 miles

La Jolla
Get back to nature along 'the Jewel' coast

6

35 miles

5

Ocean Beach

**Mission Beach &
Pacific Beach**
Old-fashioned carnival fun and kinetic beaches

Embarcadero

2

0 miles

1

START

Coronado
White-sand beaches strung along a blissful getaway 'island'

22 miles

Balboa Park
Find out who's who at San Diego's wild zoo

283

Most Americans work all year for a two-week vacation. San Diegans work all week for a two-day vacation at the beach. Family-fun attractions found just off the county's gorgeous coastal highways include the USS Midway Museum, Balboa Park zoo and Legoland theme park, along with dozens of beaches from ritzy to raucous. With SoCal's most idyllic weather, it's time to roll down the windows and chillax, dudes.

25 miles to
Oceanside 26 78
Carlsbad 9 *San Elijo Lagoon*
FINISH
Ba I
Leucadia
Encinitas
Cardiff-b the-S
Sol Be
Del

La J

PACIFIC OCEAN

TRIP HIGHLIGHT

1 Coronado

With the landmark 1888 Hotel del Coronado and one of America's top-rated beaches, the city of Coronado sits across San Diego Bay from downtown. It's miles away from the concrete jumble of the city and the chaos of more crowded beaches further north. After crossing the bay via the curved Coronado Bay Bridge, follow the tree-lined, manicured median strip of Orange Ave a mile toward Ocean Blvd, then park your car and walk around. Sprawling in front of the 'Hotel Del' is postcard-perfect **Coronado Municipal Beach**. Less than 5 miles further south, **Silver Strand State Beach** (📞619-435-5184; www.parks.ca.gov; 5000 Hwy 75; entry per car $10-15; 👶) also offers calm waters for family-friendly swimming. The strand's long, narrow sand spit connects back to the mainland, though people still call this 'Coronado Island.'

🍴 🛏 p290

The Drive » Follow Hwy 75 south of Silver Strand past San Diego National Wildlife Refuge, curving inland by Imperial Beach. Merge onto the I-5 northbound, then exit onto Hwy 163 northbound toward Balboa Park. Take exit 1C and follow the signs for the park and zoo.

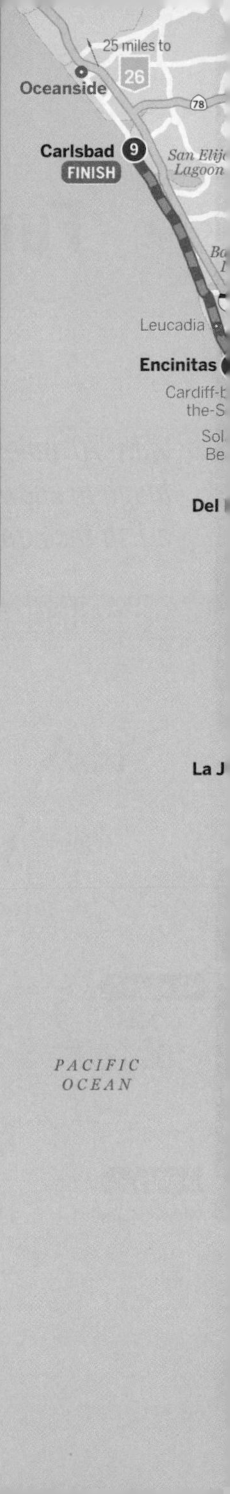

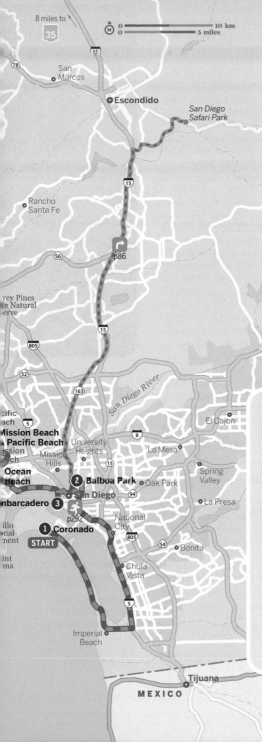

TRIP HIGHLIGHT

② Balboa Park

Spanish Revival–style pavilions from the 1915–16 Panama-California Exposition add a dash of the exotic to a day spent in **Balboa Park** (for our walking tour, see p292). This 1200-acre urban retreat is home to gardens, theaters, 15 museums and one giant outdoor organ pavilion. Without a doubt, the highlight is the **San Diego Zoo** (☏619-231-1515; www.sandiegozoo.org; 2920 Zoo Dr; adult/child entry with guided bus tour & aerial tram ride $42/32; ☺9am-5pm or 6pm daily, extended summer & holiday hr; 🚶). If it slithers, crawls, stomps, swims, leaps or flies, chances

---

§ LINK YOUR TRIP

26 Disneyland & Orange County Beaches

Cruise north on I-5 to Dana Point for another kid-friendly trip, combining knockout beaches with Disney's Magic Kingdom.

35 Temecula, Julian & Anza-Borrego

Escape to wine country, apple farms and desert resorts, starting 35 miles inland from Carlsbad via Hwy 78 east to I-15 north.

285

are you'll find it in this world-famous zoo. Conservation-minded signs guide visitors through multilevel walkways, where face-to-snout encounters aren't uncommon. Arrive early, when the animal denizens are most active.

 p290

The Drive >> Exit Balboa Park to the east via Zoo Pl, turning right onto Florida Dr and right again onto Pershing Dr. Merge onto I-5 north for over a mile, then take exit 17A. Drive almost another mile west on Hawthorn St toward the waterfront, then turn left onto Harbor Dr.

---

❸ Embarcadero

The Coronado ferry and cruise ships moor along downtown San Diego's waterfront **Embarcadero**. Well-manicured ocean-promenades stretch along Harbor Dr, where a line-up of historical sailing ships points the way to the **Maritime Museum** (📞619-234-9153; www.sdmaritime.org; 1492 N Harbor Dr; adult/child $15/8; ⊙9am-8pm, to 9pm late May-Aug; 🚻). Climb aboard the 1863 *Star of India* and don't miss seeing the B-39 Soviet attack submarine. More massive is the **USS Midway Museum** 📞619-544-9600; http://midway.org; 910 N Harbor Dr; adult/child $18/10; ⊙10am-5pm, last entry 4pm; 🚻). The Navy's longest-serving aircraft carrier (1945–92), it saw action in WWII, Vietnam and the Gulf War. Though *Top Gun's* Goose and Maverick may spring to mind at the sight of this floating city, a self-guided tour is the best way to experience history: crawl into berthing spaces, the galley and sick bay and, of course, peer over the flight deck with

WILCOX / CORBIS ©

its restored aircraft, including an F-14 Tomcat.

 🛏 p290

The Drive >> Follow Harbor Dr northwest for 3 miles as it curves along the waterfront past the airport. Turn right onto Nimitz Blvd for another mile, then left onto Chatsworth Blvd and right on Narragansett Ave. After a mile, you'll intersect Sunset Cliffs Blvd in Ocean Beach.

---

❹ Ocean Beach

San Diego's most bohemian seaside community, OB is a place of seriously scruffy haircuts and tattooed and pierced body art.

DETOUR: SAN DIEGO SAFARI PARK

Start: ❷ Balboa Park

Take a walk on the 'wild' side at **San Diego Safari Park** (📞760-747-8702; www.sandiegozoo.org; 15500 San Pasqual Valley Rd, Escondido; adult/child incl Africa Tram tour $42/32, combo ticket with San Diego Zoo $76/56; ⊙9am-5pm, extended summer & holiday hr; 🚻), where giraffes graze, lions lounge and rhinos romp more or less freely inside giant outdoor enclosures. For that safari feel, board the Africa Tram. The park is in Escondido, 30 miles north of Balboa Park via Hwy 163 and I-15 northbound; alternatively, it's 25 miles east of coastal Carlsbad (p289) via Hwy 78.

San Diego Orangutan

Newport Ave, the main drag, runs perpendicular to the beach through a downtown district of bars, street-food eateries, surf and music shops, and vintage-clothing and antiques boutiques. Half-mile-long **Ocean Beach Pier** has all the architectural allure of a freeway ramp, but at its end you'll get a great perspective on the coast. A bait-and-tackle shop rents fishing poles if you want to try your luck. Further north on **Dog Beach**, pups chase birds around the marshy area where the river meets the sea, or you could walk a few blocks south of the pier to **Sunset Cliffs Park** for surfing and yes, brilliant sunsets.

✗ 🛏 p290

The Drive » Follow stop-and-go Sunset Cliffs Blvd north Merge onto W Mission Bay Dr, which crosses over the water twice and curves past SeaWorld. Less than 4 miles from Ocean Beach, you'll intersect Mission Blvd; turn left to reach the main beach and Belmont Park.

- - - - - - - - - - - -

TRIP HIGHLIGHT

❺ Mission Beach & Pacific Beach

This is the SoCal of the movies: buffed surfers and bronzed sun worshippers pack the 3-mile-long stretch of beach from South Mission Jetty north to Pacific Beach Point. San Diego's best people-watching is along **Ocean Front Walk**, the boardwalk that connects the two beaches. For old-fashioned carnival fun in Mission Beach, **Belmont Park** (www.belmontpark. com; unlimited rides adult/child $27/16; ⊘ from 11am daily, closing times vary; 👪) has been giving kids a thrill with its Giant Dipper wooden roller coaster since 1925. There's also a large indoor pool and wave machines for faux-surfing, plus bumper cars, a tilt-a-whirl, carousel and other classic rides. At the ocean end of Garnet Ave in Pacific Beach, **Crystal Pier** is a mellow place to gaze out to sea or fish. Play beach volleyball and fly a kite inland at **Mission Bay Park** (www.sandiego.gov/park-and-recreation; 1775 E Mission Bay Dr; 🚻🚼).

✗ 🛏 p290

The Drive » Heading north of Pacific Beach on Mission Blvd, turn left onto Loring Ave, which curves right onto La Jolla Blvd. Winding through several traffic circles, the boulevard streams along the coast for 3 miles to downtown La Jolla, stretched along Pearl St east of the beach.

- - - - - - - - - - - - - -

TRIP HIGHLIGHT

❻ La Jolla

Sitting pretty and privileged on one of SoCal's loveliest sweeps of coast, La Jolla (Spanish for 'the jewel'; say la-*hoy*-ah, if you please) is a ritzy town of shimmering beaches, downtown fashionista boutiques and clifftop mansions. Take advantage of the sunshine by kayaking and snorkeling at **La Jolla Cove**, or go scuba diving and snorkeling in **San Diego-La Jolla Underwater Park**, a protected ecological zone harboring a variety of marine life, kelp forests, reefs and canyons. You can walk down 145 spooky steps to **Sunny

Jim Cave, accessed via the **Cave Store** (📞858-459-0746; www.cavestore.com; 1325 Coast Rd; adult/child $4/3; ⊙10am-5pm).

Heading north along La Jolla Shores Dr, the oceanfront **Birch Aquarium at Scripps** (📞858-534-3474; http://aquarium.ucsd.edu; 2300 Exhibition Way; adult/child $14/9.50; ⊙9am-5pm; 🚻) has kid-friendly tidepool displays. Another 5 miles further north, **Torrey Pines State Natural Reserve** (📞858-755-2063; www.torreypine.org, www.parks.ca.gov; 12600 N Torrey Pines Rd; entry per car $10-15; ⊙8am-dusk) is a haven for the endangered Torrey pine tree and offers nature walks above a state beach, where hang gliders dramatically soar in for a landing.

✗ p291

The Drive » Driving below the natural preserve next to Torrey Pines State Beach, panoramic ocean views open up as the coastal highway narrows and crosses over a lagoon, then climbs the sandstone cliffs toward Del Mar, just over 2 miles away.

- - - - - - - - - - - - - -

❼ Del Mar

The ritziest of North County's seaside suburbs is home to the pink, Mediterranean-style **Del Mar Racetrack & Fairgrounds** (📞858-755-1141; www.dmtc.com; tickets from $6; ⊙race season mid-Jul–early Sep), cofounded

in 1937 by celebrities Bing Crosby, Jimmy Durante and Oliver Hardy. It's worth braving the crowds on opening day, if nothing else to see the amazing spectacle of the ladies' over-the-top hats. Brightly colored hot-air balloons are another trademark sight in Del Mar – book ahead for a sunset flight with **California Dreamin'** (📞800-373-3359; www.californiadreamin.com; per person $190-280). Downtown Del Mar (sometimes called 'the village') extends for about a mile along Camino del Mar. At its hub, **Del Mar Plaza** (www.delmarplaza.com; 555 Camino del Mar) shopping center has restaurants, boutiques and upper-level terraces that look out to sea. At the west end of 15th St, **Seagrove Park** has grassy beach front lawns, perfect for picnicking.

✗ 🛏 p291

The Drive » Continue up the coast on Camino del Mar, leading onto S Coast Hwy 101 into Solana Beach, where the arts, fashion and antiques shops of Cedros Ave Design District are just one block inland. Continue north on S Coast Hwy 101 into Encinitas, about 6 miles north of Del Mar.

- - - - - - - - - - - - - -

❽ Encinitas

Technically part of Encinitas, the southern satellite of **Cardiff-by-

the-Sea has groovy restaurants, surf shops and new-agey businesses lined up along the coast. Known for its surfing breaks and laid-back crowds, Cardiff sits by the **San Elijo Lagoon** (☎760-623-3026; www.sanelijo.org; 2710 Manchester Ave; admission free; ⏰nature center 9am-5pm), an ecological preserve popular with bird-watchers and hikers.

Since Paramahansa Yoganada built his **Self-Realization Fellowship Retreat** (☎760-753-1811; www.yogananda-srf.org; 215 K St; admission free; ⏰meditation garden 9am-5pm Tue-Sat, 11am-5pm Sun) by the sea here in 1937, Encinitas has been a magnet for healers and spiritual seekers. Its gold lotus domes border **Swami's**, a powerful reef break favored by territorial local surfers. Apart from outdoor cafes, bars, restaurants and surf shops, downtown's main attraction is the 1928 **La Paloma Theatre** (☎760-436-7469; www.lapalomatheatre.com; 471 S Coast Hwy 101), often screening indie, international and cult films (call for schedules).

✗ p291

The Drive » About 4 miles north of Encinitas, S Coast Hwy 101 becomes Carlsbad Blvd,

---

> **LOCAL KNOWLEDGE: CHILDREN'S POOL**
>
> Local dad Paul Anderson recommends taking kids to the Children's Pool, south of Ellen Browning Scripps Park along the coast in La Jolla. But not for swimming. Seals and sea lions have taken to lolling on the protected beach in recent years, and children now come to watch the pinnipeds and their pups. The pool has garnered headlines recently, as some local activists want the seals removed and the pool returned to its intended status as a swimming beach for children. Stay tuned. The beach and cove are off Coast Blvd, just north of the contemporary-art museum.

slowly rolling north along the ocean cliffs for just over 5 miles into Carlsbad Village. If you go too far, you'll hit Oceanside, largely a bedroom community for Camp Pendleton Marine Base.

- - - - - - - - - - - -

❾ Carlsbad

One of California's last remaining tidal wetlands, **Batiquitos Lagoon** (☎760-931-0800; www.batiquitosfoundation.org; 7380 Gabbiano Ln; ⏰nature center 9am-12:30pm Mon-Fri, to 3pm Sat & Sun) separates Carlsbad from Encinitas. Go hiking here to see prickly pear cactus, coastal sage scrub and eucalyptus trees, as well as great heron and snowy egrets. Then detour inland past the blossoming springtime flower fields of **Carlsbad Ranch** (☎760-431-0352; www.theflowerfields.com; 5704 Paseo del Norte; adult/child $11/6; ⏰usually 9am-6pm Mar–mid-May) to **Legoland** (☎760-918-5346; http://california.legoland.com; 1 Legoland Dr; adult/child $72/62, incl water park $87/77; ⏰usually 10am-5pm Thu-Mon, extended daily summer & holiday hr; 🚼), a fun fantasy park of rides, shows and attractions for the elementary school set. Back at the coast, you can go beachcombing for seashells on long, sandy **Carlsbad State Beaches** (☎760-483-3143; www.parks.ca.gov; entry per car $10; ⏰dawn-sunset), off Carlsbad Blvd. The beaches run south of Carlsbad Village Dr, where a free beach boardwalk beckons for sunset strolls.

✗🛏 p291

Eating & Sleeping

Coronado ❶

✖ MooTime Creamery Dessert $

(www.nadolife.com/mootime; 1025 Orange Ave; dishes $3.50-7; ⏱11am-9pm Sun-Thu, to 10pm Fri & Sat; ♿) Hand-rolled waffle cones and homemade ice cream, sherbet and fro-yo mixed with fruits, nuts and candy are a cool treat.

🛏 Hotel Del Coronado Resort $$$

(☎619-435-6611, 800-468-3533; www.hoteldel.com; 1500 Orange Ave; r from $300; ❄@🛜♿♿) Reserve a room in the original Victorian building for the most historic experience, then sip sunset cocktails on the ocean-view patio or feast on California seafood at romantic 1500 Ocean restaurant.

Balboa Park ❷

✖ Prado Californian $$$

(☎619-557-9441; 1549 El Prado; mains lunch $10-18, dinner $22-35; ⏱11:30am-3pm Mon-Fri, 11am-3pm Sat & Sun, dinner from 5pm Tue-Sun) Eclectic fusion cooking by a renowned chef shows off chipotle beef tamales, farmers-market salads and Szechuan spiced duck. Go for happy-hour bites and margaritas on the verandah.

✖ Tea Pavilion Japanese $

(2215 Pan American Way; mains $6-8; ⏱10:30am-3pm Mon, to 4pm Tue-Sun; 🍴♿) Enjoy a quick, spicy noodle bowl or a simple cup of green tea at the umbrella-shaded tables beside the peaceful Japanese Friendship Garden.

Embarcadero ❸

✖ Escape Fish Bar Seafood $

(☎619-702-9200; www.escapefishbar.com; 738 5th Ave; mains $14-20; ⏱11am-11pm Sun-Thu, to 2am Fri & Sat; ♿) For market-fresh grilled fish to tempura-battered fish and chips, East-West fusion seafood *tacones* and coconut-milk seafood chowder, turn away from the ocean toward the trendy Gaslamp Quarter.

🛏 Best Western Plus Island Palms Motel $$

(☎619-222-0561, 800-922-2336; www.islandpalms.com; 2051 Shelter Island Dr; r $149-249; ❄@🛜♿♿) Just across the harbor from downtown, palm trees shade the lobby and grounds of these well-kept Polynesian-esque buildings with spacious rooms overlooking the marina. Free bicycles to borrow.

Ocean Beach ❹

✖ South Beach Bar & Grill Californian, Mexican $$

(☎619-226-4577; www.southbeachob.com; 5059 Newport Ave; mains $8-14; ⏱11am-1am Sun-Thu, to 2am Fri & Sat) Maybe it's the lightly fried mahimahi. Or the kickin' white sauce. Whatever the secret, the fish tacos rock at this watering hole.

🛏 Inn at Sunset Cliffs Motel $$$

(☎619-222-7901, 866-786-2543; http://innatsunsetcliffs.com; 1370 Sunset Cliffs Blvd, Point Loma; r/ste from $175/215; ❄@🛜♿♿) Hear the surf crashing onto the rocky shore at this breezy retro charmer wrapped around a flower-bedecked courtyard.

Mission Beach & Pacific Beach ❺

✖ Kono's Surf Club Cafe $

(☎858-483-1669; 704 Garnet Ave; dishes from $5; ⏱7am-2pm Mon-Fri, to 3pm Sat & Sun; ♿) Enormous breakfast burritos, egg scrambles, burgers and fries mean it's always crowded on the beach-view patio.

✖ Mission Californian, Mexican $

(☎619-488-9060; www.themissionsd.com; 3795 Mission Blvd; mains $7-13; ⏱7am-3pm; 🍴♿) Fork into famously homemade cinnamon-bread French toast and berry pancakes, or spice it up with eggy Latino dishes like *chilaquiles* and *rancheros verde*.

📛 Crystal Pier Hotel Cottage $$$

(📞800-748-5894; www.crystalpier.com; 4500 Ocean Blvd; ste & cottages $165-500; @ 🐾) Cape Cod–style 1930s cottages with flowerboxes and loads of charm (but no air-con) are built right over the ocean; hotel suites are cheaper. All have kitchenettes. Book up to 11 months in advance, or cross your fingers for last-minute cancellations.

La Jolla ⑥

🍴 George's at the Cove Californian, Seafood $$

(📞858-454-4244; www.georgesatthecove.com; 1250 Prospect St; mains $11-50; 🕐11am-10pm Sun-Thu, to 10:30pm Fri & Sat) Euro-Cal cooking is as dramatic as the oceanfront location thanks to the chef's wild imagination. Three different venues let you enjoy it all at varying price points. No reservations required for George's Bar.

🍴 whisknladle Locavarian $$

(📞858-551-7575; www.wnlhosp.com; 1044 Wall St; mains $10-32; 🕐11:30am-9pm Mon-Thu, 11:30am-10pm Fri, 10am-10pm Sat, 10am-9:30pm Sun) Seasonal 'slow food' is on the daily-changing menu at this neighborhood bistro. Brunch is the big-deal meal, or come for chorizo and date fritters and charred bone marrow at dinner.

Del Mar ⑦

🍴 Zel's Californian $$

(📞858-755-0076; www.zelsdelmar.com; 1247 Camino Del Mar; mains $9-18; 🕐brunch 9am-2pm Sat & Sun, dinner 5pm-10pm Mon-Thu, to 11pm Fri & Sat, to 9pm Sun; 🐾) Longstanding Del Mar family keeps alive the tradition of flatbread pizzas, locally ranched burgers and microbrewed beers, with weekend music too.

📛 Hotel Indigo Boutique Hotel $$$

(📞858-755-1501, 877-859-5095; www.ichotelsgroup.com; 710 Camino del Mar; d incl breakfast $159-379; ❄@📶☔🐾🐶) With the bones of a two-story courtyard motel, this beachy hotel sports seashell murals in its kitchenette rooms and suites.

Encinitas ⑧

🍴 Las Olas Mexican $$

(📞760-942-1860; www.lasolasmex.com; 2655 S Coast Hwy 101, Cardiff-by-the-Sea; mains $9-19; 🕐11am-9pm Mon-Thu, 11am-9:30pm Fri, 10am-9:30pm Sat & 10am-9pm Sun; 🐾) This cantina is so popular it has its own traffic light. Come here for fish tacos with ocean views, or order Puerto Nuevo–style lobster and pineapple-chili margaritas.

🍴 Swami's Café Cafe $

(📞760-944-0612; 1163 S Coast Hwy 101; mains $5-10; 🕐7am-5pm; 🥗🐾) For acai berry bowls, fruit smoothies, multigrain pancakes, stir-fries, salads and ohm-lets, you can't beat this breezy patio. Vegetarians will be oh so happy here.

Carlsbad ⑨

🍴 Pizza Port Pizzeria, Pub $$

(📞760-720-7007; www.pizzaport.com; 571 Carlsbad Village Dr; mains $8-20; 🕐11am-10pm Sun-Thu, to midnight Fri & Sat; 🐾) Everybody swings by this surfboard-adorned miniwarehouse for craft beers and thick, buttery slices of 'anti-wimpy' gourmet pies.

📛 Carlsbad Inn Beach Resort Resort $$$

(📞760-434-7020, 800-235-3939; www.carlsbadinn.com; 3075 Carlsbad Blvd; r/ste from $149/209; ❄@📶☔🐾) This upscale Tudor-style timeshare hotel sits right across from the beach. Borrow beach gear and bicycles, or sign up for a la carte activities like stand-up paddle boarding.

📛 West Inn & Suites Hotel $$$

(📞760-448-4500, 866-431-9378; www.westinnandsuites.com; 4970 Avenida Encinas; r incl breakfast $159-359; ❄@📶☔🐾🐶) Midway between Legoland and Carlsbad Village, you'll think you should be paying much more for your pillow-top king-sized bed, fresh orchids and complimentary Aveda bath products.

STRETCH YOUR LEGS
SAN DIEGO

Start/Finish California Quadrangle

Distance 2.5 miles

Duration 2–6 hours

The zoo, museums and gardens of sun-drenched Balboa Park, originally built for the 1915–16 Panama-California Exposition, make it a highlight of any San Diego stopover. Explore fantastical architecture along its curved walking paths.

Take this walk on Trips

[1] [27] [28]

California Quadrangle

East of Cabrillo Bridge, El Prado passes under an archway into the **California Quadrangle**. Just north, the anthropological **Museum of Man** (☏619-239-2001; www.museumofman.org; adult/child $12.50/5; ☺10am-4:30pm) is one of the park's most ornate Spanish Colonial Revival creations, its landmark **Tower of California** richly decorated with blue and yellow tiles. Exhibits focus on Native American artifacts from around the US Southwest.

The Walk » Amble east under the white colonnades along the south side of El Prado. Duck into the formally hedged Alcazar Garden on your right, then continue east toward the spritzing fountain in Plaza de Panama.

Plaza de Panama

The exterior of the **San Diego Museum of Art** (☏619-232-7931; www.sdmart.org; 1450 El Prado; adult/child $12/4.50; ☺10am-5pm Mon-Tue, Thu & Sat, 10am-9pm Fri, noon-5pm Sun) was designed in 16th-century Spanish plateresque style. Nearby, the **Timken Museum** (☏619-239-5548; www.timkenmuseum.org; 1500 El Prado; admission free; ☺10am-4:30pm Tue-Sat, 1:30pm-4:30pm Sun) has an impressive collection of artworks by European masters, while the **Mingei International Museum** (☏619-239-0003; www.mingei.org; 1439 El Prado; adult/child $8/5; ☺10am-4pm Tue-Sun) exhibits folk art from around the globe.

The Walk » Stroll north alongside the lily pond into the Botanical Building greenhouse. Back outside, cut east to Village Pl, then turn left and walk north past the giant Moreton Bay fig tree and the shops of the Spanish Village Art Center.

San Diego Zoo

Since its grand opening in 1916, **San Diego Zoo** (☏619-231-1515; www.sandiegozoo.org; 2920 Zoo Dr; adult/child entry with guided bus tour & aerial tram ride $42/32; ☺9am-5pm or 6pm daily, extended summer & holiday hr; ☝) has pioneered ways to house animals that mimic their natural habitat, in the process also becoming one of the country's great botanical

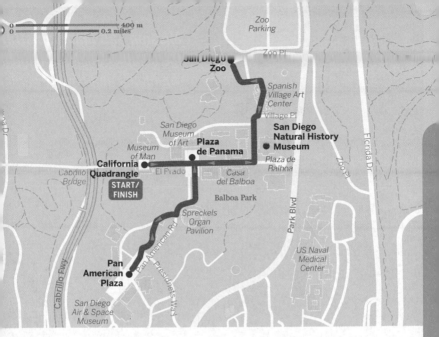

gardens. A guided double-decker bus tour gives you a good overview of the zoo – sitting downstairs puts you even closer to the animals.

The Walk » Retrace your steps south to El Prado, turning left and walking straight ahead to Bea Evanson Fountain. Backtrack a short distance west to the natural history museum's entrance.

San Diego Natural History Museum

With its giant-screen cinema and mega traveling exhibitions, the **Nat** (San Diego Natural History Museum; ☎619-232-3821; www.sdnhm.org; 1788 El Prado; adult/child $15/9; ⏱10am-5pm Sun-Fri, 9am-5pm Sat; 👪) houses 7.5 million specimens, including rocks, fossils, taxidermy animals and skulls, as well as an educational and eco-conscious exhibit on SoCal's water resources.

The Walk » Backtrack west along El Prado, passing the Casa del Balboa, which houses photography, city history and model-railroad museums, on your left. Turn left at Plaza del

Panama, heading south past the Japanese Friendship Garden and Spreckels Organ Pavilion.

Pan American Plaza

Fast-food stands and ice-cream vendors set up shop on Balboa Park's central plaza. The **UN gift shop** (☎619-233-5044; ⏱10am-4:30pm) sells globally minded crafts, jewelry and souvenirs, donating profits to worldwide children's charities. Nearby, the **House of Pacific Relations** (☎619-234-0739; www.sdhpr. org; 2191 W Pan American Rd; admission free; ⏱noon-4pm Sun; 👪) actually comprises 15 cottages, inside which you can view furnishings, artworks and museum-like displays from an Olympian mix of countries. Farther south is the famous **San Diego Air & Space Museum** (☎619-234-8291; www.sandiegoairandspace.org; adult/child $17.50/7; ⏱10am-4:30pm; 👪).

The Walk » Make a U-turn and walk back up Pan American Rd all the way northeast to Plaza de Panama. Turn left onto El Prado and head west back to California Quadrangle, where your walk began.

Mission San Juan Capistran
the complex encloses bubblir
fountains and flowery garde

Mission Trail

28

Follow the path of early Spanish colonists from San Diego to Sonoma, embracing the most intriguing of California's original missions, with atmospheric inns and eateries along the way.

TRIP HIGHLIGHTS

555 miles

San Francisco
Take time out in the soulful Mission District

FINISH
Sonoma
7

6

455 miles

San Juan Bautista
A ghostly, earthquake-rattled, old mission town

San Luis Obispo

215 miles

Santa Barbara
Spanish colonial outpost by the sea

4 Ventura

Los Angeles

2

San Diego
START

San Juan Capistrano
Justifiably nicknamed 'the Jewel of the Missions'

65 miles

5 DAYS
615 MILES/990KM

GREAT FOR...

BEST TIME TO GO
April to October for sunny skies.

ESSENTIAL PHOTO
Swallows returning to San Juan Capistrano.

BEST FOR FOODIES
San Francisco's mestizo Mission District.

28 Mission Trail

It took over 50 years for a chain of 21 missions to be established along El Camino Real ('the Royal Rd'), first forged by Spanish conquistador Gaspar de Portolá and Franciscan priest Junípero Serra in the late 18th century. Each mission was just a day's ride on horseback away from the next, but today you can drive the entire route in less than a week.

FINISH 8 S
1
San Francisco 7
San Mateo
Redwood City
San Jo
Santa Cruz
Sa
Monter

❶ San Diego

On July 1, 1769, a forlorn lot of about 100 Spanish soldiers and missionaries straggled ashore at San Diego Bay. After sailing for weeks up the coast from Baja California, many were sick and over half had died. It was an inauspicious beginning for **Mission Basilica San Diego de Alcalá** (☏619-281-8449; www.missionsandiego.com; 10818 San Diego Mission Rd; suggested donation $3; ☺9am-4:45pm), the oldest in California's chain of missions.

West atop Presidio Hill, the **Serra Museum** (☏619-297-3258; www. sandiegohistory.org; 2727 Presidio Dr; adult/child $6/3; ☺10am-4pm or 5pm Sat & Sun, call for weekday hr; ⊞) recounts Native American struggles with mission life. Where the colonists' original military fort and church once stood, this 1920s Spanish Revival building echoes early mission architecture.

Nearby, you can visit **Old Town San Diego State Historic Park** (☏619-220-5422; www. parks.ca.gov; admission free; ☺visitor center & museums 10am-4pm, to 5pm May-Sep) preserves buildings from the Spanish, Mexican and early American periods, with an old-fashioned plaza surrounded by shops and cafes.

*PACIFIC
OCEAN*

For our walking tour, see p292.

✖ ⊨ p301

The Drive » El Camino Real, which is marked throughout California by free-standing bronze mission bells erected in the 1920s, follows I-5 north from San Diego. After more than 60 miles, exit onto Hwy 74 (Ortega Hwy), turn left and drive west to Mission San Juan Capistrano.

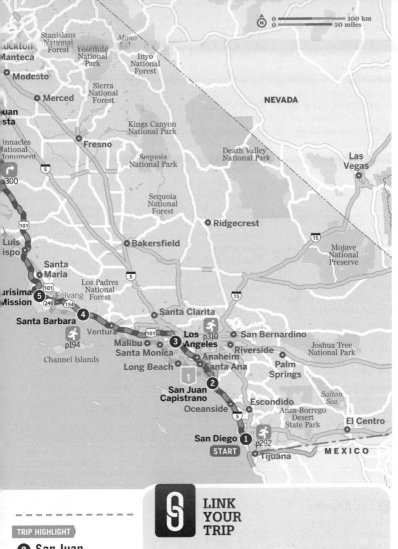

TRIP HIGHLIGHT

❷ San Juan Capistrano

Archaeologists, engineers and restoration artists have done an exquisite job of keeping alive **Mission San Juan Capistrano** (☏949-234-1300; www.missionsjc.com;

🔗 LINK YOUR TRIP

❶ Pacific Coast Highways

California's mission trail intersects with the classic coastal route at San Diego, Los Angeles, Santa Barbara and San Francisco.

❻ Sonoma Valley

Where this trip ends at Sonoma Plaza, you can start exploring Northern California's rustic-chic wine country.

26801 Ortega Hwy; adult/child $9/5; ⏱8:30am-5pm; ♿). Built around a series of 18th-century arcades, the mission complex encloses bubbling fountains and flowery gardens. The Serra Chapel, where the padre celebrated mass in 1783, is considered California's oldest building, and even the mighty San Andreas Fault hasn't been able to topple it yet. Every year on March 19, the Festival of the Swallows celebrates the birds' return from their Argentine sojourn to make their nests in the mission's walls. One block west, by the train depot, the tree-shaded **Los Rios Historic District** collects quaint cottages and adobes housing cafes and gift shops.

✗ p301

The Drive » Get back on I-5 north for the often traffic-jammed 50-mile drive to downtown Los Angeles. Take the Alameda St/Union Station exit, turn right onto Main St and look for metered street parking or pay-parking lots.

- - - - - - - - - -

❸ Los Angeles

Setting out from the valley's Mission San Gabriel Arcángel, just a few dozen Spanish colonists founded the 'City of Angels' in 1781, near the site of today's **El Pueblo de Los Angeles Historical Monument** (📞213-628-1274; http://elpueblo.lacity.org; 125 Paseo de la Plaza; admission free; ⏱museums 11am-3pm Tue-Sat, restaurants & shops 10am-8pm daily; ♿). Peek inside 19th-century historical buildings like the Avila Adobe and 'La Placita' plaza church and jostle down crowded block-long Olvera St, an open-air marketplace lined with Mexican food vendors and folklorico shops, then unwind in front of the wrought-iron bandstand, where mariachis often play on sunny weekend afternoons. Nearby, **La Plaza de Cultura y Artes** (📞213-542-6200; www.lapca.org; 501 Main St; admission free; ⏱noon-7pm Wed-Mon) vibrantly chronicles the Mexican American experience in LA.

To see more sights on foot, try our walk (see p310).

✗ p301

The Drive » Follow Hwy 101 north of Downtown LA past Hollywood and west through the suburban San Fernando Valley all the way to the Pacific coast. North of Ventura, another SoCal mission town with beautiful beaches, lies Santa Barbara, about 100 miles from LA.

- - - - - - - - - -

TRIP HIGHLIGHT

❹ Santa Barbara

After a magnitude 6.3 earthquake hit Santa Barbara in 1925, downtown's **State St** was entirely rebuilt in Spanish Revival style, with whitewashed adobe walls and red-tile roofs.

Head north to hillside **Mission Santa Barbara** (📞805-682-4713; http://santabarbaramission.org; 2201 Laguna St; adult/child $5/1; ⏱9am-5pm), another victim of historical quakes. From the front of its imposing Doric facade, itself a homage to an ancient Roman chapel, you can look up at the unique twin bell towers. Founded in 1786 on the feast day of Saint Barbara, the mission has been continuously occupied by Franciscan priests, having escaped Mexico's enforced policy of secularization that destroyed most of California's other missions. Artwork by Chumash people adorns the chapel. Look for a centuries-old cemetery out back.

For a great walk, see p194.

✗ 🛏 p301

The Drive » El Camino Real follows Hwy 101 north. For a more scenic route, take winding Hwy 154 up into the mountains and wine country. Turn left onto Hwy 246 (Mission Dr) toward the Danish village of Solvang, which has a pretty little mission, then keep driving west across Hwy 101 almost to Lompoc. It's a 50-mile trip from Mission Santa Barbara.

- - - - - - - - - -

❺ La Purísima Mission

Drive through the hills outside Lompoc, past vineyards and

Mission San Juan Bautista Main altar

commercial flower fields, to **La Purísima Mission State Historic Park** (☎805-733-3713; www.parks. ca.gov, www.lapurisimamission. org; 2295 Purisima Rd, Lompoc; entry per car $6; ☺9am-5pm). Resurrected by the Civilian Conservation Corps (CCC) during the Depression era, almost a dozen buildings here have been restored to their original 1820s appearance. Amble past Spanish soldiers' living quarters, a weaving room and a blacksmith's shop, all beside grassy fields where cows, horses and goats graze.

The Drive » Follow scenic rural Hwy 1 north to Pismo Beach, then rejoin Hwy 101 north to San Luis Obispo, a peaceful mission town that's a convenient place to break your journey (p180). The next day, follow Hwy 101 north for 140 more miles past Salinas to Hwy 156, connecting east to San Juan Bautista.

TRIP HIGHLIGHT

❻ San Juan Bautista

Unknowingly built atop the San Andreas Fault, **Mission San Juan Bautista** (☎831-623-4528; www.oldmissionsjb.org; 406 2nd St; adult/child $4/2; ☺9:30am-4:30pm) has the largest church among

California's historical missions. The original chapel was toppled by the 1906 San Francisco earthquake. Scenes from Alfred Hitchcock's 1960s film *Vertigo* were shot here, although the climactic bell tower was just a special-effects prop. The old Spanish plaza opposite the mission anchors **San Juan Bautista State Historic Park** (☎831-623-4881; www.parks.ca.gov; museum entry adult/child $3/free; ☺10am-4:30pm Tue-Sun). A short walk away, dusty downtown is crowded with Mexican restaurants and antiques shops.

DETOUR:
PINNACLES NATIONAL
MONUMENT

Start: ⑤ La Purísima Mission

Named for the towering spires that rise abruptly out of the chaparral-covered hills, this **park** (☎831-389-4486; www.nps.gov/pinn; entry per car $5) is a study in geological drama, with its craggy monoliths, sheer-walled canyons and ancient volcanic remnants. Besides hiking and rock climbing, the park's biggest attractions are its talus caves and endangered California condors. It's best visited during spring or fall; summer's heat is too extreme. Camping is available near the east entrance off Hwy 25 between San Juan Bautista and King City, accessed via Hwy 101 north of San Luis Obispo.

The Drive » Backtrack west on Hwy 156 to Hwy 101, which speeds north past the garlic farms of Gilroy past San Jose and Silicon Valley, then curves along the west side of San Francisco Bay. After 90 miles, you'll arrive in San Francisco: exit at Duboce St, turn left on Guerrero St, then right on 16th St to arrive at Mission San Francisco de Asís.

TRIP HIGHLIGHT

⑦ San Francisco

Time seems to stand still at **Mission San Francisco de Asís** (☎415-621-8203; www.missiondolores.org; 3321 16th St; adult/child $5/3; ☺9am-4pm, to 4:30pm May-Oct), also known as Mission Dolores. With its gold-leafed altar and redwood beams decorated with Native American artwork, this the only intact original mission chapel in California, its adobe walls having stood firm in the 1906 earthquake. Today it's overshadowed by the ornate 1913 basilica, where stained-glass windows commemorate the 21 original California missions. The graveyard out back, where Kim Novak wandered in a daze in Hitchcock's *Vertigo,* is where 5000 Ohlone and Miwok who died in measles epidemics are said to be buried, along with early Mexican and European settlers. In the surrounding Mission District, a bohemian neighborhood known for its contemporary art murals, Mexican *taquerías* mix with California farm-to-table kitchens.

Continue exploring San Francisco on our walking tour (p58).

✕ ⊨ p301

The Drive » Hwy 101 rolls up and down San Francisco's famous hills, from the Mission District to the Marina, finally exiting the city via the Golden Gate Bridge. North of the mission town of San Rafael, follow Hwy 37 east to Hwy 121 north, then take Hwy 12 north into downtown Sonoma, over a 40-mile drive from San Francisco.

⑧ Sonoma

The wine country town of Sonoma is not only the site of the last Spanish mission established in California. It also happens to be the place where American settlers declared independence from Mexico in 1846. Mission San Francisco Solano is now part of **Sonoma State Historic Park** (☎707-938-9560; www.parks.ca.gov; 20 E Spain St; adult/child $3/2; ☺10am-5pm Tue-Sun), which preserves military barracks and a mid-19th-century Mexican general's home. Its petite adobe chapel, dating from 1841, is also the finish line for El Camino Real.

✕ ⊨ p300

Eating & Sleeping

San Diego ❶

🍴 El Agave · Mexican $$$

(☎619-220-0692; www.elagave.com; 2304 San Diego Ave; dinner mains $21-39; ⏱11am-10pm) With nods to Spanish, Mexican and Hispanic traditions, El Agave's hybrid menu is best known for soulful mole sauces. The bar's 2000 types of tequila will make you swoon.

🛏 Cosmopolitan Hotel · B&B $$$

(☎619-297-1874; www.oldtowncosmo.com; 2660 Calhoun St; r incl breakfast $185-290; ❄🤶) Service may be spotty, but this 1870s hotel livens up Old Town's atmosphere with its saloon and restaurant. Overnight upstairs in antique-furnished rooms, some with balconies.

San Juan Capistrano ❷

🍴 Ramos House Café · Californian $$

(www.ramoshouse.com; 31752 Los Rios St; mains $13-18, weekend brunch $35; ⏱8:30am-3pm Tue-Sun) Famous for earthy comfort food flavored with herbs from the garden round back, this 1881 adobe is across the railroad tracks from the mission.

Los Angeles ❸

🍴 Philippe the Original · American $

(www.philippes.com; 1001 N Alameda St; mains $4-12; ⏱6am-10pm; 👶) From LAPD officers to suited-up attorneys, everyone loves Philippe's, where the French-dip sandwich was invented over a century ago. Order at the counter, then hunker down at communal tables above a sawdust-covered floor. Cash only.

Santa Barbara ❹

🍴 Bouchon · Californian $$$

(☎805-730-1160; www.bouchonsantabarbara. com; 9 W Victoria St; mains $25-36; ⏱5:30-9pm Mon-Thu, 5-10pm Fri & Sat, 5-9pm Sun) French

cooking with a California fusion spin marries farm-fresh produce, locally ranched meats and regional wines in a flowery setting.

🛏 Inn of the Spanish Garden · Boutique Hotel $$$

(☎805 564 4700, 866 564 4700; http:// spanishgardeninn.com; 915 Garden St; d incl breakfast $250-525; ❄@🤶🏊) Elegant Spanish Revival style downtown hotel has two dozen romantic luxury rooms and suites facing a gracious fountain courtyard.

San Francisco ❼

🍴 Pancho Villa · Mexican $

(www.sfpanchovilla.com; 3071 16th St; mains $5-9; ⏱10am-midnight) The savior of cash-strapped Mission District hipsters, this *taquería* delivers tinfoil-wrapped San Francisco–style 'super burritos' with a worthy condiments bar. Long lines move fast.

🛏 Inn San Francisco · B&B $$

(☎415-641-0188, 800-359-0913; www.innsf. com; 943 S Van Ness Ave; r incl breakfast $120-285; @🤶) Well maintained and packed with antiques, this peaceful Victorian mansion has a garden hot tub and genteel guestrooms (some shared baths) with comfy beds.

Sonoma ❽

🍴 Cafe La Haye · Californian $$$

(☎707-935-5994; www.cafelahaye.com; 140 E Napa St; mains $19-30; ⏱5:30pm-9pm Tue-Sat) Dishing up earthy New American cooking, the tiny dining room gets filled cheek-by-jowl, but its flavor-packed locavarian menu is worth reserving well ahead for.

🛏 El Dorado Hotel · Boutique Hotel $$$

(☎707-996-3220; www.eldoradosonoma.com; 405 1st St W; r $165-225; ❄🤶🏊) Ultra-stylish design touches make up for compact rooms, as do private balconies overlooking the courtyard. Book ahead for the Californian wine-country kitchen downstairs.

Huntington Beach *The SoCal surf hotspot*

SoCal Pop Culture

29

Pretend to be the star of your own reality-TV travel show on this whirlwind tour of SoCal, which samples eye-popping film sets, superstar hangouts and Hollywood's cult of celebrity.

TRIP HIGHLIGHTS

145 miles

Santa Barbara
Movie stars' mansions mix with cinematic scenery

6

235 miles

Burbank
Peek behind the real cameras of 'the Industry'

7

Santa Monica

Hollywood
FINISH

60 miles

Venice
SoCal's freakiest pop-culture trends on parade

4

3

Newport Beach

START

Laguna Beach

Huntington Beach
Livin' the ultimate beach-bum or surfer's dream

15 miles

**3 DAYS
250 MILES/400KM**

GREAT FOR...

BEST TIME TO GO
Year-round, although winter can be rainy.

ESSENTIAL PHOTO
Your favorite star on the Hollywood Walk of Fame.

BEST FOR MOVIE FANS
Burbank's behind-the-scenes studio tours.

303

29 SoCal Pop Culture

This trip starts in SoCal's epicenter of pop culture, Orange County, with its cinematic beaches. Zoom north along the Pacific Ocean past the skater punks of Venice Beach, Hollywood moguls' mansions in Malibu and famous TV and movie film locations in Santa Barbara. Swing back to LA's San Fernando Valley for a TV and movie studio tour, then wind up in Hollywood with a cruise down the rockin' Sunset Strip.

❶ Laguna Beach

When it comes to SoCal pop culture, you can't just ignore the reality-TV phenomenon, including MTV's *Laguna Beach*. Lauren Conrad and the show's other botoxed beauties are focused on scoring magazine covers, but the city's most wealthy residents are more about bohemian bonhomie than Hollywood elitism, so don't be shy. Shop the chic boutiques in downtown's **village**, then strike a pose on **Main**

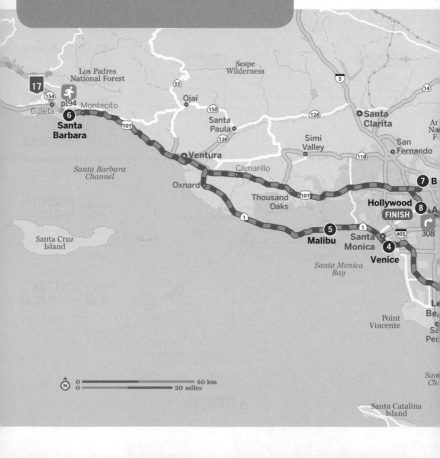

Beach in your teeny-weeny bikini. Jealously guarded by locals, **Thousand Steps Beach** (off 9th Ave) is hidden off Hwy 1 just south of Mission Hospital, where a stairway leads down to a rocky beach, postcard-perfect for sunbathing.

The Drive » Join Hwy 1, aka Pacific Coast Hwy (PCH), for the quick 10-mile trip north to Newport Beach, passing oceanfront Crystal Cove State Park. Exit onto Newport Blvd, following it down onto the Balboa Peninsula.

➋ Newport Beach

Next up are the superficial charms of glitzy Newport Beach. Primetime soap *The OC* may be long over, but the angst-ridden adventures of its glamorous teens have given a hipper, youthful sheen to the city's longstanding image as a paradise for yachtsmen and their trophy wives. On the **Balboa Peninsula**, the two-mile oceanfront strip between **Balboa Pier** and **Newport Pier** teems with young glamazons. Inland, more lifestyles of the rich and famous revolve around **Fashion Island** (www.shopfashionisland.com; 401 Newport Center Dr), a posh outdoor mall that's one of the OC's biggest shopping meccas.

✗ p309

The Drive » Keep going north up Hwy 1, often crawling with bumper-to-bumper traffic on summer weekends when everyone's heading to the beach. Relax, it's only 4 miles to Huntington Beach, at the intersection of Main St and PCH.

TRIP HIGHLIGHT

➐ Huntington Beach

Time to make the pop-cultural switch from the boob tube to surfing. **Huntington Beach** has been *the* SoCal surf hotspot since George Freeth first demonstrated the Hawaiian sport of wave-riding here a century ago. The city recently trademarked its nickname 'Surf City USA' (the moniker from Jan and Dean's 1963 pop-music hit). Surfing is seriously big business in HB, with buyers for major retailers coming here to see what surfers are wearing and then marketing the look, while beautiful blondes blithely play volleyball on the golden sand and skaters whiz past the oceanfront pier.

The Drive » Keep going north for 12 miles on Hwy 1 passing Sunset Beach (p309). Then join the I-405 north, driving past industrial areas of Los Angeles. Take the Hwy 90 westbound exit toward Marina del Rey, slingshot

🔗 LINK YOUR TRIP

17 Santa Barbara Wine Country

Follow Hwy 154 up into the mountains of the Santa Ynez Valley, where *Sideways* wine country is ready for its close-up.

26 Disneyland & Orange County Beaches

If you can't get enough of the OC's sunny sands, keep cruising coastal Hwy 1, then hit Disneyland.

around the marina to Pacific Ave by the beach, turn right and roll north to Venice.

TRIP HIGHLIGHT

④ Venice

Created in 1905 by eccentric tobacco heir Abbot Kinney as an amusement park, the 'Venice of America' became complete with Italian *gondolieri* poling the canals. Now new-age hippies, muscled bodybuilders à la Arnold Schwarzenegger, goth punks, tribal drummers and freaks have taken over **Ocean Front Walk** (you may recognize it from the opening scenes of *Three's Company*), where the crazy side of SoCal really lets it all hang out. Imagine an experimental human zoo, and strap on those rollerblades, hop on a fluorescent-painted beach cruiser or just shake what yo' mama gave you. Venice is also the birthplace of SoCal skater-punk culture, as chronicled in the movie *Lords of Dogtown*.

✗ ⌂ p309

The Drive » Drive north on Ocean Ave and rejoin PCH past the I-10. Cruise past Santa Monica's carnival pier with its solar-powered Ferris wheel. Keep following Hwy 1 (PCH) north as it curves alongside the ocean to Malibu, just over a dozen miles away.

⑤ Malibu

Measured mile for fabulous oceanfront mile, Malibu may have the densest collection of celebrities anywhere in SoCal. Keep your eye peeled for the paparazzi, especially at the **Malibu Country Mart** (www. malibucountrymart.com; 3900 Cross Creek Rd) mini-mall, where the A-list crowd sips iced lattes as they shop. About 15 miles further west, pull into **Leo Carrillo State Park** (www.parks.ca.gov; 35000 W Pacific Coast Hwy; entry per car $12; ☺8am-10pm;). This beach's hidden coves made a romantic backdrop in *Pirates of the Caribbean, The Karate Kid* and *50 First Dates*. Beware of rough surf: John Travolta and Olivia Newton-John almost got swept out to sea here in the opening scene of *Grease*.

The Drive » Hug the coast by following Hwy 1 north, which turns inland to intersect Hwy 101, a multilane freeway that swings back to the coast at Ventura, then flows past ocean cliffs and beaches northwest to Santa Barbara, about a 90-minute trip from Malibu without traffic jams.

TRIP HIGHLIGHT

⑥ Santa Barbara

A Mediterranean vibe and red-roofed, white-stucco buildings give credence to Santa Barbara's claim of being

the 'American Riviera.' Spanish Colonial Revival buildings clustered along downtown's **State St** (for our walking tour, see p194) have made cameos in countless movies, including *It's Complicated*. A 45-minute drive up into the mountains via scenic Hwy 154, Santa Barbara's **wine country** (see p187) sets the hilarious scene for the Oscar-winning 2004 hit film *Sideways*. Just east of Santa Barbara off Hwy 101, celeb-heavy **Montecito** is a leafy suburb tucked between the mountains and the

Ocean Front Walk

Pacific. Heavy hitters like Oprah Winfrey, Steve Martin and Steven Spielberg have homes here and occasionally venture out along the boutique-and-patio-lined main drag, Coast Village Rd.

✗ ⊨ p309

The Drive » Take Hwy 101 south back to Ventura, then head up into the mountains via the steep Conjeo (Camarillo) Grade. Leveling off, Hwy 101 zooms east through the San Fernando Valley. Veer left onto Hwy 134 toward Burbank, almost 90 miles after leaving Santa Barbara.

TRIP HIGHLIGHT

❼ Burbank

Long ago, the TV and movie biz (locals just call it 'the Industry') decamped from Hollywood into the San Fernando Valley. Scores of Hollywood blockbusters, from *The Terminator* to *Chinatown,* have been shot on location here. (Infamously, 'the Valley' is also ground zero for SoCal's XXX porn-movie industry.) It also birthed 1980s 'Valley Girl' speak (gag me with a spoon!) and popularized SoCal's

ubiquitous mall rat culture.

Take a look behind the scenes on the **Warner Bros VIP Studio Tour** (☎877-492-8667; www. wbstudiotour.com; 3400 Riverside Dr; tours $49; ⊙ open daily, hr vary), or take your screaming tweens and teens to **Universal Studios Hollywood theme park** (☎800-864-8377; www. universalstudioshollywood. com; 100 Universal City Plaza; adult/child $77/69; ⊙ open daily, hr vary; 🚻) to ride a tram tour past working soundstages and pick up free tickets for a live TV show taping from

DETOUR:
LA LIVE

Start: ❽ Hollywood

Next to downtown's **Staples Center**, a saucer-shaped sports and entertainment arena, **LA Live** is a shiny corporate entertainment hub. Glimpse larger-than-life statues of Magic Johnson and Wayne Gretzky, and party at the Conga Room co-owned by Will I Am. But only after you pay homage to the **Grammy Museum** (☎213-765-6800; www.grammymuseum.org; 800 W Olympic Blvd; adult/child $13/11; ⊙11:30am-7:30pm Sun-Fri, 10am-7:30pm Sat). Music lovers will get lost in interactive exhibits, where sound chambers let you try mixing and remixing, singing and rapping. Glimpse GnR's bass drum, Yo-Y Ma's cello and MJ's glove enshrined like holy relics. It's 7 miles southeast of Hollywood via Hwy 101 and the I-110 south (exit at 8th St).

Audiences Unlimited (www.tvtickets.com). To buy cast-off TV and movie star fashions, stop off at **It's a Wrap!** (www.itsawraphollywood.com; 3315 W Magnolia Blvd; ⊙10am-8pm Mon-Fri, 11am-6pm Sat & Sun).

The Drive ≫ It's a quick 3-mile trip south on Hwy 101 from Universal Studios to Hollywood. Take the Highland Ave exit and drive south on Highland Ave, which intersects Hollywood Blvd.

- - - - - - - - - -

❽ Hollywood

Like an aging starlet making a comeback, this once-gritty Los Angeles neighborhood is undergoing a rebirth of cool with hip hotels, restored movie palaces and glitzy velvet-roped bars and nightclubs.

Even though you aren't likely to see any real celebrities, the pink-starred **Hollywood Walk of Fame** still attracts millions of wide-eyed visitors every year. Snap a souvenir photo outside **Grauman's Chinese Theatre** – go ahead, we know you can't resist. Step inside the slightly musty **Hollywood Museum** (☎323-464-7776; www.thehollywoodmuseum.com; 1660 N Highland Ave; adult/child $15/5; ⊙10am-5pm Wed-Sun), crammed with costumes, memorabilia and props from Charlie Chaplin to *Glee*. Cruise west along the **Sunset Strip**, packed with celeb-slumming bars and dog-eared rock venues where the Rolling Stones and the Doors once tore up the stages. For late-night star-peeping, sneak into the lobby lounge at the **Chateau Marmont**, cosseting A-listers like Bono, Brad Pitt and Angelina Jolie.

✕ ⌷ p309

Eating & Sleeping

Newport Beach ❷

✗ Crab Cooker   Seafood $$

(☏949-673-0100; www.crabcooker.com; 2200
Newport Blvd; mains $11-30; ⊙11am-9pm
Sun-Thu, to 10pm Fri & Sat; 🐾) Expect to wait
for a heaping paper plate of fresh seafood
at this red-and-white vinyl tablecloth joint, a
1950s landmark. Don't miss the delish chowder,
loaded with clams.

Sunset Beach

✗ Harbor House Café   American $$

(www.harborhousecafe.com; 16341 Pacific Coast
Hwy; mains $6-19; ⊙24hr; 🐾) High-school
skaters, beach bums and old-timers mix under
ramshackle walls slapped with movie posters at
this classic neon-lit roadside diner, a quick drive
north of HB.

Venice ❹

✗ Abbot's Pizza Company   Pizzeria $

(www.abbotspizzaco.com; 1407 Abbot Kinney
Blvd; slices $3-5, pizzas $12-29; ⊙11am-11pm
Sun-Thu, to midnight Fri & Sat; 🐾) Join the flip-
flops crowd at this shoebox-sized pizza kitchen
for habit-forming gourmet bagel-crust pies.

🛏 Hotel Erwin   Boutique Hotel $$$

(☏310-452-1111, 800-786-7789; www.jdvhotels.
com; 1697 Pacific Ave; r $239-399; ✻ @ 🛜)
Steps from the beach, chic rooms feature
contemporary art and honor bars holding
sunglasses and retro sodas. The rooftop sunset
lounge makes up for traffic noise.

Santa Barbara ❻

✗ Jeannine's Bakery Café   Cafe $$

(http://jeannines.com; 1253 Coast Village Rd;
mains $9-13; ⊙6:30am-4pm Mon-Thu, 6:30am-
4:30pm Fri, 7am-4:30pm Sat & Sun) Nab a table
on the outdoor patio and watch socialites stroll
past. From-scratch kitchen goodness includes
challah French toast with bananas caramelized
in Kahlua.

🛏 Four Seasons Biltmore   Hotel $$$

(☏805-969-2261; www.fourseasons.com/
santabarbara; 1260 Channel Dr; r from $425;
✻ @ 🛜 ⛱ 🐾) Armani swimsuits and Gucci
sunglasses abound at pretty sunset-view
Butterfly Beach, hidden below this discrete
clifftop luxury hotel built in the Roaring
Twenties.

Hollywood ❽

✗ Musso & Frank Grill   Steakhouse $$$

(☏323-467-7788; www.mussoandfrank.com;
6667 Hollywood Blvd; mains $8-40; ⊙11am-
11pm Tue-Sat) Movie-star history hangs thick in
the air at Hollywood Blvd's oldest eatery, where
waiters balance platters of steaks, chops and
pastas. Service is smooth – so are the martinis.

✗ Pink's   Fast Food $

(www.pinkshollywood.com; 709 N La Brea Ave;
dishes $3.50-8; ⊙9:30am-2am Sun-Thu, to 3am
Fri & Sat) Everyday folks have been queuing
here for the specialty hot dogs named after
celebrities since 1939. Lines get long, especially
late at night.

🛏 Magic Castle Hotel   Motel $$

(☏323-851-0800, 800-741-4915; www.
magiccastlehotel.com; 7025 Franklin Ave; d incl
breakfast from $135; ✻ 🛜 ⛱ 🐾) Renovated
apartment building with family-friendly
courtyard suites also gives guests access to a
private magic club. Cool!

🛏 Hollywood Roosevelt   Hotel $$$

(☏323-466-7000, 800-950-7667; www.
hollywoodroosevelt.com; 7000 Hollywood Blvd;
r from $249; ✻ @ 🛜 ⛱) Hosting elite players
since the first Academy Awards were held here
in 1929, the reborn Roosevelt pairs a palatial
Spanish lobby with sleek rooms and a rockin'
poolside and after-dark social scene.

STRETCH YOUR LEGS
LOS ANGELES

Start/Finish Union Station

Distance 3.5 miles

Duration 4–5 hours

Nobody walks in LA? That's just not true in Downtown's historic core. Sample the jumbled sights, sounds and tastes of the city's Mexican, Asian and European heritage, with iconic architecture and famous TV and film locations, on this half-day ramble.

Take this walk on Trips

Union Station

This majestic 1939 **edifice** (www.amtrak. com; 800 N Alameda St; admission free; ⊘24hr) was the last of America's grand railway stations to be built. Walk into the waiting room, its glamorous interior glimpsed in dozens of movies and hit TV shows from *Speed* to *24*. Bordered by tall palm trees, the stately exterior is a uniquely Californian fusion of Mission revival and art deco streamline moderne styles.

The Walk >> Walk a block up N Alameda St,cross over W Cesar E Chavez Ave and walk west a half block. Turn left down the passageway of Olvera St.

El Pueblo de Los Angeles

Compact, colorful and car-free, this historical district sits near the spot where LA's first Spanish colonists plunked down in 1781. Preserving some of the city's oldest buildings beside tiny museums and churches, El Pueblo is a microcosm of LA's multiethnic immigrant history. Join a free guided walking tour at the **visitors center** (☏213-628-1274; www.lasangelitas.org; Sepulveda House, 622 N Main St; ⊘tours usually 10am, 11am & noon Tue-Sat) near the old firehouse.

The Walk >> Northwest of the open-air bandstand, cross Main St. To your right is 'La Placita,' LA's oldest Catholic church (1884). After peeking inside, walk back down Main St a half block.

La Plaza de Cultura y Artes

Open since 2011, **La Plaza de Cultura y Artes** (☏213-542-6200; www.lapca.org; 501 N Main St;admission free; ⊘noon-7pm Wed-Mon) tells the whole truth about the Mexican American experience in LA, from Zoot Suit Riots to the Chicana movement. Calle Principal recreates Main Street in the 1920s. Rotating gallery exhibitions showcase Latino art, documentary films and oral history.

The Walk >> Continue southwest along Main St, crossing over Hwy 101 toward LA's City Hall (1928). Turn left onto E Temple St, right onto Los Angeles St and left onto E 1st St, entering Little Tokyo.

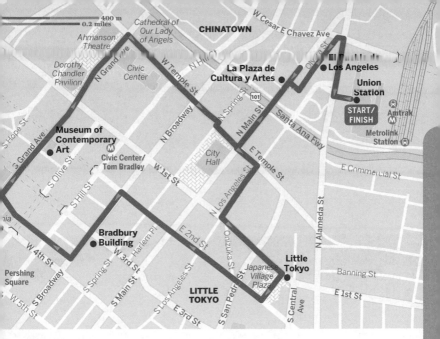

Little Tokyo

Walk past ramen shops and *izakaya* (gastropubs) over to the **Japanese American National Museum** (☏213-625-0414; www.janm.org; 369 E 1st St; adult/child $9/5; ⊙11am-5pm Tue-Wed & Fri-Sun, noon-8pm Thu). The exhibits deal with WWII internment camps and life for immigrant families. Around the corner, the **Geffen Contemporary at MOCA** (☏213-626-6222; www.moca.org; 152 N Central Ave; adult/child $12/free; ⊙11am-5pm Mon & Fri, 11am-8pm Thu, 11am-6pm Sat & Sun) houses experimental art installations.

The Walk 》 West of Central Ave, turn left to walk through Japanese Village Plaza. Turn right onto E 2nd St, walk five blocks uphill to S Broadway, then turn left and walk a block southwest to W 3rd St.

Bradbury Building

A favorite of movie location scouts since *Blade Runner* was shot here, the 1893 **Bradbury Building** (www.laconservancy.org; 304 S Broadway; admission free; ⊙usually 9am-5pm) is one of LA's architectural treasures. Its red-brick facade conceals a glass-roofed atrium with inky filigree grillwork, a rickety birdcage elevator and brick walls that look golden in the afternoon light.

The Walk 》 Opposite, walk through LA's Grand Central Market, with its multicultural food stalls. Ride Angels Flight funicular (25¢) uphill to California Plaza, veering northwest to Grand Ave. Turn right and walk a block northeast.

Museum of Contemporary Art

With collections from the 1940s to the present day, including works by Mark Rothko and Joseph Cornell, **MOCA** (☏213-626-6222; www.moca.org; 250 S Grand Ave; adult/child $12/free; ⊙11am-5pm Mon & Fri, to 8pm Thu, to 6pm Sat & Sun) inhabits a geometrically postmodern building designed by Arata Isozaki.

The Walk 》 Continue northeast up Grand Ave, passing the Walt Disney Concert Hall. Turn right on Temple St and roll downhill past the Cathedral of Our Lady of the Angels to City Hall, retracing your steps north through El Pueblo de Los Angeles back to Union Station.

Route 66 *Road trip through ghost towns, whistle-stops and the Cajon Summit*

Route 66

30

Search for the American dream along Route 66, America's 'Mother Road.' This is a trip of retro roadside relics, vintage motor lodges and milkshakes from mom-and-pop diners.

TRIP HIGHLIGHTS

300 miles

Hollywood
Get your kicks in Tinseltown

80 miles

Amboy
The big sky and empty byways are starkly photogenic

START
Needles

3

Victorville

San Bernardino

10

11 Los Angeles

FINISH

Santa Monica
End this epic trip on the Pacific shore

310 miles

3–4 DAYS
223 MILES/375KM

GREAT FOR...

BEST TIME TO GO
Spring, when you can cruise with the windows down before the heat of summer.

ESSENTIAL PHOTO
Laying down on the faded blacktop next to the Route 66 signs.

BEST ROAD
National Trails Hwy between Goffs and Amboy is the quintessential middle-of-nowhere cruise.

For generations of Americans, California, with its sparkling waters and sunny skies, was the promised land for road-trippers on Route 66. Follow their tracks through the gauntlet of Mojave Desert ghost towns, railway whistle-stops like Barstow and Victorville, and across the Cajon Summit. Finally, wind down the LA Basin, and put it in park near the crashing ocean waves at the end of Santa Monica Pier.

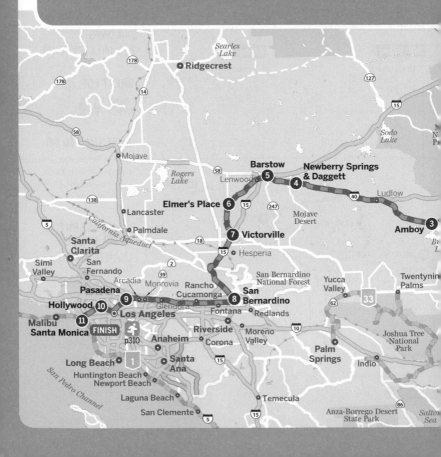

❶ Needles

At the Arizona border south of I-40 the **Old Trails Arch Bridge** (off I-40 exit 1, east of the California-Arizona border; 🕐 no public access) welcomes the Mother Road to California under endless blue skies. You might recognize the bridge: the Depression-era Joad family used it to cross the Colorado River in the movie version of John Steinbeck's novel *Grapes of Wrath*. Drive west past **Needles**, a dusty throwback railroad town with a historic depot down by the river. Frozen in a half-restored state, the **El Graces Depot** is one of only a few frontier-era Harvey Houses left standing in the American West. The Harvey Houses were a chain of railway hotels and restaurant popular in the late 19th and early 20th centuries that were famed for traveling waitresses – portrayed by Judy Garland in the 1949 MGM musical *The Harvey Girls*. Head a bit south on Broadway and you'll pass a freshly restored **66 Motel Sign** at the corner of Desnok Street – a great photo.

The Drive » West of Needles, follow Hwy 95 north of I-40 for 6 miles, then turn left onto Goffs Rd. You'll inevitably be running alongside a long locomotive – this is a primary rail shipping route to the West Coast.

❷ Goffs

The shade of cottonwood trees make the 1914 Mission-style **Goffs Schoolhouse** (📞760-733-4482; www.mdhca.org; 37198 Lanfair Rd; donations welcome; 🕐 usually 9am-4pm Sat & Sun) a soothing stop along this sun-drenched stretch of highway. It stands as part of the best-preserved pioneer settlement in the Mojave Desert (although to be quite honest it looks a bit like an empty Taco Bell). Browsing the black-and-white photographs of hardscrabble Dust Bowl migrants gives an evocative glimpse into tough life on the edge of the Mojave.

The Drive » Keep going on Goffs Rd through Fenner, crossing under I-40. Turn right onto National Old Trails Hwy (which is also known as National Trails Hwy on some maps and signs) and drive for about an hour. This is some of the coolest stretch of road, with abandoned graffiti-covered service stations, vintage signs rusting in the sun and huge skies.

LINK YOUR TRIP

33 Palm Springs & Joshua Tree Oases

After this scorching drive through the desert, cut south on I-10 out of San Bernardino and head for the breezy palms and art deco hotels of Palm Springs.

1 Pacific Coast Highways

This route along the edge of the continent is equally classic and allows a cruise along the equally iconic numbered route: Highway 1. When you finish Route 66, follow Hwy 1 north.

Classic Trip

TRIP HIGHLIGHT

③ Amboy

Potholed and crumbling in a romantic way, the USA's original transnational highway was established in 1912, more than a decade before Route 66 first ran through here. The rutted highway races through tiny towns, sparsely scattered across the Mojave. Only a few landmarks interrupt the horizon, including **Roy's Motel & Cafe** (www.rt66roys. com; National Old Trails Hwy; admission free; ⊙vary), a landmark watering hole for decades of Route 66 travelers. If you'll believe the lore, Roy once cooked his famous Route 66 double cheeseburger on the hood of a '63 Mercury. Although the motel is abandoned, the gas station and cafe are occasionally open. It's east of **Amboy Crater** (☑760-326-7000; www.blm.gov/ca; admission free; 1 mile west of Amboy; ⊙sunrise-sunset), an almost perfectly symmetrical volcanic cinder cone. You can hike to the top, but it's best to avoid the midday sun – the 1.5-mile hike doesn't have a stitch of shade.

The Drive ≫ From Amboy travel along National Old Trails Highway to Ludlow, a trip of 30 miles. At Ludlow, turn right onto Crucero Rd and pass under I-40, then take the north frontage road west and turn left at Lavic Rd. Back on the south side of I-40, keep heading west on the National Old Trails Hwy. This entire trip will take about one hour and 45 minutes.

④ Newberry Springs & Daggett

The highway passes under I-40 again on its way through **Daggett**, site of the harsh California inspection station faced by Dust Bowl refugees in *Grapes of Wrath*. Today, there ain't much action, but it's a windswept, picturesque place. Pay your respects to early desert adventurers at the old **Stone Hotel** (National Old Trails Hwy, Daggett; ⊙no public entry). This late-19th-century hotel once housed miners, desert explorers and wanderers, including Sierra Nevada naturalist John Muir and Death Valley Scotty. Then make your way out of town to visit the **Calico Ghost Town** (☑800-862-2542; www.calicotown.com; 36600 Ghost Town Rd, Yermo; adult/child $6/5; ⊙9am-5pm; 🚻). This endearingly hokey Old West attraction sets a cluster of reconstructed pioneer-era buildings amid ruins of a late-19th-century silver mining town. You'll pay extra to go gold panning, tour the Maggie Mine or ride a narrow-gauge railway. Old-timey heritage celebrations include Civil War reenactments and a bluegrass 'hootenanny.'

The Drive ≫ Drive west to Nebo Rd, turning left to rejoin I-40. You'll drive about 15 minutes before taking the exit for Barstow Road.

⑤ Barstow

Exit the interstate onto Main St, which runs through Barstow, a railroad settlement and historic crossroads, where murals adorn empty buildings

---

✓ TOP TIP: NAVIGATING THE MOTHER ROAD

As you might imagine, nostalgia for the Mother Road draws its shares of completists who want to drive every inch. For Route 66 enthusiasts who need to cover every mile, a free turn-by-turn driving guide is available online at www.historic66.com. Also surf to www.route66ca.org for more historical background, photos and info about special events.

downtown. Follow 1st St north across the Mojave River over a trestle bridge to the 1911 Harvey House, nicknamed 'Casa del Desierto,' designed by Western architect Mary Colter. Next to a small railroad museum is the **Route 66 'Mother Road' Museum** (☏760-255-1890; http://route66museum.org; 681 N First Ave, Barstow; donations welcome; ☉10am-4pm Fri-Sun Apr-Oct, 11am-4pm Fri-Sun Nov-Mar), displaying black-and-white historical photographs and odds and ends of everyday life in the early 20th century. Back in the day, it was also a Harvey House.

✖ p321

The Drive ≫ Leaving Barstow via Main St, rejoin the National Old Trails Hwy west. It curves alongside the Mojave River through Lenwood. After 25 minutes you'll arrive at Elmer's Place.

- - - - - - - - - -

❻ Elmer's Place

Loved by Harley bikers, this rural byway is like a scavenger hunt for Mother Road ruins, including antique filling stations and tumbledown motor courts. Colorful as a box of crayons, **Elmer's Place** (24266 National Old Trails Hwy, Helendale; ☉24hr) is a roadside folk-art collection of 'bottle trees,' made from recycled soda pop and beer containers, telephone poles and railroad signs. Elmer

Long, who was a career man at the cement factory you'll pass just out of town, is the proprietor and cracked artistic genius. If you see someone with a long white beard and leathery skin cementing a statue of a bronze deity to some elk antlers, you've found the right guy. Want to leave a little part of yourself along Route 66? Bring a little something for Elmer Long's colorful forest, constructed lovingly out of little pieces of junk.

The Drive ≫ Cross over the Mojave River on a 1930s steel-truss bridge, then roll into downtown Victorville, a trip of about 20 minutes.

- - - - - - - - - -

❼ Victorville

Opposite the railroad tracks in quiet little Victorville, visitors poke around a mishmash of historical exhibits and contemporary art inside the **California Route 66 Museum** (☏760-951-0436; www.califrt66museum.org; 16825 'D' St; donations welcome; ☉10am-4pm Thu-Mon, sometimes 11am-3pm Sun). The museum building itself was once the Red Rooster Cafe, a famous Route 66 roadhouse. It's a bit of a cluttered nostalgia trip – piled with old signs and roadside memorabilia – but worth a quick look.

The Drive ≫ Get back on I-15 south over the daunting Cajon

Summit. Descending into San Bernardino, take I-215 and exit at Devore. Follow Cajon Blvd to Mt Vernon Ave, detour east on Base Line St and go left onto 'E' St. This trip takes about 40 minutes. If you're hungry, pull off in Hesperia at the Summit Inn, a classic diner (p321).

- - - - - - - - - -

❽ San Bernardino

Look for the Golden Arches outside the **First McDonald's Museum** (☏909-885-6324; 1398 N 'E' St; donations welcome; ☉10am-5pm). It was here that salesman Ray Kroc dropped in to sell Dick and Mac McDonald a mixer. Eventually Kroc bought the rights to the brothers' name and built an empire. Half of the museum is devoted to Route 66, with particularly interesting photographs and maps. Turn west on 5th St, leaving San Bernardino via Foothill Blvd, which continues straight into the urban sprawl of greater Los Angeles. It's a long haul west to Pasadena, with stop-and-go traffic most of the way, but there are more than a handful of gems to uncover. Cruising through Fontana, birthplace of the Hells Angels biker club, pause for a photo by the **Giant Orange** (15395 Foothill Blvd, Fontana; ☉no public entry), a 1920s juice stand of the kind that was once a fixture alongside SoCal's citrus groves.

🛏 p321

WHY THIS IS A CLASSIC TRIP
NATE CAVALIERI, AUTHOR

Maybe it goes back to the transient vagabonds who founded this country, but there's a persistent call, deep in the American psyche, that compels us to hit the open road. And no road is quite as satisfying as the endless two-lane blacktop of Route 66. The subject of sing-alongs and fodder for daydreams, traveling this classic trail to the Pacific shore is an essentially American experience.

Top: Locomotive at museum, Barstow
Left: Classic car, Barstow
Right: Sign for Calico Ghost Town

DANITA DELIMONT / GETTY IMAGES ©

The Drive ≫ Stay on Route 66 as it detours briefly onto Alosta Ave. Take lunch in Glendora (p321), and shortly after 66 rejoins Foothill Blvd in Azusa. Continue onto Huntington Dr in Duarte, where a boisterous Route 66 parade happens in mid-September.

---

❾ Pasadena

Just before you reach Pasadena, you'll pass through Arcadia, home to the 1930s **Santa Anita Park** (📞626-574-7223, tour info 📞626-574-6677; www.santaanita.com; 285 W Huntington Dr; tours free, race tickets $5-10; 🕑live racing Thu-Mon Dec 26-Apr 20). This track is where the Marx Brothers' *A Day at the Races* was filmed (and more recently the HBO series *Luck*) and where legendary thoroughbred Seabiscuit once ran. Stepping through the soaring art deco entrance into the grandstands, you'll feel like a million bucks – even if you don't win any wagers. During race season, tram tours go behind the scenes into the jockeys' room and training areas; reservations required. Continue along Colorado Blvd into wealthy **Old Pasadena**, a bustling 20-block shopping district west of Arroyo Pkwy, where boutiques and cafes are housed in handsomely restored historic Spanish Colonial buildings.

✕ 🛏 p321

Classic Trip

The Drive » Join the jet-set modern world on the Pasadena Fwy (Hwy 110), which streams south into LA. If you're not quite ready for the trip to end, take a stroll through the glittering charms of LA (see p310). One of the first freeways in the US, it's a truck-free State Historic Freeway – the whole trip will take 20 minutes.

TRIP HIGHLIGHT

⑩ Hollywood

Like a resurrected diva of the silver screen, **Hollywood** is making a comeback. Although it hasn't recaptured the Golden Age glamour that brought would-be starlets cruising here on Route 66, this historic neighborhood is still worth visiting for its restored movie palaces, unique museums and the pink stars on the **Walk of Fame**. The exact track Route 66 ran through the neighborhood isn't possible to follow these days (it changed officially a couple times and has long been paved over) but an exploration of the **Hollywood & Highland** complex, north of Santa Monica Blvd is a good place to get in the center of the action. The **Hollywood Visitor Information Center** (www.discoverlosangeles. com) is upstairs. Travelers looking for a fun, creepy communion with stars

of yesteryear should stroll the **Hollywood Forever Cemetery** (www. hollywoodforever.com; 6000 Santa Monica Blvd; ⊙8am-5pm; 🅿) next to Paramount Studios, which is crowded with famous 'immortals,' including Rudolph Valentino, Tyrone Power, Jayne Mansfield and Cecil B DeMille. Pick up a map ($5) at the flower store near the entrance. They also offer **film screenings** here.

✕ ⏰ p321

The Drive » Follow Santa Monica Blvd west for 11 miles to reach the end of the road – it makes a junction with the Pacific Coast Highway (Hwy 1). The pier is a few blocks to the south. Just north is Palisades Park.

TRIP HIGHLIGHT

⑪ Santa Monica

This is the end of the line: Route 66 reaches its finish, over 2200 miles from its starting point in Chicago, on an ocean bluff in **Palisades Park**,

where a Will Rogers Hwy memorial plaque marks the official end of the Mother Road. Celebrate on **Santa Monica Pier** (📞310-458-8900; www. santamonicapier.org; west of Ocean Ave; admission free; ⊙24hr; 🚻🎠), where you can ride a 1920s carousel featured in *The Sting,* gently touch tidepool critters at the **Santa Monica Pier Aquarium** (📞310-393-6149; www. healthebay.org; 1600 Ocean Front Walk; adult/child $5/free; ⊙2-6pm Tue-Fri, 12:30-6pm Sat & Sun; 🚻), and soak up a sunset atop the solar-powered Ferris wheel at **Pacific Park** (📞310-260-8744; www.pacpark.com; unlimited rides over/under 42in tall $20/11; 380 Santa Monica Pier; ⊙call for hr; 🚻). Year-round carnival rides include the West Coast's only oceanfront steel roller coaster – a thrilling ride to end this classic trip.

⏰ p321

Eating & Sleeping

Barstow ⑤

✕ Idle Spurs Steakhouse   Steakhouse $$
(☏760-256-8888; www.idlespurssteakhouse.com; 690 Hwy 58; mains $13-27; ⏱11am-9pm Mon-Fri, 4-9pm Sat & Sun) This Old West steakhouse and fully stocked saloon (it's even got microbrews) will slake your desert cottonmouth. The ambience? Well, there's a tree growing inside the dining room.

Hesperia

✕ Summit Inn   Diner $
(☏760-949-8688; 5960 Mariposa Rd, Hesperia; mains $5-10; ⏱6am-8pm Mon-Thu, to 9pm Fri & Sat) Truckers aren't the only ones who know to take the Oak Hill Rd exit for the Summit Inn. Surrounded by transportation memorabilia, this old-fashioned truck stop serves ostrich and buffalo burgers and date shakes.

San Bernardino ⑧

⛏ Wigwam Motel   Motel $
(☏909-875-3005; www.wigwammotel.com; 2728 W Foothill Blvd, Rialto; r $65-80; 🏊) Rescued from its run-down state, this vintage motor court lets travelers sleep inside concrete tepees, which have been Route 66 icons since 1949.

Glendora

✕ Hat   Drive-In $
(☏626-857-0017; 611 W Route 66; mains $3-8; ⏱10am-1am; 🚻) This drive-in has been piling up hot pastrami sandwiches since 1951 – they're served on French bread topped with Thousand Island dressing.

Pasadena ⑨

✕ Fair Oaks Pharmacy   Diner $
(☏626-799-1414; www.fairoakspharmacy.net; 1526 Mission St; mains $4-8; ⏱9am-9pm Mon-Fri, 9am-10pm Sat, 10am-7pm Sun; 🚻) Road weary? Stop by this early 20th-century soda fountain for egg creams, hand-dipped malts and gooey-good chili cheeseburgers.

⛏ Saga Motor Hotel   Hotel $
(☏626-795-0431, 800-793-7242; www.thesagamotorhotel.com; 1633 E Colorado Blvd; r $92-108; 🚻🏊) Take a dip in the heated outdoor swimming pool surrounded by Astroturf, and pretend it's the 1950s. The vintage Saga Motor Hotel still hands out quaint metal room keys to its guests, living up to its motto 'timeless appeal with modern luxuries.'

Hollywood ⑩

✕ Hungry Cat   Seafood $$
(☏323-462-2155; www.thehungrycat.com; 1535 Vine St; mains $10-27; ⏱lunch & dinner; 🅿) This kitty is small and sleek and hides out in the heart of Hollywood. It fancies fresh seafood and will have you salivating for hunky lobster roll, portly crab cakes and savory fish-du-jour specials. There's a second location by the beach in **Santa Monica** (☏310-459-3337, 100 W Channel Rd; ⏱dinner nightly, brunch Sat & Sun).

⛏ Farmer's Daughter Hotel   Motel $$$
(☏323-937-3930; www.farmersdaughterhotel.com; 115 S Fairfax Ave; r $219-269; ❄@🛜 🏊🚻) Opposite the Original Farmers Market, Grove and CBS Studios, this perennial pleaser gets high marks for its sleek 'urban cowboy' look. Adventurous lovebirds should ask about the No Tell Room...

Santa Monica ⑪

⛏ Sea Shore Motel   Motel $$
(☏310-392-2787; www.seashoremotel.com; 2637 Main St, Santa Monica; r $105-175; 🏊) Say 'So long!' to your retro Route 66 road trip at the time-warped Sea Shore Motel. Although the noisy, no-frills rooms have seen better days, they're so close to the beach that you can inhale the sea-salted breezes.

Big Bear Lake Weekenders fle
this low-key mountain res

Big Bear & Rim of the World Scenic Byway

31

Let the SoCal mountain scenery scroll past your windshield as you escape to cooler elevations by alpine lakes and waterfalls in summer, or put on snow tires and chains for a winter ski trip.

TRIP HIGHLIGHTS

35 miles

Lake Arrowhead
Pleasure cruises, waterskiing and shoreline drives

65 miles

Big Bear Discovery Center
Nature lessons and forest adventures for families

Mormon Rocks
Silverwood Lake State Recreation Area
START
Lake Gregory

4

6
5

60 miles

Big Bear Lake
Laidback mountain town with year-round outdoor action

FINISH

7

Valley of the Falls
Road's-end canyon views and hiking trails

120 miles

2–3 DAYS
150 MILES/240KM

GREAT FOR...

BEST TIME TO GO
May to September for sunshine and swimming.

ESSENTIAL PHOTO
Valley of the Falls scenic viewpoint.

BEST FOR FAMILIES
Big Bear Lake's cabins and beaches.

323

Big Bear & Rim of the World Scenic Byway

A favorite weekend getaway for stressed-out city dwellers, Big Bear Lake and Lake Arrowhead are just a two-hour drive from LA, although these green forested mountain retreats look a world away from the hazy, smog-choked metro area. Outside winter, take the scenic route to Big Bear via the Rim of the World Scenic Byway for hair-raising cliff drop-offs and postcard canyon views.

❶ Mormon Rocks

Before you get motoring along the Rim of the World Scenic Byway, follow Hwy 138 west of I-15 at Cajon Junction toward those strange-looking sandstone outcroppings. Eroded by wind, water and time, these boulders are pocked with small holes and caves, where lizards scurry and owls hoot. For a quick 1-mile nature walk marked with educational signs that illustrate the rocks' geology and natural

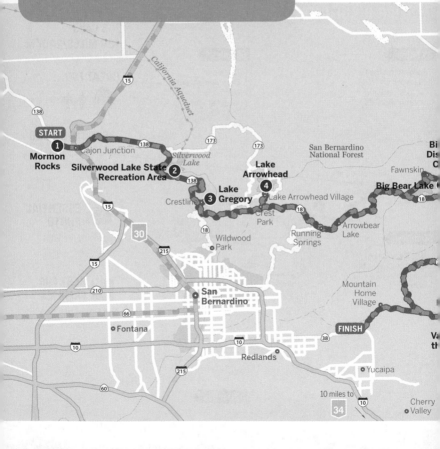

history, park at the US Forest Service (USFS) trailhead near Mormon Rocks Fire Station, about 2 miles west of I-15. The trailhead is just west of Lone Pine Canyon Rd, which grants views of California's rolling, earthquake-prone San Andreas Fault.

The Drive » Backtrack east on Hwy 138 and cross over I-15, continuing eastward as the road twists and turns uphill into the San Bernardino Mountains. Scrubby desert brush beside a railroad line slowly gives way to mountain forests over the 10-mile trip to Silverwood Lake Vista Point. Continue downhill across the Mojave River bridge for almost another 6 miles.

- - - - - - - - - - - -

❶ Silverwood Lake State Recreation Area

About 4 miles past USFS Cottonwood Station, turn left into the Miller Canyon Unit of **Silverwood Lake State Recreation Area** (☏760-389-2281; www.parks.ca.gov; entry per car $10; ☺7am-5pm Fri-Tue, extended daily hr Jun-Aug). Surrounded by native Californian chaparral, this artificial reservoir gets packed on weekends when scores of families show up for picnicking, swimming, boating and fishing along its 13-mile shoreline below Cedar Springs Dam. For a quiet hike or to do some bird-watching, come on a weekday in spring or fall. The Miller Canyon Trail meanders for 3.5 miles from Miller Canyon group camping area to Serrano Beach, passing

Devils Pit swimming hole and Lynx Point for panoramic views of the San Bernardino and San Gabriel Mountains, before meeting a paved lakeside cycling path by the marina.

The Drive » Back uphill at Hwy 138, turn left and drive southeast toward Crestline. Bordered by stately pine and oak trees, the highway narrows and twists further into the deep forest, gaining elevation. After less than 5 miles, veer right onto Knapp's Cutoff Rd (signposted as 'Lake Gregory 1 mile'), then left again onto Lake Dr, which reaches the lakeshore.

- - - - - - - - - - - -

❸ Lake Gregory

A relaxing family vacation spot, where kids can splash around in the calm water all summer long, this reservoir was built by the Works Progress Administration (WPA) during the Depression era. In what SoCal citrus-growing magnate Arthur Gregory once romantically called the Valley of the Moon,

LINK YOUR TRIP

30 **Route 66**
California's original road trip, the 'Mother Road' follows I-15 over Cajon Pass, intersecting with the Rim of the World Scenic Byway.

34 **Palms to Pines Scenic Byway**
South of Hwy 38 and Yucaipa, take I-10 eastbound to Banning to drive this roller-coaster mountains-and-desert route in reverse.

today **Lake Gregory Regional Park** (☏909-338-2233; http://cms.sbcounty.gov/parks; 24171 Lake Dr, Crestline; swimming beach admission $3, water-slide ride $1, rowboat rental per half-day $20) is perennially popular for its sandy beaches and water slides. Get out and stretch along the paved shoreline walking trail shadowed by fragrant pine and cedar trees. Private boats are banned, but you can rent a rowboat, aquacycle, paddleboat or stand-up paddle boarding set (SUP) when the weather allows. By the lake, the tiny town of **Crestline**

has burger shops, pizza parlors and coffee shops for a break from the road.

✗ ⊨ p329

The Drive ⟩⟩ Backtrack uphill to Hwy 138, turn left onto Hwy 18 and continue south on the Rim of the World Scenic Byway. Overlooks along the scenic route let you pull over for dizzying canyon views. After about 4 miles, turn left onto Hwy 173 leading down to Lake Arrowhead.

- - - - - - - - - - -

TRIP HIGHLIGHT

❹ Lake Arrowhead

Called Little Bear Lake until the 1920s, Lake Arrowhead is Big Bear's wealthy cousin.

Filled with fashionable shops and cafes, **Lake Arrowhead Village** looks more like a Tahoe ski resort than a rustic SoCal mountain retreat. This lake, which soaks up 300 days of sunshine every year, is privately owned. Public access is limited to taking a cruise on the **Lake Arrowhead Queen** (☏909-336-6992; http://lakearrowheadqueen.com; tickets: Leroys Boardshop, Lake Arrowhead Village, 28200 Hwy 189; adult/child $16/10; ☺ call for schedules), zooming around with **McKenzie Water Ski School** (☏909-337-3814; www.mckenziewaterskischool.

com; Lake Arrowhead Village; ride/lesson/cruise from $45/55/60) and rambling the village's shoreline boardwalk. Or you can just drive the scenic 15-mile lake loop by starting on Hwy 173, then turning left on Grass Valley Rd. West of town, the 1930s **Strawberry Peak Fire Lookout** (www. nationalforestassociation. org/strawberry.php; 1029 Strawberry Lookout Rd, off Bear Springs Rd; ⏰7am-5pm May-Dec, weather permitting) lets you inspect its fire-finding tools and photograph 360-degree mountain landscapes.

✕ ⛺ p329

The Drive ≫ Back on Hwy 18, drive east and buckle up for the most jaw-dropping stretch of the scenic byway, with vast canyon views and crazy-steep drop-offs that will have you clutching the wheel white-knuckled. Veer right at Running Springs and again at Big Bear Lake Dam to stay on Hwy 18 into Big Bear Village.

- - - - - - - - - - - -

TRIP HIGHLIGHT

5 Big Bear Lake

Weekenders flood the low-key mountain resort of Big Bear Lake. Snowy winters lure scores of ski bunnies and snowboarders to its two mountains (with 55 runs and 26 ski lifts), while

summers bring hikers, mountain-bikers and water-sports enthusiasts looking to escape LA's stifling heat. The main thoroughfare, Big Bear Blvd (Hwy 18), streams past roadside motels and cabins and skirts pedestrian-friendly **Big Bear Village**, with its souvenir shops and busy restaurants. **Swim Beach**, near the village, has lifeguards, making it popular with families. For more privacy, rent a boat, kayak or waverunner and get out on the water. Big Bear's winter ski resorts, **Bear Mountain & Snow Summit** (☎800-232-7686;

TOP TIP: SAFE DRIVING

It's dangerous to drive Hwy 18 – especially the tricky stretch between Lake Arrowhead and Big Bear Lake – during whiteout fog or snowstorms, when you can't see the car in front of you or the steep cliff and canyon drop-offs. In winter, come prepared with snow tires and tire chains.

www.bearmountainresorts. com; 2-park lift ticket adult/child $56/46; ☉ usually Dec-Apr), are east of the village off Hwy 18. During summer, their chair lifts and mountain trails swarm with mountain bikers.

✖ ⊨ p329

The Drive ›› Follow Hwy 18 east of Big Bear Village toward Big Bear City. Turn left onto Stanfield Cutoff and drive north across the bridge over the lake. Take another left onto North Shore Dr (Hwy 38), continuing just over a mile ahead to the Big Bear Discovery Center on your right.

TRIP HIGHLIGHT

❻ Big Bear Discovery Center

On the quieter side of Big Bear Lake, North Shore Dr (Hwy 38) passes by shady public campgrounds, calm swimming beaches and myriad forest trails. Just inland from the lake's north shore, the US Forest Service (USFS) **Big Bear Discovery Center** (☎909-382-2790; www. bigbeardiscoverycenter.com; 40971 North Shore Dr/Hwy 38, Fawnskin; ☉8:30am-4:30pm Thu-Mon) is a one-stop outdoor education and information center for help finding campgrounds, hiking and mountain-biking trails, plus self-guided driving tours of **Holcomb Valley**, an 1860s gold-mining camp. Ask about ranger-led nature walks and snowshoe tours on weekends, or lace up your hiking boots and head up the Castle Rock or Cougar Crest Trail, both popular routes with hawk's-eye views.

✖ p329

The Drive ›› After making the 15-mile scenic loop drive around the lake, turn left on Hwy 18 and drive back east. About 6 miles past Big Bear Village, turn right onto Hwy 38, which switchbacks down through national forest for 33 miles. At Valley of the Falls Dr, turn left and slowly drive 5 miles to the road's end.

TRIP HIGHLIGHT

❼ Valley of the Falls

Beyond the mountain hamlet of **Forest Falls**, the valley road continues gently rolling up and down, stealthily gaining elevation until it dead-ends at **Valley of the Falls** scenic lookout and picnic area. With its cliffside waterfalls, aromatic pine trees and craggy mountain views, SoCal denizens call this spot a 'little Yosemite Valley'. Although that's a stretch, the San Gorgonio Wilderness views are inspiring, and several hiking trails start nearby. Even the road here itself is a treat, following fault-born Mill Creek Canyon with its toweringly steep sides. The road's end is closed by snow in winter, so either visit from late spring through early fall or bring snowshoes.

The Drive ›› Backtrack to Hwy 38, turning left to continue downhill and south another 6 miles to the official end of Rim of the World Scenic Byway at USFS Miller Creek Ranger Station, situated beside a meadow off Mill Creek Rd.

Eating & Sleeping

Lake Gregory ❸

✖ Stockade · · · · · · · · · · · · · · · Barbecue $$

(23881 Lake Dr, Crestline; mains $10-20; ⏰11am-2pm & 5-10pm Mon-Fri, 11am-10pm Sat & Sun) When they fire up the wood-chip smoker outside this divey biker bar, swing by for baby back ribs slathered in BBQ sauce, mighty fine burgers and damn cheap beer.

🛏 North Shore Inn · · · · · · · · · · · Inn $$

(☎909-338-5230, 800-300-5230; www.thenorthshoreinn.com; 24202 Lake Dr, Crestline; r $70-175; ❄🛜🛗👪) A hospitable innkeeper makes this simple country guesthouse a worry-free place to lay your head with tidy, just-like-home rooms, some of which have private lake-view patios.

Lake Arrowhead ❹

✖ Belgian Waffle Works · · · · · · American $

(http://belgianwaffle.com; Lake Arrowhead Village, 28200 Hwy 189; mains $7-10; ⏰8am-4pm Mon-Thu, to 5pm Fri-Sun, extended summer hr) Classic dockside breakfast and brunch spot serves hot waffles piled with whipped cream all day, plus patty melts, fried-fish sandwiches and California-style salads.

✖ Lake Arrowhead Sports Grille · · · · · · · · · · · · · Pub $$

(http://lasportsgrille.com; 27200 Hwy 189, Blue Jay; mains $8-20; ⏰11am-10pm Mon-Thu, 11am-11pm Fri & Sat, 10am-10pm Sun) Step inside this jovial sports bar for barbecue chicken wings, burgers, flatbread pizzas and craft beers on tap.

🛏 Lake Arrowhead Resort & Spa · · · · · · · · · · · Hotel $$$

(☎909-336-1511; www.laresort.com; 27984 Hwy 189; r $179-249; ❄🛜🛗) Most of these rustic-chic lodge rooms close to the lakeshore have

private balconies. Additional daily resort fee includes spa and fitness-center access.

Big Bear Lake ❺

✖ Himalayan · · · · · · · · · · · South Asian $

(www.himalayanbigbear.com; 672 Pine Knot Ave; mains $8-17; ⏰11am-9pm Sun-Tue, to 10pm Fri & Sat; 🚹🛗) In the busy village, this kitchen cooks up authentic Nepali and Indian dishes, including flaming-hot tandoori grills and mellow momo (Tibetan dumplings). Standoffish but quick service.

🛏 Bear Creek Resort · · · · · Motel, Cabin $$

(☎877-428-9335; http://bearcreek-resort.com; 40210 Big Bear Blvd/Hwy 18; r $109-169, cabins $209-309; ❄@🛜♨🛗👪) Right off the highway (expect some traffic noise), tidy renovated studio cabins have wood-burning fireplaces and kitchenettes. The sister property, Wolf Creek Resort, is closer to the ski resorts.

🛏 Switzerland Haus · · · · · · · · · B&B $$

(☎909-866-3729, 800-335-3729; www.switzerlandhaus.com; 41829 Switzerland Dr; r incl breakfast $125-249; @🛜) King sleigh beds, private mountain-view patios and a Nordic sauna on the deck are among the perks at this friendly, well-kept five-room inn. Snow Summit ski resort is next door.

Big Bear Discovery Center ❻

✖ North Shore Café · · · · · · · · American $

(☎909-866-5879; www.dininginbigbear.com; 39226 North Shore Dr/Hwy 38, Fawnskin; breakfast & lunch mains $6-12; ⏰8am-4pm Wed-Thu, 8am-9pm Fri, 7am-9pm Sat, 7am-6pm Sun, also 8am-4pm Mon May-Sep; 🛜🛗) This homey north-shore cabin is a heart-warming breakfast or brunch stop for homemade corned-beef hash, custardy French toast and fluffy pancakes.

Death Valley Hike rolling fields of sand dunes

Life in Death Valley

32

Drive where California pioneers and gold miners once rolled their wagons in Death Valley National Park, where the magnum forces of natural and human history collide.

TRIP HIGHLIGHTS

330 miles

Scotty's Castle
Tour a historic oasis in Grapevine Canyon

10 FINISH

8

270 miles

Rhyolite
Explore a ghostly Wild West mining town

Stovepipe Wells Village

Panamint Springs

Furnace Creek

6

3

5 miles

Emigrant & Wildrose Canyons
Follow early pioneers' desperate escape route

Tecopa

Badwater
Plant your feet at the USA's lowest elevation

110 miles

Baker
START

**3 DAYS
380 MILES/610KM**

GREAT FOR...

BEST TIME TO GO
February to April for wildflowers and cooler temperatures.

ESSENTIAL PHOTO
Elevation sign at Badwater Basin.

BEST FOR HISTORY
Guided tours of Scotty's Castle.

331

Classic Trip

32 Life in Death Valley

The name itself evokes all that is harsh, hot and hellish – a punishing, barren and lifeless place of Old Testament severity. Ghost towns and abandoned mines are proof of the human struggle to survive here. Yet a scenic drive through the park reveals that in Death Valley, nature is spectacularly alive: 'singing' sand dunes, water-sculpted canyons, boulders mysteriously moving across the desert floor, extinct volcanic craters and palm-shaded oases.

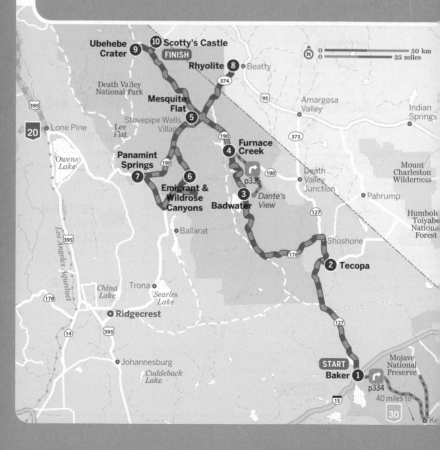

❶ Baker

Death Valley is a land of extremes – you'll find the lowest elevation in North America here, not far from Mt Whitney, the highest peak in the US outside Alaska. More infamously, Death Valley is the hottest place in the nation. Just take a look at the **World's Largest Thermometer**, off I-15 next to Bob's Big Boy diner. It stands 134ft tall to commemorate the record-breaking temperature of 134°F measured in Death Valley on July 10, 1913. Often broken these days, the thermometer is still an eye-catching tower of roadside kitsch.

The Drive ›› From Baker, follow Hwy 127 (Death Valley Rd) north for almost 50 miles,

LINK YOUR TRIP

20 Eastern Sierra Scenic Byway

From Panamint Springs, it's 33 miles to Lone Pine, gateway to lofty Sierra Nevada peaks, via Hwys 190, 136 and 395.

30 Route 66

From Baker, drive through the Mojave National Preserve and across I-40 to meet California's original road trip.

crossing railroad tracks and zooming through a sere desert landscape. Turn right onto Old Spanish Trail Hwy and drive 4 miles east toward Tecopa, turning left onto Tecopa Hot Springs Rd for the hot-springs resorts.

❷ Tecopa

Even when the desert looks bone-dry, you can still find oases in the dusty outpost of Tecopa. In the middle of town at **Tecopa Hot Springs Resort** (www.tecopahotsprings.org; 860 Tecopa Hot Springs Rd; public bathhouse entry $10; ☺ usually 7am-9pm Oct-May), you can soak in the natural mineral springs used by Native Americans for centuries. Sex-segregated bathhouses let tribal elders, snowbird RVers and curious travelers all soak together, or you could rent a private pool. Outside town, **China Ranch Date Farm** (www.chinaranch.com; ☺9am-5pm) is a refreshingly green refuge where you can go hiking or bird-watching, then stock up on fresh dates or try their yummy date shakes. To get to the ranch, follow the Old Spanish Trail Hwy east of Tecopa Hot Springs Rd, turn right onto Furnace Creek Rd, then right again onto China Ranch Rd. The last stretch is unpaved, steep and winding, sometimes requiring 4WD.

🛏 p339

The Drive ›› Backtrack west on the Old Spanish Trail Hwy to Hwy 127. Turn right and drive north to Shoshone (p339), your last chance for gas, drinks and snacks until Furnace Creek, over 70 miles away. Turn left onto Hwy 178 (Jubilee Pass Rd), which wrenches right at Ashford Junction, becoming Badwater Rd and curving lazily north along the valley floor.

TRIP HIGHLIGHT

❸ Badwater

Cresting Jubilee Pass (1290ft), the highway at last dips down into Death Valley itself. Despite its harsh name, the valley is actually a thriving wildlife habitat and has supported human life for millennia, from Shoshone tribespeople to Old West pioneers, gold seekers and borax miners. It's the silence and solemnity of the vast expanse that inspires today. That cracked, parched-looking salt pan extending across the valley floor, which suddenly sears your retinas with its dazzling white light, is **Badwater**. At 282ft below sea level, it's the lowest point in North America. A boardwalk hovers over the constantly evaporating bed of salty, mineralized water, almost alien in its beauty. Prehistoric Lake Manly, which covered the entire valley during the last ice age, reappeared here in 2005 for the first time in recorded human history. Although the lake

Classic Trip

evaporated again within weeks, its reemergence just goes to show the tenacity of life in this valley that appears deceptively barren.

The Drive >> About 8 miles north of Badwater, past the turnoff to the Natural Bridge trailhead on your right and the bizarre salt crystals of the Devils Golf Course on your left, detour right onto Artists Drive, a one-way 9-mile scenic loop (no vehicles with trailers or over 25ft long). Rejoining Badwater Rd, drive 5 miles north, then turn left onto Hwy 190 to Furnace Creek.

---

❹ Furnace Creek

At Furnace Creek Ranch, the park's busiest tourist hub, the **Borax Museum**

(admission free; Hwy 190; ⊙ usually 10am-5pm) lets you poke around historical exhibits about mining and the famous 20-mule teams that hauled mineral ore out of Death Valley. Out back are authentic pioneer-era wagons and stagecoaches. A short drive north of the park's **Furnace Creek Visitor Center** (📞760-786-3200; www.nps.gov/deva; Hwy 190; ⊙8am-5pm), walk in the footsteps of Chinese laborers as you examine the adobe ruins of the 1880s **Harmony Borax Works** on a scenic side-trip loop through twisting **Mustard Canyon**.

✕ ⌖ p339

The Drive >> If you didn't fill up outside the park, Furnace Creek has an expensive gas station with 24-hour credit-card pumps. Head north from

Furnace Creek on Hwy 190. After less than 20 miles, turn left to stay on Hwy 190 west toward Stovepipe Wells Village. Just over 5 miles later, pull into the Mesquite Flat parking lot on your right.

---

❺ Mesquite Flat

It's time to take up another strand of history in Death Valley: the story of the lost '49ers. When the California gold rush took off in 1849, a small group of pioneers chanced what they hoped would be a shortcut to the California goldfields, leaving behind the Old Spanish Trail. Exhausted, dangerously running out of food and water, and struggling with broken wagons and worn-out pack animals, the woeful group arrived near Furnace Creek on Christmas Eve. Failing to get their wagons across

---

⮕ DETOUR:
MOJAVE NATIONAL PRESERVE

Start: ❶ Baker

For even more Wild West history than you'll find in Death Valley's abandoned mines and ghost towns, head into the lonely **Mojave National Preserve** (📞760-252-6100; www.nps.gov/moja; admission free; ⊙24hr), southeast of Baker off I-15. Start by touring the beautifully restored Kelso Depot, with its modern museum of local history and lore. Drive south to scramble around the Kelso Dunes, a field of 'singing' sand that makes strange music when the wind blows just so. Further east at Hole-in-the-Wall, scale the cliffs Native Americans used to escape Western ranchers, then drive through Wild Horse Canyon or follow the old Mojave Rd blazed by Spanish missionaries, fur trappers and traders and, oddly enough, camels on an 1867 military expedition. North of Cima look for the trailhead for Teutonia Peak, a 3-mile round-trip hike through the world's largest forest of Joshua trees, ending with panoramic desert views peppered with colorful cinder cones.

the Panamint Mountains, the survivors slaughtered their oxen and burned their wagons near what today is the **Mesquite Flat**. Get out of the car to hike up and down across the rolling field of sand dunes that look like a mini Sahara.

The Drive » You can fill up the gas tank and buy food and drinks at Stovepipe Wells Village, 2 miles further west along Hwy 190. Heading west, you'll pass the side road to Mosaic Canyon on your left before reaching Emigrant Canyon Rd after 9 miles. Turn left and start winding uphill toward Emigrant Pass.

TRIP HIGHLIGHT

6 Emigrant & Wildrose Canyons

Faced with no other choice, the '49er pioneers eventually walked out of torturous Death Valley over **Emigrant Pass**. As they left, one woman reputedly looked back and fatalistically uttered the words: 'Good-bye, death valley.' Later pioneers flooded back when gold was discovered in Death Valley, including at **Skidoo**, a boomtown that went bust in the early 20th century, and where the influential silent movie *Greed* was filmed in 1923. Nothing remains of the ghost townsite today. Farther south, the ruined **Eureka Mine** is en route to vertigo-inducing **Aguereberry Point**, where you can see the

↱ **DETOUR: DANTE'S VIEW**

Start: 4 Furnace Creek

For spectacular valley views across Death Valley's golden badlands eroded into waves, pleats and gullies, drive 3.5 miles east of the Furnace Creek Inn on Hwy 190 to **Zabriskie Point**. Escape the valley's midday heat or catch a memorable sunset by continuing up to **Dante's View**. There you can simultaneously view the highest (Mt Whitney) and lowest (Badwater) points in California. The 22-mile drive takes about 1½ to two hours round-trip.

Funeral Mountains and the parched valley spread out below. Both of these side trips travel on rough, rutted dirt roads (high-clearance 4WD vehicles recommended). Turn left onto Wildrose Canyon Rd to reach the abandoned **charcoal kilns**. Built in the 1876, these beehive-shaped kilns made the fuel miners needed to process Death Valley's silver and lead ore. The landscape is subalpine, with forests of piñon pine and juniper; it can be covered with snow, even in spring.

The Drive » Backtrack downhill, turning left at the intersection with Emigrant Canyon Rd onto Wildrose Canyon Rd, which snakes through a flash-flood zone (don't attempt this road except during dry weather). At Panamint Valley Rd, turn right and drive north to Hwy 190, then turn left. The longer all-weather route is to backtrack down Emigrant Canyon Rd to Hwy 190, then turn left for the 22-mile drive to Panamint Springs.

7 Panamint Springs

At the park's far western edge, **Panamint Springs** is a remote base camp. In spring, you can drive the 2-mile graded gravel road, followed by a mile-long cross-country hike, to **Darwin Falls**, where a hidden natural-spring cascade plunges into a gorge, embraced by shady willows and migratory birds. Or get more adventurous and follow roughshod Saline Valley Rd out to **Lee Flat**, where Joshua trees thrive. Or play it safe and stay on the paved highway 6 miles west of Panamint Springs Resort to **Father Crowley Point**, which peers deep into Rainbow Canyon, created by lava flows and scattered with painterly volcanic cinders.

The Drive » Turn around and drive back downhill east on Hwy 190. About 7 miles east of Stovepipe Wells Village, turn

WHY THIS IS A CLASSIC TRIP
SARA BENSON, AUTHOR

Most people think of sunny beaches when you mention Southern California road trips. But some of the most epic scenery I've ever witnessed through my car's windshield has been in the Mojave Desert. In every season, Death Valley's landscape looks startlingly different. You'll never forget your first view of hillsides painted in spring wildflower blooms or when vanished prehistoric lakes suddenly reappear in the salt flats after heavy winter rains.

Top: Mojave Desert
Left: Salt plates, Badwater
Right: Rhyolite

WITOLD SKRYPCZAK / GETTY IMAGES ©

WITOLD SKRYPCZAK / GETTY IMAGES ©

left and then right onto Daylight Pass Rd for 16 miles, exiting the park and following Hwy 374 into Nevada for 5 miles to the signposted turn-off for Rhyolite on your left.

- - - - - - - - - - -

TRIP HIGHLIGHT

❽ Rhyolite

Just 4 miles west of Beatty (p339), Nevada, **Rhyolite** (www.rhyolitesite. com; Hwy 374; ☉sunrise-sunset) was the queen of Death Valley's mines during its heyday. It epitomizes the hurly-burly, boom-and-bust story of Western gold-rush mining towns. Don't miss the 1906 'bottle house' or the skeletal remains of a three-story bank. Also here is the bizarre **Goldwell Open Air Museum** (www. goldwellmuseum.org; ☉24hr), a trippy art installation started by Belgian artist Albert Szukalski in 1984. One favorite piece: the giant-sized miner with a pet penguin.

The Drive » Backtrack down Daylight Pass Rd, turning right onto Scotty's Castle Rd, which winds for over 33 miles through the valley, shadowed by the Grapevine Mountains. Turn left near the ranger station at Grapevine Junction onto the side road leading 6 miles northwest toward Ubehebe Crater.

- - - - - - - - - - -

❾ Ubehebe Crater

West of Grapevine Junction, a rough dirt road rumbles out to an overlook of 600ft-deep

ED NORTON / GETTY IMAGES ©

Ubehebe Crater, formed by the explosive meeting of fiery magma and cool groundwater. Once thought to be an ancient volcano, scientists have come to believe that this volcano exploded possibly as recently as just 300 years ago. Hikers can make a loop around the rim and over to younger **Little Hebe Crater**, for astounding views into the volcanic depths and over rainbow-colored cinder fields lying scattered over the valley floor.

The Drive » Backtrack along Ubehebe Crater Rd to Grapevine Junction ranger station, then turn left and continue another 3 easy miles east along Scotty's Castle Rd to the Scotty's Castle parking lot, snack bar and gift shop, all on your left.

- - - - - - - - - - -

TRIP HIGHLIGHT

❿ Scotty's Castle

No trip to Death Valley would be complete without a tour of

SUMMER SURVIVAL TIPS

When the mercury can climb over 120°F, a car with reliable air-con is essential and outdoor explorations in Death Valley should be limited to the early morning and late afternoon. Spend the hottest part of the day poolside or at higher elevations. Always carry extra water in case you get stranded. Fill up the gas tank whenever you can. An underinflated tire can overheat quickly, so check the tire pressure, too. Watch the engine temperature gauge as you drive. If it rises into the red zone, turn off the air-con, turn on the heater and roll down windows. Or pull over, face the car's front into the wind, carefully pop the hood and idle the engine. If the engine gets hotter, shut it off immediately.

Scotty's Castle (☎760-786-2392, reservations 877-444-6777; www.recreation.gov; Hwy 267; adult/child $15/7.50; ☉ open daily, tour schedules vary). Guides in authentic period dress lead curious visitors around the Spanish-inspired villa named for 'Death Valley Scotty,' a gifted tall-tale teller who captivated people with his fanciful stories of gold. Scotty's most lucrative friendship was with Albert and Bessie Johnson, insurance magnates from Chicago. Despite knowing that Scotty was a freeloading liar, they bankrolled the construction of this eccentric desert estate. Restored to the glory of its 1939 appearance, the historic home has sheepskin drapes, carved California redwood, handmade tiles, elaborately wrought iron, woven Shoshone baskets and a bellowing pipe organ upstairs. If you haven't reserved a tour at least a day in advance, show up early – limited same-day tour tickets are sold on a first-come, first-served basis.

Eating & Sleeping

Tecopa ❷

🛏 Cynthia's   Hostel, B&B $

(☎760-852-4580; www.discovercynthias.
com; 2001 Old Spanish Trail Hwy; dm $22-25,
r $75-140, tepee $165; 🛜) Match your budget
to the bed: an eclectically decorated room
or dormitory in a vintage trailer, or a canvas
tepee with fire pits and a comfy king-size bed.
Reservations essential.

Shoshone

🍴 Cafe C'est Si Bon   Coffee Shop $

(Hwy 127; mains $6-8; ⊙usually 8am-4pm Wed-
Mon; 🛜🚹) At this solar-powered coffee and
teahouse with a world-music beat, the genial
chef-owner cooks 'flexitarian' breakfasts and
lunches like sweet crêpes and savory quiche.

Furnace Creek ❹

🍴 19th Hole Bar & Grill   American $

(www.furnacecreekresort.com; Furnace Creek
Golf Course, off Hwy 190; mains $8-12; ⊙kitchen
10:30am-3:30pm Oct-May, bar till 4pm Mon-Fri,
5pm Sat & Sun) By the golf pro shop, this
verandah grill with views of the Panamint Range
has the juiciest burgers around.

🍴 49'er Cafe   American $$

(www.furnacecreekresort.com; Ranch at Furnace
Creek, Hwy 190; mains $8-25; ⊙7am-10:45am
& 11:30am-9pm Oct-May, 4-9pm only Jun-Sep;
🛜🚹) Be prepared for long waits and crowded
tables, but surprisingly decent California fare,
at this Old West family-style restaurant next to
the general store.

🛏 Inn at Furnace Creek   Hotel $$$

(☎760-786-2345, 800-236-7916; www.
furnacecreekresort.com; Hwy 190; r $340-455;
⊙mid-Oct–mid-May; ❄🛜🏊) At this hilltop
adobe hotel with an elegant cocktail bar, the
1920s Mission-style buildings lie among palm-
shaded garden terraces with panoramic valley
views and a natural spring-fed swimming pool.
Stripped-down rooms are hardly sumptuous.

🛏 NPS Campgrounds   Campground $

(reservations ☎877-444-6777; www.nps.gov/
deva, www.recreation.gov; campsites free-$18;
⊙some campgrounds year-round; 🚹🐕) Of
the park's nine campgrounds, only Furnace
Creek accepts reservations (from mid-October
through mid-April only). At peak times, like
during the spring wildflower bloom, all park
campsites fill by mid-morning.

🛏 Ranch at
Furnace Creek   Motel, Cabin $$

(☎760-786-2345, 800-236-7916; www.
furnacecreekresort.com; Hwy 190; r $135-215;
❄🛜🏊🚹) When sunset makes Death Valley
look aflame, check into the rustic motel rooms
and cabins at the ranch, which also has a natural
hot-springs swimming pool, horseback-riding
stables and the world's lowest-elevation golf
course.

Mesquite Flat ❺

🍴🛏 Stovepipe Wells Village   Motel $$

(☎760-786-2387; www.escapetodeathvalley.
com; Hwy 190; r $100-160, mains $8-25;
❄🛜🏊🚹🐕) Newly spruced-up rooms
feature quality linens beneath cheerful Native
American–patterned bedspreads. The small
pool is cool, while the cowboy-style Toll Rd
Restaurant delivers three square all-American
meals a day.

Beatty

🛏 Stagecoach Hotel   Motel $

(☎775-553-2419, 800-424-4946; www.
bestdeathvalleyhotels.com; 900 E Hwy 95 N,
Beatty; r $60-110; ❄🏊🛜🚹🐕) Rooms are
bland but comfy enough for an overnight stay
in the podunk casino town of Beatty, just a few
miles east of the Rhyolite site.

Joshua Tree National Park A wonderland o
rocks and sandy Joshua tree forests

Palm Springs & Joshua Tree Oases

33

Southern California's deserts can be brutally hot, barren places — escape to Palm Springs and Joshua Tree National Park, where shady fan-palm oases and date gardens await.

TRIP HIGHLIGHTS

60 miles

Keys View
Capture sunset panoramas sweeping from summit to sea

50 miles

Hidden Valley
Cool off inside Joshua Tree National Park

Joshua Tree

Twentynine Palms

4

Desert Hot Springs

5

1 START

Coachella Valley ● ● Indio

FINISH

7

Palm Springs
Fabulously hip resort town with Mid-Century Modern style

0 miles

Cottonwood Spring
Where fan-palm trees shade the desert sun

120 miles

2–3 DAYS
185 MILES/300KM

GREAT FOR...

BEST TIME TO GO

February to April for wildflowers and cooler temperatures.

ESSENTIAL PHOTO

Sunset from Keys View.

BEST FOR SOLITUDE

Hike to the Lost Palms Oasis.

341

33 Palm Springs & Joshua Tree Oases

Just a short drive from the chic resorts of Palm Springs, the vast Mojave and Sonoran Deserts are serenely spiritual places. You may find that what at first looked like desolate sands transform on foot into perfect beauty: shady palm tree and cactus gardens, tiny wildflowers pushing up from hard-baked soil in spring, natural hot-springs pools for soaking, and uncountable stars overhead in the inky dark.

TRIP HIGHLIGHT

❶ Palm Springs

Hollywood celebs have always counted on Palm Springs as a quick escape from LA. Today, this desert resort town shows off a trove of well-preserved Mid-Century Modern buildings. Stop at the **Palm Springs Visitor Center** (☎760-778-8418; www.visitpalmsprings.com; 2901 N Palm Canyon Dr; ☻9am-5pm), inside a 1960s gas station by modernist Albert Frey, to pick up a self-guided

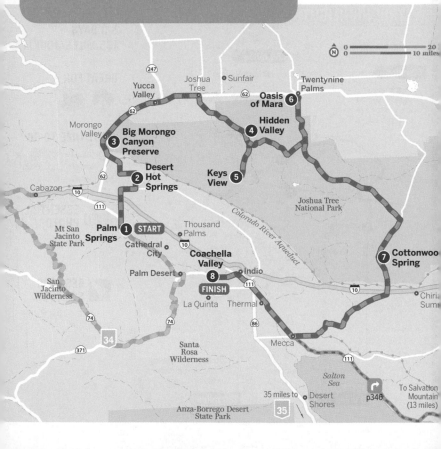

architectural tour map. Then drive uphill to clamber aboard the **Palm Springs Aerial Tramway** (☎888-515-8726; www.pstramway.com; 1 Tram Way; adult/child $24/17; ☺10am-8pm Mon-Fri, 8am-8pm Sat & Sun, last tram down 9:45pm daily; ⊕), which climbs nearly 6000 vertical feet from the hot Sonoran Desert floor to the cool, even snowy San Jacinto Mountains in less than 15 minutes. Back down on the ground, drive south on Palm Canyon Dr, where you can hop between art galleries, cafes, cocktail bars and chic boutiques like fashionistas' find **Trina Turk** (www.trinaturk.com; 891 N Palm Canyon Dr; ☺10am-

5pm Mon-Fri, 10am-6pm Sat, noon-5pm Sun).

 p347

The Drive » Drive north out of downtown Palm Springs along Indian Canyon Dr for 8 miles, passing over the I-10. Turn right onto Dillon Rd, then after 2.5 miles turn left onto Palm Dr, which heads north into central Desert Hot Springs.

---

❷ Desert Hot Springs

In 1774 Spanish explorer Juan Bautista de Anza was the first European to encounter the desert Cahuilla tribe. Afterward, the Spanish name Agua Caliente came to refer to both the indigenous people and the natural hot springs, which still flow restoratively today through the town of **Desert Hot Springs** (www.visitdeserthotsprings.com), where newly hip boutique hotels have appeared atop healing waters bubbling up from deep below. Imitate Tim Robbins in Robert Altman's film *The Player* and have a mud bath at **Two Bunch Palms Resort & Spa** (☎800-472-4334; www.twobunchpalms.com; 67425 Two Bunch Palms Trail; ☺by reservation only), which sits atop an actual oasis. Bounce between a variety of pools and sunbathing areas (including clothing-optional), but maintain the code of silence.

🛏 p347

The Drive » Head west on Pierson Blvd back to Indian Canyon Dr. Turn right and drive northwest through the dusty outskirts of Desert Hot Springs. Turn right onto Hwy 62 eastbound toward Yucca Valley; after about 4 miles, turn right onto East Dr and look for signs for Big Morongo Canyon Preserve.

---

❸ Big Morongo Canyon Preserve

Another oasis hidden in the high desert, **Big Morongo Canyon Preserve** (☎760-363-7190; www.bigmorongo.org; admission by donation; 11055 East Dr, Yucca Valley; ☺7:30am-sunset) is a bird-watching hotspot. Tucked into the Little San Bernardino Mountains, this stream-fed riparian habitat is flush with cottonwood and willow trees. Start from the educational kiosk by the parking lot, then tramp along wooden boardwalks through marshy woodlands as hummingbirds flutter atop flowers and woodpeckers hammer away.

The Drive » Rejoin Hwy 62 eastbound past Yucca Valley (p347), with its roadside antiques and vintage shops, art galleries and cafes, to the town of Joshua Tree 16 miles away, where you'll find places to sleep and eat (p347). At the intersection with Park Blvd, turn right and drive 5 miles to Joshua Tree National Park's west entrance. Make sure you've got a full tank of gas first.

LINK YOUR TRIP

34 Palms to Pines Scenic Byway

Starting just outside Palm Springs, drive this twisting highway from the desert floor up into the cool green mountains.

35 Temecula, Julian & Anza-Borrego

From the Coachella Valley, drive along the Salton Sea's western shore, then head inland to Borrego Springs, a 50-mile trip.

MOMATIUK · EASTCOTT / CORBIS ©

TRIP HIGHLIGHT

④ Hidden Valley

It's time to jump into **Joshua Tree National Park** (☎760-367-5500; www.nps.gov/jotr; 7-day entry permit per car $15; ◷24hr; ⚑), a wonderland of jumbo rocks interspersed with sandy forests of Joshua trees. Related to agave plants, Joshua trees were named by Mormon settlers who thought the twisted, spiky arms resembled a prophet's arms stretching toward God. Revel in the scenery as you drive along the winding park road for about 7 miles to Hidden Valley picnic area. Turn left and drive past the campground to the trailhead for **Barker Dam**. Here a kid-friendly nature trail loops for a mile past a pretty little artificial lake and a rock incised with Native American petroglyphs. If you enjoy history and Western lore, reserve ahead for a 90-minute guided walking tour of nearby **Keys Ranch** (☎760-367-5555; adult/child $5/2.50; ◷usually 10am & 1pm), where 19th-century pioneer homesteaders tried their hand at cattle ranching, mining and desert farming.

🛏 p347

The Drive » Backtrack to Park Blvd, turn left and head south again past jumbled rock formations and fields of spiky Joshua trees. Take the well-signed right turn toward Keys View. You'll pass several trailheads and roadside interpretive exhibits over the next 5.5 miles leading up to the viewpoint.

TRIP HIGHLIGHT

⑤ Keys View

Leave Hidden Valley at least an hour before sunset for the drive up to **Keys View**, where

Cottonwood Spring

panoramic views look into the Coachella Valley and reach as far south as the shimmering Salton Sea or, on an unusually clear day, Mexico's Signal Mountain. Looming in front of you are Mt San Jacinto and Mt San Gorgonio, two of Southern California's highest peaks, often snow-dusted even in spring. Down below snakes the shaky San Andreas Fault.

The Drive » Head back downhill to Park Blvd. Turn right and wind through the park's Wonderland of Rocks, where boulders call out to scampering kids and serious rock jocks alike,

passing more campgrounds. After 10 miles, veer left to stay on Park Blvd and drive north for 7 miles toward the town of Twentynine Palms onto Utah Trail.

- - - - - - - - - -

6 Oasis of Mara

Detour to the National Park Service (NPS) **Oasis Visitor Center** (www.nps.gov/jotr; 74485 National Park Dr, Twentynine Palms; ⊙8am-5pm; 👫) for its educational exhibits about Southern California's desert fan palms. These palms are often found growing along fault lines, where cracks in the earth's crust allow subterranean water

to surface. Outside the visitors center, a gentle half-mile nature trail leads around the **Oasis of Mara**, where Serrano peoples once camped. Ask for directions to the trailhead off Hwy 62 for the 3-mile round-trip hike to **49 Palms Oasis**, where a sun-exposed dirt trail marches you over a ridge, then drops you into a rocky gorge, doggedly heading down past barrel cacti toward a distant speck of green.

🛏 p347

The Drive » Drive back south on Utah Trail and re-enter the park. Follow Park Blvd south,

345

DETOUR: SALTON SEA

Start ⑦: Cottonwood Spring

Driving along Hwy 111 southeast of Indio, it's a most unexpected sight: California's largest lake in the middle of its largest desert. In 1905 the Colorado River breached, giving birth to the Salton Sea. Marketed to mid-20th-century tourists as the 'California Riviera' with beachfront vacation homes, the Salton Sea has been mostly abandoned because of the stinky annual fish die-offs caused by chemical runoff from surrounding farmland. An even stranger sight is folk-art **Salvation Mountain** (www. salvationmountain.us), an artificial hill covered in acrylic paint and found objects and inscribed with Christian religious messages. It's in Niland, about 3 miles east of Hwy 111.

turning left at the first major junction onto Pinto Basin Rd for a winding 30-mile drive downhill to Cottonwood Spring.

- - - - - - - - - - - - -

TRIP HIGHLIGHT

⑦ Cottonwood Spring

On your drive south to Cottonwood Spring, you'll pass from the high Mojave Desert into the lower Sonoran Desert. At the **Cholla Cactus Garden**, handily labeled specimens burst into bloom in spring, including unmistakable ocotillo plants, which look like green octopus tentacles adorned with flaming scarlet flowers. Turn left at the **Cottonwood Visitor Center** (www.nps.gov/jotr; off Cottonwood Springs Rd; ☺8am-4pm) for a short drive east past the campground to **Cottonwood Spring**. Once used by the Cahuilla, who left behind archaeological evidence such as mortars and clay pots, the springs became a hotbed for gold mining in the late 19th century. The now-dry springs are the start of the moderately strenuous 7.2-mile round-trip

trek out to **Lost Palms Oasis**, a fan-palm oasis blessed with solitude and scenery.

🛏 p347

The Drive » Head south from Cottonwood Springs and drive across the I-10 to pick up scenic Box Canyon Rd, which burrows a hole through the desert, twisting its way toward the Salton Sea. Take 66th Ave west to Mecca, then turn right onto Hwy 111 and drive northwest ('up valley') toward Indio.

- - - - - - - - - - - - -

⑧ Coachella Valley

The hot but fertile Coachella Valley is the ideal place to find the date of your dreams – the kind that grows on trees, that is. Date farms let you sample exotic-sounding varieties like halawy, deglet noor and golden zahidi for free, but the signature taste of the valley is a rich date shake from certified-organic **Oasis Date Gardens** (www.oasisdate.com; 59-111 Grapefruit Blvd, Thermal; ☺9am-4pm) or the 1920s pioneer **Shields Date Garden** (www.shieldsdate garden.com; 80-225 Hwy 111, Indio; ☺9am-5pm).

Eating & Sleeping

Palm Springs ❶

✖ Cheeky's
Californian $$

(http://cheekysps.com; 622 N Palm Canyon Dr; mains $7-14; ⊙8am-2pm Wed-Mon) Waits can be long, but this cafe's farm-to-table menu dazzles with witty inventiveness. Dishes change weekly, with chilaquile towers and bacon bar 'flights' making regular appearances.

✖ Sherman's
Deli, Bakery $$

(www.shermansdeli.com; 401 E Tahquitz Canyon Way; mains $8-17; ⊙7am-9pm; 🐾) With a breezy sidewalk patio and Hollywood celebrity headshots hanging on the walls, this 1950s Jewish deli feeds an all-ages crowd on mile-high sandwich boards and homemade pies.

🛏 Horizon Hotel
Boutique Hotel $$

(☎760-323-1858, 800-377-7855; www.thehorizonhotel.com; 1050 E Palm Canyon Dr; r $169-249; ❄❄🛰🐾) Designed by modernist architect William F Cody, this intimate retreat had Marilyn Monroe and Betty Grable lounging poolside back in the day. Adults only.

🛏 Parker Palm Springs
Resort $$$

(☎760-770-5000; www.theparkerpalmsprings.com; 4200 E Palm Canyon Dr; r from $199; ❄🛰❄🐾) Once the star of a Bravo reality TV series, this posh full-service resort boasts whimsical decor by Jonathan Adler. Drop by the luxe spa or for cocktails at Mister Parker's steakhouse.

Desert Hot Springs ❷

🛏 El Morocco Inn & Spa
Boutique Hotel $$

(☎760-288-2527, 888-288-9905; www.elmoroccoinn.com; 66814 4th St; r incl breakfast $159-249; ❄🛰❄) Heed the call of the Kasbah in a drop-dead spa hideaway with 10 fantastically furnished rooms. Sip cocktails or homemade mint ice tea in the garden.

🛏 The Spring
Boutique Hotel $$

(☎760-251-6700; www.the-spring.com; 12699 Reposo Way; r incl breakfast $179-229; ❄🛰❄) This 1950s motel has morphed into a chic, whisper-quiet spa retreat with natural hot-springs pools. The 10 blissful rooms are minimalist in design but not in amenities.

Yucca Valley

✖ Ma Rouge Coffee House
Cafe $

(www.marouge.net; 55844 Hwy 62; mains $5-10; ⊙7am-7pm; 🛰) At the corner of Pioneertown Rd, this locals' stop pours organic coffee and dishes up quiche, pastries, sandwiches and salads.

Joshua Tree

🛏 Hicksville Trailer Palace
Motel $$

(☎310-584-1086; www.hicksville.com; d $100-225; ❄🛰❄) Eight outlandishly decorated vintage trailers are parked around a saltwater swimming pool. All but two share bathrooms. Reservations required; address given out only to guests.

🛏 Spin & Margie's Desert Hideaway
Inn $$

(☎760-366-9124; www.deserthideaway.com; ste $125-175; ❄🛰) This inn's five boldly colored suites are an eccentric symphony of corrugated tin, old license plates and cartoon art. Each has a kitchenette or kitchen. Reservations required; address given out only to guests.

Joshua Tree National Park ❹❻❼

🛏 NPS Campgrounds
Campground $

(reservations ☎877-444-6777; www.nps.gov/jotr, www.recreation.gov; Joshua Tree National Park; campsites $10-15; 🐾❄) Pitch a tent near Joshua Tree's jumbo rocks or in shady canyons at several designated campgrounds along the park's main roads. Most campgrounds don't accept reservations and sites fill up before noon on busy weekends during spring and fall.

Palm Springs The byway is or
day (or overnight trip) a

Palms to Pines Scenic Byway

34

From Spanish padres to Hollywood cowboys, SoCal's mountains and desert landscapes are legendary. This time, in the same terrain seen in scores of car commercials, you're the driver.

TRIP HIGHLIGHTS

15 miles

Palm Desert
Meet the desert's iconic wildlife at the zoo

0 miles

Palm Springs
Hike Native American canyons, or take a treetop tram ride

Banning • • Cabazon **FINISH**

START ①

②

6

Santa Rosa & San Jacinto Mountains National Monument

Lake Hemet

Idyllwild
Arty, musical mountain hideaway with cooler weather

55 miles

**2 DAYS
100 MILES/160KM**

GREAT FOR...

BEST TIME TO GO

May, September and October for cooler temperatures and snow-free roads.

ESSENTIAL PHOTO

Desert canyons from Cahuilla Tewanet Vista Point.

BEST FOR RELAXING

Small-town Idyllwild's cabins, shops and cafes.

Palms to Pines Scenic Byway

An easy day or overnight trip from Palm Springs, this scenic byway ascends to piney forests and descends back to the desert floor in a mere couple of hours. Up in the mountains, watch for bald eagles, prairie falcons, bighorn sheep and mule deer. Stretch your legs along the Pacific Crest Trail before taking a time out at the lakes, meadows and mountains around Idyllwild.

❶ Palm Springs

Take a ride on the **Palm Springs Aerial Tramway** (☎888-515-8726; www. pstramway.com; adult/child $24/17; ☺10am-8pm Mon-Fri, 8am-8pm Sat & Sun, last tram down 9:45pm; ♿). It's 30°F to 40°F cooler as you step out into pine forest at the top, so bring some warm clothing – the trip up from the sun-baked desert floor is said to be the equivalent (in temperature) of driving

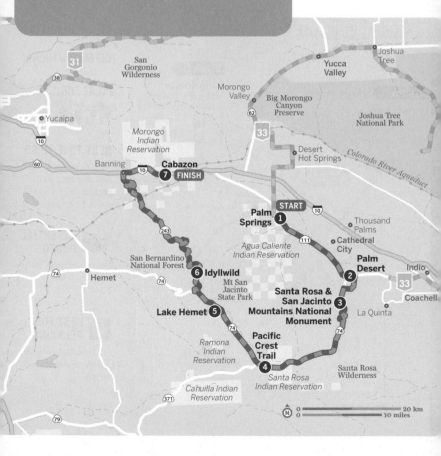

from Mexico to Canada. From the top of the tramway, 54 miles of hiking, snowshoeing and cross-country skiing trails await inside **Mt San Jacinto State Park** (📞951-659-2607; www.parks. ca.gov, www.msjnha.org).

Streams flowing from the San Jacinto Mountains sustain a rich variety of plant life in the desert canyons around Palm Springs. On the outskirts of downtown PS, take a hike in **Indian Canyons** (📞760-323-6018; www. indian-canyons.com; adult/ child $9/5, incl guided hike $12/7; off South Palm Canyon Dr; ⏱8am-5pm, Fri-Sun only Jun-Sep), where sculpted cliffs overlook fan-palm oases, or in **Tahquitz Canyon** (📞760-416-7044; www.tahquitzcanyon.com; 500 W Mesquite Ave; adult/child $12.50/6; ⏱7:30am-5pm, last entry 3:30pm, Fri-Sun only Jul-Sep), featured in Frank Capra's 1937 classic film *Lost Horizon*.

✖ 🛏 p355

The Drive » Follow stop-and-go Hwy 111 (E Palm Canyon Dr) a dozen miles slowly southeast through the built-up Coachella Valley to Palm Desert. Past the turn-off to Hwy 74 (Palms to Pines Scenic Byway), turn right onto Portola Dr; head south just over a mile to the zoo, on your left.

- - - - - - - - - - - - -

TRIP HIGHLIGHT

❷ Palm Desert

While glamorous downtown Palm Desert is all about the fashionable shopping street **El Paseo**, you can get back to nature at the **Living Desert** (📞760-346-5694; www. livingdesert.org; 47900 Portola Ave; adult/child $14.25/7.75; ⏱9am-5pm, last entry 4pm, Oct-May, 8am-1:30pm, last entry 1pm, Jun-Sep; 🚼). This acclaimed zoo and botanical garden harbors a variety of desert plants and animals from North America (including bighorn sheep, mountain lions and birds of prey) and Africa (gazelles, oryx and more), accompanied by exhibits on desert geology and Native American culture. Kids love the walk-through wildlife hospital and African-themed village with a storytelling

grove. Over 1000 acres of undisturbed desert surround the zoo, where dirt hiking trails grant views of the earthquake-rattled San Andreas Fault.

The Drive » Head a mile south on Portola Dr, continuing on Mesa View Dr for almost another mile through a residential neighborhood. At Hwy 74 (Palms to Pines Scenic Byway), turn left and drive about 2.5 miles uphill toward the mountain peaks. Look for the BLM visitor center on your left.

- - - - - - - - - - - - -

❸ Santa Rosa & San Jacinto Mountains National Monument

Just after the start of the scenic byway, pull over at the **Santa Rosa & San Jacinto Mountains National Monument BLM Visitor Center** (📞760-862-9984; 51-500 Hwy 74; ⏱9am-4pm Thu-Tue Oct–mid-Jun, 8am-3pm daily late Jun-Sep; 🚼). Browse the thoughtful displays about the history of this young federal parkland, established in 2000 with the cooperation of Native American tribes. Stretching vertically from desert canyons at sea level to the peak of Mt San Jacinto, the monument most comes alive at native fan-palm oases and beside streams that trickle through the mountains. Look for bighorn sheep ranging across the craggy desert here at the northern edge of the Peninsular

LINK YOUR TRIP

31 Big Bear & Rim of the World Scenic Byway

From Cabazon, drive I-10 west to join Hwy 38 and follow this scenic byway in reverse up to Big Bear Lake.

33 Palm Springs & Joshua Tree Oases

Loop back to Palm Springs to explore desert hot springs, date farms and wildlife havens.

Ranges, which extend south to Mexico. The visitor center and bookstore stock maps and information about all kinds of outdoor activities. One easy nature trail with bird-spotting opportunities conveniently starts right outside.

The Drive » Hwy 74 winds steeply uphill as the eroded canyons of the Sonora Desert

floor slowly give way to ponderosa forests, with valley towns spread out below. It's about 10 miles to the dramatic Cahuilla Tewanet Vista Point. After 10 more miles, look for the inconspicuously signed Pacific Crest Trail intersection.

- - - - - - - - - - - -

❹ Pacific Crest Trail

The Pacific Crest Trail (PCT) treks along the continent's edge from Mexico to Canada. This

national scenic trail measures 2650 miles and passes through the majority of North America's different biospheres on its way, starting in Southern California. Right here you've got a chance to put your own two feet on a short section of the PCT as it passes out of the Sonoran Desert and scales the

Cabazon

backbone of the San Jacinto Mountains before dipping back down to the San Gorgonio Pass and intersecting the I-10. Although only 300 people hike the entire PCT each year, there's nothing stopping you from taking a short day hike along the dirt path, just so you can say that you've done it.

The Drive » Get back on Hwy 74 westbound, passing the Hwy 371 junction after another mile. After another 9 miles of winding through national forest lands, you'll arrive at the Lake Hemet turnoff.

---

⑤ Lake Hemet

A pretty little reservoir set in a mountainous valley, **Lake Hemet** (📞951-659-2680; www. lakehemet.org; 56570 Hwy 74, Mountain Center; day-use entry per car $12; ⊘6am-9pm Sun-Thu, to 10pm Fri & Sat Apr-Sep, reduced hr Oct-Mar) is the kind of old-fashioned resort where rambunctious kids run wild while parents snooze on the beach or cast a fishing line for rainbow trout. You can rent a kayak or rowboat to paddle out

353

✓ **TOP TIP:
ALL-WEATHER DRIVING**

During summer, keep the air-con off as you drive around the desert and climb into the mountains, to keep your vehicle's radiator from overheating. Approaching Idyllwild in winter, tire chains or 4WD with snow tires may be required. Check current road conditions before starting out with the **California Department of Transportation** (☏800-427-7623; www.dot.ca.gov).

into the cool waters, or just splash around the shoreline on a hot day. In summer, outdoor movies play after dark by the campground.

⌂ p355

The Drive » Get back on Hwy 74 by turning left, heading northwest to Mountain Center. After a few miles, veer right onto Hwy 243 for 4 more miles, following the signs into Idyllwild's town center.

TRIP HIGHLIGHT

❻ Idyllwild

Just when you think you can't go one more mile without a break, traffic slows down as the scenic byway reaches the mile-high mountain hamlet of **Idyllwild**. Where Cahuilla people once camped during the summer, escaping from the stifling heat of the Coachella Valley, hippies rediscovered homesteading in the 1960s (acid-tripping guru Timothy Leary once owned a ranch

nearby). Today Idyllwild is best known for its arts scene and live music, especially its plein-air art shows and the Jazz in the Pines festival in late August. Year-round, you can stroll the groovy little downtown village, brimming with art galleries, shops, cafes and alternative-thinkers' hangouts where crystals and tarot-card reading have never gone out of style. Or you could go rock climbing, hiking, mountain biking and camping in the nearby forests, where Hollywood movies have been shot since the silent-film era.

✕ ⌂ p355

The Drive » Resume your journey northwest on Hwy 243, passing trailheads, campgrounds and ranger stations. After less than 10 miles, stop at Indian Vista scenic overlook before reaching Lake Fulmor Picnic Area. The highway drops over Banning Pass, then rapidly twists and turns downhill over the next 15 miles to Banning, the official end of the

scenic byway. Merge onto I-10 eastbound.

❼ Cabazon

Just half dozen miles east of Banning, you might do a double take when you see a giant T. Rex and apatosaurus standing on the north side of the I-10. These concrete behemoths, the **World's Biggest Dinosaurs** (☏951-922-0076; www. worldsbiggestdinosaurs.com; 50770 Seminole Dr; self-guided tour adult/child $7/6; ☺usually 10am-5:30pm), were created in the 1960s by Claude K Bell, a sculptor for Knott's Berry Farm. Today they're owned by Christian creationists. In the gift shop in the belly of the brontosaurus, alongside the sort of dino-swag you might find at science museums, you can read about alleged hoaxes and fallacies of Darwinism and the theory of evolution, alongside biblical quotes. Also nearby Cabazon's outlet mall and casino, **Hadley Fruit Orchards** (☏951-849-5255; www. hadleyfruitorchards.com; 48980 Seminole Dr; ☺9am-7pm Mon-Thu, 8am-8pm Fri-Sun) farmstand makes a less contentious claim: they say they invented hikers' trail mix.

⌂ p355

Eating & Sleeping

Palm Springs ❶

✕ Koffi — Coffee Shop $

(www.kofficoffee.com; 515 N Palm Canyon Dr; snacks & drinks $3-6; ⏱5:30am-7pm; 🛜) Between the art galleries and vintage consignment shops, this minimalist cafe serves strong organic coffee. A more architecturally mod branch stands at 1700 S Camino Real, off E Palm Canyon Dr.

✕ Manhattan in the Desert — Diner, Bakery $$

(http://manhattaninthedesert.com; 2665 E Palm Canyon Dr; mains $9-20; ⏱7am-9pm Sun-Thu, to 10pm Fri & Sat; 🚻) It feels like Nu Yawk inside this old-school Jewish deli with vinyl booths. Simply massive slices of cake mirror the enormity of the sandwiches.

🛏 Caliente Tropics — Motel $$

(☎760-327-1391, 800-658-6034; www.caliente tropics.com; 411 E Palm Canyon Dr; r $55-205; ❄🛜🏊🚻🐕) Impeccably kept tiki-style motor lodge, where Elvis once frolicked poolside, is a premier budget pick with spacious rooms and beds with dreamy mattresses.

🛏 Orbit In — Boutique Hotel $$

(☎760-323-3585, 877-996-7248; www. orbitin.com; 562 W Arenas Rd; r $149-259; ❄🏊🛜) Swing back into the 1950s during complimentary 'Orbitini' happy hour at this fabulously retro hotel. Throwback touches include LP turntables and Mid-Century Modern furnishings.

Lake Hemet ❺

🛏 Lake Hemet — Campground $

(☎951-659-2680; www.lakehemet.org; 56570 Hwy 74, Mountain Center; tent/RV sites from $21/35; 🚻🐕) Offering more amenities than national forest campgrounds closer to Idyllwild, these lakeshore campsites, with outdoor play areas and hot showers, are designed for families.

Idyllwild ❻

✕ Café Aroma — Californian $$

(☎951-659-5212; 54750 N Circle Dr; mains $10-24; ⏱7am-9pm Sun-Thu, to 10pm Fri & Sat; 🛜🚻) Inside a country cabin sheltered by pine trees, a classically trained chef puts new spins on his Italian grandmother's recipes. The outdoor deck has panoramic mountain views.

✕ Nature's Wisdom — Health Food $

(54235 Ridge View Dr; dishes $5-10; ⏱11am-5:30pm; 🛜🍴) Inside a health-food store, locals chat over fresh-baked Danishes and strudels with steaming cups of chai tea or juicy smoothies. Order a homemade panini and veggie soup for a take-out picnic.

🛏 Fireside Inn — Inn $$

(☎951-659-2966; www.thefiresideinn.com; 54540 N Circle Dr; d $65-145; 🚻🐕) Clean, tidy cabins and cottages, some with wood-burning fireplaces, air-conditioning and kitchens, are an easy walk from Idyllwild's town center.

🛏 Quiet Creek Inn — B&B $$

(☎951-468-4208, 800-450-1516; www.quiet creekinn.com; 26345 Delano Dr; d $90-160; @🛜🚻) Eco-conscious creekside duplex cabins, with studios and air-con suites, beckon you to unwind in hammocks on decks overlooking woodsy acres. Grab popcorn and borrow DVD movies from the converted-barn lounge.

Cabazon ❼

🛏 Morongo Casino Resort & Spa — Hotel $$

(☎951-849-3080, 800-252-4499; www. morongocasinoresort.com; 49500 Seminole Dr; r $109-299; ❄@🛜🏊🚻) Over 300 cookie-cutter rooms and suites accommodate gamblers and weary road-trippers inside a high-rise tower. Scarf cheap eats at the casino's buffet or 24-hour cafe.

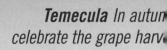

Temecula In autum
celebrate the grape harve

Temecula, Julian & Anza-Borrego

35

Make a weekend getaway from San Diego to Temecula's Wild West wine country; Julian, a gold-mining town surrounded by hills of fruit orchards; and the desert resort of Borrego Springs.

TRIP HIGHLIGHTS

0 miles

Temecula
Taste the grapes outside this Wild West town

125 miles

Borrego Springs
Sleep under starry desert skies

1 START

Palomar Mountain

4

Ocotillo Wells

Santa Ysabel

3

6

85 miles

Julian
Stop for historical gold mines and sweet apple pie

FINISH

Ocotillo

Blair Valley
See hidden treasures in Anza-Borrego Desert State Park

210 miles

**3 DAYS
300 MILES/485KM**

GREAT FOR...

BEST TIME TO GO

February to April for wildflowers and moderate temperatures.

ESSENTIAL PHOTO

Font's Point in Anza-Borrego Desert State Park.

BEST FOR FAMILIES

Julian's apple pie and gold mine tours.

35 Temecula, Julian & Anza-Borrego

In just about any season, incredible scenery will roll past your windshield on this SoCal sojourn. In spring, the desert comes alive with a riot of wildflowers and crazy ocotillo plants with scarlet blooms. In autumn, you can pick apples in Julian's pastoral orchards and celebrate the grape harvest in Temecula's vineyards. For a winter warm-up, escape to Borrego Springs' desert resorts. In summer, cool off in the mountains outside Julian.

TRIP HIGHLIGHT

❶ Temecula

Luiseño peoples, who were present when the first Spanish missionary visited in 1797, called this desert place *temecunga* ('place of the sun'). It became a ranching outpost for Mission San Luis Rey in the 1820s, and later a stop along the Butterfield stagecoach line and California Southern railroad. Hiding behind the Old West facades lining **Old Town's** Front St today are

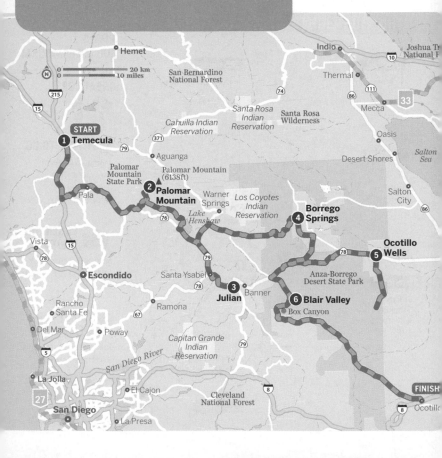

antique shops and wine-tasting bars. **Temecula Olive Oil Company** (www.temeculaoliveoil.com; 28653 Old Town Front St; ⊙10am-5pm) offers free samples of its herb and citrus-infused oils, some pressed from the same types of olives that Spanish priests cultivated at 18th-century California missions.

Although you may imagine there's nothing but desert down here, Temecula is only 20 miles inland from the Pacific. Every night, coastal fog and ocean breezes blow inland to cool down the valley's citrus groves and vineyards. Wine grapes flourish, especially sun-seeking Mediterranean varietals. A 10-minute

LINK YOUR TRIP

27 Fun on the San Diego Coast

San Diego's sunny and bodacious beach towns are only an hour's drive southwest of Temecula's vineyards.

33 Palm Springs & Joshua Tree Oases

From Borrego Springs, drive east toward the Salton Sea, then north to the Coachella Valley's date farms, a 50-mile trip.

drive east of Old Town along Rancho California Rd, you'll find the most popular **wineries** (www.temeculawines.org) with patio views of vine-planted hillsides. If you don't like crowds, start your wine tasting fairly early in the day, especially on weekends. Visit family-owned wineries with less crowded tasting rooms by following the **De Portola Wine Trail** (www.deportolawinetrail.com).

✕ 🍴 p363

The Drive » From Temecula, take the I-15 south 11 miles to the Pala exit. Turn left onto Hwy 76 eastbound, which winds through wide green valleys bordered by citrus groves, protea farms and mountains. After about 20 miles, take the signposted left turn onto County Rd (CR) S6, aka South Grade Rd, which climbs 11.5 miles up Palomar Mountain.

- - - - - - - - - - - - - -

❷ Palomar Mountain

Run by Pasadena's prestigious California Institute of Technology (CalTech) university, white-domed **Palomar Observatory** (📞760-742-2119; www.astro.caltech.edu/palomar; 35899 Canfield Rd; ⊙9am-4pm, to 3pm early Nov–mid-Mar) has a lofty perch atop Palomar Mountain. On weekends, guided tours focus on the dome's history and current scientific research. They'll also let

you peek at the 200in Hale Telescope, once the world's largest until the Keck I opened on Hawaii's Mauna Kea. Bring a fleece jacket – temperatures inside the observatory hover just above around freezing during some months of the year. Call ahead to check road conditions and opening hours before making the long, winding drive here. Even if you're not a science geek, the sprawling views of the San Diego backcountry from the summit are worth the trip. To stretch your legs, nearby **Palomar Mountain State Park** (📞760-742-3462; www.parks.ca.gov; off CR S7; entry per vehicle $8; ⊙dawn-dusk) has forested hikes along panoramic-view trails where wildflowers bloom in early summer.

The Drive » Drive 4.5 miles back down CR S6, then turn left onto CR S7, which winds southeast 11 miles down the mountainside. Turn left onto Hwy 76 and drive east past Lake Henshaw recreational area to Hwy 79. Turn right and head south toward Santa Ysabel, where you can stop for a bite to eat (p363), then take a left onto Hwy 78 to Julian.

- - - - - - - - - - - - - -

TRIP HIGHLIGHT

❸ Julian

Winding through pine-covered mountains and tree-shaded valleys, you'll finally arrive at Julian. Settled by

CAROL POLICH PHOTO WORKSHOPS / GETTY IMAGES ©

ex-Confederate soldiers after the Civil War, flecks of gold were found in the creek here in 1869, sparking a short-lived burst of speculation. Be regaled with tales of the hardscrabble life of early pioneers at **Eagle and High Peak Mine** (🕿760-765-0036; end of C St; adult/child $10/5; 🕙10am-2pm Mon-Fri, to 3pm Sat & Sun; 🚻), where tour guides lead you through the underground tunnels of an authentic 19th-century hard-rock mine.

Although not much mineral ore was ever extracted from Julian's hills, more lasting riches were found in its fertile soil. Today apple orchards fill the surrounding countryside. The Apple Days harvest festival takes place in early October, but crowds descend year-round on Julian's pint-sized **Main Street**, where false-fronted shops along the wooden sidewalks all claim to make the very best apple pie – you'll have to be the judge of that.

✗ ⊨ p363

The Drive » Backtrack 7 miles west of Julian on Hwy 78. Turn right onto Hwy 79 northbound through Santa Ysabel toward

Anza-Borrego Desert State Park Hikers

Warner Springs. Turn right onto CR S2, then almost 5 miles later take a left onto CR S22 (Montezuma Valley Rd), which twists and turns its way down to Borrego Springs, revealing panoramic desert views.

- - - - - - - - - - - -

TRIP HIGHLIGHT

④ Borrego Springs

Lonely, wind-buffeted Borrego Springs is the only settlement to speak of in **Anza-Borrego**

Desert State Park
(☎760-767-4205; www.parks. ca.gov; visitors center 200 Palm Canyon Dr; ☉24hr, visitors center 9am-5pm daily Oct-Apr, Sat, Sun & hol only May-Sep; ♿), the largest US state park outside Alaska, comprising almost a fifth of San Diego County and extending almost all the way to Mexico. Pick up information on hiking trails and

road conditions at the educational visitors center.

Northeast of Borrego Springs, where CR S22 takes a 90-degree turn to the east, there's a pile of rocks just north of the road. This, the **Peg Leg Smith Monument**, commemorates Thomas Long Smith: mountain man, fur trapper, horse thief, liar and Wild West

WATCHING WILDFLOWERS

Depending on winter rains, wildflowers bloom brilliantly, albeit briefly, in Anza-Borrego Desert State Park starting in late February, making a striking contrast to the desert's usually subtle earth tones. Call the **Wildflower Hotline** (☎760-767-4684) or check the **park website** (www.parks.ca.gov) to find out what's blooming right now.

legend. Show up on the first Saturday of April for the hilarious Peg Leg Smith Liars Contest.

Further east of Borrego, a signed 4-mile dirt road, sometimes passable without a 4WD (check conditions at the visitors center), heads south of CR S22 to **Font's Point**, where the desert seemingly drops from beneath your feet. Views stretch over the entire Borrego Valley to the west and the park's eroded badlands to the south.

The Drive » From Christmas Tree Circle in Borrego Springs, follow Borrego Springs Rd south onto Yaqui Pass Rd, which dramatically twists down a narrow pass into the desert badlands below, passing hiking trailheads and campgrounds. Turn left onto Hwy 78 and drive 16 miles east to Ocotillo Wells. By the airport, turn right and drive south on Split Mountain Rd.

⑤ Ocotillo Wells

To escape the roaring off-highway vehicles (OHVs) around Ocotillo Wells, follow Split Mountain Rd back onto

state park land. About 6 miles south of Hwy 78, you'll pass the **Elephant Trees Discovery Trail**. Related to myrrh, these fragrant trees were thought not to exist in the Colorado Desert until a full-fledged hunt was launched in 1937. Today few living trees are left, although you'll encounter plenty of other desert flora along this 1.5-mile loop hike. Another 4 miles south along Split Mountain Rd is the dirt-road turnoff for primitive Fish Creek campground. A 4WD road continues for another 6 miles right through **Split Mountain**, its 600ft-high walls created by earthquakes and erosion. At the gorge's southern end, a steep trail leads up to delicate wind caves carved into the sandstone outcrops.

The Drive » Retrace your drive on Split Mountain Rd to Hwy 78, turning left and heading back west past the Yaqui Pass turnoff for another 7 miles to Scissors Crossing. Turn left onto CR S2 south, which passes ranchlands for the next 6 miles

before reaching the signed Blair Valley turnoff on your left.

TRIP HIGHLIGHT

⑥ Blair Valley

This peaceful desert valley abounds with Native American pictographs and *morteros* (hollows in rocks used for grinding seeds), which you can see along hiking trails leading off the dirt road that loops around the valley east of CR S2. A steep 1-mile scramble leads to **Ghost Mountain** and the remains of a Depression-era homestead occupied by the family of desert recluse Marshal South. On the north side of the valley at Foot and Walker Pass, a roadside historical monument marks a difficult spot on the Butterfield Overland Mail Route. A few miles further south along CR S2 at **Box Canyon**, you can still see the marks where wagons had to hack through the rocks to widen the Mormon pioneers' original trail.

The Drive » Keep following CR S2 south through the park, winding downhill though Oriflamme Canyon grassy valleys that look like oases, and county-run campgrounds and parks. About 26 miles after leaving Box Canyon, look for the Carrizo Badlands Overlook pull-off on your left. From there, it's just 13 miles south to the I-8, which heads back to San Diego.

Eating & Sleeping

Temecula ❶

✕ Restaurant at Ponte   Californian $$$

(📞951-252-1770; www.pontewinery.com; Ponte Family Estate, 35053 Rancho California Rd; mains $12-34; ⏰11am-3pm Mon-Thu, 11am-8pm Fri & Sat, 11am-5pm Sun) Farm-fresh cuisine melds with Italian flavors at this busy winery bistro, a favorite for weekend brunch on the airy patio.

✕ Swing Inn Cafe   Diner $$

(www.swinginncafe.com; 28676 Old Town Front St; mains $7-14; ⏰5am-9pm; 🖐) A proud local institution since 1927, with red leatherette seating and windows from which you can watch the world go by. This cafe serves three square meals, but everyone goes for breakfast – luckily, it's served all day.

🛏 South Coast Winery Resort & Spa   Hotel $$$

(📞951-587-9463; www.wineresort.com; 34843 Rancho California Rd; r $199-329; ✳🖐🛜) Villa rooms dot the edge of the vineyards, some with gas fireplaces and spa tubs. Your room key comes with a wine glossary; rates include a complimentary bottle of wine and free tastings.

Santa Ysabel

✕ Dudley's Famous Bakery   Deli $

(http://dudleysbakery.com; 30218 Hwy 78; snacks & sandwiches $3-8; ⏰8am-5pm Thu-Sun, sometimes 9am-1pm Mon; 🖐) Generations of San Diegans have stopped by Dudley's to pick up picnic lunches and fresh-baked loaves of bread in over a dozen different flavors.

✕ Round Up BBQ Grill   Barbecue $$

(www.roundupbbq.com; 26439 Hwy 76; mains $9-23; ⏰usually 11am-9pm Mon-Thu, 7am-10pm Fri-Sun; 🖐) Fuel up after your trip up Palomar Mountain with a huge platter of rib-sticking Western barbecue. It's across the road from Lake Henshaw.

Julian ❸

✕ Julian Pie Company   Bakery $

(www.julianpie.com; 2225 Main St; snacks & pies $3-15; ⏰9am-5pm; 🖐) Family-owned bake shop churns out cider and cinnamon-dusted cider donuts alongside apple-filled pastries and pie.

🛏 Julian Gold Rush Hotel   B&B $$

(📞760-765-0201, 800-734-5854; www.julianhotel.com; 2032 Main St; d incl breakfast $135-210; 🛜) This 1897 hostelry welcomes with Victorian furnishings, quilt-covered beds and complimentary afternoon tea. A historical landmark, its original owner was a freed slave.

Borrego Springs ❹

✕ Carlee's Place   American $$

(660 Palm Canyon Dr; mains $7-23; ⏰11am-9pm, bar till late) Despite décor that looks stuck in the 1970s, Carlee's, near Christmas Circle, is the locals' top pick for burgers, pastas, pizzas and steak dinners, plus the rowdy bar's pool table.

🛏 Borrego Palm Canyon Campground   Campground $

(reservations 📞800-444-7275; www.reserveamerica.com; tent/RV sites $25/35; 🖐🛜) Near the state park's visitors center, this campground has award-winning toilets (no kidding!), close-together campsites and an amphitheater for natural-history programs.

🛏 Borrego Valley Inn   Boutique Hotel $$$

(📞760-767-0311, 800-333-5810; www.borregovalleyinn.com; 405 Palm Canyon Dr; r incl breakfast $190-275; ✳🛜🖐) This Southwestern-style adobe inn with Native American weavings is an intimate adults-only spa retreat (one pool is clothing-optional). Most rooms have a gas fireplace and kitchenette.

California Driving Guide

With jaw-dropping scenery and one of the USA's most comprehensive highway networks, California is an all-star destination for a road trip any time of year.

Driving Fast Facts

➡ **Right or left?** Drive on the right
➡ **Legal driving age** 16
➡ **Top speed limit** 70mph (some interstate and state highways)
➡ **Best bumper sticker** Mystery Spot, Santa Cruz

DRIVER'S LICENSE & DOCUMENTS

Out-of-state and international visitors may legally drive a car in California for up to 12 months with their home driver's license. If you're driving into the USA from Canada or Mexico, bring your vehicle's registration papers, liability insurance and home driver's license; an International Driving Permit (IDP) is a good supplement but isn't currently required.

If you're from overseas, an IDP will have more credibility with traffic police and simplify the car-rental process, especially if your license doesn't have a photo or isn't written in English. International automobile associations can issue IDPs, valid for one year, for a fee. Always carry your home license together with the IDP.

The American Automobile Association (AAA) has reciprocal agreements with some international auto clubs (eg Canada's CAA, AA in the UK), so bring your membership card from home.

INSURANCE

California law requires liability insurance for all vehicles. When renting a car, check your home auto-insurance policy or your travel-insurance policy to see if rental cars are already covered. If not, expect to pay about $20 per day for liability insurance when renting a car.

Insurance against damage to the car itself, called Collision Damage Waiver (CDW) or Loss Damage Waiver (LDW), costs another $20 per day for rental cars. The deductible may require you to pay up to the first $500 for any repairs. If you decline CDW, you will be held liable for all damages up to the full value of the car.

Some credit cards cover CDW/LDW, provided you charge the entire cost of the car rental to that card. If you have an accident, you may have to pay the rental-car company first, then seek reimbursement. Most credit-card coverage isn't valid for rentals over 15 days or for 'exotic' models (eg convertibles, 4WD Jeeps).

RENTAL VEHICLES

To rent your own wheels, you'll typically need to be at least 25 years old, hold a valid driver's license and have a major credit card, *not* a check or debit card.

Road Distances (miles)

	Anaheim	Arcata	Bakersfield	Death Valley	Las Vegas	Los Angeles	Monterey	Napa	Palm Springs	Redding	Sacramento	San Diego	San Francisco	San Luis Obispo	Santa Barbara	Sth Lake Tahoe
Arcata	680															
Bakersfield	130															
Death Valley	285	705	235													
Las Vegas	265	840	285	140												
Los Angeles	25	650	110	290	270											
Monterey	370	395	250	495	535	345										
Napa	425	265	300	545	590	400	150									
Palm Springs	95	760	220	300	280	110	450	505								
Redding	570	140	440	565	725	545	315	190	650							
Sacramento	410	300	280	435	550	385	185	60	490	160						
San Diego	95	770	230	350	330	120	465	520	140	665	505					
San Francisco	405	280	285	530	570	380	120	50	490	215	85	500				
San Luis Obispo	225	505	120	365	405	200	145	265	310	430	290	320	230			
Santa Barbara	120	610	145	350	360	95	250	370	205	535	395	215	335	105		
Sth Lake Tahoe	505	400	375	345	460	480	285	160	485	260	100	600	185	390	495	
Yosemite	335	465	200	300	415	310	200	190	415	325	160	430	190	230	345	190

Rates generally include unlimited mileage, but expect surcharges for additional drivers and one-way rentals. Airport locations may have cheaper rates but higher fees; if you get a fly-drive package, local taxes may be extra when you pick up the car. Child or infant safety seats are compulsory; reserve them when booking your car.

Major car-rental companies:

Alamo (www.alamo.com)

Avis (www.avis.com)

Budget (www.budget.com)

Dollar (www.dollar.com)

Enterprise (www.enterprise.com)

Fox (www.foxrentacar.com)

Hertz (www.hertz.com)

National (www.nationalcar.com)

Thrifty (www.thrifty.com)

Some major car-rental companies offer 'green' fleets of hybrid or biofuel rental cars, but they're in short supply; make reservations far in advance and expect to pay significantly more for these models. Many companies rent hand-controlled vehicles and vans with wheelchair lifts at no extra charge, but you must also reserve these well in advance.

For independent car rentals, check:

Simply Hybrid (www.simplyhybrid.com) Hybrid car rentals in LA.

Zipcar (www.zipcar.com) Car-sharing club with two dozen California locations.

Car Rental Express (www.carrental express.com) Search for independent car-rental agencies.

Rent-a-Wreck (www.rentawreck.com) Rents to younger drivers, mainly in the LA and San Francisco Bay areas.

Super Cheap! Car Rental (www.super cheapcar.com) Rents to younger drivers in LA, Orange County and San Francisco Bay Area.

Wheelchair Getaways (www.wheelchair getaways.com) Rents wheelchair-accessible vans in San Francisco, LA and San Diego.

Motorcycles

Motorcycle rentals and insurance are very expensive. Discounts may be available for three-day and weekly rentals.

Warning!

As of February 2012, the **US State Department** (http://travel.state.gov) has issued a travel warning about increasing drug-trafficking violence and crime along the US–Mexico border. Travelers should exercise extreme caution in Tijuana, avoid large-scale gatherings and demonstrations, and refrain from venturing out after dark, especially in cars with US license plates.

Eagle Rider (www.eaglerider.com) Motorcycle rentals in the LA and San Francisco Bay areas, San Diego, Orange County, Palm Springs, Fresno and Lake Tahoe.

Dubbelju Motorcycle Rentals (www.dubbelju.com) In San Francisco.

Route 66 (www.route66riders.com) Harley Davidson rentals in LA's South Bay.

Recreational Vehicles & Campervans

Book Recreational Vehicle (RV) and campervan rentals as far in advance as possible. Rental costs vary by size and model; rates often don't include mileage, bedding or kitchen kits, vehicle prep or taxes. Pets are sometimes allowed (surcharge may apply).

Cruise America (www.cruiseamerica.com) Over 20 RV-rental locations statewide.

El Monte (www.elmonterv.com) Almost 20 RV-rental locations in NorCal and SoCal.

Road Bear (www.roadbearrv.com) RV rentals in San Francisco and LA.

Happy Travel Campers (www.camperusa.com) Rentals in San Francisco and LA.

Vintage Surfari Wagons (www.vwsurfari.com) LA-based rentals.

BORDER CROSSING

California is an important agricultural state. To prevent the spread of pests and diseases, certain food items (including meats, fresh fruit and vegetables) may not be brought into the state. Bakery items and hard-cured cheeses are admissible. If you drive across the border from Mexico or the neighboring states of Oregon, Nevada or Arizona, you may have to stop for a quick agricultural inspection.

If you're driving across the Mexican border, check the ever-changing passport and visa requirements with the **US Department of State** (http://travel.state.gov) beforehand. **US Customs & Border Protection** (http://apps.cbp.gov/bwt) tracks current wait times at every border crossing. Between San Diego and Tijuana, Mexico, San Ysidro is the world's busiest border crossing. US citizens do not require a visa for stays in Mexico of 72 hours or less within Baja California's border zone.

Unless you're planning an extended stay in Tijuana, taking a car across the Mexican border is more trouble than it's worth. Instead, ride the trolley from San Diego or leave your car on the US side of the border and walk across. If you drive across, you must buy Mexican car insurance either beforehand or at the border crossing.

MAPS

Visitor centers and tourist information offices distribute free (but often very basic) maps. GPS navigation cannot be entirely relied upon, especially in remote desert or mountain areas. If you are planning on doing a lot of driving, you'll need a more detailed road map or atlas. Benchmark Maps' comprehensive *California Road & Recreation Atlas* ($25) is the gold standard, showing campgrounds, recreational areas and topographical land features, although it's less useful for navigating congested urban areas. Members of the American Automobile Association (AAA) or its international affiliates can pick up free driving maps from any of AAA's California offices.

ROAD HAZARDS & CONDITIONS

For highway conditions, including road closures and construction updates, dial ☎800-427-7623 or visit www.dot.ca.gov.

In places where winter driving is an issue, snow tires and tire chains may be required, especially on mountain highways. Ideally, carry your own chains and learn how to use them before you hit the road. Otherwise, chains can usually be bought (but not cheaply) on the highway, at gas stations or in nearby towns. Most car-rental companies don't permit the use of chains. Driving off-road, or on unpaved roads, is also prohibited by most car-rental companies.

In rural areas, livestock sometimes graze next to unfenced roads. These areas are typically signed as 'Open Range,' with the silhouette of a steer. Where deer or other wild animals frequently appear road-side, you'll see signs with the silhouette of a leaping deer. Take these signs seriously, particularly at night or in the fog.

In coastal areas, thick fog may impede driving – slow down and if it's too soupy, get off the road. Along coastal cliffs and on twisting mountain roads, watch out for falling rocks, mudslides and snow avalanches that could damage or disable your car if struck.

ROAD RULES

➡ Drive on the right-hand side of the road.

➡ Talking or texting on a cell (mobile) phone while driving is illegal.

➡ The use of seat belts is required for drivers, front-seat passengers and children under 16.

➡ Infant and child safety seats are required for children under eight years old unless they are at least 4ft 9in tall.

➡ High-occupancy vehicle (HOV) lanes marked with a diamond symbol are reserved for cars with multiple occupants, sometimes only during rush hours.

➡ Unless otherwise posted, the speed limit is 65mph on freeways, 55mph on two-lane undivided highways, 35mph on major city streets and 25mph in business and residential districts.

➡ At intersections, U turns are permitted unless otherwise posted.

➡ Except where indicated, turning right at red lights after coming to a full stop is permitted, although intersecting traffic still has the right of way.

➡ At four-way stop signs, cars proceed in the order in which they arrived. If two cars arrive simultaneously, the one on the right has the right of way. When in doubt, wave the other driver ahead.

Driving Problem-Buster

What should I do if my car breaks down? Call the roadside emergency assistance number of your car-rental company or, if you're driving your own car, your automobile association. Otherwise, call information (☎411) for the number of the nearest towing service or auto-repair shop.

What if I have an accident? If it's safe to do so, pull over to the side of the road. For minor fender benders with no injuries or significant property damage, exchange insurance information with the other driver and file a report with your insurance provider as soon as possible. For major accidents, call ☎911 and wait for the police and emergency services to arrive.

What should I do if I am stopped by the police? If you are stopped by the police, be courteous. Don't get out of the car unless asked. Keep your hands where the officer can see them (eg on the steering wheel). For traffic violations, there is usually a 30-day period to pay a fine; most matters can be handled by mail. Police can legally give roadside sobriety checks to assess if you've been drinking or using drugs.

What should I do if my car gets towed? Call the police nonemergency number for the town or city that you're in and ask where to pick up your car. Towing and hourly (or daily) storage fees can quickly total hundreds of dollars.

What if I can't find anywhere to stay? If you're traveling during summer and/or holiday periods, always book accommodations in advance, as beds fill up fast. If you're stuck and it's getting late, it's best not to keep driving on aimlessly – just pull into one of those ubiquitous roadside chain motels or hotels.

California Playlist

Surfer Girl Beach Boys

(Sittin' On) The Dock of the Bay
Otis Redding

California Love 2Pac & Dr Dre

California Dreamin' The Mamas &
the Papas

California Phantom Planet

California Gurls Katy Perry featuring Snoop Dogg

➡ When emergency vehicles (ie police, fire or ambulance) approach from either direction, carefully pull over to the side of the road.

➡ If a police car is pulled off on the shoulder of the road, drivers in the right-hand lane are legally required to merge left, as long as it's safe to do so.

➡ It's illegal to carry open containers of alcohol inside a vehicle, even empty ones. Unless containers are full and still sealed, store them in the trunk.

➡ California has strict antilittering laws; throwing trash from a vehicle may incur a $1000 fine.

PARKING

Parking is plentiful and free in small towns and rural areas, but scarce and expensive in big cities. You can pay municipal parking meters and centralized pay stations with coins (eg quarters) or sometimes credit or debit cards. When parking on the street, read all posted regulations and restrictions (eg street-cleaning hours, permit-only residential areas) and pay attention to colored curbs, or you may be ticketed and towed. Expect to pay at least $2.50 per hour or $25 overnight at a city parking garage. Flat-fee valet parking at hotels and restaurants is common in cities; tip the valet attendant at least $2 when your keys are handed back to you.

FUEL

➡ Gas stations in California, nearly all of which are self-service, are everywhere, except in national parks and remote desert and mountain areas.

➡ Gas is sold in gallons (one US gallon equals 3.78L). In 2012, the cost for midgrade fuel ranged from $3.75 to $5.

ROAD TRIP WEBSITES

Driving Conditions & Traffic

California Department of Transportation (www.dot.ca.gov/cgi-bin/roads.cgi) Highway conditions, construction updates and road closures.

511.org (www.511.org) San Francisco Bay Area traffic updates.

go511.com (www.go511.com) LA and Southern California traffic updates.

Automobile Clubs

American Automobile Association (www.aaa.com) Emergency roadside assistance (24-hour), free maps and travel discounts for members.

Better World Club (www.betterworldclub.com) Ecofriendly auto-club alternative to AAA.

Maps

Google Maps (http://maps.google.com) Free online maps and driving directions.

National Park Service (www.nps.gov/state/ca/index.htm) Links to individual park sites for road condition updates and free downloadable PDF maps.

Road Rules

California Department of Motor Vehicles (www.dmv.ca.gov) Statewide driving laws, driver's licenses and vehicle registration.

BEHIND THE SCENES

OUR READERS

Many thanks to the travelers who used the last edition and wrote to us with helpful hints, useful advice and interesting anecdotes: Steffen Beck, Filip Bosmans, Sara Camici.

AUTHOR THANKS

SARA BENSON

Without everyone at Lonely Planet and my California coauthors, this book would not have been so much fun. Big thanks to my Golden State friends and family, especially the Picketts for their hospitality. PS to MSC Jr: Only 185,000 miles?!

NATE CAVALIERI

Thanks much to Suki Gear and the Oakland publishing team, who are a joy to work with, and to all the fellows in Lonely Planet's Oakland warehouse, who are always kind enough to let me rummage around.

BETH KOHN

The biggest round of applause goes to Sara Benson and Suki Gear, plus cheers to Laura Stansfeld, carto queen Alison Lyall and coauthor Nate Cavalieri. Thanks to Alexis Averbuck, Dominique Channell, John Vlahides and Ryan Ver Berkmoes for their work on previous editions. Lots of love to Claude.

PUBLISHER THANKS

Climate map data adapted from Peel MC, Finlayson BL & McMahon TA (2007) 'Updated World Map of the Köppen-Geiger Climate Classification', *Hydrology and Earth System Sciences*, 11, 163344.

Cover photographs: Front (clockwise from top): Pacific Ocean landscape with Bixby Canyon bridge. Big Sur, California, John Elk III/Lonely Planet Images; Golden Gate Bridge, San Francisco, California, Sabrina Dalbesio/Lonely Planet Images; 1948 Chevrolet Fleetmaster Woody Wagon with surfboards Car Culture/Corbis. Back: Yosemite Falls, Yosemite National Park, California, Radius Images/Lonely Planet Images

THIS BOOK

This 2nd edition of California's Best Trips was researched and written by Sara Benson, Nate Cavalieri and Beth Kohn. Ryan Ver Berkmoes, Alexis Averbuck and Amy C Balfour also contributed some of the text. This guidebook was commissioned in Lonely Planet's Oakland office, and produced by the following:

Commissioning Editor Suki Gear **Coordinating Editor** Sophie Splatt **Coordinating** **Cartographer** Corey Hutchison **Coordinating Layout Designer** Mazzy Prinsep **Managing Editors** Annelies Mertens, Angela Tinson **Managing Cartographers** Mark Griffiths, Alison Lyall, Diana Von Holdt **Managing Layout Designer** Jane Hart **Assisting Editors** Cathryn Game, Helen Koehne **Assisting Cartographer** Karusha Ganga **Assisting Layout Designers** Clara Monitto, Jessica Rose **Cover Research** Timothy O'Hanlon **Internal** **Image Research** Nicholas Colicchia

Thanks to Sasha Baskett, Jennifer Bilos, Lucy Birchley, Laura Crawford, Janine Eberle, Ryan Evans, Jennye Garibaldi, Joshua Geoghegan, Chris Girdler, Liz Heynes, Laura Jane, Jennifer Johnston, David Kemp, Gabriel Lindquist, Wayne Murphy, Trent Paton, Martine Power, Kirsten Rawlings, Raphael Richards, Cameron Romeril, Mik Ruff, Julie Sheridan, Laura Stansfeld, Matt Swaine, John Taufa, Gerard Walker, Juan Winata

INDEX

17-Mile Drive 172

Aztec Hotel 320

A

accidents 367
accommodations 25
Agate Beach 128
Aguereberry Point 335
Ahjumawi Lava Springs
   State Park 143
Alabama Hills 218
Alcatraz 51
Amador County Wine
   Country 231-3, 235
Amboy 316
American Valley 248
Ancient Bristlecone Pine
   Forest 222
Anderson Valley wineries 110
Andrew Molera State Park
   155
Angels Camp 230
Año Nuevo State Park 165
Anza-Borrego Desert State
   Park 361
Aptos 65
Arcadia 319
Arcata 122-3, 126, 138, 139
architecture (Scotia) 119
Armstrong Redwoods State
   Reserve 102-3
Arnold 239
Avenue of the Giants
   118-19, 121
Avila Beach 181-3

B

Badger Pass 209
Badwater 333-4
Baker 333
Bakersfield 266, 267
Bakersfield Sound 264, 266
Balboa Island 278
Balboa Park 285-6, 290
Balboa Peninsula 305
Banning 354
Barker Dam 344
Barstow 316, 321
Bartholomew Park 96
Bass Lake 53
Bassetts 249
Bay Bridge 64
beaches 22
Bear Flag Republic 94
Bear Valley 72, 239-40
Beatty 337, 339
beer 138
Berkeley 64, 67, 75, 77
Big Basin Redwoods State
   Park 166
Big Bear Discovery Center
   328, 329
Big Bear Lake 327-8, 329
Big Morongo Canyon
   Preserve 343
Big Pine 220
Big River 110-11
Big Sur 17, 41, 153-59

Big Sur village 155, 159
Bigelow Meadow 144
Bishop 220-1
Bixby Bridge 154-5
Black Sand Beach 117
Blair Valley 362
Bodega 102
Bodega Bay 101-2
Bodie 223
Bodie State Historic Park
   223-4
Bohemian Hwy 101, 105
Bolinas 53, 54, 56-7
Boonville 109, 113
border crossings 366
Borrego Springs 361-2, 363
Box Canyon 362
Bridgeport 224
Buck Rock Lookout 212
Buellton 190
Bunny Flat 135, 145
Burbank 307-8
business hours 25
byways 23

C

Cabazon 354, 355
Calaveras Big Trees State
   Park 239, 243
California Cavern State
   Historical Landmark 230
Calistoga 83, 84, 85-6, 89
Cambria 39
car insurance 364

car rental 24, 364-6
Cardiff-by-the-Sea 288-9
Carlsbad 289, 291
Carmel Valley 174
Carmel-by-the-Sea 172-3, 175
Carquinez Strait Regional
  Shoreline 258
cars, see driving
Carson River 242
Castle Lake 146
Cayucos 39
Cedar Grove 212, 215
cell phones 24
Central Valley 261-7
Chester 247
Chez Panisse 52, 75
children, travel with 23
Chowchilla 264
Clarksburg 255, 259
climate 24
Coachella Valley 346
Coleman Valley Rd 101
Coloma 234
Columbia 229-30, 235
condors 155
Cornerstone Gardens 92-6, 97
Corona del Mar 279
Coronado 36, 284, 290
costs 25
Cottonwood Spring 346
Crescent City 130
Crestline 326
Crystal Bay 202
Crystal Cave 213
Crystal Cove State Park 38,
  279, 281
Curry Village 207, 209

D

Daggett 316
Daly City 66
Dana Point 280
dangers, see safety

Dante's View 335
Dean, James 184
Death Valley 331-9
Del Mar 288, 291
Del Norte Coast Redwoods
  State Park 130
Delta Loop 256-7
DeRose Winery 66
Desert Hot Springs 343, 347
Dewey Point 209
Disneyland 14, 275, 276, 281
Disney's California
  Adventure 275, 276
DL Bliss State Park 199, 203
Donner Lake 200
Dorrington 239
Downieville 250, 251
driving 364-8
  accidents 367
  breakdowns 367
  car rental 24, 364-6
  documents 364
  driver's license 364
  fuel 24, 368
  insurance 364
  maps 366
  parking 368
  road conditions 39, 354
  road distances 365
  road rules 366, 367-8
  safety 366-7
  towing 367
  traffic violations 367
  websites 25, 368
Dry Creek Valley 104
Duarte 319
Dunsmuir 136

E

Eagle Lake 250
East Fort Baker 52
Eastern Sierra Scenic Byway
  217-25
Ebbetts Pass 241-2

Ebbetts Pass Scenic Byway
  237-43
Edna Valley 181
elephant seals 41, 165
Elmer's Place 317
Embarcadero 286, 290
Emerald Bay 199
emergencies 24
Emigrant Canyon 335
Empire Mine State Historic
  Park 234
Encinitas 288-9, 291
Esalen Institute 158
Eureka 44, 47, 126

F

Fall River Mills 143
Fanette Island 199
Father Crowley Point 335
Feather River 246
Feather River Scenic Byway
  245-51
Felton 166
Fern Canyon 129
Ferndale 120, 121
Ferry Building Marketplace
  72-4, 76
flag, California 94
Fontana 317
food 22, 25
Fort Bragg 43-4, 47, 112
Fortuna 120
Founders Grove 118
Foxen Canyon 190-2
Freestone 101
fuel 24, 368
Furnace Creek 334, 339

G

Garberville 116-17, 121
gas 24, 368
gay travellers 104
General Sherman Tree 212

Ghost Mountain 362
Giant Forest 212-13, 215
Gilroy 300
Glacier Point 209, 215
Glen Ellen 54, 57, 95, 97
Glendora 319, 321
Goffs 315
Gold Country 227-35
gold rush 231
Golden Gate Bridge 14, 43
Golden Gate Park 42-3
Grammy Museum 308
Grant Grove 211-12, 215
gray whales 54
Grizzly Redwoods State
    Park 43
Grover Hot Springs State
    Park 242
Guadalupe 39
Guerneville 103, 105
Gundlach-Bundschu winery
    93

H

Haggard, Merle 264
Half Dome 207, 208
Half Moon Bay 164, 167
harbor seals 54, 102
Hawk Hill 51
Healdsburg 104, 105
Hearst Castle, around 39, 47
Heart Lake 146, 147
Hell's Kitchen Vista Point
    239
Henry Cowell Redwoods
    State Park 166
Henry Miller Library 157-8,
    159
Hermit Valley 241
Hesperia 317, 321
Hetch Hetchy 207, 214
Hidden Valley 344
highlights 8-11, 12-21
Highway 18 328

hiking
    Lost Coast 120
    Natural Bridges 232
    Yosemite National Park 208
history 22
Hog Island Oyster Company
    72
Holcomb Valley 328
Hollister 66
Hollywood 308, 309, 320,
    321
Homewood winery 93
Hope Valley 242, 243
Hopland 108-9
hot springs 86, 223
Howland Hill Scenic Drive
    130
Humboldt Lagoons State
    Park 128, 131
Humboldt Redwoods State
    Park 118-19, 121
Huntington Beach 38, 277-8,
    281, 305-6
Hwy 18 328

I

Idyllwild 354, 355
Imagery Estate 94-5
Incline Village 202
Independence 220
insurance 364
internet access 24
Isleton 256, 259

J

Jack London State Historic
    Park 96
Jade Cove 158
James Dean Memorial 184
Jamestown 228-9
Jedediah Smith Redwoods
    State Park 130, 131
Jenner 102, 105
Joshua Tree 343, 347

Joshua Tree National Park
    20, 344, 347
Julia Pfeiffer Burns State
    Park 158
Julian 359-61, 363
June Lake 223
June Lake Loop 223

K

Kenwood 96
Keys View 344-5
King Range 117
Kings Beach 201-2
Kings Canyon National Park
    209, 211-12
Kingsburg 265-6, 267
Knott's Berry Farm 278
Knott's Soak City USA 278

L

La Jolla 37, 288, 289, 291
LA Live 308
La Purísima Mission 298-9
Laguna Beach 38, 279-80,
    281, 304-5
Lake Almanor 247-8, 251
Lake Alpine 240, 243
Lake Arrowhead 326-7, 329
Lake Gregory 325-6, 329
Lake Hemet 353-4, 355
Lake Manly 333-4
Lake Tahoe 19
Lake Tahoe Nevada State
    Park 202
Lakes Basin 248-9, 251
Lassen Volcanic National
    Park 142-3, 147
Lava Beds National
    Monument 146
Lazy Bear Weekend 104
Legoland 289
lesbian travellers 104
Lewiston 137, 139
Lewiston Lake 137

Locke 255-6, 259
Lodi 263-4, 267
Lompoc 298-9
London, Jack 96
Lone Pine 218-19, 225
Long Beach 38, 46
Los Angeles 28, 298, 301
Los Olivos 39, 190, 192, 193
Los Padres National Forest 158, 159, 189
Lost Coast 115-21

M

Malibu 38-9, 46, 306
Mammoth Lakes 221-2, 225
Manzanar National Historic Site 220
maps 366
Marin Headlands 51, 54
Mariposa Grove 209-11
Markleeville 242, 243
Mattole River 117
McArthur-Burney Falls Memorial State Park 143-4, 147
McCloud 144-5, 147
McWay Falls 158
Mendocino 43-4, 47, 111-12, 113
Mendocino Headlands State Park 112
Merced River 207
Mesquite Flat 334-5, 339
Mexico, travel to/from 366
microbreweries 138
Mineral King Valley 213
Mission Beach 37, 287-8, 290
Mission District 74-5, 77
Mission Trail 295-301
mobile phones 24
Mojave National Preserve 334
Mokelumne Hill 230
money 25

Mono Lake 223, 225
Montaña de Oro State Park 183-4
Montecito 306-7
Monterey 19, 41-2, 47, 170-1, 175, 176-7
Montgomery Woods State Reserve 112
Mormon Rocks 324-5
Morro Bay 39, 184, 185
Moss Beach 162-4
Moss Landing 174, 175
motorcycles, *see* driving
Mt Hoffman 210
Mt Shasta 134-5, 139, 145, 147
Mt Whitney 219-20
Mt Williamson 220
mud baths 86
Muir Woods 52-3, 74
Murphys 238-9, 243
music 368

N

Napa 55, 81, 88
Napa Valley 55, 57, 79-89
national & state parks 23
Natural Bridges 232
Navarro River 109
Needle Rock 117
Needles 315
Nevada City, around 234, 235
Newberry Springs 316
Newport Beach 38, 278-9, 281, 305, 309
Newton B Drury Scenic Parkway 130
Niland 346
Nobel Lake 241

O

Oak Hill Farm 94-5
Oakland 64-5

Oakville 81-2, 88-9
Oasis of Mara 345
Occidental 101
Ocean Beach 286-7, 290
Oceanside 289
Ocotillo Wells 362
Olmsted Point 208
opening hours 25
Orange County 273-81
Oregon 144
Oroville 246-7, 251
Orr Hot Springs 112, 113
Owens, Buck 264

P

Pacific Beach 287-8, 290-1
Pacific Coast Hwy 35-47
Pacific Crest Trail 241, 352-3
Pacific Grove 171-2, 175
Pacific Marine Mammal Center 280
Pacifica 162
Palisades Park 320
Palm Desert 351
Palm Springs 14, 342-3, 347, 350-1, 355
Palms to Pines Scenic Byway 349-55
Palo Alto 66, 67
Palomar Mountain 359
Palos Verdes Peninsula 38
Panamint Springs 335-7
parking 368
Pasadena 319-20, 321
Paso Robles Wine Country 184, 185
Patrick's Point State Park 127-8, 131
Pebble Beach 172
Pescadero 164, 167
Petaluma 71
Petrified Forest 86
petrol 24, 368
Pfeiffer Beach 156-7

Pfeiffer Big Sur State Park 155-6, 159

Philo 109-10, 113

Pigeon Point 164-5, 167

Pinnacles National Monument 300

Pismo Beach 39, 46, 181, 185

Placerville 233-4, 235

Plymouth 231

Point Arena, around 43, 47

Point Lobos State Natural Reserve 173

Point Reyes 54, 57

Point Reyes National Seashore 42, 54, 63-4, 67, 72, 76

Point Reyes Station 71-2, 76

Point Sur State Historic Park 155

Port Costa 258, 259

Port San Luis 182

Q

Quincy 248, 251

R

Rainbow Falls 222

Redding 136, 139

Reds Meadow 222-3

Redwood National Park 44, 128-30, 131

Reedley 265

Reno 224, 225

Rhyolite 337

Rich Bar 247

Rim of the World Scenic Byway 323-9

Rio Vista 256, 259

Ritter Range 222

road conditions 39, 354

road distances 365

road rules 366, 367-8

roadside oddities 21

Robert Louis Stevenson State Park 87

Rockefeller Forest 118-19

Rough and Ready Island 258

Route 66 313-21

Rubicon Trail 199

Russian River 102, 104

Rutherford 82

S

Sacramento 254-5, 259, 262, 267

Safari West 87

safety 366-7

Salinas 174

Salmon Creek Falls 158

Salton Sea 346

Salvation Mountain 346

Samoa Dunes Recreation Area 126

Samoa Peninsula 126, 131

San Bernardino 317-19, 321

San Clemente 38

San Diego 29, 36-7, 46, 292-3, 296, 301

San Diego Safari Park 286

San Diego's beaches 21

San Francisco 26-7, 42-3, 47, 50, 56, 58-9, 62-3, 67, 72-5, 76-7, 300, 301

San Juan Bautista 299-300

San Juan Capistrano 297-8, 301

San Luis Obispo 180-1, 185

San Rafael 300

Sand Harbor 202

Santa Barbara 39, 46, 188-9, 193, 194-5, 298, 306-7, 309

Santa Cruz 42, 47, 65-6, 67, 166, 167

Santa Cruz Mountains 166

Santa Monica 19, 40, 320, 321

Santa Monica Pier 40, 320

Santa Rita Hills 190

Santa Rosa & San Jacinto Mountains National Monument 351-2

Santa Ynez 192

Santa Ynez Valley 192

Santa Ysabel 359, 363

Sausalito 51-2, 56

scenic routes 15

Schulman Grove 222

Scotia 119, 120

Scotty's Castle 338

sea lions 54

Sea Ranch 43

Seal Beach 275-7

seals
 harbor 54, 102
 elephant 41, 165

Sebastopol 100-1, 105

Selma 264-5

Sequoia & Kings Canyon National Park 209, 211-12

Shasta Lake 135-6, 139

Shelter Cove 117, 121

Shoshone 333, 339

Sierra City 249-50, 251

Sierra Nevada 220, 240, 242

Silverado Trail 87

Silverwood Lake State Recreation Area 325

Skidoo 335

Skunk Train 112

small towns 17

SoCal 303-9

Solana Beach 288

Solvang 189-90, 192, 193

Sonoma 93-4, 97, 300, 301

Sonoma Coast 43

Sonoma Valley 20, 54, 91-7

Sonora 228-9, 235

South Bay 38

South Lake Tahoe 198-9, 203

South Yuba River State Park 234

Spooner Lake 202

Squaw Valley 199-200
Squaw Valley Creek Trail 144-5
St Helena 82-3, 89
state & national parks 23
Steinbeck, John 174
Stevenson, Robert Loius 83, 86, 87
Stewart Mineral Springs 146, 147
Stockton 258
Sunset Beach 277, 309
Sutter Creek 231, 235

T

Tahoe City 199
Tahoe Meadows 202
Tahoe Rim Trail 202
Tahoe Vista 201-2, 203
Tecopa 333, 339
telephone services 24
Temecula 358-9, 363
Tenaya Lake 208
tipping 25
Tomales Bay 64
towing 367
Traintown 93
transport 25
trees 128
Trinidad 126, 131
Trinity Alps Wilderness 137
Trinity Scenic Byway 133-9
Truckee 200-1, 203

Tulare 266, 267
Tunnel View 207
Tuolumne Meadows 208, 214-15
Turlock 264

U

Ubehebe Crater 337-8
Universal Studios Hollywood 307-8

V

Vacaville 70-1
Valley of the Falls 328
Van Damme State Park 110, 113
Venice 306, 309
Ventura 39, 298
Victorville 317
Virginia City 224
Volcanic Legacy Scenic Byway 141-7
Volcano 230-1, 235

W

Waddell Beach 165-6
Walk of Fame 320
Warner Bros VIP Studio Tour 307
Waters, Alice 69-77
Wawona 209
weather 24

Weaverville 137-8, 139
websites 25, 368
Weed 146
whale watching 102
whales, gray 54
Whiskeytown Lake 136
Whiskeytown National Recreation Area 136-7
White Mountain 220
Whitney Portal 219-20
wi-fi 24
wildflowers 362
wildlife watching 54
Wildrose Canyon 335
Willow Creek 138
wine 22
  Anderson Valley 110
  Napa Valley 82, 83
  tasting 55, 192
Wingfield Park 224
winter activities 209

Y

Yosemite National Park 15, 207, 208, 209, 210
Yosemite Valley 207, 209, 214
Yosemite Village 207
Yountville 81, 88
Yucca Valley 343, 347

Z

Zumwalt Meadow 212

Beth Kohn A lucky long-time resident of San Francisco, Beth lives to be playing outside or splashing in big puddles of water, and there's always a California atlas stashed in her red pickup truck in case a back road looks particularly promising. An author of Lonely Planet's *Yosemite, Sequoia & Kings Canyon National Parks, Mexico* and *California* guides, you can see more of her work at www.bethkohn.com.

My Favorite Trip 20 Eastern Sierra Scenic Byway Who can get enough of those hot springs and mountain views?

OUR WRITERS

OUR STORY

A beat-up old car, a few dollars in the pocket and a sense of adventure. In 1972 that's all Tony and Maureen Wheeler needed for the trip of a lifetime – across Europe and Asia overland to Australia. It took several months, and at the end – broke but inspired – they sat at their kitchen table writing and stapling together their first travel guide, *Across Asia on the Cheap*. Within a week they'd sold 1500 copies. Lonely Planet was born.

Today, Lonely Planet has offices in Melbourne, London and Oakland, with more than 600 staff and writers. We share Tony's belief that 'a great guidebook should do three things: inform, educate and amuse'.

Sara Benson After graduating from college, Sara jumped on a plane to California with just one suitcase and $100 in her pocket. She has bounced around the Golden State ever since, including in the Sierra Nevada, where she worked as a seasonal park ranger. The author of over 50 travel and nonfiction books, Sara also coordinated Lonely Planet's *California* guide. Follow her adventures online at www.indietraveler.blogspot.com, www.indietraveler.net and @indie_traveler on Twitter.

My Favorite Trip `21` **Highway 49 Through Gold Country** I explored the last lonely stretches of a California highway I'd never driven before. Eureka!

Read more about Sara at:
www.lonelyplanet.com/members/Sara_Benson

Nate Cavalieri Born and raised in rural Michigan, Nate Cavalieri has a sentimental soft spot for the piquant cow pastures, political radicals and sleepy one-stoplight towns of Northern California. One of his favorite trips traced the stunning Feather River and into the exotic wilds of the northeastern corner of the state. He authors guides for Lonely Planet on the US, Central America and the Caribbean, writes about music and maintains several fictional twitter accounts about professional cycling. He lives in Oakland. Look him up at www.natecavalieri.com.

My Favorite Trip `30` **Route 66** Driving California's Mother Road – windows down, radio blasting, endless blue skies all around – offered the most iconic road trip experience.

← MORE WRITERS

Published by Lonely Planet Publications Pty Ltd
ABN 36 005 607 983
2nd edition – Feb 2013
ISBN 978 1 74179 810 4
© Lonely Planet 2013
Photographs © as indicated 2013
10 9 8 7 6 5 4 3 2 1
Printed in China

Although the authors and Lonely Planet have taken all reasonable care in preparing this book, we make no warranty about the accuracy or completeness of its content and, to the maximum extent permitted, disclaim all liability arising from its use.

MIX
Paper from responsible sources
FSC™ C021741

Paper in this book is certified against the Forest Stewardship Council™ standards. FSC™ promotes environmentally responsible, socially beneficial and economically viable management of the world's forests.